Koprivnica

NORTHERN
COUNTIES

CROATIA

Sisak

SLAVONIA AND
BARANJA

Osijek

Đakovo

Slavonski Brod

Central Croatia
Pages 172–183

Slavonia and Baranja
Pages 184–201

**The Northern
Counties**
Pages 202–219

Split

Dubrovnik

0 kilometres   50
0 miles   50

EYEWITNESS TRAVEL

CROATIA

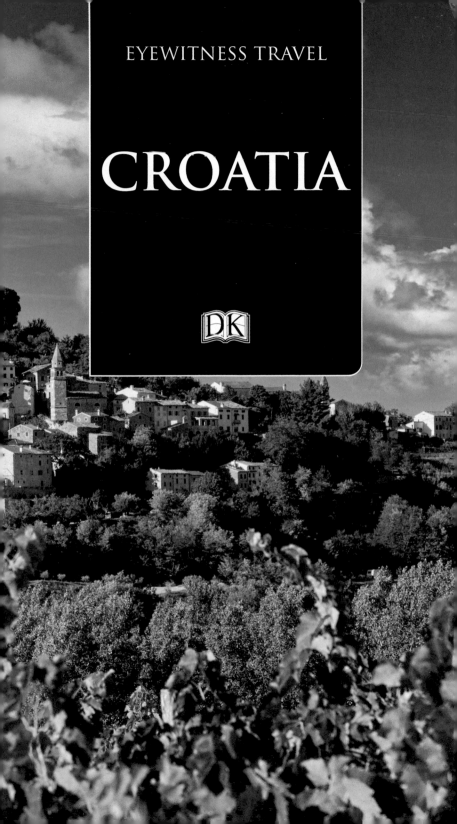

EYEWITNESS TRAVEL

CROATIA

DK

LONDON, NEW YORK,
MELBOURNE, MUNICH AND DELHI
www.dk.com

Produced by Fabio Ratti Editoria Srl, Milan, Italy
Project Editor Donatella Ceriani
Art Editor Oriana Bianchetti
Editors Sara Cattel, Emanuela Damiani, Alessandra Lombardi Giovanna Morselli,
Federica Romagnoli

Main Contributors Leandro Zoppé,
Gian Enrico Venturini (Travel Information and Practical Guide) Other Contributors
Božidarka Boža Gligorijević, Iva Grgic, Sanja Rojić

Photographer
Adriano Bacchella, Aldo Pavan, Lucio Rossi, Leandro Zoppé

Cartographers Grafema Cartografia Srl, Novara
LS International Cartography snc, Milano

Illustrators Modi Artistici

English Translation Susan Andrews

Dorling Kindersley Limited
Editors Hugh Thompson, Fiona Wild
Consultant Jane Foster
Senior DTP Designer Jason Little
Production Melanie Dowland

Reproduced by Fabio Ratti Editoria Srl, Milan
Printed and bound in China

First published in Great Britain in 2003
by Dorling Kindersley Limited
80 Strand, London WC2R 0RL

15 16 17 18 10 9 8 7 6 5 4 3 2 1

Reprinted with revisions 2005, 2007, 2009, 2011, 2013, 2015

Copyright © 2003, 2015 Dorling Kindersley Limited, London
A Penguin Random House Company

A CIP catalogue record is available from the british library.
ISBN 978-1-4093-6956-1

Floors are referred to throughout in accordance with european usage;
ie the "first floor" is the floor above ground level.

MIX
Paper from
responsible sources
FSC
www.fsc.org   FSC™ C018179

Front cover main image: The old town of Korčula, Dalmatia

◀ Motovun, one of the fortified hilltop towns of Istria

Roški falls, Krka National Park, Dalmatia

Contents

Naive painting of the Hlebine School,
Koprivnica Gallery

Croatia Area by Area

Statue by Contieri, church of
St Andrew, Mošćenice

Travellers' Needs

Buzara, a typical Dalmatian dish of
shellfish in tomato sauce

Survival Guide

The bustling harbour of Makarska

The church of
St Donat in Zadar

HOW TO USE THIS GUIDE

The detailed information and tips given in this guide will help you to get the most out of your visit to Croatia. *Introducing Croatia* maps the country and sets it in its historical and cultural context. The six sections, one dedicated to Zagreb, describe the main sights using maps, photographs and illustrations. In Istria, Kvarner and part of Dalmatia, two languages are spoken (Croatian and Italian) and two place names may refer to the same town. Where both names are officially recognized, the Croatian name is given first, then the Italian in brackets. Restaurant and hotel recommendations can be found in the section *Travellers' Needs*, together with information about shopping and entertainment. The *Survival Guide* has tips on everything from transport to making a phone call, as well as other practical matters.

Croatia Area by Area

Croatia has been divided into six main areas, each one identified by its own colour code. On the inside front cover is a general map of the country showing these six areas. All the most interesting places to visit are located on the Regional Map in each chapter.

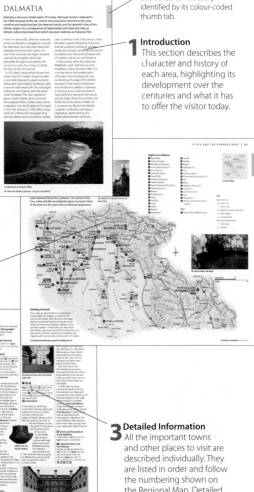

Each area can be easily identified by its colour-coded thumb tab.

1 Introduction
This section describes the character and history of each area, highlighting its development over the centuries and what it has to offer the visitor today.

2 Regional Map
This shows the road network and provides an illustrated overview of the whole region. The most interesting places to visit are numbered, and there are useful tips on getting around the region by car and public transport.

3 Detailed Information
All the important towns and other places to visit are described individually. They are listed in order and follow the numbering shown on the Regional Map. Detailed information is given about the most important sights.

The Visitors' Checklist provides practical information about transport, opening times, events and the closing dates of places of particular interest.

4 Detailed Information on Each Sight

The main attractions are listed for each place. A map shows the main towns, villages and beaches on the larger islands.

5 Main Towns

All the main towns have an individual section where the museums, monuments and other places of interest are listed. All the sights of major interest are located on the town map.

The town map shows the main roads, stations, car parking areas and tourist offices.

6 Street-by-Street Map

This gives a bird's-eye view of the key areas of interest in the main towns and cities with photographs and captions describing the sights.

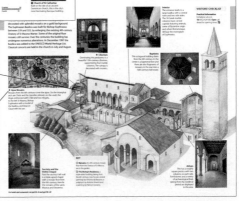

7 Croatia's Top Sights

These are given two full pages. There are cutaways or reconstructions of historic buildings, maps of national parks with information about trails and facilities available, and there are floorplans of the major museums. There are also photographs of the main sights.

Stars indicate the sights that no visitor should miss.

INTRODUCING CROATIA

DISCOVERING CROATIA

The itineraries on the following pages have been designed to take in as many of Croatia's highlights as possible, while keeping long-distance travel manageable. First come a pair of two-day tours *(see p12)*: one of Dubrovnik, the romantic city on the Adriatic, packed with historical monuments; the other taking in the national capital Zagreb and its absorbing mix of museums and cultural diversions.

These itineraries are perfect for a short break, or can be used to enhance one of our longer tours, such as ten days spent island-hopping on the magnificent Dalmatian coast *(p13)*. Finally, our two-week tour of Croatia's riches *(pp14–15)* packs a feast of historical sights and natural wonders into an exhilarating fortnight. Choose or combine your favourite tours, or simply dip in and out for inspiration.

Hvar town, capital of Hvar island
Peaceful bays, a mild climate and lavender-covered hillsides characterize the islands off the Dalmatian coast.

Two Weeks in Croatia

- Spend a day getting to know **Zagreb**, the nation's vibrant capital.
- Wander the cobbled streets of chic **Rovinj**, Istria's most charming seaside town.
- Admire Roman ruins in **Pula**, the unofficial cultural capital of the Istrian peninsula.
- Venture into Croatia's most dramatic lakeland landscape, the **Plitvice Lakes National Park**.
- Roam the centre of **Zadar**, famous for its mixture of medieval and contemporary architecture.
- Stroll the narrow alleyways of medieval **Šibenik** on the way to its stunning cathedral.

- Cool down and splash around beneath the cascading waterfalls of the **Krka National Park**.
- Enjoy the stone-paved squares and streets of Renaissance **Trogir**, one of the Adriatic's most picturesque towns.
- Revel in the energy of **Split**, Dalmatia's biggest port and liveliest seaside city.
- Explore historic **Hvar** island, home to well-preserved towns and contemporary nightlife.
- Mix beach life with medieval history on the green island of **Korčula**.
- Leave plenty of time at the end of the trip to explore the fascinating walled city of **Dubrovnik**.

ISTRIA

Rovinj

Pula

Krk

Cres
Lopar
Rab
Rab
Stinica

Lošinj

Adriatic Sea

Olib
Pag

Zadar

Dugi Otok

Korčula island
Forested mountain slopes lead down to sandy beaches on Korčula, once a prize fought over in historic naval battles.

South Croatian Coast
Many of Croatia's coastal towns and villages have yet to become the high-rise resorts of other holiday destinations.

Ten Days on the Dalmatian Islands

- Explore the bustling port city of **Split** before heading for quiet, unspoiled **Šolta**.

- Hit the spectacular beaches of **Brač**, largest and most developed of the Dalmatian islands.

- Head for **Hvar** and its quiet villages and idyllic coves, then enjoy Hvar town's characterful local restaurants and lively nightlife.

- Soak up the unique, far-from-the-crowds atmosphere of **Vis**, the main jumping-off point for excursions to the Blue Cave of **Biševo**.

- Enjoy medieval towns, pebbly coves and great food on the slender green island of **Korčula**.

- Spend a day walking or cycling on Mljet, home to the lakes and forests of the **Mljet National Park**.

- Relax as you take a voyage by sea to the captivating walled city of **Dubrovnik**, your last stop on the tour.

Zagreb

Sava

Kupa

Plitvice Lakes
National Park

DALMATIA

Krka
National Park

Šibenik

Trogir   Split

Rogač   Supetar
Šolta   Brač
         Bol

Hvar Town   Jelsa
Vis Town   Hvar
Komiža
Biševo   Vis   Pelješac

Korčula Town
Korčula   Ston

Polače
Lastovo   Mljet   Dubrovnik

*Adriatic
Sea*

0 kilometres   50

0 miles   50

Key

— Two Weeks in Croatia

— Ten Days on the Dalmatian Islands

Two Days in Dubrovnik

This perfectly preserved walled city is compact and easy to explore, providing a wonderful opportunity for leisurely walking.

- **Arriving** Dubrovnik's airport is 22 km (13 miles) east of the city at Čilipi. A bus runs to the Old Town every 90–120 minutes.

- **Moving on** The bus station and ferry port, 3 km (1 mile) west of the Old Town at Gruž, offer services to the Dalmatian coast and islands.

Decorative grotto at Trsteno Arboretum, just outside Dubrovnik

Day 1
Morning Start with a tour of the **city walls** *(p148)*, a popular destination that can get crowded later in the day. Follow this with a stroll along the **Stradun** *(p150)*, the Old Town's main street and the site of many of its cafés. At the eastern end of Stradun, the **Church of St Blaise** *(p151)* honours the city's patron saint. Visit the nearby **Dominican Monastery** *(p152)* for its quiet cloisters and Renaissance paintings.

Afternoon The former **Rector's Palace** *(p151)* houses an intriguing museum. Also nearby is the **Cathedral** *(p151)*, its treasury packed full of intriguing relics. Behind the cathedral lie some of the Old Town's most atmospheric alleyways, perfect for leisurely strolling.

Day 2
Morning Take the ten-minute boat trip from the Old Port to the island of **Lokrum** *(p152)*, the site of a ruined monastery, botanical gardens and numerous coves perfect for bathing. Returning to the mainland, take a look at the medieval quarantine buildings of the **Lazareti** *(p148)* before taking a lunch break.

Afternoon Cool off on an out-of-town trip to the lush gardens of **Trsteno** *(p152)* just up the coast. Early evening is a good time to ride the **Dubrovnik Cable Car** *(p152)* up to Mount Srđ to take in its stunning panoramic views.

> **To extend your trip…**
> Spend a day hopping your way around the unspoiled **Elaphite Islands** *(p152)* just offshore, using the local passenger ferry as transport.

Two Days in Zagreb

Art, culture and a vibrant café scene are the keynotes of this easy-going Central European metropolis. Close in style to Vienna and Budapest, the Croatian capital is very different to the Mediterranean-flavoured towns of the Adriatic coast.

- **Arriving** Zagreb Pleso airport is 15 km (9 miles) south of the city. Buses run to the city bus station every 30–60 minutes.

- **Getting around** Zagreb's tram system is efficient and comprehensive. Tickets can be bought from any newspaper kiosk.

Day 1
Morning Begin your first day on Trg bana Jelačića, the city's central square, perpetually busy with pedestrians and passing trams. From here it's a short walk to the Neo-Gothic **Cathedral** *(p158)* and then the **Dolac Market** *(p159)*, one of Central Europe's most colourful collections of fruit-and-veg stalls. Stroll up Radićeva street to the **Upper Town** *(pp160–61)*, a well-preserved Baroque quarter where the Church of **St Mark's** is a popular landmark.

Afternoon The **City Museum** *(p162)* will fill you in on Zagreb's eventful history, while the nearby **Tower of Lotrščak** *(p165)* offers impressive views of the downtown area. Descend to Ilica, the main shopping street, and the **Croatian National Theatre** *(p166)* in its pretty square. Return to the main square via Cvjetni trg or "Flower Square", where many of Zagreb's liveliest cafés can be found.

Day 2
Morning Stroll south from the main square to the **Archaeological Museum** *(p168)*, strong on prehistory and Egyptology. The nearby **Gallery of Old Masters** *(pp170–71)* is a

The Dubrovnik Cable Car, offering stunning views of the walled city

For practical information on travelling around Croatia see pp274–81

superb collection of European paintings. Northwest of here, Teslina and Masarykova streets are full of lunching opportunities.

Afternoon Choose between the spectacular **Museum of Contemporary Art** *(p169)*, a tram ride south of the river Sava, or the woodland delights of **Maksimir Park** *(p169)*, a short tram journey to the east. If it's the park you choose, return to the centre via **Mirogoj Cemetery** *(p169)* with its rich variety of memorial sculptures.

Museum of Contemporary Art, Zagreb

Ten Days on the Dalmatian Islands

- **Airports** Arrive at Split and depart from Dubrovnik – although this itinerary can just as easily be followed in reverse.

- **Transport** Split is the main ferry port for the Dalmatian islands, while Dubrovnik is connected to some of the southern islands in the group. Island-to-island routes are operated by passenger-only boat services in season.

Day 1: Split
Split *(pp120–25)* is the main ferry port of the Croatian Adriatic, and although you may pass through it more than once in the course of your island-hopping trip, it's well worth spending a day exploring this multi-layered city. The Roman remains that form the heart of modern Split provide eternally fascinating points of reference.

Day 2: Šolta
Nearest of the islands to Split, **Šolta** *(p126)* is also the least visited, and has consequently retained a great deal of charm. Ancient, stone-built villages characterize the fertile interior, while the slow-paced fishing ports of Stomorska and Maslinica offer swimming and relaxation.

Day 3: Brač
You'll have to return to Split to catch a ferry to **Brač** *(p126)*, largest of the Dalmatian islands and best-known when it comes to beach holidays. Supetar, on the northern coast, boasts broad pebble bays, while Bol to the south is the site of the spectacular Zlatni rat, a spit of fine shingle that is one of the most breathtaking bathing spots in the Adriatic.

Days 4 & 5: Hvar
A catamaran service connects Bol with the port of Jelsa on **Hvar** *(pp130–33)*, an island that cries out for a stay of two days

or more. The main settlement, Hvar town, is famous for its hip bars, trendy clubs and yachting scene. A short distance away, the comparatively sleepy former fishing ports of Jelsa or Stari Grad offer a much more laid-back, family-attuned experience.

Days 6 & 7: Vis
Hop from Hvar to **Vis** *(pp128–9)* to enjoy one of the Adriatic's most characterful islands. Vis favours independent tourists rather than large hotels, and has a correspondingly relaxed atmosphere. The ports of Vis town and Komiža are beautifully unspoiled, and there are some wonderful coves for swimming. Accessible by boat from Komiža, the islet of **Biševo** is famous for the Blue Cave, a sea grotto filled with water-filtered light.

Days 8 & 9: Korčula
East of Vis, **Korčula** *(pp138–9)* is one of the most varied of the islands, with chic, fashionable Korčula town rubbing shoulders with rustic inland villages and semi-secret beaches. A popular day-trip from Korčula, Mljet is a sparsely populated, forested island taken up in large part by **Mljet National Park** *(pp142–3)*. Inside the park are saltwater lakes, woodland trails and plenty of places to hire bikes.

Day 10: Dubrovnik
The sea journey from Korčula to **Dubrovnik** *(pp146–53)* passes many smaller islands and offers stunning views of the south Dalmatian coast – the perfect way to wind up your tour.

Small boats moored at Maslinica on the island of Šolta

Plitvice Lakes National Park, perfect for a lakeside walk or a bracing hike

Two Weeks in Croatia

- **Airports** Arrive at Zagreb and depart from Dubrovnik.
- **Transport** Mainland Croatia is covered by a fast and efficient bus network. You will need to use ferries to get to the islands: Split is the main passenger port for Hvar and Korčula.

Day 1: Zagreb
Croatia's laid-back capital city, **Zagreb** (pp154–71) is the ideal place to unwind after your inward journey. A walk round the atmospheric Upper Town sheds light on the country's eventful history, while the pedestrianized streets around Zagreb's main square, filled with pavement cafés, are alive with strollers and socializers. If you only have time for one sightseeing destination then make it the excellent Museum of Contemporary Art, showpiece of a restless and forward-looking culture.

Day 2: Rovinj
Thanks to recent road improvements Zagreb is only a few hours' drive from the northern coast, where the heart-shaped Istrian peninsula juts into the Adriatic. Istria is studded with Venetian-style coastal towns and **Rovinj** (p59) is the most charming of the bunch. With its well-preserved medieval centre, quirky gallery scene and some of Croatia's best restaurants, Rovinj is the epitome of Adriatic chic.

Day 3: Pula
Standing at the southern apex of the Istrian peninsula, the port city of **Pula** (pp62–5) is dominated by the 1st-century Roman arena that stands in its centre, one of the largest surviving amphitheatres in the world. There are dramatic rocky beaches right on the outskirts of town, and Pula's restaurants are famous for offering the best of a regional cuisine rich in fish, shellfish and truffles.

Day 4: Rab
There are several inviting islands in the northern Adriatic but few are quite as idyllic as **Rab** (pp84–5). Rab town, the historic island capital, is famous for its medieval churches and their soaring belfries, while the nearby villages of Lopar and Kampor sit beside some of the most spectacular sandy beaches and shallow bays in Croatia. Don't forget to try the local delicacy, Rapska torta (Rab cake), a delicious combination of light pastry and marzipan.

Day 5: Plitvice Lakes National Park
Returning to the mainland, scenic roads wind their way over the Velebit mountain range, a dramatically dry and rocky place on its seaward side, lush and forested further east. On the far side of the Velebit's main ridge lies the stunning **Plitvice Lakes National Park** (pp88–9), a frothing sequence of waterfalls, lakes and streams. Walkways weave their way around the water, while trails lead into the wilder, woodland parts of the park in the surrounding hills.

Prettily painted houses dividing turquoise sea and sky, Rovinj

For practical information on travelling around Croatia see pp274–81

Rab town, capital of the island of Rab, with its distinctive bell towers

Day 6: Zadar

A short drive southwest of Plitvice, **Zadar** (pp94–9) is the main seaport serving the northern Dalmatian islands. It is also one of the rising stars of Adriatic tourism, with bold new public artworks such as *Sea Organ* and *Greeting to the Sun* by architect Nikola Bašić giving the seafront of this vibrant peninsula city a uniquely contemporary feel. There is a wealth of Roman and medieval monuments to explore, and the main food market is one of the liveliest on the coast. An evening stroll along the promenade is compulsory: sunsets here are spectacular.

Day 7: Šibenik

The main town of mid-Dalmatia, **Šibenik** (pp108–11) is steeped in history, with a warren of picturesque alleyways jostling below an impressive ensemble of hilltop fortresses. Local restaurants serve outstanding fresh seafood and superb local wines, especially the dry red Babić from nearby Primošten.

Day 8: Krka National Park

Šibenik is the ideal base from which to visit the spectacular **Krka National Park** just inland (pp106–7), an extensive natural wonderland that you will need a whole day to explore. The pretty town of Skradin is the gateway to Skradinski buk, where you can bathe beside waterfalls and visit old watermills. Boat trips take you deeper into the park, through lakes and canyons.

Day 9: Trogir

Lying between Šibenik and Split, **Trogir** (pp114–17) is one of the most delightful small towns of the Croatian Adriatic, not least because of the medieval cathedral that towers above the Old Town. Trogir's perfectly preserved web of tiny streets and small squares is ideal for long evening walks; plentiful harbour-side cafés will help you unwind.

Day 10: Split

The unofficial capital of the Adriatic and its main passenger port, **Split** (pp120–25) is one of those Mediterranean cities that simply bubbles with character. It was founded as a retirement home by the Roman emperor Diocletian, and the remains of his palace still form the core of the Old Town. Crammed with cafés and bars, this buzzing hive of daytime and night-time activity represents maritime Croatia at its most vivacious.

Day 11: Hvar

A short ferry ride from Split, **Hvar** (pp130–33) is an outstanding example of what makes the new Croatia so popular with visitors. Cocktail bars and yacht marinas add contemporary swank to the Renaissance backdrop of Hvar town, while elsewhere on the island, sleepy villages and pebble-beached coves offer up a soothing blend of rest and relaxation.

Palms and parasols outside the Church and Monastery of St. Dominic, Trogir

Day 12: Korčula

The turreted medieval town of **Korčula** (pp138–9) is one of the coast's historic gems, its solid-stone core of ancient houses split by tiny stepped streets. Some of Croatia's best beaches lie just out of town at Lumbarda. Korčula is known for fine wines and seafood, although many village restaurants in the island's interior serve up delicious roast meats. Don't leave without sampling cukarin, a delicious local citrus-flavoured biscuit.

Days 13 & 14: Dubrovnik

After a short ferry-hop from Korčula, travelling to **Dubrovnik** by land takes you along the Pelješac peninsula, famous for its red wines and oysters – stop for lunch at Ston (p137) to enjoy both. Once in Dubrovnik itself you will need at least a day and a half to get the best out of this enchanting city: see the two-day itinerary on p12 for ideas.

Pula's Roman amphitheatre, now used to stage concerts and other events

Putting Croatia on the Map

Covering an area of 56,594 sq km (21,825 sq miles), Croatia has a population of approximately 4,290,600 with an average of 76 inhabitants per square kilometre. Since the break-up of the former Yugoslavia, and Croatian independence, the country has been bordered by Slovenia, Hungary, Bosnia-Herzegovina and the two now independent republics of Serbia and Montenegro. It is not a large country, but it has a wide variety of natural and man-made environments. From a topographical point of view the country is made up of three types of terrain. Much is mountainous, with peaks up to 2,000 m (6,560 ft) high, mostly covered with forest and pasture. The vast Pannonian Plain lies between the rivers Drava, Sava and the Danube. Coastal Croatia is nearly 600 km (372 miles) long, but over 2,000 km (1,242 miles) long when the indented coastline is taken into account, and twice that when the hundreds of islands are included.

Europe

Key

	Motorway
	Motorway under construction
	Major road
	Minor road
	Railway line
	International border
	Ferry route

For keys to symbols *see back flap*

A PORTRAIT OF CROATIA

Croatia forms a meeting point between the Mediterranean and central Europe, and between the Alps and the Pannonian Plain. Its relatively small territory is made up of a wide variety of landscapes. A stunningly beautiful country, it has re-emerged from the difficult years of conflict and regained its role as a popular holiday destination.

Croatia seceded from the Federal Socialist Republic of Yugoslavia in 1990, following the first free elections since World War II. However, the brutal conflict that quickly followed had disastrous effects on the economy and led to the damage and destruction of many historic monuments and treasures. The United Nations administered disputed territories until 1995, and the last region, Eastern Slavonia, was returned to Croatian administration only in January 1998.

The resolution of the conflict recreated a country which had lost its autonomy long ago in 1102, when Croatian nobles handed the vacant crown to King Koloman. Under Koloman, Croatia became part of Hungary and remained so for 900 years, until 1918. At the end of World War I, Croatia declared independence but, under pressure from greater powers, agreed to become part of the kingdom of Yugoslavia. From the ruins of the Habsburg empire emerged Yugoslavia: a new state of Serbs, Croatians and Slovenes.

Few people live in the steep mountainous areas and as a result the forests of this region, among the most beautiful in southern Europe, are unspoilt. The coast and larger islands are more densely populated and the income from tourism is important to many. The political upheavals of the last decade of the 20th century have caused a shifting of the population and many Serbs have moved away.

Zrmanja river valley, running below the Velebit mountains, Dalmatia

◀ Pretty quayside on the island town of Krk

Fisherman mending his nets in the port of Fažana

Population

According to a census carried out in 2011, Croatia has a population of 4,290,612. Compared with the census of 2001, this is a decrease of nearly 150,000 in the population. These figures, a reflection of the upheavals of the 1990s, reduce the numbers to the population levels of 1968. Two different factors were responsible for these changes: firstly, the departure of thousands of Serbians (partially offset by the return of Croatians resident in other parts of former Yugoslavia), and secondly, the emigration of many young people in search of work in other countries in Europe, America or Australia.

The tragic events of the 1990s have also altered the distribution of the population, emptying villages and concentrating populations in large urban centres. Changes to the size of many towns and cities, the result of enlarging their territorial boundaries, make detailed analysis difficult, particularly with regard to Zagreb, Rijeka, Split, Osijek and Zadar.

Woman in the typical costume of Konavle

Economy

Manufacturing industries are concentrated in the larger cities and employ 20 per cent of the population. The service industry is being overhauled

and provides employment for an increasing number of workers, mainly in the tourist sector, which has recovered after a decade of recession and neglect: 7 per cent of the population is employed in this area. Demand for fresh fish to supply the tourist resorts means that the fishing industry has revived and mussel farming has also expanded, in particular along the Limski Channel and around Ston. The privatization of much agricultural land, and the introduction of modern machinery and the rationalization of crops, have reduced the number of farm workers. However, the production of fruit and wine grapes has recovered, and overall quality is improving significantly.

The urgent need to rebuild public and privately owned buildings damaged during the conflict in the 1990s and the ever-increasing demand for tourist facilities keeps the numbers employed in the building trade high: 7 per cent of the workforce is involved in the construction industry. However, in spite of an improved standard of living for most of the population, unemployment is still high. Croatia hopes to resolve most of its employment problems now that it has joined the European Union, offering land, energy and labour at competitive costs. The building of a modern road network with the construction of new motorways, the modernization of the railways and plans to improve the ports will also help to alleviate high unemployment levels.

Traditions and Customs

Since the rebirth of the Croatian state, all kinds of traditional festivals have reappeared. These festivals, ceremonies or games commemorate historical, religious and military events. Some festivals are expressions of primitive or ancient faith, and mix Christianity with ancient pagan rites; others are linked to the religious calendar. Traditional costumes and jewellery, carefully preserved by the older generation, are worn on these occasions. The materials may sometimes be new but the designs stay faithfully traditional.

Other expressions of popular culture are the rites linked to the rhythms of farming: harvesting, bringing flocks down from the mountains, felling trees. The Feast of St Blaise, the patron saint of Dubrovnik, is magnificent. People from local and surrounding parishes gather, dressed in splendid costumes and displaying ancient banners in honour of the saint. Even the communists were unable to suppress this tradition. Another spectacular festivity is the Olympics of Ancient Sports in Brođanci, when young people parade in gold-embroidered costumes, followed by groups of musicians. Other important events are the Festival of the Bumbari in Vodnjan with its donkey race, the Folk Festival in Đakovo and the Moreška and Kumpanija festivals in Korčula, commemorating battles against the Ottoman Turks.

One of many religious events in Split

Language

The attempt to fuse the Croatian and Serbian languages lasted more than a century, but in 1991 the official language of Croatia became Croatian, and this is now part of the constitution. The language has always been a fundamental part of Croatian identity, even under foreign domination. The people continue to use three basic dialects, *štokavski* in southern and eastern Croatia, *čakavski* in Istria and parts of Dalmatia, and *kajkavski* in Zagreb and the north. A dialect similar to Venetian is spoken along the coast.

Religion

Religious feeling has always been important to Croatians. Religion was relegated to a secondary role during the communist period but the great sanctuaries are once again centres of spirituality. In the 2001 census, over 90 per cent declared they were Christian (88 per cent Catholic, 4 per cent Orthodox), with a Muslim minority, mostly Bosnians, and a Protestant minority, mostly Hungarians. The Orthodox community has shrunk due to the fall in the number of Serbians.

The lively centre of Split, a popular meeting place

The Landscape and Wildlife of Croatia

A wide variety of landscapes can be found in Croatia, from wild uninhabited craggy gorges to steep river valleys and a stunningly beautiful indented coastline stretching into the lower Adriatic, dotted with hundreds of islands. A plateau stretches from the Istrian peninsula towards Gorski kotar and ends in the hilly vine-growing region of Zagorje. The geological formations produced by the porous limestone terrain called karst are found in Gorski kotar and continue to nearby Istria and the Velebit mountains, where the combination of wind, rain and rock has created strange shapes called *kukovi*. Nicknames and legends have been created by folklore for these rock formations, and for the thousands of rocky islands off the coast, remnants of an ancient mountain chain.

Seagull perched on a rocky outcrop near the island of Pag

Mountains

Mountains form 40 per cent of Croatia and rise to nearly 2,000 m (6,560 ft) high. The higher land is given over to sheep farming and the breeding of livestock. The forests are mixed, with pine, fir, chestnut and beech, depending on altitude and microclimate. The wildlife includes bears, wolves, wild boar, lynxes, badgers, foxes, roebucks and chamois. Forestry management aims to control deforestation.

The Plain

The plain is bordered by wide rivers which also define Croatia's borders for much of their length. The vast Pannonian Plain is the breadbasket of Croatia. Maize, wheat, soya and tobacco are grown here and at the fringes are vine-covered hills. At one time there were forests here, dominated by the Slavonian oak, much sought-after in Europe for the quality of its wood. A few isolated remnants of these forests can still be seen.

The forests are a precious resource in Croatia. Thick vegetation covers more than 30 per cent of the country.

The oak of Slavonia, famous since ancient times, was used to build most of the ships in the Venetian and Dubrovnik fleets, because of its extraordinary strength.

The chamois was thought to have disappeared from Croatia but there are now a dozen or so animals originating from Slovenia.

The Croatian plain is one of the most fertile areas in Europe. Some agricultural produce is exported.

National Parks

Croatia began protecting wildlife areas of particular importance in 1949 by setting up the Plitvice Lakes National Park on the Lika plateau. A few years later, the Risnjak National Park was founded north of Rijeka, then in 1985 the Krka National Park north of Šibenik. The Paklenica National Park, at the heart of the Velebit mountain chain, dates from 1949. In 1978 it was declared a world biosphere reserve by UNESCO and later included on the list of World Heritage Sites. It is home to over 2,400 species of plant. There are four national parks in the Adriatic. the Mljet National Park, founded in 1960,

Risnjak National Park with its thick forests of fir and beech

the Kornati National Park (1980), the Brijuni National Park (1983) and the North Velebit National Park (1999). There are also nature reserves, oases, biotopes (environments characterized by particular conditions) and two marshes: Kopački rit and Lonjsko polje. In 2008, Stari Grad Plain on the island of Hvar was declared a UNESCO World Heritage Site.

The Coast

The coast's appearance is determined by the extent of its exposure to the fierce, northeast bora wind. Mediterranean flora flourishes on the sheltered side, with olives, lemon trees and vines. Low-growing vines are cultivated along the central part of the coast and on some of the islands, sheltered from the wind by stone walls. Two common plants along the coast and on the islands are lavender, particularly on Hvar, and broom.

Lakes and Rivers

The lakes of Croatia are not large, but some are truly spectacular, as for example those of Plitvice and those formed by the River Krka. The rivers are another of Croatia's valuable resources. The Danube, Drava, Sava and Kupa are all navigable and form international transport routes (although traffic is currently partly interrupted). The rivers abound with a variety of fish and are a big attraction for fishing enthusiasts.

The marine life is extraordinarily varied, with a wide range of species including sea-horses.

Waterlilies are in flower in late spring, particularly in Lonjsko polje and Kopački rit.

Broom is a common sight in Croatia. In spring, it bears bright yellow flowers.

Storks live near the rivers as well as in protected nature reserves in Croatia. The wetlands make an ideal habitat for the rare black stork.

Art and Artists in Croatia

For centuries Croatian art has combined elements from eastern and western Europe. The coast was ruled by Venice for 400 years, and between the Middle Ages and the 17th century, Croatia was in regular contact with the other side of the Adriatic. Italian artists came to the islands to work, and the Dalmatians crossed the sea and brought Romanesque, Gothic and Renaissance styles back to their country. After the expulsion of the Turks at the end of the 17th century, many churches were rebuilt in the Baroque style, and acquired rich ornamentation. The 20th century saw the advent of Naive painting, an important artistic trend, and sculptor Ivan Meštrović was confirmed as Croatia's most famous contemporary artist (see p163).

Maria Banac, sculpture by Ivan Meštrović

Sculpture

The art of sculpture in Croatia has ancient origins and may have been inspired by the local stone, used to construct some of the most important Roman monuments in Pula and Split, which became models for future generations of Adriatic sculptors.

Sculpture and stone carving reached the height of expression with the Romanesque style. Dating from this time are the cathedral doors of Trogir and Split, the rose windows of Zadar and Rab, the capitals in the cloisters in Dubrovnik and Zadar, and much church statuary. The technical skills of the Renaissance period are documented in Šibenik cathedral, with masterpieces by Juraj Dalmatinac, Nikola Firentinac and Andrija Aleši.

The stonemasons should also be remembered, particularly those of Korčula. Decades of skilled work went into Korčula cathedral and the masons' work can be seen in hundreds of other Croatian towns and cities.

Sculpture again reached a peak in the 20th century with Ivan Meštrović, the chief figure in a group of great artists which included Antun Augustinčić.

Andrija Buvina

All that is known of this sculptor is that he was born in Split and lived in the

Wooden panel by Andrija Buvina in Split cathedral

13th century. The great door of the cathedral of his native city is testament to his skill. This masterpiece from 1214 consists of 28 wooden panels depicting scenes from the Gospels of the life of Christ, and uses simple lines allied to a wealth of detail.

Master Radovan

The sculptor Master Radovan was of Dalmatian origin and

The door of the cathedral of Trogir by Master Radovan

lived in the 13th century. His name appears on the door of the cathedral in Trogir, which he started in about 1240 and which was later completed by other artists. This complex masterpiece has columns, arches, sculpted relief figures and rich decoration. It is possible to discern scenes from the life of Christ such as the nnunciation, the Flight to Egypt, and the Martyrdom on Golgotha, while other sculptures represent the months of the year. The artist's expressive skill is revealed in the figures of Adam and Eve in particular.

Juraj Dalmatinac

Juraj Dalmatinac, also known as Giorgio Orsini, was an ambassador for Dalmatian art, which was greatly influenced by Venice. The artist was born in Zadar in about 1400 and died in 1475. He was active in Dalmatia and in Italy as a sculptor and an architect. The cathedral of St James in Šibenik (see pp110–11), to which he contributed, is regarded as a masterpiece of the Croatian Renaissance. Dalmatinac sculpted the faces on the upper part of the base of the apses and also the statues of Adam and Eve at either side of the Door of Lions.

Face by Dalmatinac in the cathedral of Šibenik

Artists

Painting in Croatia cannot boast a history equal to that of sculpture since it was only after contact with the Venetian school at the end of the 16th century that Croatian painting emerged in Istria and Dalmatia. The monasteries and cathedrals commissioned Venetian masters to make altarpieces and in emulating these models the great artists of Dubrovnik developed.

In the late 17th and 18th centuries, the Baroque style predominated in inland Croatia in architecture as well as art. Baroque originated in German-speaking areas and inspired local artists; the Austrian artist Ivan Ranger *(see p210)* was a key figure. Interest in religious paintings then dwindled, and in the 19th century, young artists were inspired by pan-European culture. In the 1930s and 1940s Naive Art developed.

Dance of Death by Vincent od Kastva

Vincent od Kastva

One of the most expressive cycles of frescoes in Istria bears the signature of this Istrian painter, Vincent od Kastva (Vincenzo da Castua), who lived in the 15th century. The frescoes are hidden away in the small church of St Mary (Sv. Marija na Škriljinah) in Beram. The brightly coloured frescoes on the side walls and the inside façade were painted, with assistants, in about 1471 and have a primitive but vigorous style. The *Life of Christ and the Virgin* has figures of saints; the best-known work is the *Dance of Death*, where Death, holding a scythe, punishes sinners, here represented by all the most powerful people on earth (from the pope to lords of the manor).

Lovro Dobričević

Little is known of Lovro Marinov Dobričević (Lorenzo de Boninis), pupil of Paolo Veneziano, who lived in the 15th century and is regarded as one of the most significant exponents of the Dubrovnik school. Two of his great works are in Dubrovnik: the *Baptism of Christ* (c.1448) is in the Dominican Museum and the polyptych *Virgin, Christ and the Saints Julian and Nicholas* (1465) is in the church of St Mary of Dance (Sv. Marije na Dančama).

Detail, polyptych by Lovro Dobričević in the church of St Mary of Dance

Julije Klović

Julije Klović (Giulio Clovio) was one of the most famous Renaissance miniaturists. A native of Croatia (he was born in Grižane in 1498), his most significant works are found outside the country. The painter developed his craft in Venice, and was then summoned to work in Rome, Mantua, Perugia and numerous monasteries. He died in Rome in 1578.

Miniature by Klović

The Hlebine School

Krsto Hegedušić (1901–75), Expressionist painter and later a Naive artist, founded a group of artists called Zemlja ("Earth"). He encouraged the work of two amateur painters from the village of Hlebine, near Koprivnica: Ivan Generalić and Franjo Mraz, who depicted their local world on glass and canvas in fresh, vivid style. Together with Mirko Virius they founded the Hlebine School which flourished from 1930 to the beginning of World War II. Many other painters, including Ivan Večenaj, Dragan Gaži, Franjo Filipović and Josip Generalić, followed their ideas, concentrating on depicting the lives of outcasts, the poor, and working folk. The Hlebine School became a worldwide phenomenon with the 1952 Venice Biennale and exhibitions in Brazil and Brussels. Naive works are on show at the Hlebine Gallery in Koprivnica and the Museum of Naive Art in Zagreb.

Woodcutters by Generalić, Museum of Naive Art, Zagreb

Architecture in Croatia

Croatian architecture, like its art, has also been influenced by Croatia's position in Europe. Secular and religious buildings display a fusion of elements from nearby Italy and Germany and other forms originating in the Byzantine or Slavic worlds. This blending of influences was first noticeable in the time of the Romans and still continues today. Some styles became particularly important: for example the impressive cathedrals of the Adriatic coast, the legacy of many centuries of Venetian rule. In inland Croatia Baroque architecture prevails, characterized by exuberant decoration and expansive forms.

The Byzantine Euphrasian Basilica in Poreč

Pre-Romanesque and Romanesque

True Croatian architecture begins with pre-Romanesque and dates back to the time of Duke Branimir (879–92), who created the first state of Croatia. Contact with the Byzantine world influenced the look of religious buildings in Istria and Dalmatia but some decorative elements reveal the first signs of Romanesque: small churches with irregular ground-plans appear in areas inhabited by Croatian tribes. The founding of Šibenik (1066) saw the first Romanesque buildings, introduced by the Cistercians. The style spread and remained popular until the end of the 16th century, and three-aisle cathedrals with apses were built as well as monasteries with cloisters, public buildings, town halls and loggias.

The façade consists of vertical and horizontal lines: the upper order is decorated with blind arcades and rose windows.

Romanesque rose window

The arched main door, richly decorated

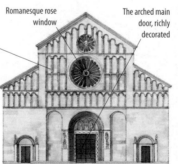

The Cathedral of St Anastasia in Zadar *(see p96)*, founded in the 9th century but rebuilt in the 12th–13th, shows the links between Croatian and Italian Romanesque, particularly in the façade, similar to churches found in Pisa and Lucca in Italy.

The Church of the Holy Cross in Nin *(see p102)*, one of the most interesting examples of the pre-Romanesque and known as the world's smallest cathedral, was built in the 9th century. It has a Greek cross ground-plan with three apses. It is positioned to ensure that the sun's rays fall in pre-planned positions on the floor and act as a clock.

Gothic

The Gothic style, more than any other in Croatia, is lasting evidence of the long rule of the Venetians along the Istrian and Dalmatian coasts. It developed following the Venetian conquest of the Adriatic coast (1420) and is a fundamental expression of the close contact that was established. Venetian Gothic not only influenced the design of Dalmatian and Istrian churches but also mansions in Pula, Rab, Pag, Zadar, Šibenik and Split.

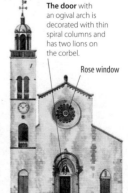

The door with an ogival arch is decorated with thin spiral columns and has two lions on the corbel.

Rose window

Façade of the Town Hall in Split

The Cathedral of St Mark in Korčula *(see p138)* is of Romanesque origins – the bell tower is evidence of this. The façade shows similarities with churches in Puglia in southern Italy. Gothic elements include the pointed arches over the entrance door, which was the work of Bonino of Milan.

Renaissance

The Renaissance style was only able to develop in those parts of the country which did not fall under Turkish rule. The most important architects and artists of the time were Juraj Dalmatinac *(see p24)*, Nikola Firentinac and Andrija Aleši, who worked mainly along the Adriatic coast. They were all involved in the construction of churches and public buildings. The cathedral of St James in Šibenik *(see pp110–11)* became a model for the churches of St Stephen in Hvar, St Mary in Zadar and St Saviour in Dubrovnik. Renaissance buildings also appeared in the north of Croatia, both in the form of private residences (Varaždin and Čakovec) and castles (Trakošćan and Veliki Tabor).

The second storey, with windows and a statue of the city's patron saint, St Blaise, in the centre, was a later addition.

The windows in Venetian Gothic symbolize the ties between Dubrovnik and Venice.

Sponza Palace in Dubrovnik *(see p150)* has both Gothic and Renaissance elements, a reflection of the time it took to build. It was begun in 1312 (the beautiful Gothic windows on the first floor date from this period) and remodelled in 1516–22, when the Renaissance arcaded loggia on the ground floor was added.

Baroque

This was the style that characterized the legitimization of Christian worship in Croatia after the expulsion of the Turks at the end of the 17th century. The signs of Ottoman rule were eradicated and architects, mainly of German extraction, constructed public and private buildings, enriching them with ornate decorations equal to those of the churches, castles and sanctuaries. The most notable examples of the Baroque style can be found in Varaždin, Požega, Osijek, Križevci, Ludbreg and Krapina.

Vojković-Oršić-Kulmer-Rauch Palace, now home of the Croatian Historical Museum *(see p164)*, is one of many fine Baroque buildings in Zagreb. The façade and interior have the sumptuous decorations of the time with elegant columns, scalloped windows and a decorated tympanum.

Modernism

By the 19th century Zagreb had become the centre of political and cultural life in Croatia, which gave it a prominent role as leader in the architectural field. Much experimentation took place in the following century in the capital, inspired first by the Viennese Secession style and later by Modernism. The church of St Blaise and Villa Krauss are interesting examples of the latter style.

The Neo-Renaissance Mimara Museum in Zagreb

The typically elegant building is functional and symmetrical

The decorations in Secession style are stylized and not figurative.

On the façade are sculptures and bas-reliefs by the Croatian artists Robert Frangeš-Mihanović and Rudolf Valdec.

The former National and University Library in the centre of Marulić Square in Zagreb was designed by a local architect, Rudolf Lubinsky. It is regarded as the most significant work in the Secession style in Croatia.

CROATIA THROUGH THE YEAR

The upheavals of the decade from 1991 to 2000 inevitably affected the calendar of events which characterized the cultural life of Croatia. However, concerts, theatre seasons and sporting events have now largely been resumed along with religious festivals and a variety of events linked to local traditions. The different stages in the agricultural year, such as the grape harvest and the threshing, fishing and hunting seasons, are also marked. In addition, every town celebrates its patron saint's day and the "town's day", which is linked to episodes in the town's history. Zagreb offers a rich calendar of cultural events all through the year, while the festivals in the towns and villages along the coast are generally held during the summer season.

Spring

The arrival of spring in Croatia coincides with a series of important dates in the religious calendar. Spring brings warmer weather and also sees the beginning of a series of festivals and events which continue throughout the summer. Catholic churches are especially busy around Easter time, with its associated rituals.

Procession during Holy Week on the island of Korčula

March

Holy Week *(Easter)*. On Korčula Easter is celebrated with processions of brother-hoods performing mystery plays and singing.
Dora Pejačević Memorial, Našice *(Mar)*. Music festival commemorating this Croatian composer, with concerts and competitions.

April

Musical Biennial of Zagreb *(Apr)*. Festival of modern music.
St George's Day, Senj *(23 Apr)*.
St Vincenca's Day, Korčula *(28 Apr)*. The Kumpanjija dance, which commemorates an ancient battle, is performed. At the finale local girls in costume dance in a circle.
Regatta Rovinj–Pesaro– Rovinj, Rovinj *(late Apr/early May)*. Sailing race to Italy and back, with various associated events.

May

Croatian Wine Exhibition, Kutjevo *(May)*. Displays of Croatian wines plus a folklore and music programme.
Days of Hvar Theatre, Hvar *(May)*. Annual celebration of Croatian literature and theatre, as well as scientific themes and presentations by scientists from other countries.
St Mark's Festival, Zagreb *(May)*. Sacred music at various venues.
Tournament of Rab *(9 May)*. Parade of costumed riders with crossbows.
Festival of the Small Theatre, Rijeka *(first half of May)*. Groups from all over Europe participate.
Josip Štolcer Slavenski Memorial, Čakovec *(first half of May)*. Musical festival dedicated to the great 20th-century Croatian composer.
Festival of Croatian Tambour Music, Osijek *(mid-May)*. Festival of ancient music with period instruments, including the tambour.
Croatian One-Minute-Film Festival, Požega *(end May)*. Screenings of short amateur films and videos.

Summer

As this is the season when most tourists visit Croatia, particularly Istria and Dalmatia, this is also the period when the calendar of events is busiest. There are festivals dedicated to music, theatre and dance, as well as many traditional festivals. The folk festivals held throughout the summer are particularly colourful events.

June

Dance Week, Zagreb *(end May/Jun)*. International festival of dance, movement and mime, organized in collaboration with European associations.
Music events, Pula *(all summer)*. Various events in the Roman amphitheatre.
Festival of Satire, Zagreb *(Jun)*. International festival celebrating the satirical.
Brodsko kolo, Slavonski Brod *(mid-Jun)*. Displays of

The festival of Brodsko Kolo, Slavonski Brod

Average Daily Hours of Sunshine

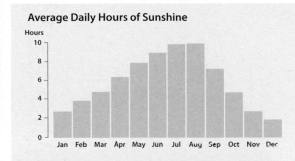

Hours

Bar chart showing average daily hours of sunshine by month (Jan–Dec), with values ranging from about 2.5 hours in December/January up to approximately 10 hours in July and August.

Sunshine
The Dalmatian coast is one of the sunniest parts of Europe, and the island of Hvar holds the record with its 2,700 hours of sun a year. The summers along the coast are hot and dry, while the inland areas have a continental climate with hot summers and cold winters.

Đakovački Vezovi, a folklore and embroidery festival in Đakovo

folk dancing in costume, shows and exhibitions of regional produce.
Đakovački vezovi, Đakovo *(mid-Jun–early Jul)*. Folklore displays and exhibition of local embroidery.
Summer of Margherita, Bakar *(Jun/Jul)*. Concerts and performances in the local *čakavski* dialect.
International Children's Festival, Šibenik *(end Jun–beginning Jul)*. Festival dedicated to the creativity of the very young. Music, dance, theatre and film.

July
Summer Festival, Hvar *(Jul)*. A fun festival of music, theatre, folklore and dancing.
Festival klapa, Omiš *(Jul)*. Celebration of traditional Dalmatian songs performed by groups of five to ten men.
Rapska fjera, Rab *(Jul)*. For three days the historic town of Rab is returned to

medieval times, with craft displays, public preparation of traditional dishes and an archery tournament.
International Jazz Festival, Grožnjan *(Jul)*. International jazz artists participate in this festival in the picturesque Istrian town of Grožnjan.
Summer Carnival, Novi Vinodolski *(Jul)*.
International Festival of Theatre, Pula *(Jul)*. Multimedia festival with the participation of other European groups.
St Theodore's Day, Korčula *(29 Jul)*. Features the Moreška, a dance re-enacting a battle between Christians and Muslims.
International Tennis Tournament, Umag *(end Jul)*.
International Folklore Festival, Zagreb *(end Jul)*. Croatian music and dance with international guests.
Pag Carnival, Pag *(end Jul)*. Traditional dancing, *kolo*, and various shows with the local people in traditional costumes.

Labin Art Republic, Labin *(Jul–Aug)*. Classical and folk concerts.
Musical Evenings in St Donat, Zadar *(mid-Jul–beginning Aug)*. Church, theatre and instrumental music.
Osor Music Festival, Osor *(mid-Jul–mid-Aug)*. Chamber music.
Split Summer *(mid-Jul–mid-Aug)*. A programme of opera, concerts, dance, theatre and performances of the first plays written in the Croatian language.
Dubrovnik Summer Festival, Dubrovnik *(mid-Jul–end Aug)*. The oldest international festival in Croatia: music, theatre, folklore, ballet, with performers from many countries.
Krk Summer Festival, Krk *(Jul–Aug)*. Music and prose, concerts, ballet, performances by young artists and folklore.
Concerts in the Basilica of Euphrasius, Poreč *(Jul–mid Sep)*. Performances of church and secular music given by Croatian and European musicians.

The Moreška dance, St Theodore's Day, Korčula

Average Monthly Rainfall

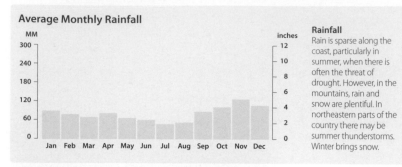

Rainfall
Rain is sparse along the coast, particularly in summer, when there is often the threat of drought. However, in the mountains, rain and snow are plentiful. In northeastern parts of the country there may be summer thunderstorms. Winter brings snow.

Costumed jousters on horseback during the folk festival, Sinj

August

Pag Art Festival, Pag *(Aug)*. This small island's world-famous pianist, Lovro Pogorelić, organizes a two-week programme of classical music concerts and other artistic events, attracting international performers.
Sinjska alka, Sinj *(beginning Aug)*. Folklore festival commemorating victory over the Turks, with jousting competitions for horse riders. Parades, dancing, folk music and displays of regional produce.
Baljanska noć, Bale *(first Sun in Aug)*. Festival of the city.
Festival of the Bumbari, Vodnjan *(2nd Sat in Aug)*. "Bumbari" is what the local people call themselves. A folk festival in costume with an unusual donkey race and the preparation of *crostoli*, cakes of Venetian origin.
St Roch's Day, Žrnovo and Postrana (on Korčula) *(16 Aug)*.

Events include the Mostra, a traditional sword dance. At one time the festivities ended with the sacrifice of an ox.
Trka na prstenac, Barban *(3rd weekend in Aug)*. Jousting tournament, dating back to 1696.
Olympics of Ancient Sports, Brođanci *(last Sun in Aug)*. Folk festival with traditional games, costumes and musicians playing in the streets.

Festival of Vinkovačke Jeseni, Vinkovci

Autumn

Visiting Croatia in this season means there are fewer crowds, even along the busy Adriatic coast. However this season also offers an unexpectedly rich and varied calendar of events. Many of the events are cultural but there are also several festivals celebrating wine and food – offering an ideal opportunity to discover some of the local produce of this country.

September

Festival of the Golden Strings of Slavonia, Požega *(Sep)*. Festival of folk and modern music using the traditional Slavonian instrument, the *tamburica*.
Lace Exhibition, Lepoglava *(Sep)*. Exhibition of traditional hand-made lace, still made according to ancient methods.
Week of Kajkavian Culture, Krapina *(Sep)*. Festival of Kajkavian poetry, folk music and painting.
International Doll Festival, Zagreb *(Sep)*.
Vinkovačke jeseni, Vinkovci *(Sep)*. Festival of music and folk traditions. Parades in costume.
Grape Festival, Buje *(3rd weekend in Sep)*.
Baroque Evenings in Varaždin, Varaždin *(second half of Sep–first half of Oct)*. Festival of Baroque music with the participation of top Croatian and European musicians.

Average Monthly Temperature

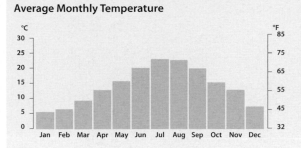

Temperature
The climate in Croatia is typically Mediterranean along the coast, with mild winters and hot, dry summers. Inland the climate is continental with hot summers and cold winters. The mountainous areas have an alpine climate.

October
Bela nedeja, Kastav *(first Sun in Oct)*. Wine festival.
Marunada, Lovran *(mid-Oct)*. Chestnut festival.
Olive Days, Punat *(Oct)*. A great opportunity to participate in the olive harvest festivities on the island of Krk. Visitors can pick olives to the strains of fluting *sopile* music, then enjoy an olive-based feast, prepared by competing cooks from all over Croatia, in the evening.

November
St Martin's Day, Dugo Selo, Samobor, Sv. Ivan Zelina, Velika Gorica, Zagreb County *(Nov)*. A traditional wine festival that celebrates the period when the must is turned into wine.
The Town's Day, Lipik *(4 Nov)*. Traditional festival celebrating the town.

Winter
The cold makes itself felt throughout Croatia, with the temperatures in Zagreb and Slavonia dropping well below freezing point and the cold bora wind sweeping across Istria and Dalmatia. But Croatians still love to go out and enjoy themselves and attend cultural events.

December
The Town's Day, Osijek *(2 Dec)*. Celebration of Osijek's main feast day with music and dancing.

Costume at the Carnival of Lastovo

January
St Vincent's Day, Međimurje *(late Jan)*. Join local growers to toast the patron saint of wine, with tastings, food and music.

February
Feast of St Blaise, Dubrovnik *(3 Feb)*. Processions celebrating the town's saint.
Shrovetide sezona, Kraljevica. Traditional masked ball.
Carnival of Rijeka, Rijeka. Colourful parade in elaborate costumes.
Carnival of the Riviera, Opatija. **International Violin Competition (Vaclav Huml)**, Zagreb *(first half of Feb)*. For violinists under 30.
Carnival, Lastovo.

Croatian Holidays
New Year's Day 1 Jan
Epiphany 6 Jan
Easter Sunday and Monday Mar or Apr
Labour Day 1 May
Corpus Christi May or Jun
Anti-Fascist Victory Day 22 Jun
Statehood Day 25 Jun
Victory and National Thanksgiving Day 5 Aug
Assumption Day 15 Aug
Independence Day 8 Oct
All Saints' Day 1 Nov
Christmas 25 Dec
Boxing Day 26 Dec

A Baroque music ensemble playing in the cathedral, Varaždin

THE HISTORY OF CROATIA

Situated between eastern and western Europe, Croatia has long been a land of passage but also a point of contact between different worlds and cultures. Diverse events and cultural influences have all contributed to the country's history. Croatia is particularly proud of its close ties to the West; for more than a century, parts of the country struggled to free themselves from harsh Turkish domination. The history of Croatia goes back almost as far as man's first appearance on earth.

Prehistory

Early in the 19th century ancient human remains were found at Krapina in the north of Croatia. Dating from the Neanderthal period, "Krapina man" places human presence in Croatia in the middle-Palaeolithic. Other traces of prehistoric cultures have been found in Croatia. The richest site is probably Vučedol, near Vukovar, where the Neolithic "Vučedol Dove" *(see p192)* was found.

The Illyrians

Around 1200 BC, tribes of Indo-European origin settled on the Pannonian Plain, the larger islands and along the coast. The tribes had different names (Istrians, Liburnians, Dalmatians, Japods) depending on where they settled, but the area was known under one name, Illyria. They traded amber and had dealings with other Mediterranean people and northern European traders. Traces of ancient walls on some hilltops confirm their presence.

The Celts

In the 4th century BC, the Celts began to search for new lands when Gaul became overpopulated. Some tribes followed the River Danube to present-day Bohemia; some went as far as the Greek border. In the same period the Greeks founded fortified colonies on some Dalmatian islands, including Vis and Hvar and in the area of Trogir and Salona. Greek historians claim the Celts fought against Alexander the Great in 335 BC on the southern banks of the Danube. A century later, they attacked Delphi and on their return stopped at the Paludes Volcae, an area between the rivers Sava, Drava and Danube. These people were called Scordisci and mixed with the Illyrians. The Celts and Illyrians were defeated by the Romans in the 2nd century BC. After a number of rebellions, some people were expelled, but those remaining adopted their conquerors' customs and became thoroughly Roman.

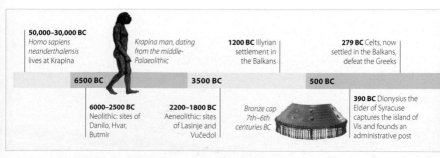

50,000–30,000 BC Homo sapiens neanderthalensis lives at Krapina	Krapina man, dating from the middle-Palaeolithic	1200 BC Illyrian settlement in the Balkans	279 BC Celts, now settled in the Balkans, defeat the Greeks
6500 BC	3500 BC		500 BC
6000–2500 BC Neolithic: sites of Danilo, Hvar, Butmir	2200–1800 BC Aeneolithic: sites of Lasinje and Vučedol	Bronze cap 7th–6th centuries BC	390 BC Dionysius the Elder of Syracuse captures the island of Vis and founds an administrative post

◀ St Paul and St Blaise, patron saint of Dubrovnik, in a triptych by Nikola Božidarević

The Roman Conquest

The Romans conquered Croatia at different times and in different ways. First, they wanted to put an end to attacks on their merchant ships, which were falling into the hands of the Liburnians or the Dalmatians, so they subdued the coastal towns by landing Roman legions transported by the fleet. The first battle took place in 229 BC, when Teuta, the queen of the Illyrians, put to death a Roman ambassador who had tried to persuade her to put an end to the acts of piracy. Roman revenge was fierce and the towns of Epidaurum, Lissa and Pharos were attacked, conquered and forced to pay taxes to Rome. However, despite promises to the contrary, acts of piracy continued and Rome decided to deploy its legions based in Aquileia, east of Venice, a fortified town founded in 181 BC.

Symbol of the Roman Empire, Sisak

The legions succeeded in subduing Istria, a process completed by 177 BC. Twenty years later Publius Scipio Nasica inflicted the first defeat on the Dalmatians at Delminium and again on the Dalmatians and the Japods who inhabited the area of the delta of the River Neretva. In 107 BC the Romans defeated the Scordisci and the Illyrians and conquered the town of Segestica (Sisak). In 87 BC another war broke out between the Romans and the Illyrians which lasted for three years and was won by the Romans. In 48 BC the Illyrians sided with Pompey in the fight against Caesar, providing ships and men. Pompey's defeat also at first appeared to be the decisive defeat of the Illyrians.

However, many Illyrians, still determined to fight, fled to inland forests not occupied by the Romans. A few decades later, in 6 AD, the Illyrian people staged their greatest united rebellion yet, under the command of Batone. The first battles were won by the Illyrians, who soon began to march towards Italy. After three further years of war, the Romans managed to get the better of Batone's exhausted, famished army, thanks to better military organization.

Over the years that followed, Caesar Augustus made the Balkans part of the Roman Empire. After a military campaign waged by Tiberius and completed in AD 12, the Illyrian defences were dismantled and cities were founded, linked by roads wide enough for marching armies. The inhabitants became Roman citizens and were allowed to stand for public office. Indeed, Illyria produced several emperors, including Septimius Severus, Aurelian, Claudius II, Probus, Valens, Valentinian and, perhaps most famous of all, Diocletian.

Roman Roads

The roads were the first great public works built by the Romans. They allowed them to move legions quickly and in fact the Roman

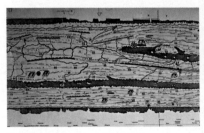

The Tabula Peutingeriana showing Roman roads

229 BC The Roman army destroys Illyrian forts, subdues the Greek colonies of Lissa and Pharos and forces Illyrians to pay taxes

107 BC Decisive Roman victory over the Scordisci who are driven from the region; Rome owes the victory to Quintus Minucius Rufus

300 BC　　　　　　　**200 BC**　　　　　　　**100 BC**

177 BC The Roman fleet is attacked by Istrians; Rome sends an army which defeats them and drives them out

One of the many Roman fragments from the city of Sisak

119 BC The Dalmatian Lucius Metellus defeats the Scordisci and Dalmatian tribes near Segestica (Sisak); Romans settle in Salona and begin work on the Via Gabina from Salona to Andretium

road network remained the principal means of communication in this part of the Balkans for many centuries.

Two important arteries led from Aquileia: one towards the Istrian peninsula to Pula, the other in the direction of Aemona (Ljubljana). The main communication link in Dalmatia began in Aenona (Nin), went on to Zadar and continued, connecting Scardona (Skradin), Tragurium (Trogir), Salona, Narona, Epidaurum (Cavtat) and finally Catarum (Kotor). Other roads branched off inland from this coastal road: the busiest was that from Salona, which went towards present-day Bosnia, through Klis and Sinj, near the town of Aequum (Čitluk). Another road followed the river Narenta (Neretva) to Sirmium, the present-day Sremska Mitrovica, which would become one of the capitals of the Roman Empire.

The inland roads were no less important: these followed the rivers Sava, Drava and the Danube. In the centre of Pannonia, one town which grew in importance was Siscia (Sisak), from which roads led towards Andautonia (Šćitarjevo), Mursa (Osijek), Cuccium (Ilok), Marsonia (Vinkovci) and the thermal spas of Aquae Salissae (Daruvar), Aquae Valissae (Lipik) and Aquae Iasae (Varaždinske Toplice), which were used by the emperors.

Relief in the Baths in Varaždinske Toplice

Founding of Towns

The Romans initially founded the Istrian towns of Poreč, Rovinj and Pula, which became a place of great importance in the 2nd century. Later the existing Illyrian towns

Pula in Roman times, in an engraving from 1819

on the main islands and along the coast were turned into Roman towns. The main towns were Senia (Senj), Aenona (Nin), Jadera (Zadar), Delminium (now a village east of Salona with few remains), Promona (a village near Makarska, with parts of the Roman walls), Burnum (the remains of the ancient town are near Kistanje along the road between Knin and Benkovac), Blandona (which no longer exists, near the lake of Vrana), Scardona (today Skradin), Narona (at the mouth of the Neretva near Vid), Tragurium (Trogir) and, lastly, Salona (near Split). The towns had walls, forums, triumphal arches and aqueducts, the remains of which can often still be seen. The best-preserved aqueduct, built to serve Salona, was extended by Diocletian as far as Split and is, for the most part, still in use.

The principal Roman monuments remaining today in Croatia are in Pula, with its magnificent Roman amphitheatre (see pp64–5), and in Split, site of the extraordinary Palace of Diocletian (see pp122–3).

A statue of Emperor Augustus

AD 6–9 Augustus conquers all of Pannonia and begins construction of forts along the rivers; later the region becomes part of the Roman Empire with the name Provincia Pannoniae

AD 12 Final defeat of the Illyrians. In Rome Tiberius celebrates his triumph with a solemn procession, at the front of which is Batone, chief of the rebels, now a prisoner

271 Aurelian defines the border of the Empire as the Danube, unable to defeat the Dacians who live along the river

284 Diocletian becomes emperor; some years later work begins on the palace in Split, to which he retires in 304

AD 1   **100**   **200**

Aerial view of the ancient Roman ruins of the city of Salona, destroyed in 614

The Barbarian Invasions and the Crisis of the Roman Empire

In 378, after a century of relative peace, the Goths invaded Pannonia and then turned towards Italy. From that time, and for the entire 5th century, the Balkans were attacked by the Huns, Vandals, Visigoths and Longobards, which finally caused the fall of the Roman empire in 476.

The Avars and Slavs in the Balkans

The beginning of the 6th century saw invasion by the Avars, who were followed by other Slavic tribes. Those Roman inhabitants who did not manage to flee to the mountains or the islands were captured and sold as slaves. In 582 the Avars conquered and destroyed Sirmium (Sremska Mitrovica), one of the ancient capitals of the Roman Empire. Later they also subdued other nomadic tribes and organized a powerful army to conquer

Constantinople, but they were defeated by the Byzantines. Some of the troops returned to the Asiatic steppes, while others settled between the Danube and Tisza rivers, leaving the field clear for the Slavs who occupied Moravia and Bohemia to push southwards and towards the Adriatic, conquering all the Roman cities and destroying Salona (614). The Slavs settled in the countryside or in what remained of the sacked cities. These people cultivated the land and bred livestock and formed extended family groups (*županija*) with a *župan* at the head of each.

The Bulgars and the Byzantine Reconquest

The Slavs' expansion to the south was halted by the Bulgars, a people of Turkish origin, who settled along the final stretch of the Danube. After the fall of the Western Empire, Byzantium attempted to reconquer the

Roman bust recovered from ancient Mursa

380 With the Edict of Thessalonica, Theodosius the Great divides the Roman Empire in four parts

476 The Ostrogoths of Odoacer depose Romulus Augustulus, the last Roman emperor

300

400

500

378 Ostrogoths conquer and destroy Mursa (Osijek)

437 Dalmatia comes under the rule of Constantinople; the Huns invade and conquer Pannonia

500 The Slavs occupy Pannonia, which would become Slavonia

Balkans and inflicted various defeats on the Slavs, while at the same time trying to make them part of the empire. The Byzantine fleet was able to move the army rapidly and in this way Greece, part of Macedonia and the Dalmatian islands and cities were retaken. Inland areas remained in Slav possession.

The Croats

At the beginning of the 7th century, perhaps summoned by the Byzantine emperor Heraclius, the Croats, a Slavic people possibly from what is now Iran, settled in upper Pannonia and Dalmatia, mixing with the native Roman people or refugees from the interior. In the 8th and 9th centuries, the Croats set up territorial bases in the inland regions, while the coastal cities and the islands were governed by Byzantine officials with a fleet based in Zadar. In the 9th century, the Croats established a fledgling state in a hilly area now called Biskupija on the Dalmatian plateau, far from the Byzantine-controlled coast and away from central Croatia, subject to the Franks. Several churches were built here and the small settlement was named Pet Crikvah. Recent archaeological digs have unearthed the foundations of religious buildings. The finds are now in Split and Knin.

The Franks

Towards the end of the 8th century the Franks, led by Charlemagne, succeeded in conquering what is now northern Croatia, Bohemia, Istria, Slovenia and part of

Foundations of one of the churches in Biskupija

Dalmatia. The area was divided into counties which were entrusted to loyal nobles or bishops. The Aquileian patriarch assumed particular importance for these lands when, in the 9th century, he sent monks and priests from Byzantium to spread the gospel and convert the Croats to Christianity. Among the priests were Cyril and Methodius, who devised the Glagolitic script to spread the word in a language intelligible to the Slavs.

The First Croatian Towns

During the 8th and early 9th centuries, the first Croatian towns were built next to the Byzantine-governed towns. Many (Dubrovnik, Zadar, Split and Trogir) were inhabited by people of mainly Roman origin. Biograd was founded near Zadar, and the town of Knin was repopulated by Croats under Prince Višeslav. Later, the town of Šibenik was founded. In Pannonia, the Roman town of Siscia (now Sisak) and the town of Mursa (Osijek) were revived by Prince Vojnomir.

The baptismal font of Prince Višeslav, found near Nin

Bust of Charlemagne (742–814)

614 The Slavs and Avars conquer and destroy Salona; the Roman population seeks refuge in Split and the nearby islands

From 820 Croats found the cities of Biograd, Šibenik and Knin; Sinj and Osijek revive

600

700

800

Early 7th century The Croats settle in upper Pannonia and Dalmatia

799 Charlemagne defeats and subdues Croats in Laurana (Lovran); beginning of Croats' conversion to Christianity. Their cultural centre is in Aenona (Nin); first writing in Croat appears

The Hungarians

The situation in the Balkans seemed stable enough towards the end of the 9th century. However, Hungarians from the Urals came to Europe and, under the leadership of King Arpad, settled along the middle stretches of the Danube and in the valleys of Transylvania, forcing out the Slavs and other tribes. They carried out military raids in Italy and Austria but were defeated in 955 by Emperor Otto I at Lechfeld in Augsburg, Bavaria, and were forced to retreat to what are today the borders of Hungary and Transylvania. This Hungarian invasion was the last great invasion of the first millennium.

Statue of the alleged first Croat king, Tomislav

The Kingdom of the Croats

In the meantime, in 845, under Prince Trpimir, the Croats obtained a tacit autonomy from the Franks and formed a state which also controlled part of Dalmatia. This was recognized by the pope while

Relief of King Zvonimir in the baptistry of St John in Split

Duke Branimir (879–92) was its leader. Prince Tomislav was allegedly crowned king in 925 and his death, in 928, was followed by years of anarchy until King Petar Krešimir IV (1058–74) came to power and united Croatia. Krešimir

also conquered the islands of Dalmatia. In 1054, with the schism of the Roman and Byzantine churches, Croatia sided with Rome. After the death of Petar Krešimir IV, his successor Zvonimir, who had married the sister of the Hungarian king Ladislaus, was crowned king by Pope Gregory VII and declared himself subject to Rome. The Croat nobles refused to participate in the war against the Turks and killed Zvonimir in 1089.

The Union with Hungary

Claiming the right of succession, Koloman (1102–1116), the Hungarian king, came to power after Ladislaus. He conquered Croatia and was crowned king of Dalmatia and Croatia. In 1102 an agreement united the two states under one dynasty. A Croatian parliament (Sabor) was set up, to be ruled by a royally appointed Ban (governor), and the state was divided into counties governed by Croatian and Hungarian nobles. In the following century, to deal with the Tartar raids, King Bela IV reorganized the state into two parts (Croatia and Slavonia), each ruled by a Ban. New cities were founded and some were granted the privileges of a free city.

The Royal Free Cities

These cities, defended by walls, moats and towers, were built mainly in Pannonia and the northern counties. Varaždin, founded at this time, became one of the area's busiest trading centres and, for a long period, the

896 Hungarians settle between the Tisza and the Danube

901 Prince Tomislav defeats the Hungarians and forces them beyond the Sava. He obtains from Byzantium the authority to administer the cities of Dalmatia

956 Branimir, prince of Croatia, rebels against the Byzantines. He obtains the title of king of Croatia with the pope's blessing

850   **900**   **950**   **1000**

899 Hungarians enter the Balkans and destroy the cities of the Croats, who seek refuge in Dalmatia

930 The Byzantines renew the union with the coastal towns and cities that pay taxes to the emperor

925 Tomislav allegedly becomes king of the Croats with the pope's blessing

1000 Venice's first armed naval expedition against pirates near mouth of Neretva river; towns on islands and coast of Istria and Dalmatia declare allegiance to Venice

The Golden Bull of 1242 declaring Zagreb (Gradec) a Free Royal City

seat of the Sabor. The cities which emerged from the ruins of old Roman towns were fortified: for example Križevci, proclaimed a royal city in 1252; Koprivnica, declared a free town in 1356; and Ludbreg, which became a free town in 1320 and played an important role in the region's defences. The lower stretch of the Drava was strengthened, with a rebuilt Sisak and, further south, a new Slavonski Brod. Zagreb became a free royal city in 1242; Vukovar became a free town in 1231. Thanks to tax advantages and non-subjection to feudal lords, these towns prospered and attracted foreign merchants and artisans.

The Defences

King Bela IV built forts in strategic positions which were directly dependent on royal power or granted to the great feudal lords. Impressive ruins remain of these forts, including the famous one of Ružica near Orahovica in Slavonia. Samobor, in central Croatia, was enlarged and given a fort, as were Klis, Knin and Sinj in Dalmatia. Several noble families were also given the task of building and

manning forts, as was the case with the Bribir counts, who moved to Zrin (taking the name of Zrinski). This intense programme strengthened a state which was threatened on many sides: after the danger of the Tartars had passed, threat of a Turkish invasion loomed.

Venice, Istria and Dalmatia

The Adriatic coast fared differently; Its fate was linked to that of Venice. Much of Istria belonged to the Aquileian patriarchate, which held civil and ecclesiastical jurisdiction. From the year 1000, many coastal towns had agreements of mutual assistance with Venice, which had a powerful fleet for defence against attacks by pirates. Venice needed the Istrian cities, which often had fortified ports, for mooring its merchant fleets, which plied the Croatian coast on their expeditions to the East. In the 13th century, some cities asked to come under Venetian rule for defence reasons, a process which in most cases took place peacefully. In Zadar, however, this was not the case and two warring factions forced Venice to employ crusaders on their way to the Holy Land to subdue the city (1202). In 1204 Zadar surrendered, and a year later Venice also conquered Istria and the city of Dubrovnik.

The taking of Zadar by the Venetians depicted by Andrea Vicentino

The Republic of Ragusa in a contemporary illustration

The Republic of Ragusa

The story of the city of Dubrovnik, for a long time known as Ragusa, takes up an entire chapter in Croatia's history. The city was founded by exiles from Epidaurum, which had been destroyed by the Avars. It became an important trading port, thanks to its central position in the Adriatic and its safe mooring. In 1205, it came under Venetian rule. This lasted for 150 years and resulted in the city's current appearance. In 1358, Hungary's Louis I of Anjou defeated the Venetians and reunited the Croatian territories, but in 1382 Ragusa bought its freedom by means of a treaty with the king of Hungary. It became an independent republic and flourished as a great power and a thriving spiritual and cultural centre. In 1808, Napoleon Bonaparte's troops entered the city and the republic came to an end.

Turkish Domination

The Kingdom of Hungary went through a long period of dynastic crisis when the house of Arpad died out after the death of Andrew III in 1301. There were numerous contenders for the crown, provoking fierce battles until 1308 when Charles Robert of Anjou, of the Neapolitan royal family, came to the throne. Under the Angevin dynasty, with Matthias Corvinus (1458–90), the Hungarian-Croatian kingdom enjoyed long periods of prosperity, competing with Venice for possession of the coast and Adriatic islands. However, a Turkish invasion was imminent and after the battle of Kosovo Polje in 1389, the Turks conquered nearby Bosnia and part of Serbia. In 1463, the Sultan Mohammed II began to invade Croatia from Bosnia. The Croatian army was defeated in 1493 at the battle of Krbavsko Polje. In the Battle of Mohács, on 29 August 1526, the Hungarian king, Louis II, died without heirs, leaving the way clear for the Turks of Suleyman II the Magnificent to conquer almost all of Croatia and much of Hungary.

Ottoman army in the Battle of Mohács

Venice and the Purchase of Dalmatia

The wars with Venice over coastal Dalmatia continued until 1409 when Ladislaus of Anjou, the King of Naples, renounced all rights over Dalmatia and sold it for 100,000 gold ducats to Venice. The towns and islands stayed under Venetian rule from 1409 until 1797, when Venice surrendered to Napoleon. As well as the territories purchased by Venice, other towns wanted to become Venetian possessions. They were given a great deal of autonomy by Venice, whose principal interest was in the security of the ports and their defence, building the ramparts which today characterize these towns. During the wars of the early 18th century, Venice conquered the whole of Dalmatia, except for Dubrovnik, then an independent republic, and a small stretch of coast, extending its borders to the Velebit passes, which still separate Croatia from Bosnia-Herzegovina today.

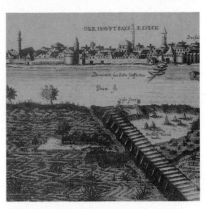

View of Osijek at the time of liberation from the Turks in 1687

Ties with the Habsburgs

In 1527, Croatian and Hungarian nobles granted what remained of the kingdom to Archduke Ferdinand of Habsburg, who then concentrated all power in the court, depriving the nobility of control of the cities and border areas. In 1578, he established the Military Frontier *(Vojna Krajina)* which was administered by the military governor of Vienna. This was to serve as a buffer zone against the advancing Turks. To populate this frontier,

Fran Krsto Frankopan, beheaded in 1671

Serb, Morlach and Bosnian refugees were brought in and integrated with the military garrisons. For some decades there was a truce, then the Turkish offensive against Vienna resumed, but the Turks were pushed back, first in 1664 and again in 1683. The slow retreat of the "infidels" from Croatia began at this point. Croatia was liberated ten years later, while Bosnia remained under the Turks. The liberated areas became border lands and remained so until 1881. Vienna's heavy taxation and centralized rule caused discontent, but in 1670 a plan to detach Croatia from Hungary and Vienna, devised by some of Croatia's most influential families (including the Frankopans and Zrinskis) *(see p181)*, resulted in the beheading of Ban Petar Zrinski and Fran Krsto Frankopan and the other two rebel leaders in 1671, halting any attempt at revolt.

1566 Suleyman II besieges Siget, which, led by Nikola Zrinski, resists for five weeks

1573 Peasant revolt in Zagorje, against nobles and emperor, put down with much bloodshed

1670 Attempted revolt by the Croatian princes Petar Zrinski and Krsto Frankopan against Leopold of Austria

1718 Treaty of Passarowitz (Požarevac): Turkey loses Serbia and part of inland Dalmatia

1550	1600	1650	1700	1750

Nikola Zrinski, Ban of Croatia

1592 The Turks capture Bihać and extend the borders to the river Kupa, which still separates Bosnia from Croatia

1688 Pope Innocent XI promotes Holy League against Turks; the battle of Petervaradino brings Turkish defeat and liberation of all of Croatia

1683 Siege of Vienna by the Turks; Austria wins and reconquers Buda and Pannonia

Drawing showing the Congress of Vienna

The Kingdom of the Illyrian Provinces

The Napoleonic wars also affected Croatia, where the Kingdom of Illyrian Provinces was established in 1809, governed by the French marshal, Marmont. This relatively short period (five years) saw the introduction of important economic and legal reforms that left a deep impression on Croatian culture. With the mood of growing nationalism in Europe, people felt inspired to rebuild a united state. However, at the Congress of Vienna (1815), Croatia supported the expansionist aspirations of Austria, which annexed all the Istrian and Dalmatian territories which had belonged to Venice, and the Republic of Dubrovnik.

The Illyrian Movement

Croatian aspirations were apparent in movements which also influenced and politicized the newly emerging working class, a product of early industrialization. The origins of this nationalist trend can be dated to the 1834 writings of Ljudevit Gaj (1809–72), known as

"the Illyrian". Moving against this trend, however, was the expansion of Hungary, which tried to extend its influence in frontier zones by imposing the use of the Magyar language in administrative affairs and schools. In the former Venetian territories, on the other hand, pro-Italian nationalism, with ideas of unification, was spreading among the middle classes in the Dalmatian and Istrian cities. The Austrian government opposed all these movements and continued to govern without compromise. Indeed, they tried to introduce the teaching of German in schools. Any possible unification of Croatian territories was blocked by maintaining the *Krajina*, the military border, and by customs barriers between the various areas. Major public works, the expansion of the ports of Rijeka and Pula, which became a base for the Austrian fleet, and a renewed road network were all made to promote Austrian interests.

From the Revolt of 1848 to Austro-Hungarian Reign

After 1847, when the Sabor (parliament) of Zagreb managed to proclaim Croatian as the official language and abolished feudalism, the revolt of the Hungarian people and the hopes aroused by the Italian revolution in 1848 also involved Croatian political movements. The failure to understand the Hungarian rebels and ambiguous Austrian policy forced the Ban, Josip

Ban Josip Jelačić, a Croatian national hero

1809 Napoleon Bonaparte founds kingdom of Illyrian Provinces

Napoleon Bonaparte

1830 Ljudevit Gaj publishes *Essential Rules of Croatian-Slavic Spelling*, introducing to the script the signs missing from the Latin alphabet

Ljudevit Gaj, he of the Croatian national revival

1800	1810	1820	1830	1840	1850

1815 Treaty of Vienna: Austria is allotted all the territories of the Republic of Venice

1832 Janko Drašković publishes *Dissertation* against Hungarian and Austrian supremacy, introduces idea of Illyria as the "mother" of Croats

1847 The Illyrian Movement gains majority in Croatian Parliament and proclaims Croat the official language

1848–50 Hungarian uprising against Austria: Vienna abolishes local autonomy, dissolves Sabor and makes German the official language

Jelačić, into war against Hungary, now ruled by rebels. The Austrian monarchy was saved but then became, if anything, even more keen on centralization. In 1867, Franz Joseph, the Austrian emperor, modified the structure of the state and established the Austro-Hungarian empire. Hungary was granted autonomy and a corridor to the sea. Rijeka and the hinterland became part of the Magyar state. However, under pressure from the Sabor, in 1868 the Austrian emperor granted Croatia the status of "a nation with territory within the Austro-Hungarian Empire", and Zagreb became its cultural and political centre. In 1863 the bishop of Đakovo, Josip Juraj Strossmayer, founded the Croatian Academy of the Arts and Sciences and the University (1874), the first in the Balkans.

Political contention continued to develop along different lines. Some people dreamed of a confederation of states within the Habsburg monarchy, others felt that the moment had come to unite the Slav peoples in one state, and lastly, others felt it was time for Croatian independence.

Tension increased in 1878 when Bosnia and Herzegovina came under Austrian

Bishop Josip Juraj Strossmayer, founder of the University of Zagreb

rule, sparking reaction from the Kingdom of Serbia, which had been established in 1882 after the expulsion of the Turks. The Serbian ruling classes aspired to unify the southern Slavs and intended to extend their territories towards Dalmatia and Slavonia, which they regarded as Serbian land. In the last decade of the 19th century a political battle developed in Dalmatia and Istria. It formed between a movement supported by the bourgeoisie in the cities formerly under Venetian rule, which pushed for autonomy, and other groups which aimed at a union with Serbia. Austria, which as always took advantage of these internal controversies, did not concede any form of autonomy.

World War I

In 1914, with the assassination of Archduke Franz Ferdinand in Sarajevo, World War I broke out, which caused the dissolution of the Habsburg Empire. Croatians paid dearly for their involvement in the war, as did many other countries, but finally the Croatian population was able to free itself from foreign rule.

Flag of the Hungarian-Croatian Imperial regiment

1860 Austrian emperor reinstates the Sabor

1881 Vienna dissolves the *Vojna Krajina* and those areas are part of the Croatian state again

1904 Antun and Stjepan Radić found the People's Peasant Party

1914 Assassination in Sarajevo; World War I begins

| 1860 | 1870 | 1880 | 1890 | 1900 | 1910 |

1868 Birth of United Kingdom of Croatia and Slovenia supported by Emperor Franz Joseph

Emperor Franz Joseph

1908 Austria annexes Bosnia and Herzegovina

1912 Slavko Cuvaj proclaimed Ban of Croatia, dissolves the Sabor and abolishes the Constitution

Assassination of King Alexander in Marseilles (1934)

From the State of Slovenes, Croats and Serbs to the Kingdom of Yugoslavia

Croatia proclaimed independence in 1918, but a few months later agreed to be part of a state formed by Slovenes and Serbs under the Serbian dynasty of Karađorđević. The Treaty of Rapallo (1920) allotted Istria, Zadar, the islands of Cres, Lošinj, Lastovo and Palagruža to Italy, followed in 1924 by Rijeka. The discontent of Croatians led many to join the People's Peasant Party, led by Stjepan Radić until he was shot and fatally wounded in parliament in Belgrade in 1928. The revolts which broke out in Croatia were repressed and in 1929 King Alexander abolished the constitution and then established the Kingdom of Yugoslavia. The assassination of the king in Marseilles (1934) by a member of a Macedonian revolutionary group working with the Ustaše (Croatian fascists), led by Ante Pavelić, increased tension, and in an attempt to suppress the uprising and placate the discontented, in 1939 the government of Belgrade established the Banovina of Croatia within the Kingdom of Yugoslavia. However, a few days later World War II began.

World War II

Initially, Yugoslavia supported the Axis, but a military revolt removed the king of Yugoslavia, and the country was then invaded by Nazi troops. A kingdom of Croatia was established, which was to be governed by Aimone of Savoy, but in reality it was an independent state led by Pavelić. Italy took control of the islands and cities of the Dalmatian coast. Resistance gained ground in all of Yugoslavia led by the Communist Party and its chief, Marshal Tito: from 1941 to 1945 Croatia was bloodied by war and internal conflicts that caused hundreds of thousands of deaths.

Marshal Tito

At the end of the war the state of Yugoslavia was reunited, and regained land granted to Italy after World War I *(see p51)*, as well as the area of Prekomurje and a part of Baranja, which were both Hungarian at the time. In 1948, the break between the Yugoslav Communist Party

Tito with his wife and son in a photo from 1927

and the Soviet Union led Marshal Tito to employ a policy of mediation and neutrality between the opposing international factions of the Cold War. Tito held together the country's various ethnic groups (with great difficulty) and these ties showed signs of strain after he died in 1980. The reform of the constitution, aimed at weakening Serbia's dominance over the other states, did not alter the resentment of the Croats and Slovenes who sought support for opposition to the regime in religion and nationalism.

Ivo Josipović, elected president in 2010

The Dissolution of the Socialist Republic of Yugoslavia

The fall of the Berlin Wall (November 1989) and the break-up of the Soviet Union at the end of 1991 convinced the governments of Slovenia, Croatia (under its first president, Franjo Tuđman) and Macedonia that they should dissolve federal ties and proclaim independence, after a referendum which was won by a wide margin by the secessionists (May 1991). However, a Serb faction, supported by the Yugoslav People's Army (JNA) from Belgrade, stirred up rebellion and war broke out. In Slovenia the war lasted only ten days, but the battle in Croatia was prolonged. Under the pretext of defending the Serbs, parts of Slavonia and Baranja were occupied by the JNA, and in Krajina the Serbian Republic of Krajina was created with Knin as its capital. A fifth of Croatia fell to Serb soldiers, and the city of Dubrovnik was held under a seven-month siege.

The Independent State of Croatia

Five years later the land occupied by the Serbs was liberated by the Croatian army and the Erdut Agreement (1995) sanctioned reunification, although the disputed territories (Slavonia and Krajina) were overseen by the UN until 1998.

Croatia joined the World Trade Organization and elections held in December 2000 voted in a coalition of democratic parties. As a result steps were taken for Croatia's entry into the European Union. In March 2002, the Italian bank, UniCredito, bought the important Croatian bank, the Zagrebačka Bank, bringing it into the European circuit. However, in 2005, after failing to hand over an indicted general, Croatia was accused of not co-operating fully with the international war crimes tribunal at the Hague and negotiations for entry to the EU stalled. Soon after, the general was captured and talks resumed, and eventually, Croatia joined the European Union on 1 July 2013.

Bombed houses in Vukovar during the war of 1991–95

	1980 President Tito dies and conflict between the various nationalities begins	**1998** The restitution of Slavonia and Krajina reunites a now free Croatia	**2000** On 7 February Stipe Mesić is elected President of the Republic	**2009** The accession of Croatia to NATO
				2013 Croatia joins EU on 1 July
1980		**1990**	**2000**	**2010**	**2020**

1991 Slovenia and Croatia abandon Republic, Croatian land inhabited by Serbs is occupied by Yugoslav People's Army: war between Serbia and Croatia begins

1995 Erdut Agreement: Slavonia and Krajina are administered by the United Nations

2010 Ivo Josipović elected President

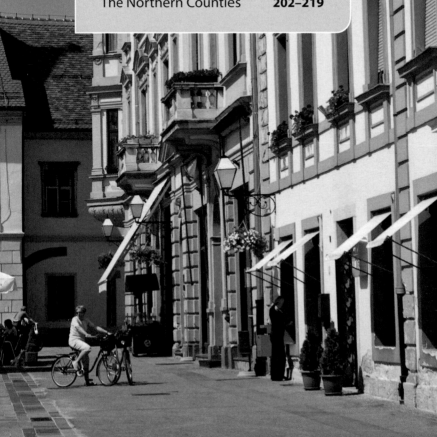

CROATIA AREA BY AREA

Croatia at a Glance

Croatia is a fascinating country with great ethnic, historical and architectural diversity as well as varied topography. The north had close ties with the former Austrian empire, and the bell towers alongside 19th-century Baroque churches and buildings have a Viennese look. The eastern side marks the start of the Hungarian plain with broad rivers and houses with overhanging roofs. The Adriatic coast is quite different, with its indented coastline fringed with lovely islands. The coastal cities reflect the centuries-old Venetian culture with churches, monasteries, palaces and forts testifying to the brilliance of the late Middle Ages and the greatness of the Renaissance period.

St Mark's Square *(pp160–61)*, with its Gothic church of the same name, is the heart of the Gornji Grad district in Zagreb and the city's oldest square.

Euphrasian Basilica in Poreč *(pp56–7)* has marvellous mosaics, some of the best-preserved examples of Byzantine art in Croatia.

ISTRIA AND THE KVARNER AREA *(see pp50–89)*

Poreč
Barban
Pula
Rijeka
Ogulin
Senj
Jablanac
Lički Osik

Amphitheatre, Pula *(pp64–5)*

Zagreb
ZAGRE
(see pp154–

Karlovac

Plitvice Lakes National Park *(pp88–9)* is one of nature's natural wonders with 16 lakes surrounded by woods. The cascading waterfalls create an impressive display of light and colour.

Otr
Posedarje
Zadar

DALMAT
(see pp90–15

Šib•

Kornati National Park *(pp100–1)* is made up of over 150 islands with underwater caves and sheltered coves. The park covers an area of about 300 sq km (115 sq miles) and is surrounded by clear seas. These wooded, rocky islands present an unforgettable sight.

◄ Pavement cafés in Varaždin, once a seat of the Croatian Parliament

Zagorje, west of Varaždin, towards the border with Slovenia, is a fascinating area with vine-covered hills, thermal spa towns and castles.

Kopački Rit Park
(pp198–9) is an oasis of great ornithological interest. In spring and summer the Danube overflows, transforming this area into a large lake attracting more than 200 bird species.

araždin

E NORTHERN COUNTIES
(see pp202–19)

0 kilometres   50

0 miles   50

Virovitica

ENTRAL ROATIA
(see pp172–83)

isak

SLAVONIA AND BARANJA
(see pp184–201)

Osijek

Đakovo

Slavonski Brod

Lonjsko Polje Nature Park
(p180)

The Tvrđa in Osijek *(pp196–7)*, the fortified nucleus of the city, has 18th-century military buildings. Initially Roman, then Hungarian, Turkish and lastly Austrian, the city retains traces of most of these diverse cultures.

The Palace of Diocletian in Split *(pp122–3)* was built by Emperor Diocletian at the end of the 3rd century. The city of Split grew up in and around it. Almost in its original state, it is the largest Roman building in the Adriatic.

Sinj

Split

Makarska

The city of Dubrovnik
(pp146–52) is situated on the coast. It is surrounded by fortifications begun in the 8th century and enlarged over the years.

Ploče

Dubrovnik

ISTRIA AND THE KVARNER AREA

The Istrian peninsula, nestling at the northern end of the Adriatic Sea, and the islands that tumble down the Kvarner gulf are some of the most sought-after holiday destinations in Europe. The coast is spectacular and the towns and cities are fascinating. Three National Parks – the Brijuni Islands, the Plitvice Lakes and Risnjak – preserve the natural charm of the area.

Until 1000 BC, the region was inhabited by Illyrians. From 42 BC Istria became part of the Roman empire, when the Province of Dalmatia was founded. Cities were built along the coast and on the islands, and many traces of Roman presence remain. Pula has a well-preserved amphitheatre dating back to the 1st century, the sixth-largest arena of its kind in the world.

With the fall of the western Roman Empire, much of the eastern Adriatic coast came under the control of Byzantium. The intricate, well-preserved golden mosaics of the 6th-century basilica of St Euphrasius in Poreč survive from that time.

In 1420 the area came under Venetian rule, a situation which was to last until 1797, when Napoleon dissolved the Venetian Republic. Nearly 400 years of Venetian rule are recorded by 15th-century open-air loggias, elegant bell towers and buildings with Venetian-Gothic windows, built by wealthy merchants.

With the Treaty of Vienna in 1815, Austria-Hungary extended its domain to include Venetian lands. Rijeka developed into an industrial port under Austro-Hungarian rule and is still today a hub for Croatian shipping. Close by in Opatija the Habsburgs built elegant villas and planted lush gardens for their winter holidays.

In 1918 Istria briefly became part of the new kingdom of Serbs, Croats and Slovenes, which subsequently became Yugoslavia in the same year.

Many Istrian towns have two official names, an Italian and a Croatian one, a legacy from 1920, when Istria was given to Italy as a reward for having joined the Allies in World War I. During World War II, the region became a stronghold for Italian partisans. After 1943, most of Istria was given back to Yugoslavia.

The Roman amphitheatre at Pula, one of the best preserved Roman theatres in the world

◀ Lake and falls, Plitvice Lakes National Park

Exploring Istria and the Kvarner Area

Istria is a triangular peninsula, traditionally divided into three areas. White Istria is a central plateau of karst or limestone with sparse areas of oak, pine and ash trees; grey Istria consists of a strip of eroded limestone with rich soil, used for vines and olive trees; and red Istria is a plateau furrowed by the rivers Mirna and Raša, farmed for cereals and vegetables. The most popular destinations in Istria are Poreč, Rovinj, Pula and the Brijuni National Park. The Kvarner area includes the city of Rijeka and the coastline as far as Jablanac. Woods cover the northern hinterland, with the Risnjak National Park to the north, and the Plitvice Lakes National Park to the southeast. The islands of Krk, Cres, Lošinj and Rab are delightful places to explore. Many of the towns on the coast have an Italianate appearance.

The Cathedral of St Mary the Great on the island of Rab

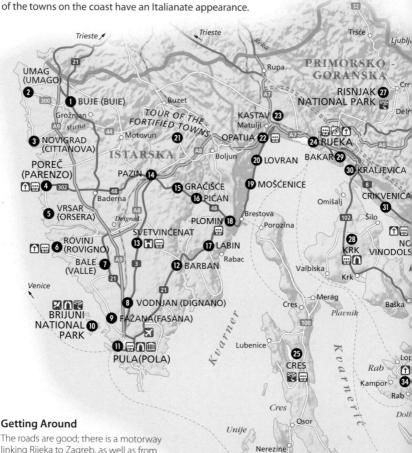

Getting Around

The roads are good; there is a motorway linking Rijeka to Zagreb, as well as from Pula to the border with Slovenia. The larger islands can be reached by tourist and local ferries and there are frequent sailings in the summer season – these take cars also. Buses link all the main towns and there's a bus that runs from Pula to Trieste, while trains link Rijeka and Zagreb, with connections to the south of Croatia.

For hotels and restaurants see pp226–8 and pp238–40

Sights at a Glance

Locator Map

Key

▬▬	Motorway
▬	Major road
═══	Minor road
═ ═	Motorway under construction
▬▬	Main railway
▬▬	County border
▬▬	International border
‐ ‐	Ferry route
△	Summit

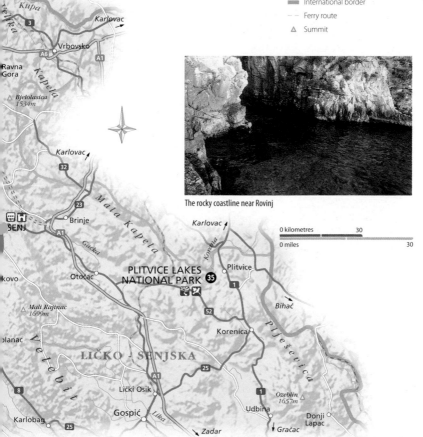

The rocky coastline near Rovinj

0 kilometres   30
0 miles   30

Façade of the Church of St Servelus, Buje

❶ Buje (Buie)

Map A2. ⛰ 6,000. ✈ Pula, 70 km (43 miles) S. 🚌 from Pula, Rijeka, Kopar, Trieste, Padova, Zagreb, Rovinj, Poreč. ℹ 1 svibnja 2, (052) 773 353. 🎭 Grape festival (3rd weekend Sep). 🅦 **coloursofistria.com**

On an isolated hill, among flourishing vineyards, stands Buje, the ancient Roman settlement of Bullea. Formerly a Frankish feudal village, in 1102 it became part of the Patriarchate of Aquileia and in 1412 the town came under Venetian rule.

The town still retains the outline of the ancient walled castle and has kept its original medieval layout, with narrow alleys and lanes leading to the main square. The Cathedral of **St Servelus** (Sv. Servol) and its Aquileian bell tower stand here. The church was built in the 16th century over the remains of a Roman temple, of which a few columns and pieces survive.

Inside the church are wooden statues from the 14th and 15th centuries (*Madonna with Child* and *St Barbara*), sculptures representing St Servelus and St Sebastian (1737) by Giovanni Marchiori, and an organ by Gaetano Callido (1725–1813).

A 15th-century Venetian Gothic palace and a 16th-century loggia with a frescoed façade also face the square.

Outside the walls is the Church of **St Mary** (Sv. Marija), erected in the 15th century: a wooden statue of the Virgin and a *Pietà* are from the same period. Some of the paintings of biblical scenes are by Gasparo della Vecchia (early 18th century).

The **Civic Museum** houses some interesting handicrafts and pieces made by local craftsmen.

🏛 **Civic Museum**
Trg Josipa Broza Tita 6. **Tel** (052) 773 075. **Open** Jul & Aug: 9am–1pm, 5–9pm Mon–Sat; Sep–Jun: by appt.

Environs
Perched on a hilltop, 8 km (5 miles) southeast of Buje, is the medieval town of **Grožnjan** (Grisignana).

The town was first documented in 1102 when it became the property of the patriarch of Aquileia. In 1358 the Venetians bought the town from Baron Reiffenberg and since that time it has been the administrative and military centre of the surrounding area. A tower, some parts of the walls and two doors are all that remain of the old town.

Within the walls are a 16th-century loggia, in the main square, and the Baroque Church of St Vitus and St Modest. The church has splendid altars and an impressive marble choir.

After World War II, the majority of the inhabitants, nearly all of them Italian, abandoned the town. In 1965, however, it was declared a "City of Artists". Contemporary artists work and exhibit their art in the various local galleries and workshops.

❷ Umag (Umago)

Map A2. ⛰ 13,000. ✈ Pula, 83 km (51 miles). 🚌 Joakima Rakovca bb, (060) 317 060. ℹ Trgovačka 6, (052) 741 363. 🎭 Feast of St Pilgrim (weekend nearest 23 May); International tennis tournament (end Jul); concerts in summer. 🅦 **coloursofistria.com**

This town is located on a narrow peninsula which frames a small bay. It was founded by the Romans and given the name of Umacus. In 1268, it became an important port when it passed into Venetian hands. Later, in the 14th century, a wall and towers were built, some of which still remain.

The town still has many 15th- and 16th-century stone houses, some with ornate Gothic windows. On the left outer wall of the 18th-century Church of **St Mary** (Sv. Marija) is a relief of St Pilgrim and the fortified town of Umag, and inside the church is a 15th-century Venetian-school polyptych.

15th-century polyptych, church of St Mary, Umag

Today Umag is a busy seaside resort with numerous hotels. It has become known for its well-equipped sports centres, and major tennis tournaments are held here.

View of the ancient wall and port of Umag

Boats in the harbour at Poreč

❸ Novigrad (Cittanova)

Map A2. 🏔 4,000. ✈ Pula, 60 km (37 miles). 🚌 Pazin, 41 km (25 miles). 🚊 Mandrač 29a, (052) 757 075. 🎭 GnamGnam Fest: Novigrad Scallop Evening (first Fri in Jun), Patron saint's day, St Pelagius (weekend nearest 28 Aug). 🌐 **coloursofistria.com**

Originally a Greek colony and later a Roman one called Aemonia, Novigrad stands at the mouth of the River Mirna. In the Byzantine period (6th century) when it was enlarged, it was called "New Town" (Neopolis). From the early Middle Ages until 1831 it was an episcopal seat. In 1277 it passed into Venetian hands and oak from the Motovun forests was shipped to Venetian dockyards.

In the 13th century the town was walled for defence, but it was unable to withstand a Turkish attack in 1687 and the town was partially destroyed along with many works of art.

Evidence of the Venetian period can be seen on the façades of the houses in the narrow lanes which lead to the main square (Veliki Trg). An 18th-century loggia stands here. Of the early Christian basilica of **St Pelagius** (Sv. Pelagij), rebuilt in the 16th century, only the Romanesque crypt from the 11th century remains. In the present-day Baroque church are paintings from the Venetian school of the 18th century. Evidence of the Roman and medieval periods can be seen in the museum housed in the Urizzi Palace.

❹ Poreč (Parenzo)

Map A2. 🏔 11,000. ✈ Pula, 53 km (33 miles). 🚌 Pazin, 32 km (20 miles). 🚐 Ulica K Hoguesa 2, (060) 333 111. 🚊 Local: Zagrebačka 9, (052) 451 458; Regional: Pionirska 1, (052) 452 797. 🎭 Season of classical music (at St Euphrasius) and jazz festival (both Jul–Aug). 🌐 **to-porec.com**

Poreč was a Roman town (Colonia Julia Parentium) which, after centuries of splendour, was sacked by the Goths and fell into decline. In 539 it was conquered by the Byzantines, who founded a bishopric around the year 800. The town then became part of the kingdom of the Franks, who gave it to the Patriarchate of Aquileia. In 1267 it was the first Istrian town to choose Venetian rule, and the town acquired a Venetian look as palaces, squares and religious buildings were built.

In 1354 it was destroyed by the Genoese and later, plague, pirates and a long war greatly reduced the population. During Austrian domination it became the seat of the Istrian parliament and an important shipyard.

The old centre shelters on a narrow peninsula protected by rocks and the island of St Nicholas. Despite being a popular base for visitors to Istria, the old town has remained intact and Poreč invariably wins an annual award for "best-kept town". The layout is based on the original Roman network, with a main road

(Decumanus) and another main road at right angles (Cardo). The main monuments of the town line these roads.

Along the Decumanus stand many Gothic houses. At the easternmost point is the Baroque Sinčić Palace (18th century), which houses the **Poreč Museum** (Zavičajni Muzej Poreštine). It is dedicated to Roman and early Christian archaeology; an ethnographic section illustrates daily life in the Poreč region. Nearby in St Maurus Street (Sv. Mauro) is the House of Two Saints, all that is left of the abbey of St Cassius (12th century), with two Romanesque figures on the façade. To the west, the Decumanus leads to Trg Marafor, once the site of the forum, with houses from the 12th and 13th centuries and the remains of a pre-Roman temple.

North of the square is the church of **St Francis** (Sv. Frane, 12th–14th centuries), altered in the Baroque period. To the east is the parish house with an ornate Romanesque façade. From here there is a passage that leads to the 6th-century Euphrasian Basilica, which has marvellous Byzantine mosaics (see pp56–7).

Archaeological exhibit in the Poreč Museum

🏛 **Poreč Museum**
Sinčić Palace, Dekumanska 9. **Tel** (052) 431 585. **Closed** for restoration.

A typical trefoil window in Venetian Gothic style, Poreč

Poreč: Euphrasian Basilica
Eufrazijeva bazilika

This 6th-century church, a Byzantine masterpiece, is decorated with splendid mosaics on a gold background. The Euphrasian Basilica was built for Bishop Euphrasius between 539 and 553, by enlarging the existing 4th-century Oratory of St Maurus Martyr. Some of the original floor mosaics still survive. Over the centuries the building has undergone numerous alterations. In December 1997 the basilica was added to the UNESCO World Heritage List. Classical concerts are held in the church in July and August.

★ Ciborium
Dominating the presbytery is a beautiful 13th-century ciborium, supported by four marble columns. The canopy is decorated with mosaics.

★ Apse Mosaics
Mosaics from the 6th century cover the apse. On the triumphal arch are Christ and the Apostles *(above)*; on the vault, the Virgin enthroned with Child and two Angels, to the left St Maurus, Bishop Euphrasius with a model of the basilica, and Deacon Claud with his son.

Sacristy and the Votive Chapel
Past the sacristy's left wall is a triple-apsed chapel with a mosaic floor from the 6th century. Here lie the remains of the saints Maurus and Eleuterius.

KEY

① **Remains** of a 4th-century mosaic floor from the Oratory of St Maurus are in the garden.

② **The Bishop's Residence**, a triple-aisled building dating from the 6th century, now houses several paintings by Antonio da Bassano, a polyptych by Antonio Vivarini and a painting by Palma il Giovane.

Interior

The entrance leads to a large basilica with a central nave and two side aisles. The 18 Greek marble columns have carved capitals featuring animals, some of Byzantine origin and others Romanesque. All bear the monogram of Euphrasius.

VISITORS' CHECKLIST

Practical Information
Eufrazijeva ulica 22.
Tel (052) 429 030. **Open** call ahead for opening times.

Baptistry

This octagonal building dates from the 6th century. In the centre is a baptismal font and there are also fragments of mosaics; to the rear rises a 16th-century bell tower.

Atrium

This has a roughly square portico with two columns on each side. Tombstones and a variety of archaeological finds dating from the medieval period are displayed in this area.

The Church of St Anthony in Vrsar, built in the 17th century

❺ Vrsar (Orsera)

Map A3. 🏔 2,200. ✈ Pula, 41 km (25 miles). 🚉 Pazin, 42 km (26 miles). 🛈 Rade Končara 46, (052) 441 187. 🎭 International sculpture school, Montraker quarry (early Sep); classical music concerts (summer). 🆆 infovrsar.com

The remains of a villa, a quarry and the foundations of an early Christian building all provide evidence that Romans once settled here. In documents preceding 1000 AD, this village is mentioned as the feudal territory of the bishop of Poreč, who owned a fortified summer residence here. Until 1778 it remained under the protection of the bishop and then came under Venetian rule.

The town had an outer wall and towers which have now almost disappeared except for the West and East Town Gate and some fragments of the walls. On the harbour is the Church of **St Mary** (Sv. Marija) from the 10th century, one of the most important Romanesque monuments in Istria. Guitar concerts are held here in the summer months.

The town is dominated by the 18th-century **Vergottini Castle**, built by restructuring the bishop's former residence. Near the Romanesque gate in the medieval wall is the small church of **St Anthony**, built in the 17th century with an open portico.

Environs
Just outside Vrsar lies **Koversada**, Europe's largest naturist resort.

To the south of Vrsar, towards Rovinj, is the **Limski Channel**,

now a marine reserve. The channel is 9 km (5 miles) long and 600 m (1,970 ft) wide, with steep sides perforated by limestone caves which have been lived in from time to time since the Neolithic Age. In the early 11th century, one of the caves was the home of the hermit St Romualdo, who founded the monastery of St Michael near Kloštar.

Many of the restaurants in the area offer the oysters and mussels farmed in the channel.

Fishermen on the Limski Channel

❻ Rovinj (Rovigno)

Map A3. 🏔 13,000. ✈ Pula, 40 km (25 miles). 🚉 Pula. 🚌 Trg na lokvi, (060) 333 111. 🛈 Obala Pina Budicina 12, (052) 811 566. 🎭 Grisia, International art exhibition (2nd Sun in Aug); Patron St Euphemia's day (16 Sep). 🆆 tzgrovinj.hr

Rovinj was originally an island port built by the Romans. In 1763, Rovinj was joined to the coast by filling in the channel dividing the island from the mainland, creating a peninsula.

Initially ruled by the Byzantines and the Franks, from 1283 until 1797 the town was under Venetian control. The remains of a wall dating back to the Middle Ages can still be seen.

In the square in front of the pier is Balbi's Arch (1680), an ancient city gate, as well as a late-Renaissance clock tower. The Califfi Palace, dating from 1680, is now the **Heritage Museum**, housing 18th-century art from the Venetian school and works by modern Croatian artists.

In the roads branching off the square are Baroque and Renaissance buildings. The backs of many of these face the sea. The **cathedral**, dedicated to St Euphemia (Sv. Eufemija), dominates the town. Originating in early Christian times, it was rebuilt in 1736. The saint's remains are preserved in a Roman sarcophagus in the apse on the right of the three-aisle church. The adjacent bell tower is 62 m (200 ft) high (the second-highest in Istria), and was modelled on that of San Marco in Venice. It is crowned by a copper statue of St Euphemia.

In the east of the city is the 13th-century **Baptistry of the Holy Trinity** (Sv. Trojstvo).

Along the waterfront is the Institute of Marine Biology. It was founded in the late 19th century and has an aquarium. Nearby, Red Island (Crveni otok) is in fact two islands linked by an embankment.

South of the town is Zlatni Rt, a park planted with cedars, pines and cypresses.

🏛 Heritage Museum
Trg maršala Tita 11. **Tel** (052) 816 720, 830 650. **Open** summer: 10am–2pm, 6–10pm Tue–Fri, 10am–2pm, 7–10pm Sat & Sun; winter: 10am–1pm Tue–Sat. 🆆 muzej-rovinj.com

The port of Rovinj, dominated by the Cathedral

The Church of St Elizabeth inside the walls of Bale

● Bale (Valle)

Map A3. 🔼 900. ✈ Pula, 10 km (17 miles). 🚆 Pula, 25 km (15 miles). 🚌 Trg palih boraca. 👤 Rovinjska 1, (052) 824 270. 🎭 Night of Bale, Baljanska noć (first Sun in Aug); Castrum Vallis, art exhibition (Jul & Aug).
W bale-valle.hr

On a hill of limestone, the Illyrians constructed a fort which dominated the surrounding countryside. The Romans also built a *castrum* (Castrum Vallis) on the same site, which was renovated when the place became a feudal estate of the Patriarchate of Aquileia. During Venetian rule, which began in 1332, the town grew in size and acquired its present layout of an elliptical wall with towers enclosing two parallel rows of houses. Interesting buildings include the Gothic-Venetian Magistrates' Court with coats of arms on the portico; the loggia; and the Gothic-Renaissance **Castle** dating from the 15th century, a residence for the Soardo Bembo family. Under one of the two side towers is a gate leading to the old town.

The Church of **St Elizabeth** (Pohođenje Blažene Djevice Marije), of Romanesque origins, was reconstructed in the 16th century and again in the 19th. The church contains a splendid Romanesque crucifix, a sarcophagus, a polyptych and a crypt with a marble Renaissance altar.

There are two other churches in Bale. One dates from the 14th century and is dedicated to St Anthony; the other, dedicated to the Holy Spirit, was built in the 15th century.

● Vodnjan (Dignano)

Map A3. 🔼 4,000. ✈ Pula, 11 km (7 miles). 🚆 Željeznička ulica, (052) 511 538. 👤 Narodni trg 3, (052) 511 700. 🎭 Bumbari, a festival in costume based on the name given to the town's inhabitants (2nd Sat in Aug).
W vodnjandignano.com

The town of Vodnjan stands on a hill among vineyards and olive groves. At one time it was an Illyrian fort and later, a Roman military post known as Vicus Atinianus. From 1331 until 1797 it was under Venetian rule.

The old part of town still has various buildings in Venetian-Gothic style, including the Bettica Palace and the 18th-century Church of **St Blaise** (Sv. Blaž). In the church are some splendid statues and about 20 paintings from the 17th to 19th centuries, as well as a *Last Supper* by G Contarini (1598) and an *Encounter of Saints* attributed to Palma il Vecchio.

Seven rooms of the church are given over to religious art (730 pieces): vestments, china and silver reliquaries, statues and paintings, and a fine polyptych by Paolo Veneziano from 1351 (*Portrait of the Blessed Leon Bembo*). There are also six mummies of saints, which have survived miraculously without being embalmed. The most revered is that of St Nicolosia.

🏛 **St Blaise**
Župni trg. **Tel** (052) 511 420. **Open** by appt. Collection of Religious Art: **Tel** (052) 511 420. **Open** Jun–Sep: 9:30am–7pm Mon–Sat, noon–5pm Sun; Oct–May: by appt.

● Fažana (Fasana)

Map A3. 🔼 2,800. ✈ Pula, 8 km (5 miles). 🚆 Vodnjan, 5 km (3 miles). 🚢 to the Brijuni Islands. 👤 43 istarske divizije 8, (052) 383 727.
W infofazana.hr

This small town is known mainly as the embarkation point for the islands of the Brijuni National Park (*see pp60–61*). Its ancient name, Vasianum, derives from the production of oil and wine amphorae during the Roman period. Facing the sea is the church of **SS Cosmas and Damian** (Sv. Kuzma i Damjan), which was founded in the 11th century and has undergone various reconstructions. Inside is a painting by Jurai Ventura of *The Last Supper* (1578), and in the sacristy are remains of frescoes by Italian artists from Friuli dating from the 15th–16th centuries.

To the side of the church is a seven-storey bell tower with an octagonal spire. The Church of **Our Lady of Carmel** from the late 14th century has Gothic frescoes by unknown artists and a 17th-century loggia. Nearby is the church of **St Elys** from the 6th century, with a stone doorway and blind-arch windows, which preserves its Byzantine appearance from the 8th–9th centuries.

Thanks to the growth in numbers of visitors heading for the Brijuni Islands, the town has grown and new facilities have been built.

The façade of the Church of SS. Cosmas and Damian in Fažana

⑩ Brijuni National Park

Nacionalni park Brijuni

The Brijuni Archipelago is made up of 14 islands and was declared a national park in 1983. The two largest islands have been inhabited since the Palaeolithic era. In Roman times there were aristocratic villas and later religious communities. The islands were abandoned in 1630 because of malaria, but people returned in the following century to work the stone quarries. In the late 19th century, the islands were bought by the Tyrolean industrialist Paul Kupelwieser. After World War II they were used as a summer residence by Marshal Tito, and were visited by heads of state. Visitors are only allowed on the two main islands, Veli Brijun and Mali Brijun.

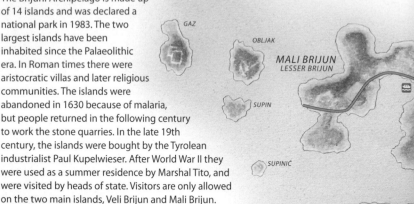

SV. MARKO

GAZ

OBLJAK

MALI BRIJUN
LESSER BRIJUN

SUPIN

SUPINIĆ

Barban

GALIJA

GRUNJ

VANGA

VRSAR

Aerial View of the Brijuni Islands
The islands are covered with lush vegetation, much of it undisturbed by human habitation.

Safari Park
Tito introduced many species of exotic animal, including zebra. Many were gifts from visiting heads of state.

Native Animals
Numerous indigenous animals also live freely in the park: fallow deer, moufflon, roe deer, hares, peacocks and about 200 species of wild bird.

Key

━━ Minor road

0 metres		800
0 yards		800

For hotels and restaurants see pp226–8 and pp238–40

Ancient Trees
Hundreds of different plant species from all over the world were planted on Brijun. Many of the trees, like this ancient olive, are now fully mature and are regarded as living monuments.

VISITORS' CHECKLIST

Practical Information
Map A3.
Brijuni National Park
Tel (052) 525 883; 525 882.
Individuals and groups must book on an excursion, which includes the boat crossing. Bicycles can be hired.
Open always, but access limited to crossing times.

w **brijuni.hr**

Transport
from Fažana.

Roman Villa
Excavations have unearthed the foundations of a Roman villa, its calidarium (hot room) and a frigidarium (cold room). A large room where the family met for banquets and ceremonies is decorated with mosaics.

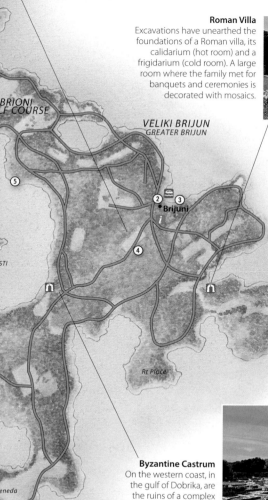

BRIONI
LF COURSE

VELIKI BRIJUN
GREATER BRIJUN

STI

Brijuni

Rt Ploče

eneda

KEY

① **The fort of Mali Brijun** is situated on the second-largest island in the archipelago. The Austro-Hungarian fort was built at the end of the 19th century

② **The museum**, opened in 1955, contains cultural and archaeological finds from the island.

③ **In the area around Brijuni harbour** hotels and a golf course have been built.

④ **The Tegetthoff Fortress** is a ruined Austrian defence system which was built in the 19th century.

⑤ **The White Villa** (Bijela Vila) dates from the Venetian period. It was restored in 1721. This was Tito's summer residence and was used for receptions and political meetings.

Byzantine Castrum
On the western coast, in the gulf of Dobrika, are the ruins of a complex of buildings dating from the Byzantine era (539–778), with towers and walls for defence.

⓫ Pula (Pola)

Pula is well known for its magnificent monuments from the Roman era, when it was a colony known as Pietas Julia. It became an episcopal seat in 425 and still has the foundations of some 5th-century religious buildings. It was destroyed by the Ostrogoths, but flourished again when it became the main base for the Byzantine fleet in the 6th and 7th centuries: the cathedral and chapel of St Mary of Formosa date from this time. In 1150 it came under Venetian rule, but by the mid-17th century the population had declined to 300. Revitalized in 1856 when Austria made it the base for its fleet, it is still one of the most important naval bases in Croatia. Today, Pula is a university town and, with Pazin (see pp66–7), the administrative centre of Istria.

The Cathedral's interior, a combination of styles and periods

Arch of the Sergii, 1st century BC

🏛 Arch of the Sergii
Slavoluk obitelji Sergijevaca
Ulica Sergijevaca.
The arch was erected in the 1st century BC on the orders of Salvia Postuma Sergia, to honour three brothers who held important positions in the Roman Empire. The arch is small with fluted columns, a winged Victory and Corinthian capitals. Its frieze has a bas-relief depicting a chariot pulled by horses.

Next door is a bar named Uliks ("Ulysses"), in memory of James Joyce, who lived here for six months in 1904.

🏛 Chapel of St Mary of Formosa
Kapela Marije Formoze
Maksimilijanova ulica.
Closed to public.

A small Byzantine chapel built on a Greek cross plan, this was once part of the large Basilica of St Mary of Formosa. Inside are remains of mosaics from the 6th century.

🏛 Church of St Francis
Sv. Frane
Uspon B. Lupetine 5.
Open Jun–Sep: 10am–1pm, 4–8pm; Oct–May: for Mass.

Built at the same time as the adjacent monastery in the late 13th century, this church has a fine doorway with a Gothic rose window. The interior is a single nave with three apses; on the main altar is a splendid wooden 15th-century polyptych of the Emilian school. Various exhibits from the imperial Roman era can be seen in the monastery cloisters.

🏛 Temple of Romae and Augustus
Augustov hram
Forum. **Tel** (052) 218 603.
Open May: 9am–9pm Mon–Fri; Jun–Aug: 9am–10pm Mon–Fri, 9am–3pm Sat & Sun; Sep–Apr: by appt. 🅿

Built in the 1st century AD, this temple stands in the square which was once the site of the Roman forum. It is a splendid example of Roman architecture,

Temple of Romae and Augustus, a jewel of Roman architecture

built on simple lines, with six plain columns and beautiful carved capitals.

🏛 Cathedral
Katedrala
Trg sv. Tome 2.
Open Jun–Sep: 10am–1pm, 4–8pm; Oct–May: for mass.

The Cathedral, dedicated to the Blessed Virgin Mary, was founded in the 5th century after Pula became an episcopal seat. Its present appearance dates back only as far as the 17th century. However, parts of the walls, some of the capitals and the windows are from the original building. On the right is a doorway from 1456, while the bell tower, which was built by 1707, contains stone blocks from the amphitheatre.

🏛 Church of St Nicholas
Sv. Nikola
Castropola 39. **Open** for mass.
ℹ (052) 212 987 (tourist office).

This church dates from the 6th century but was partially rebuilt in the 10th century. Towards the end of the 15th century it was assigned to the Orthodox community. Inside are some fine icons from the 15th and 16th centuries.

🏰 Castle & Historical and Maritime Museum of Istria
Povijesni i pomorski muzej Istre
Gradinski uspon 6. **Tel** (052) 211 566.
Open Jun–Sep: 8am–9pm daily; Oct–May: 9am–5pm daily. 🅿

This star-shaped castle with four bastions houses the Historical and Maritime Museum of Istria and was built by the Venetians in the 17th century on the ruins of the Roman Capitol in the city centre. The walls linking the four towers offer views over the city. Nearby are remains of a small, 2nd-century Roman theatre.

🏛 Twin Gate
Dvojna vrata
Carrarina.

The gate, from the 2nd–3rd centuries, has two arches with an ornate frieze. Nearby are parts of the wall which once encircled the city.

🏛 Archaeological Museum of Istria
Arheološki muzej Istre
Carrarina 3. **Tel** (052) 351 301.
Open May–Sep: 9am–8pm Mon–Fri, 10am–3pm Sat & Sun; Oct–Apr: 9am–3pm Mon–Fri. 🐾 🎫 by appt 🏛
W ami-pula.hr

This museum is housed in the former German school, within a park which is reached from the Twin Gate. On display are finds from Pula, with collections from the prehistoric era to the Middle Ages. On the ground floor are architectural remains, mosaics, altars and other exhibits from antiquity to medieval times.

The rooms on the first floor contain exhibits from the Neolithic to the Roman era. Three rooms on the second floor are dedicated to Roman antiquity (including a headless female statue found at Nesactium, near Pula). Two rooms have exhibits from the late Classical to medieval periods.

Of particular interest are pieces from Slavic tombs dating from the 7th to the 12th centuries.

Headless Statue, Archaeological Museum

VISITORS' CHECKLIST

Practical Information
Map A3. 🏘 60,000. 🛈 Tourist office: Forum 3, (052) 219 197. 🎵 Music events in Arena, Pula Amphitheatre (summer), Croatian Film Festival (summer).
W pulainfo.hr

Transport
✈ 8 km (5 miles), (052) 530 105. 🚢 Jadroagent (052) 210 431. 🚌 (052) 541 722. 🚍 43 istarske divizije, (060) 304 090.

🏛 Gate of Hercules
Herculova vrata
Carrarina.

The arched Gate of Hercules, built in the 1st century BC, is the oldest and best-preserved Roman monument in the city. At the top of the arch is a carving of the head of Hercules with a club.

🏛 Amphitheatre
See pp64–5.

Pula Town Centre

① Arch of the Sergii
② Chapel of St Mary of Formosa
③ Church of St Francis
④ Temple of Romae and Augustus
⑤ Cathedral
⑥ Church of St Nicholas
⑦ Castle & Historical and Maritime Museum of Istria
⑧ Twin Gate
⑨ Archaeological Museum of Istria
⑩ Gate of Hercules
⑪ Amphitheatre

For keys to symbols *see back flap*

Pula Amphitheatre

Amfiteatar

The elliptical arena in Pula is one of the six largest Roman amphitheatres existing today. Originally a small amphitheatre built here by Claudius, it was enlarged by Vespasian in AD 79 for gladiator fights. The amphitheatre could hold 23,000 spectators and had about 20 entrances. It remained intact until the 15th century when some of the stone was used to construct the castle and other buildings in the city. It was restored, first by the French governor of the Illyrian provinces, General Marmont, and again more recently when it was adapted for musical events. It can seat 5,000 spectators and is a venue for concerts ranging from opera to rock as well as for an annual film festival.

View of the amphitheatre today

Four Towers
The roofs of the towers were designed to collect the scented water that was sprayed onto the stalls. It is also thought that there was a structure capable of supporting large awnings as protection from the sun and rain.

Amphitheatre Wall
The well-preserved external wall of the amphitheatre has three floors on the side facing the sea, and two on the opposite side, because it was constructed on an incline. At its highest point, the external wall measures 29.4 m (96 ft).

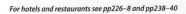

Interior of the Amphitheatre
When first built, the broad tiers could seat an audience of 23,000 people. Shows of every kind were performed, including naval battles. Today, during the summer season, operas, ballets and plays are put on here.

VISITORS' CHECKLIST

Practical Information
Flavijevska ulica. **Tel** (052) 219 028. **Open** summer: 8am–9pm daily (to midnight Jul & Aug); winter: 9am–5pm daily.
🚫 ♿ limited access.

Reconstruction

The main floor of the arena, 67.75 m (222 ft) long and 41.05 m (135 ft) wide, was originally framed by iron railings to separate spectators from the performance. Between the tiers of seats and the railings there was a space, 3m (10 ft) wide, reserved for staff. Along the main axis, under the arena, were underground corridors used by the gladiators and cages for animals. The animals were kept here before being sent into the stadium.

Arches
The first two floors have 72 arches, the third has 64 large rectangular openings. The arches lit the internal corridors which enabled spectators to move from one sector of the amphitheatre to another.

KEY

① **The various corridors** which led to the seats allowed spectators to find their places efficiently.

② **Today** the southwest tower is one of the entrances.

Underground Area
Many archaeological finds from the amphitheatre and other Roman buildings are kept in the underground passages, where there were once cages and prisons.

⑫ Barban

Map B3. 250. Pula, 28 km (17 miles). Pula. from Pula. *i* Barban 69, (052) 567 420. Trka na prstenac, Tournament of the Ring (3rd weekend in Aug). **tz-barban.hr**

A free town in the late Middle Ages, in the 13th century Barban came under the rule of the county of Pazin, and from 1516 until 1797 it was part of Venetian territory. It was granted to the Loredan family in 1535, and many buildings acquired their current Venetian look. The town still has some medieval fortifications which now incorporate several Renaissance buildings.

The Church of St **Nicholas** (Sv. Nikola) faces the square, which is reached through the Great Gate (Vela Vrata). The church has five marble Gothic altars and many Venetian paintings (16th–18th centuries), one attributed to the Italian artist Padovanino.

In the same square is the Loredan Palace from 1606 and, towards the Small Gate (Mala Vrata), the Town Hall, dating from 1555.

Outside the Great Gate is the 14th-century Church of **St Anthony** (Sv. Antun), with frescoes from the 15th century. In 1976, the Tournament of the Ring was revived and costumed lancers on horses participate in this traditional annual event.

St Nicholas
Tel (052) 567 173. **Open** by appt.

⑬ Svetvinčenat

Map A3. 300. Pazin. from Pula. *i* Svetvinčenat 20, (052) 560 349. **tz-svetvincenat.hr**

This walled village was built in the 10th century on a small hill around a much restructured fort. The main square is one of the most beautiful in Istria. Many of the main buildings in the village are found here, including the 15th-century

Church of the Annunciation which contains two paintings by Palma il Giovane and an Annunciation by Giuseppe Porto-Salviati.

The **Castle** dates from the 13th century and is one of the best preserved in the region. It belonged to the Venetian families of Castropola, the Morosini and the Grimani. In 1589, the Grimani commissioned the architect Scamozzi to convert one of the square towers into a residence for the Venetian governors, the other into a prison. High walls connecting the other two round towers enclose a large internal courtyard. This is reached through the citadel's only gate, which at one time had a drawbridge. The town's coat of arms and that of the Grimani family can also be seen here.

The town's name derives from the Romanesque church and cemetery of St **Vincent** (Sv. Vinčenat), whose walls were frescoed by an unknown 15th-century artist.

St Vincent
Cemetery. **Tel** (052) 560 004. **Open** by appt.

Environs
About 10 km (6 miles) away are the ruins of **Dvigrad** (Duecastelli), an atmospheric, abandoned walled village, surrounded by lush vegetation. Around 1000 AD, two castles

Church of the Annunciation, Svetvinčenat

were built on neighbouring hills and were later enclosed by an oval wall. A village of some 200 inhabitants grew up inside the wall around the basilica of St Sophia, built between the 11th and 12th centuries.

Although attacked and burned by the Genoese in the 14th century during the war with Venice, the village soon recovered. In the 17th century, sacking by the Uskoks (see p83) and a malaria epidemic depopulated the village. It has not been inhabited since then.

Reconstruction of a room in the Ethnographic Museum, Pazin

⑭ Pazin

Map B2. 5,300. (052) 624 310. (060) 306 040. *i* Franine i Jurine 14, (052) 622 460. **tzpazin.hr**

The town of Pazin originated in the 9th century as a fort and stands on a cliff 130 m (426 ft) high. One side of the cliff falls away to an abyss, which is 100 m (328 ft) deep and about 20 m (65 ft) wide, and is said to have inspired Dante's description of the Gateway to Hell in *Inferno*.

In the 14th century, Pazin passed into the hands of the Habsburgs, who granted it to the Montecuccoli family. They

The imposing, overgrown ruins of Dvigrad

maintained ownership of the castle after the end of the feudal regime.

The castle's present layout dates from the 16th century. The tower is reached through a doorway in the façade made in 1786. It houses the **Ethnographic Museum of Istria** (Etnografski muzej Istre) and the **Civic Museum**, where weaponry and finds from the castle are on display.

The Church of the **Visitation of the Blessed Virgin Mary** (Pohođenje Blažene Djevice Marije) and its 15th-century monastery were cultural centres for the area.

🏛 Ethnographic Museum of Istria

Castle, Trg Istarskog razvoda 1275, no 1. **Tel** (052) 622 220. **Open** 10am–6pm daily. 🏛 📷 🎥 **w** emi.hr

🏛 Civic Museum

Castle, Trg Istarskog razvoda 1275, no 1. **Tel** (052) 623 054. **Open** Apr–Oct: 10am–6pm Tue–Sun (Jul & Aug daily); Nov–Mar: 10am–3pm Tue–Thu, 11am–4pm Fri, 10am–4pm Sat & Sun. 🏛 📷 **w** muzej-pazin.hr

⑮ Gračišće

Map B2. 🏔 470. 🚊 Pazin, 7 km (4 miles). 🚌 only during school year; contact Pazin (060) 306 040. 🅸 Franine i Jurine 14, Pazin, (052) 622 460.

The small village of Gračišće stands on a hill among woods and vineyards. At one time this was a strong military garrison, which stood on the borders of the Venetian Republic and the Habsburg empire. The town has some interesting buildings, such as the 15th-century **Salamon Palace** and, to the side, the **Bishop's Chapel** (both in Venetian Gothic style) where the bishop of Pićan spent the summer.

The Church of **St Mary** (Sv. Marije) was consecrated in 1425 and has a characteristic barrel vault and several frescoes. The Romanesque Church of **St Euphemia** (Sv. Fumija) was rebuilt in the 16th century and still has a wooden crucifix from the 14th century. The loggia near the main gate dates from 1549.

The picturesque town of Pićan, once a bishop's see

⑯ Pićan

Map B2. 🏔 320. 🚌 only during school year; contact Pazin (060) 306 040. 🅸 Franine i Jurine 14, Pazin, (052) 622 460.

Known as Petena under the Romans, Pićan stands on a hilltop 350m (1,150 ft) high. It was a bishop's see from the 7th century to 1788, and has some intriguing medieval buildings. Inside the medieval walls is a cathedral dedicated to St Nicephorus, built in the 14th century, and rebuilt in the early 18th century after an earthquake. The story of the Christian martyr Nicephorus is shown in a painting by Valentin Metzinger (1699–1759) in the cathedral. The Romanesque Church of St Michael (Sv. Mihovil) in the cemetery has early 15th-century frescoes.

⑰ Labin

Map B3. 🏔 12,000. 🚌 Ulica 2, marta, (060) 333 888. 🅸 Aldo Negri 20, (052) 855 560. 🎵 Classical music concerts (Jul–Aug). **w** rabac-labin.com

The old part of Labin is made up of the medieval part inside the walls, and the part from the Venetian period around Tito Square (Titov Trg). Here stand the 19th-century Town Hall, a 17th-century bastion, a loggia (1550) and the St Flora gate (1587) with a Lion of St Mark.

In the square called Stari Trg lies the Magistrates' Court (1555) and in a street leading off the square stands the Gothic Church of the Blessed Mary's Birth (Rođenje Marijino), built in the late 14th century. A rose window decorates the façade and inside are works by Venetian artists of the 16th and 17th centuries, including a painting by Palma il Giovane.

In the same street are the Scampicchio Palace and the early 18th-century Baroque Battiala Lazzarini Palace, also Venetian-influenced, and now the **Town Museum**, with Roman and medieval finds and a lifelike reconstruction of a coal mine. Labin was Croatia's most important coal mining town until the mines were closed down in 1999. In 1921, in opposition to rising Fascism in Italy, 2,000 coalminers set up the Labin Republic, a socialist mini-state that barely lasted a month.

🏛 Town Museum

Ulica 1 maja 6. **Tel** (052) 852 477. **Open** Jun–Sep: 10am–1pm, 6–8pm Mon–Fri, 10am–1pm Sat; Oct–May: 7am–3pm Mon–Fri.

Environs

About 4 km (2 miles) from Labin is Rabac, a popular seaside resort.

Café in Tito Square, Labin

Detail of the altar in the Church of St George the Younger, Plomin

⑱ Plomin

Map B3. 🏛 140. ✈ Pula, 54 km (34 miles). 🚉 Rijeka, 55 km (34 miles). ℹ Vozilići 66, Vozilići; (052) 880 155; Regional: Pionirska 1, Poreč, (052) 452 797.

An ancient fortified town once stood here on the site of the Roman town Flanona, which was destroyed by the Avars in the 6th century. It was rebuilt after 1000 AD and took on its present look in the 13th century after it had become Venetian territory. Plomin, built on a sheer cliff 168 m (550 ft) above the bay of the same name, was once densely populated.

Houses take up nearly all the space inside the walls (from the 13th–14th centuries and only partially preserved). Worn, narrow roads climb towards the centre, where the 11th-century Romanesque Church of **St George the Elder** (Sv. Juraj Stari) stands. Inside is a tablet in Glagolitic script also dating from the 11th century, one of the oldest documents in this ancient Slavic script extant in Croatia.

The Church of the **Blessed Virgin Mary** (Crkva Blažene Djevice Marije) also contains treasures of artistic merit. The church was consecrated in 1474, but was greatly altered in the 18th century. There are three Baroque altars in carved, painted wood and a rich church treasury. A fresco by Albert, a German painter, was found on the wall during restoration work.

⑲ Mošćenice

Map B2. 🏛 330. ✈ Rijeka, 53 km (33 miles), on the island of Krk. 🚉 Rijeka. ℹ Aleja Slatina bb, Mošćenička Draga, (051) 739 166. 🌐 tz-moscenicka.hr

This small village was founded by the Liburnians on a small hilltop. The structure of the medieval town is still evident, with houses pressed against the walls, narrow streets, small alleys and courtyards. There are lovely views over the Kvarner Gulf from the village.

In the main square is the Church of **St Andrew** (Sv. Andrije), a building of medieval origin which was rebuilt in the Baroque style in the 17th century. Inside are some statues by the Paduan sculptor Jacopo Contieri. Just outside the walls are the small Church of St Sebastian from the 16th century, and the 17th-century Church of St Bartholomew.

The history of the area is documented in the **Ethnographic Museum** (Etnografski Muzej).

Statue by Contieri, church of St Andrew, Mošćenice

🏛 Ethnographic Museum
Tel (051) 737 551. **Open** summer: 9am–1pm, 6–9pm daily; winter: 11am–3pm daily. **Closed** Jan & Feb.

Environs
A series of steps leads down to Mošćenička Draga (2 km/1 mile), where there is a large pebble beach.

⑳ Lovran

Map B2. 🏛 4,000. ✈ Rijeka, 50 km (31 miles, island of Krk). 🚉 Rijeka, 20 km (13 miles). 🚌 Opatija, 6 km (4 miles). ℹ Trg slobode 1, (051) 291 740. 🎉 Asparagus Festival (Apr); Cherry Days (Jun); Marunada, chestnut festival (mid-Oct). 🌐 tz-lovran.hr

The town of Lovran (whose name derives from the laurel trees which are common throughout the area) extends along the coast until it meets the long seafront at Opatija (see p69). The old part of the town is situated on a small peninsula along the coast. The houses in the ancient fortified town lean against the enclosing walls, of which only a very few parts and sections remain: just a tower and the Stubica Gate. In the main square, as well as a medieval tower there are several houses with Venetian Gothic façades and also the Church of **St George** (Sv. Juraj), built in the 12th century and rebuilt in the Baroque period, along with a Romanesque bell tower. Inside the church, on the vault and the arch of the apse are some late-Gothic frescoes (1470–79) depicting the life of Christ and several saints. A building with a figure of St George stands in the main square and is worth a visit.

Along the coastal promenade, which extends between Lovran and the village of Ika, stand several beautiful early

Old mill at the Ethnographic Museum, Mošćenice

The Villa Angiolina in Opatija, surrounded by a splendid park

20th-century Secessionist villas *(see p27)*, surrounded by lush gardens.

🏛 St George
Open Jul & Aug: 7–9:30pm Mon, Wed & Fri.

㉑ Tour of the Fortified Towns
See pp70–71.

㉒ Opatija
Map B2. 🏘 13,000. ✈ Rijeka, 40 km (25 miles), island of Krk. 🚌 Rijeka. 🚏 Rijeka. ℹ Local: Maršala Tita 128, (051) 271 310; Regional: Nikole Tesle 2, (051) 272 988. 🎭 Carnival of the Riviera (Feb); Coffee Festival (Apr); Gourmet Story (May); Summer Festival (May–Sep); Opatija-Imperial City (Jul); Liburnia Jazz Festival (Jul); Chocolate Festival (Dec). 🌐 **opatija-tourism.hr**

The resort of Opatija takes its name from a 14th-century Benedictine abbey, around which a village was built. On the site of the monastery now stands the Church of St James (Sv. Jakov), built in 1506 and enlarged in 1937.

Tourist interest began to grow in around 1844 when a nobleman from Rijeka, Iginio Scarpa, built the grand **Villa Angiolina** here. The villa is surrounded by a large park and became the first hotel.

A few years later the Austrian Empress Maria Anna stayed here and her visit was immediately followed by visits from other court dignitaries. More luxury hotels and villas were then built and the small town became a fashionable turn-of-the-century resort. Tourism in Opatija was given a boost by the construction of the railway line which linked Austria with Rijeka, with a tram line to Opatija.

The Emperor Franz Joseph also stayed at a hotel here, often for long periods during the winter in order to enjoy the mild climate of the area. Today the coast is still lined with luxury late-19th-century hotels and villas surrounded by parks and gardens. However, it is no longer the height of fashion, although older visitors are drawn by its comparative tranquillity.

㉓ Kastav
Map B2. 🏘 10,000. ✈ Rijeka, 20 km (12 miles), island of Krk. 🚌 Rijeka, 11 km (7 miles). 🚏 Rijeka, 11 km (7 miles). ℹ Matka Laginje 5, (051) 691 425. 🎭 Bela nedelja, wine festival (first Sun in Oct). 🌐 **kastav-touristinfo.hr**

On a hill a short distance from Rijeka is the town of Kastav, which originated in the early Middle Ages. The castle was the residence of the local lord of the manor until the 16th century, and later the home of the Austrian governor. In Lokvina square stand the church of St Anthony of the Desert, which dates from the 15th century, and a loggia from 1571, restored in 1815. By the water trough a plaque recalls the drowning in 1666 of Captain Morelli, guilty of imposing excessive taxes.

Opatija, once a royal haunt and now a popular tourist destination

㉑ Tour of the Fortified Towns

The villages and towns of Istria were all fortified. The first people to build walls were the Histri (an Illyrian tribe), who put up defences on the hilltops where they settled. There are 136 such fortified towns in Istria. Many were abandoned, but evidence in some shows continuous occupation from 1000 BC up to the present day. The walls were reinforced in Roman times and rebuilt in the late Middle Ages, then enlarged when the towns came under Austrian or Venetian rule. Documents written in the ancient Glagolitic script can be seen on a detour.

③ **Hum**
This small village is protected by an oval wall, reinforced by the Venetians. The Church of St Jerome has splendid 12th-century Byzantine frescoes.

④ **Buzet**
An Illyrian fort and a Roman fortification (Pinquentum), Buzet belonged to the Venetians from 1420 onwards. They rebuilt the town wall with a Large Gate and a Small Gate (16th century). Today Buzet is known for its truffles.

Istarske Toplice

Livade

Pazin

Račice

⑤ **Draguć**
Medieval walls form the backs of the houses in this village. Ramparts were built by the Venetians after 1420. The 14th-century Church of St Roch has a series of frescoes, including a Journey of the Magi.

0 kilometres	3
0 miles	3

Key

— Tour route
--- Trail of the Glagolitics
= Other roads

⑥ **Motovun**
This medieval town stands on a hill dominating the valley. The old town is still encircled by an original 13th–14th-century wall. Later, a second wall was built around the suburbs. An internal gate, under a 15th-century tower, leads from the Lower Town to the Upper Town.

② Roč

The wall around Roč was built by the Patriarchate of Aquileia in the 14th century. Towers were added in the 1500s. Roč was an important centre for Glagolitic writing and in the 1200s the alphabet was carved on a wall in the Church of St Anthony Abbot. The Romanesque Church of St Roch contains two fresco cycles.

Tips for Walkers

Departure point: Boljun. **Distance:** 77 km (48 miles) one way. **Stopping-off points: Motovun** Konoba Mondo, (052) 681 791 (restaurant); **Hum** Humska Konoba, (052) 660 005 (restaurant); **Buzet** Restaurant Toklarija, (091) 926 67 69. **ⓘ Buzet** Šetalište Vladimira Gortana 9, (052) 662 343. **Poreč** Istria Tourist Board, Pionirska 1, Poreč, (052) 452 797.

① Boljun

The village still has some of its medieval walls, the 16th-century ramparts, a tower and a water trough from 1697. The grain store, loggia and the RomanesqueChurch of SS Cosmas and Damian are on the main road. Gothic paintings can be seen in the 14th-century Church of St Peter.

The Trail of Glagolitic Documents

The "Glagolitic Alley" (Aleja Glagoljaša) winds between Roč and Hum. It is 7 km (4 miles) long and was created from 1977 to 1985 to commemorate this ancient Slavic script. Along the way are 11 significant Glagolitic documents recalling events and people who contributed to the spread of the writing, invented in the 9th century by the saints Cyril and Methodius to translate the scriptures into Slavonic in order to disseminate Christian liturgy among Slav peoples.

Glagolitic document in stone on the trail to Roč

㉔ Rijeka

Founded by the Liburnians and conquered by the Celts, this town became a Roman city called Tarsatica. Over the centuries it frequently changed hands, and finally came under the rule of the Habsburgs. In 1719, to develop its maritime role, Ferdinand of Habsburg declared Rijeka a free port. The city became part of the kingdom of Hungary in 1870 and its economic importance continued to grow. Together with shipyards and industry, Rijeka is one of Croatia's main ports and a key rail and road junction. In February and March each year, Rijeka hosts Croatia's largest carnival celebrations.

The Korzo, a pedestrian avenue with 19th-century buildings

Exploring Rijeka

Over recent decades, the city has expanded along the coast and into the surrounding hills. However, its Central European atmosphere is still preserved in the majestic 19th-century buildings along the Korzo and the Riva, two broad avenues south of the Old Town (Stari Grad), built on land reclaimed from the sea. The Korzo is the heart of the city, lined with cafés, bars, restaurants and shops.

🏠 Capuchin Church of Our Lady of Lourdes

Kapucinski Crkva Gospe Lurdske
Kapucinske stube 5. **Tel** (051) 335 233.
Open 7am–noon, 4–8pm daily.

North of Žabica Square (Trg Žabica), the church was built between 1904 and 1929 on the orders of the abbot of the neighbouring Capuchin monastery on his return from a pilgrimage to Lourdes, to mark the 50th anniversary of the Virgin's miraculous apparition there.

🏠 Church of St Nicholas

Prvoslavna crkva hram svetog Nikolaja
Ignacija Henkea 2. **Tel** (051) 335 399.
Open 8am–1pm, 6–6:40pm daily.

This church, built by the Orthodox community in 1790, contains fine icons from Vojvodina, Serbia.

🏛 City Tower

Gradski Toranj
About halfway along the Korzo is the City Tower, first built in the Middle Ages. It has been remodelled several times, most significantly at the turn of the 18th century. The clock dates from the 17th century and the dome was added in 1890. An imposing building, it is decorated with coats of arms, including those of the city and the Habsburgs, and busts of the emperors Leopold I and Charles VI.

Detail of the Civic Tower

🏛 Town Hall

Municipij
Trg Riječke rezolucije.
In 1883, the 14th-century Augustinian monastery was turned into the Town Hall. It takes up three sides of the square and is now used as offices.

🏠 Roman Arch

Stara vrata
Trg Ivana Koblera.
In an alley leading from the north side of the square are the remains of a Roman arch, which was probably a gate to the city. It is a simple stone structure. Nearby, excavations have unearthed the foundations of a perimeter wall from the Roman period.

🏠 Church of the Assumption

Crkva Uznesenja Blažene Djevice Marije
Pavla Rittera Vitezovića 3. **Tel** (051) 214 177. **Open** 8am–noon, 4–6pm.

The Church of the Assumption, once a cathedral, preserves little of its original 13th-century aspect. It was renovated in the Baroque style in 1695 and altered in 1726 with Rococo details, and a 16th-century rose window was inserted. Inside, the altars, some paintings and the chancel are from the Baroque period. The bell tower bears the date of its construction (1377); the upper part is in Gothic style.

🏠 St Vitus Cathedral

Katedrala sv. Vida
Trg Grivica. **Tel** (051) 330 879.
Open 7am–noon, 4:30–7pm.

The Church of St Vitus, patron saint of the city, is now the cathedral. This large Baroque church was built between 1638 and 1742 by the Jesuits. Baroque altars and a Gothic crucifix from the 13th century adorn the interior.

🏛 Maritime and History Museum of the Croatian Coast

Pomorski i povijesni muzej Hrvatskog primorja
Muzejski trg 1/1. **Tel** (051) 213 578.
Open 9am–4pm Mon, 9am–8pm Tue–Fri, 9am–1pm & 4–8pm Sat, 4–8pm Sun.

This is the oldest museum in Rijeka, founded in 1876, but since 1955 housed in the

Gothic crucifix in the Cathedral of St Vitus

Governor's Palace built in 1896. The history of navigation is told through the collections of model ships, weapons and seafaring equipment from the 17th and 18th centuries. There are also rich archaeological collections from prehistory to the Middle Ages, displays of prints, furniture, paintings and an ethnographic collection.

🏛 Shrine of our Lady of Trsat
Svetište Majke Božje Trsatske
Frankopanski trg. **Tel** (051) 452 900.
Open daily.

On the opposite bank of the Rječina river, above the centre of Rijeka, is Trsat. At the top of the 561 steps from Tito Square (Titov trg) is the Shrine of Our Lady of Trsat. The church and Franciscan monastery were built in 1453 by Martin Frankopan on the site of a 12th-century church. It was in this church, from 1291 to 1294, that parts of the Holy House of Mary of Nazareth were preserved before being transferred to Loreto in Italy. To

The altar of Our Lady of Trsat, with a copy of the painting of the Virgin

compensate the local people for this loss, in 1367 Pope Urban V donated to them a *Virgin with Child*, painted by St Luke, a copy of which now stands on the main altar.

The sanctuary was visited by soldiers and sailors who left votive gifts, now kept in a chapel next to the cloisters. The church was remodelled in 1864 but retained the triumphal arch, the marble altar which sits underneath the painting of the Virgin, and tombs of the Frankopan family.

VISITORS' CHECKLIST

Practical Information
Map B2. ⚏ 130,000.
ℹ Korzo 14, (051) 335 882.
🎭 Rijeka's Summer Nights (Jun–Jul), Rijeka Carnival (Feb–Mar).
W visitRijeka.hr

Transport
✈ Krk, (051) 842 132.
🚉 Krešimirova ulica, (060) 333 444, 🚌 Trg Žabica 1, (060) 302 010. 🚢 Riva, (051) 212 696; Adriatica d.o.o.: Verdijeva 6, (051) 214 511; Jadrolinija, Riječki lukobran bb, (051) 211 444.

🏛 Trsat Castle
Trsatski kaštel
Ulica Zrinskog. **Tel** (051) 217 714.
Open summer: 8am–8pm; winter: 9am–5pm. 🅿 🖥

The Sanctuary of Our Lady leads to a castle built by the Romans to defend Tarsatica, parts of which still survive. In the 13th century, Trsat was owned by the Frankopans, who built another castle on the same site. It offers fine views over the Kvarner gulf.

Rijeka Town Centre

① Capuchin Church of Our Lady of Lourdes
② Church of St Nicholas
③ City Tower
④ Town Hall
⑤ Roman Arch
⑥ Church of the Assumption
⑦ St Vitus Cathedral
⑧ Maritime and History Museum of the Croatian Coast

㉕ Cres

The narrow island of Cres is 65 km (40 miles) long. In the north, a colony of native griffon vultures, protected by law since 1986, nests on a plateau swept by the dry, cold bora wind. The south is milder and olives and vines are grown. A single road travels from the north of Cres to the south of Lošinj, linking the islands by a bridge. Tourism focuses on just a few villages such as Cres and Osor.

Dry stone walls and olive groves overlooking the town of Cres

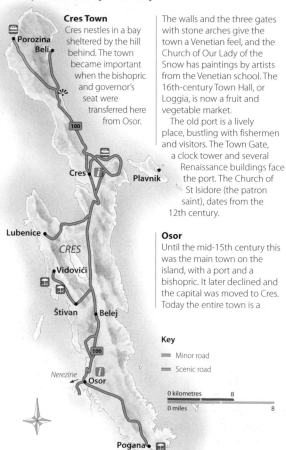

Cres Town

Cres nestles in a bay sheltered by the hill behind. The town became important when the bishopric and governor's seat were transferred here from Osor.

The walls and the three gates with stone arches give the town a Venetian feel, and the Church of Our Lady of the Snow has paintings by artists from the Venetian school. The 16th-century Town Hall, or Loggia, is now a fruit and vegetable market.

The old port is a lively place, bustling with fishermen and visitors. The Town Gate, a clock tower and several Renaissance buildings face the port. The Church of St Isidore (the patron saint), dates from the 12th century.

Osor

Until the mid-15th century this was the main town on the island, with a port and a bishopric. It later declined and the capital was moved to Cres. Today the entire town is a museum, with Bronze Age remains and some splendid monuments, making it a centre of great artistic interest.

The beautiful 15th-century Cathedral of the Assumption was completed in 1497 and is built of honey-coloured stone. The façade has an arched tympanum above a doorway with a relief of the Virgin Mary. Inside the church there is a painting of SS Nicholas and Gaudentius on the altar.

The **Cres Museum** (Creski muzej) occupies the Town Hall and has stone inscriptions and interesting finds from the Illyrian and Roman periods, and the early Middle Ages. The façade of the Bishop's Palace (second half of the 15th century) bears coats of arms of the bishops and nobles of the island and the interior is richly decorated. Some walls, foundations and mosaics are all that remain of the Church of St Peter.

🏛 **Cres Museum** Creski muzej
Petris-Arsan Palace, Ribarska 7.
Tel (051) 571 127. **Closed** for restoration. Temporary exhibitions mid-Jun–mid-Jul: 10am–noon, 7–10pm; mid-Jul–mid-Aug: 9–11am, 8–11pm; mid-Aug–mid-Jun: 10am–noon, 6–9pm. **Closed** Mon.

Key

━━ Minor road
━━ Scenic road

| 0 kilometres | 8 |
| 0 miles | 8 |

Door of the Gothic Church of Our Lady of the Snow, Cres

❷⁶ Lošinj (Lussino)

The island of Lošinj has a mild climate and sub-tropical vegetation with maritime pines, palms, oleanders and citrus trees. The main town, Mali Lošinj, was founded in the 12th century, when 12 Croat families landed here. The most famous beach is at Čikat bay, southwest of Mali Lošinj. It is 30 km (19 miles) long and a popular place for water sports.

Key

— Minor road

— Path

Interior of the church of St Anthony Abbot, Veli Lošinj

Mali Lošinj

This pretty town, which, like Cres, belonged to Venice for many centuries, has many buildings from the 18th and 19th centuries, when maritime activity was at its height. The oldest part of the town lies around the 18th-century Church of St Mary. Large hotel complexes just outside the town cater for package holiday-makers.

Veli Lošinj

Quieter than Mali Lošinj, this is a lovely town with villas hidden among the vegetation. The church of St Anthony Abbot (Sv. Antun Pustinjak) was built in the 18th century on the site of a smaller 15th-century church. It has a rich store of paintings, with examples by Bartolomeo Vivarini (1430–90), Bernardo Strozzi (1581–1644) and Francesco Hayez (1791–1882). The Baroque style is much in evidence on the seven altars.

There is a splendid view of the town and the coastline from the 16th-century tower of the Uskoks (*see p83*).

Environs

The island of **Susak** is renowned for its unusual geology: a 10-m (33-ft) layer of sand covering a calcareous platform. Vines grow well on this soil and all the islanders have vineyards; their wealth is measured by the number of vines they own. The vines, grown on terraces and protected by cane windbreaks, are further sheltered by dry-stone walls which are typical of the islands and the coastline of the upper Adriatic. The picturesque, brightly coloured women's costumes are famous. They are made by the islanders during the winter months and shown off at festivals.

The island of **Ilovik**, south of Lošinj, covers an area of nearly 6 sq km (2.3 sq miles) and is home to about 170 people, most of whom live in the village of Ilovik on the northeast coast. Vines, olives, fruit and flowers grow well in this mild climate. Nearby is the uninhabited island of Sv. Petar, where there are the ruins of a Venetian fortress and a Benedictine Abbey with a church and monastery. Prehistoric and Roman finds (mosaics, coins and other objects) have been discovered on Susak and Ilovik.

VISITORS' CHECKLIST

Practical Information
Map B3. 🚢 8,500.
ℹ️ Mall Lošinj: Riva lušinjskih kapetana 29, (051) 231 547/051) 231 884; Unije: (051) 231 547. For Susak and Ilovik, contact the Tourist Office at Mali Lošinj.
🌐 tz-malilosinj.hr

Transport
🚢 Mali Lošinj, (051) 231 765.

Unije is the largest of the lesser islands. It is hilly with little vegetation and a steep rocky coast on the eastern side, but there is a more accessible coast on the western side. The village is built around the Church of St Andrew. The islanders make their living from market gardening or fishing.

Overlooking the fishing harbour of Mali Lošinj

ⓐ Risnjak National Park: The Leska Trail

Nacionalni park Risnjak

The vast Gorski Kotor plateau, separating Croatia from Slovenia, begins north of Rijeka. Part of the area has been declared a national park in order to protect the forests and natural environment and the ecological balance of the area. The park, set up in 1953, first covered an area of 32 sq km (12 sq miles), but it is now double that size, most of it made up of forests and grasslands with many karst (limestone) features. The climatic conditions, caused by the territory's particular exposure and altitude, are very varied and about 30 different plant communities have been identified. The Leska trail was set up in 1993, and 23 information panels inform visitors about various aspects of this area.

Leska • • Crni Lug

☐ Park area
☐ The Leska trail

⑧ Silver Fir Forest
The silver fir, in great demand for boat building, has disappeared from many woods in Croatia; here it mingles with beech trees.

⑦ Chasm
Cold air from the chasm and the damp subsoil of this rocky fissure make the flora of great interest: plants which normally only grow at the higher altitudes of the park can be found here.

⑥ Feed Troughs
Feed troughs are set up here in winter to provide food for all the animals in the park.

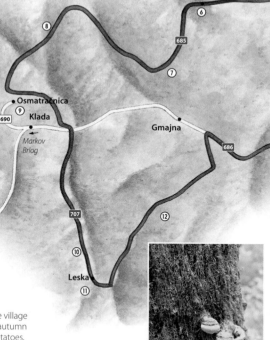

Hranilište

⑥

685

⑦

• Osmatračnica
⑨ Klada
690

Gmajna

686

↙ Markov Brlog

707

⑫

⑨ Observatory
From this viewing platform the behaviour of animals such as bears, foxes, lynxes, martens and wild cats can be observed in the woods. There are also many birds, both non-migratory and birds of passage. Towards evening at certain times of the year, eagles, hawks and crows can also be seen.

⑩
Leska
⑪

⑩ Cultivating the Countryside
Only one house is inhabited in the village of Leska. It is used from spring to autumn by farmers, who come to grow potatoes, peas and beans on specially built terraces.

⑪ Springs
Water flows under the layers of impervious rock and springs are created where the water emerges.

⑫ Tree Trunks
Fungi thrive in the cracks of old tree trunks providing a source of food for insects too.

⑤ Beech and Fir Forests
The trail goes through woods of fir and beech trees; many of the trees are very large. The undergrowth consists of hazelnut, bilberry and elder bushes.

④ Mountain Meadows
The areas which were deforested for agriculture or grazing land for animals are now mountain meadows. In late spring they explode with the varied colours of heather, purple moor grass, fescue and other grasses.

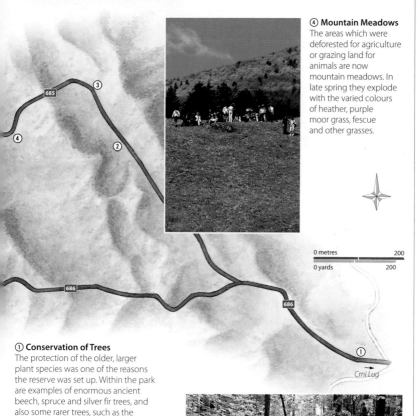

| 0 metres | 200 |
| 0 yards | 200 |

Crni Lug

① Conservation of Trees
The protection of the older, larger plant species was one of the reasons the reserve was set up. Within the park are examples of enormous ancient beech, spruce and silver fir trees, and also some rarer trees, such as the mountain elm and maple.

② Storm Damage
When strong winds blow down old or sick trees, they are left where they fall as they provide suitable growing conditions for microorganisms such as fungi.

Key

━━ Pedestrian trail

═══ Other roads

③ Karst Sinkholes
A karst sinkhole is a funnel-shaped hollow in the land. This feature is caused by water erosion of the rock and is characteristic of limestone areas.

㉘ Krk

This is the largest of the Adriatic islands, with an area of 409 sq km (158 sq miles). A bridge links the island to the mainland, built to provide good connections to the island's international airport. Along the eastern coast the island looks almost ghostly, its white rocks swept by the bora wind. Inland and on the more protected western coast, there is rich, lush vegetation.

The crystal-clear waters surrounding the island of Krk

Krk was first inhabited by the Liburnians, followed by the Romans, who founded Curicum (the present-day Krk) and Fulfinum. Traces of walls, baths and villas with floor mosaics still remain.

In the 6th century it came under Croatian rule and after the Frankish and Byzantine occupation it became part of the possessions of Venice. It was then granted to Dujam I, founder of the Frankopan family, and from 1480 to 1797 it was directly ruled by Venice.

Krk was a centre for Glagolitic script and the Baška Tablet, now in the Croatian Academy of Arts and Sciences in Zagreb, was found on the island.

Krk Town

The town of Krk developed in the Middle Ages on the site of the Roman town of Curicum. The wall and three Venetian city gates are still visible: the City Gate with a guard tower called Kamplin, the Sea Gate (Pisana) and the Upper Gate. Facing the main square are Renaissance-era buildings and in the area of the Roman baths is the Cathedral of **Our Lady of the Assumption**, dating from the 1100s but modified since. The three-aisle church has a façade of light-coloured stone. Inside are four paintings (1706) by Cristoforo Tasca, and a fine wooden Baroque pulpit.

The treasury is in the adjacent Romanesque Church of **St Quirinus** which houses the **Diocesan Museum**. This contains works from the cathedral and other churches on the island, including the silver Frankopan altarpiece depicting the *Virgin Mary in Glory* and a polyptych (1350) by Paolo Veneziano.

Behind the cathedral stands the Frankopan castle with four square towers from 1191, and a round tower from the Venetian period. Inside the walls are churches dedicated to Our Lady of Health and St Francis. The latter has an engraved wooden pulpit.

Omišalj

Omišalj lies on a headland near the site of Roman Fulfinum. The village (Castrum Musculum in the Middle Ages) was enclosed by walls, some of which survive. There is a square with a 17th-century Venetian

Map showing the island of KRK with locations: Rijeka, Omišalj, Rudine, Njivice, Klimno, Malinska, Silo, Porat, Šepići, Glavotok, Vrbnik, Valbiska, Košljun, Krk, Punat, Jurandvor, Baška, Stara Baška

Key
━ Major road
━ Minor road
━ Scenic route

0 kilometres 8
0 miles 8

For keys to symbols *see back flap*

loggia, the Church of St Helen with reproductions of Glagolitic script, and the Romanesque church of Assumption of St Mary (Uznesenja Marijina) (13th century) with a dome, bell tower and 16th-century choir, and a 15th-century triptych by Jacobello del Fiore.

Glagolitic inscription and rose window, Assumption of Mary, Omišalj

Baška

Not to be confused with isolated Stara Baška (Old Baška) Omišalj. Baška (New Baška) is on the coast and is a popular tourist resort with a beautiful beach, 2 km (1 mile) long, and clear sea. The Church of the Holy Trinity (1723) stands in a small square; inside is a fine *Last Supper* by Palma il Giovane.

Behind Baška, around a castle destroyed in the 11th century, is Stari grad, with the Romanesque Church of St John, rebuilt in 1723.

In the Church of St Lucy in Jurandvor, a short distance from Baška, is a copy of the Baška Tablet (the original is in Zagreb), the oldest document in Croatia written in Glagolitic script in 1100.

Košljun

Just offshore from Punat, this small islet is best known for its Franciscan monastery, where for centuries the monks have collected not just sacred objects, but all manner of valuable and curious items. Its zoological collection is noted for its assembly of seashells, and among the library's 30,000-odd titles is one of only three surviving copies of the atlas of Ptolemy, printed in Venice in 1511.

㉙ Bakar

Map B2. 🏛 1,600. 🛈 Primorje 39, (051) 761 111. 🎭 Margareta's Summer, concerts, sports events and shows in the *čakavski* dialect (Jun–Aug). **W tz-bakar.hr**

The demolition of a refinery and a coke plant has brought visitors back to this village, which was once a popular destination for people attracted to the landscape of the area and curious about the phenomena of the fresh-water springs. These springs originate in underground sources and flow out to the coast.

The **Frankopan Castle** and surrounding fishing village are also worth a visit. The village stands on the site of the Roman Volcera. From the 13th century until 1577 it belonged to the Frankopans who, in 1530, built a triangular-shaped castle. It is still well preserved with high windows which were salvaged when it was transformed into a palace for the Šubić-Zrinski family who lived in the property after the Frankopans.

The parish Church of St Andrew the Apostle has a painting of the *Holy Trinity* by Girolamo da Santacroce and a Crucifix from the 14th century. Evidence of the past is preserved in the **Civic Museum** which has many tombstones and sculptures dating from the Roman and early Middle Ages. Bakar keeps its naval traditions alive thanks to the prestigious Maritime Academy, which was founded in 1849.

The internal courtyard in the Frankopan castle, Kraljevica

㉚ Kraljevica

Map B2. 🏛 4,600. 🛫 Rijeka. 🚍 (051) 282 078. 🛈 Rovina bb, (051) 282 078. 🎭 Shrovetide sezona, traditional masked ball (carnival).

A well-known tourist resort on the mainland, Kraljevica is linked to the island of Krk by a long bridge which also connects with Rijeka airport (on Krk). In the old town (Stari Grad) is a castle, built in the 16th century by the family of the counts of Šubić-Zrinski. The castle walls also shelter the small Church of St Nicholas.

A village inhabited by families from the fortress of Hreljin developed around the castle. In the new district (Novi Grad), on a small promontory above the sea, is a castle built by the Frankopan family in 1650 in the late-Renaissance style. It has a square ground-plan with four round towers. It was turned into a magnificent palace in the middle of the 18th century.

In 1728, the Austrian emperor Charles VI began to create a sizeable port here, at the end of a road that went from Karlovac to the sea.

The Frankopan castle in Bakar, dominating the village

For hotels and restaurants see pp226–8 and pp238–40

❶ Crikvenica

Map B2. ⛰ 5,800. ✈ Rijeka, 16 km (10 miles), island of Krk. 🚌 Nike Veljačića 3, (051) 781 333. 🛈 Trg Stjepana Radića 3, (051) 784 101. 🎪 Trade fair of Croatian products (Jul); Town festival (Aug). 🌐 **rivieracrikvenica.com**

A Roman staging post called Ad Turres existed here at one time, with a port for trading in timber. In 1412 Nikola Frankopan (whose name derives from the noble Roman family of the Frangipani) built a castle here. It was later donated to the Pauline order, who set up a church, monastery and school. In the 16th century a wall and a round tower were built and, in 1659, the church was enlarged by adding a nave. The town, now a popular tourist resort, takes its name from the monastery. At the beginning of the 19th century, the Pauline order was dissolved and in 1893 the ancient monastery was turned into the Hotel Kaštel *(see p226)*.

The town has a long pebble beach and is one of the most popular tourist resorts along this stretch of coast. Thanks to its position, protected from the winds by the Velebit mountains, it enjoys a mild climate with dry summers and warm winters.

Gate of the former Pauline monastery, now a hotel, in Crikvenica

The altar in the Church of SS Philip and James, Novi Vinodolski

❷ Novi Vinodolski

Map B3. ⛰ 4,000. ✈ Rijeka, 28 km (17 miles), island of Krk. 🚊 Rijeka, 49 km (30 miles). 🛈 Ulica kralja Tomislava 6, (051) 791 171. 🎪 Patron saints' day, Philip and James (May); Novi Vinodolski summer carnival (1st weekend Jul). 🌐 **tz-novi-vinodolski.hr**

The old town, built on a hill overlooking the Vinodol valley, holds an important place in Croatian history. On 6 January 1288, in the castle built by the Frankopan dukes, the Vinodol Codex, one of the oldest legislative Croatian texts in the ancient Glagolitic script, was produced. The document is now in the National Library in Zagreb. It was signed by the representatives of nine communes, and established rules for the ownership and use of local land.

In 1988, the 700th anniversary of the Vinodol Codex, a fountain created by the sculptor Dorijan Sokolić was placed in the central square of Novi. The fountain bears the names of the places which participated in drawing up the laws.

The town is also remembered for the stratagem used by Bishop Kristofor to save the troops defeated by the Turks: the horses' shoes were put on backwards so as to foil their pursuers. Having reached the safety of Vinodol Castle, the bishop gave thanks by

Costume in the castle of Novi Vinodolski

rebuilding the Church of **SS Philip and James** (Sv. Filip i Jakov). He was buried here in 1499. The church, decorated in the 17th century in the Baroque style, has a magnificent altar from that period. The side altar has a Gothic Virgin Mary from the 15th century.

The 13th-century **Frankopan Castle** has been restored and is now a museum, with exhibits from the Roman and medieval periods and a rich, varied collection of traditional folk costumes.

❸ Senj

Map C3. ⛰ 8,000. ✈ Rijeka, 52 km (32 miles); Island of Krk. 🚌 Obala kralja Zvonimira 8, (060) 394 394. 🛈 Stara cesta 2, (053) 881 068. 🎪 Feast of St George (23 Apr). 🌐 **tz-senj.hr**

The cold wind known as the bora of Senj blows through a pass in the Velebit chain of mountains, making the town the chilliest place in the Adriatic. People have long been aware of it, yet despite this notoriety, Senj has always been inhabited, first by the Illyrians, then by the Romans who first created a port at Senia. This became a bishopric in 1169 and an important trading port for the transport of timber. After 1000 AD it was granted to the Templar Knights. It then passed to the Frankopans, and finally came under the direct rule of the

The Uskoks

In 1526, shortly before the Battle of Mohács, numbers of Christians from the hinterland fled to the safer coastal cities to escape the Turks. The refugees were called "Uskoks" ("the ones who jumped in") and their main desire was to fight those who had taken their land; and they carried out a highly successful guerrilla war. Initially they were organized by Venice around the fortress of Klis, from which they attacked the Turk-occupied land. In 1537 the Turks conquered Klis. Some Uskoks went to Primošten, but the main nucleus settled in Senj, under the rule of the Habsburgs, who encouraged them to procure fast boats in order to plunder the heavy Venetian ships. When Austria also slowed down operations against the Turks, the Uskoks took up piracy and started sacking coastal towns. At the end of the war between Venice and the Ottoman empire in 1617, the emperor was forced to remove the Uskoks from the coast and they and their families were transported to the west of Zagreb, to the Žumberak mountains.

Relief in the Museum of the Uskoks, Senj

Nehaj Castle, dominating the town of Senj

King of Hungary. As defence against the Turks, the Habsburgs established the first station of the Military Frontier (Vojna krajina) here. This stronghold had a powerful outer wall which is now only partly preserved.

After the Battle of Mohács in 1526, many Uskoks from Sinj and Klis came to Senj, and were co-opted by the local Austrian governor in the fight against the Turks. Their presence is recorded in **Nehaj Castle**, a fortress built on a square plan, constructed in 1553–8 by the Uskok captain Ivan Lenković on a hill a short distance from the town. It was positioned so as to sight approaching ships. The well-laid-out **Museum of the Uskoks** is on the first floor of the fort, and has an excellent view over the bay.

In the southern part of the wide bay is the main square, called Cilnica. Facing the square is the Frankopan palace, built in 1340 and altered in the 19th century. There are also large salt warehouses, and, further in, the Cathedral of St Mary (Sv. Marija), built in the 13th century and altered in

the Baroque period. It has tombstones with Renaissance reliefs and Baroque works, including an altar decorated with four marble statues.

A short distance from the square is the Vukasović Palace which houses the **Civic Museum** (Gradski muzej Senj), a museum of local history. The palace was once the residence of an Uskok captain. Flanking the roads of the town and in the Small Square (Mala placa), also known as Campuzia, are Renaissance buildings such as the Town Hall with its splendid loggia. Nearby is the Leon tower

(Leonova kula), dedicated to Pope Leo X, and the small, pretty church of St Mary.

Environs

The small village of **Jablanac** lies 37 km (23 miles) south of Senj. This bustling place is also a departure point for ferries to the island of Rab, and a good starting point for visiting the Velebit massif.

Jablanac is a well-preserved town and worth an unhurried visit. It was a county seat and its representatives met in the medieval castle. The castle was built by the Ban (governor) Stjepan Šubić, as was the church and its cemetery, both known from documents from 1251. The castle is now in ruins.

To the east of Jablanac is the Sjeverni Velebit National Park (Nacionalni park Sjeverni Velebit) where there is an interesting **Botanical Garden** (Botanički vrt) founded in 1966 on the slopes of Mount Zavižan at an altitude of 1,576 m (5,169 ft).

Jablanac, south of Senj, departure point for the island of Rab

㉞ Rab

The island of Rab lies parallel to the Velebit massif, creating a channel which was much dreaded by sailors because it forms a tunnel for the cold, dry bora wind which makes this part of the coast rocky and barren. The opposite, western side of the island is protected from the wind and the climate is mild. Here the landscape is much greener and maquis alternates with woods of pine, oak and holm oak. The Romans knew the island by the name of Arba, or Scadurna, and, after its conquest, built a settlement on the site of the present-day town of Rab. This island is a popular holiday destination with its sandy beaches, rocky coves and mild climate.

Rab Town

The main town, Rab, which gives its name to the island, became a bishopric in the early Christian period and was inhabited by Slavic people in the 6th century. After it had been conquered

View of Rab with its four bell towers

by the Franks, it was administered by Venice and a treaty of mutual defence was agreed upon which lasted until 1000 AD. Rab was at times under the rule of the Hungarian kings until 1409, when it became Venetian territory. Venice ruled the island until 1797.

The town, famous for its four bell towers which make it look like a ship with four masts, has some lovely Venetian architecture. Along the three main streets are fine aristocratic buildings with Romanesque doorways, such as the Nimira, Tudorin, Kukulić, Galzigna and Cassio Palaces. The ancient medieval walls that encircled

The Sea Gate, one of the ways into the town of Rab

the Old Town on the southern point of the peninsula were destroyed, and in the 15th century a wall was built which also enclosed the New Town, called Varoš. Part of this wall is well preserved, particularly the stretch facing the bay of St Euphemia.

▥ Loggia
Srednja ulica, Rab.

Where the main road, Srednja ulica, widens out, there is a beautiful Venetian loggia, built in 1506 in Renaissance style, and a granary *(fondak)*. To the left is the Sea Gate (Morska vrata), a tower from the 14th century. Through the gate is the town square.

▥ Prince's Palace
Knežev dvor

Trg Municipium Arba, Rab. **Tel** (051) 724 064. **Open** call for opening times.

The port and the town square are the heart of Rab, and this is also where the Prince's Palace was built in the 13th century in the Romanesque style. It was later enlarged in the Gothic style and then rebuilt in the Renaissance style. It has Venetian Gothic windows and Renaissance mullioned

windows. In the courtyard are some Roman and medieval remains.

⬆ Monastery and Church of St Andrew
Sv. Andrija

Ulica Ivana Rabljanina, Rab.

This small Romanesque church is annexed to a Benedictine convent founded in 1118. The bell tower, the oldest in Rab, is from the following century. The belfry has trefoil windows.

⬆ Cathedral of St Mary the Great
Katedrala Sv. Marija Velika

Ulica Ivana Rabljanina, Rab.

This splendid Romanesque building was consecrated by Pope Alexander III in 1177. The façade has alternating layers of pink and white stone and above the portal is a sculpted *Deposition* by Petar Trogiranin dating from 1514. The three-aisle interior, divided by columns, has a beautiful baptismal font made by the same sculptor in 1497, and a polyptych by Paolo Veneziano (1350) on the altar.

In the presbytery is a splendid altar canopy with marble columns and on the main altar, surrounded by an ornate wooden choir, is a reliquary from the 12th century with the remains of St Christopher.

The 13th-century bell tower stands 70 m (230 ft) away from the cathedral. It is the tallest of all the bell towers on the island.

The bell tower of the Cathedral of St Mary the Great

⬆ Chapel of St Anthony of Padua

Sv. Antun

Ulica ribara, Rab.

The small church of St Anthony, dating from 1675, is a good example of religious Baroque architecture. Inside is a marble inlaid altar and a 17th-century painting from the Venetian school.

⬆ Franciscan Convent of St Anthony Abbot

Sv. Antun Opat

Rab. **Tel** (051) 724 064. **Open** call for opening times.

The Church and Convent of St Anthony Abbot stand behind the cathedral at the end of the promontory. This convent, built for a closed order of nuns, was founded in 1497 by the noblewoman Magdalena Budrišić.

⬆ Church of St Francis

Sv. Frane

Park Komrčar, Rab.

The church dates from 1491 and stands to the north of the town in Komrčar Park. It is a blend of Gothic and Renaissance and has an original façade with three sculpted shells.

The altar in the Renaissance Church of St Justine in Rab

⬆ Convent and Church of St Justine

Sv. Justine

Gornja ulica, Rab. **Tel** (051) 724 064. **Open** call for opening times.

The convent and church were consecrated in 1578, and were intended for nuns from non-noble families. The bell tower with its onion dome dates from 1672. The church now houses a Museum of Holy Art, with the crucifix of King Koloman from 1112, and the reliquary of St Christopher (12th century), protector of the town. Also

VISITORS' CHECKLIST

Practical Information
Road Map B3. 🗺 9,000.
ℹ Trg Municipium Arba 8, Rab town, (051) 724 064. 🎵 musical evenings, Church of the Holy Cross (Jun–Sep); Tournament of Rab (25–27 Jul). 🌐 **tzg-rab.hr**

Transport
🚌 from Rijeka, Jablanac, Pag, Valbiska (Krk), (051) 724 122.
🚌 Palit, (060) 306 080.

on display are paintings and panels, including a polyptych by Paolo Veneziano (1350), Gospels and illuminated books in Glagolitic script.

Kampor

Kampor lies at the end of a long bay (Kamporska Draga) and has preserved its stone houses and terraces of olives and vines. Many holiday houses have sprung up around the village.

The Franciscan Convent of St Euphemia, with a small adjacent Romanesque church, is near the Church of St Bernard. The church contains two panels by Bartolomeo and Antonio Vivarini, a Byzantine panel (14th century) and other works. In the cloister there are various tombs and the sarcophagus of Magdalena Budrišić, the noblewoman who founded the convent of St Anthony Abbot in Rab.

Lopar

The village of Lopar is at the end of a rocky peninsula. It is a popular spot thanks to the sandy beaches fringed by pinewoods and the leisure facilities on offer (tennis, football and mini-golf).

Polyptych by the Vivarini, Church of St Bernard, Kampor

㉟ Plitvice Lakes National Park

Nacionalni park Plitvička jezera

The Plitvice Lakes National Park, set in the heart of Croatia, was founded in 1949. This area of 300 sq km (115 sq miles), covered in lakes and forest, has been part of the UNESCO World Heritage list since 1979. It is particularly known for its spectacular waterfalls. There are 16 lakes within the park and visitors can move around by following the paths along the shores or by using footbridges. Shuttle buses take people to the starting points of the trails and to the hotels in the park. The largest lake can be toured by electric boat. There are no towns or villages in the reserve, only hotels.

A hut by the lake shore

Footbridges
Numerous footbridges and rowing boats enable visitors to get from one shore of a lake to another and are a lovely way to access and explore the fir, pine and beech forests.

KEY

① **Dense forests** alongside the waters are home to some of the largest European species of animal, including wolves, lynxes, foxes, wild boar, roebucks, wild cats, otters and badgers.

② **The bird life** is extremely varied: 160 species have been recorded, including the eagle, marsh harrier, peregrine falcon, hoopoe, kingfisher, heron, little owl, and tawny owl.

③ **Along the banks of the River Korana**, into which the lakes drain, are a few shepherds' huts and several sawmills, which are run on hydraulic power. The river flows between steep cliffs in a spectacular natural landscape.

④ **The park vehicles**, shuttle buses, take visitors around the area on special routes.

Ciginovac

Prošćansko jezero

②

Okrugljak

Labudovac

Stubica

Galovac

Gradinsko jezero

Is

Prijeka Kosa

①

Gliborita draga

Velika Poljana

Entrance 2

Zac

| 0 metres | 500 |
| 0 yards | 500 |

VISITORS' CHECKLIST

Practical Information
Map C3. ⓘ (053) 751 014, 751
015. **Open** summer: 8am–sunset
daily; winter: 9am–sunset daily.
⬚ ⬚ ⬚ limited access.
ⓦ np-plitvicka-jezera.hr

Flora

The park flora is very varied, from waterlilies on the lakes to forests of gigantic trees. There is also a rich undergrowth of shrubs, a source of food for wildlife.

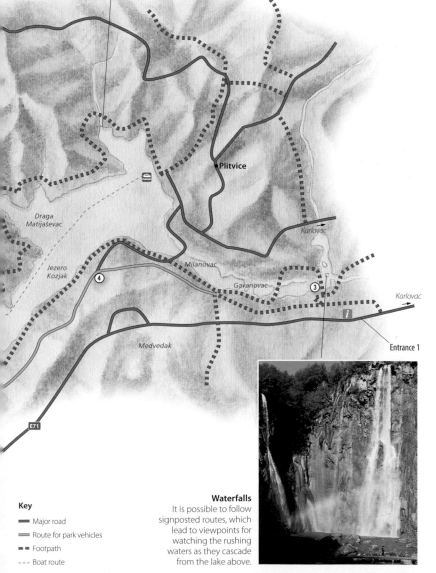

Key

━━ Major road

━━ Route for park vehicles

■ ■ Footpath

--- Boat route

Waterfalls

It is possible to follow signposted routes, which lead to viewpoints for watching the rushing waters as they cascade from the lake above.

For keys to symbols *see back flap*

DALMATIA

Dalmatia is the most visited region of Croatia. Although tourism collapsed in the 1990s because of the war, visitors have long since returned to the rocky coastline and sandy beaches, the deserted islands and the splendid cities of this Adriatic region. As a consequence of relationships and trade with Italy, an Adriatic culture developed here which has given Dalmatia an Italianate feel.

In the 1st century BC, after two centuries of war, the Romans managed to conquer the Dalmatian and Liburnian tribes and integrate them into their system. For over three centuries the region enjoyed a period of prosperity which was eventually brought to an end by the arrival of peoples from Asia, including the Slavs in the 7th century.

In 915, after a long period of wars and unrest, the first Croatian kings founded a new state, blessed by papal authority. New public and religious buildings, walls and town halls were built, the arts began to flourish, and trading with the Italian coast increased. This was a period of great cultural vitality, which survived the collapse of the Croatian state and its integration into the Kingdom of Hungary in the 12th century. In 1409, after a long series of conflicts, the Hungarian king sold the islands and many of the coastal cities to Venice. In the 16th century, there followed a second flowering of the arts, and the sculptors, architects, painters, writers and scholars of this period laid the foundations for the future development of Croatian culture, art and literature.

In late spring, when the Jadranska magistrala coast road has yet to be invaded by heavy summer traffic, this must be one of the loveliest parts of Europe. From Karlobag the road winds along the edge of the Velebit mountain chain and the Dalmatian and the Biokovo plateaux. Seawards is the long, lunar-surfaced island of Pag and further along are the islands around Zadar, those around Split, and finally the lovely island of Mljet, set in an azure sea. Behind are hillsides covered in vineyards and maquis vegetation, dominated by the bright yellow flowers of broom.

A secluded beach on the island of Mljet

◀ Walls of the Old Town, Dubrovnik – the "pearl of the Adriatic"

Exploring Dalmatia

To the north is Zadar, with its exceptional monuments, and the islands of the Zadar archipelago, the southern part of which is designated the Kornati National Park. The road travels on to Šibenik, with its perfectly preserved old town centre and splendid cathedral, and Trogir, an architectural jewel. The ruins of the Roman town of Salona are just outside the city of Split, which developed within the Palace of Emperor Diocletian. The coastal road turns inland to cross the delta of the Neretva and reaches Ston, a point of access to the peninsula of Pelješac. Finally, on a rocky spur stands the medieval city of Dubrovnik, now a UNESCO World Heritage Site.

Bell tower of the Cathedral, Zadar

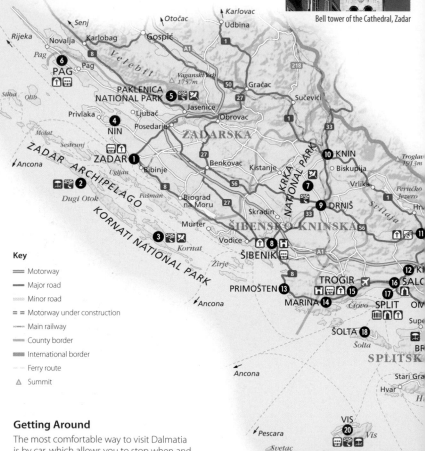

Key

─── Motorway

─── Major road

─── Minor road

= = Motorway under construction

⊷⊷ Main railway

─── County border

─── International border

-- Ferry route

△ Summit

Getting Around

The most comfortable way to visit Dalmatia is by car, which allows you to stop when and where you like. Traffic is always heavier during the summer holiday months. Cities and towns are not directly connected by railway, but buses are frequent and run between almost all the towns. The main coastal towns and the more important islands are linked by frequent ferry connections (see pp278–9). Yachts can be hired for cruising along the coast (see p258).

For hotels and restaurants see pp228–30 and pp240–45

The imposing 15th-century Minčeta Tower in Dubrovnik

Locator Map

Sights at a Glance

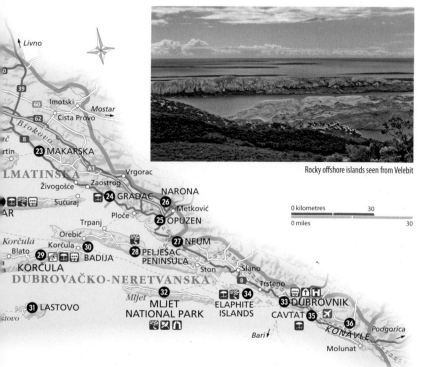

Rocky offshore islands seen from Velebit

For keys to symbols *see back flap*

❶ Zadar

Originally Illyrians inhabited this narrow peninsula, but its present layout dates back to Roman rule, when the straight roads and forum were built. It became an important *municipium*, and a port for the trading of timber and wine. In the Middle Ages it was the main base for the Byzantine fleet. Venice and the king of Hungary fought over Zadar in the 12th–13th centuries but in 1409, King Ladislaus of Hungary sold his Dalmatian islands and cities to Venice for 100,000 ducats. Zadar became Zara and enjoyed a spell of prosperity; churches and palaces were built. After World War I, Zadar was ceded to Italy by the Treaty of Rapallo, but many Italians left after the forming of Yugoslavia in 1947. Zadar was repeatedly bombed during World War II and suffered considerable damage.

Roman arch forming the Sea Gate

The medieval tower, Bablja Kula, part of the ancient wall

🏛 Land Gate and Walls
Kopnena vrata

The Land Gate was built in 1543 by the great Veronese architect Michele Sanmicheli as the entrance to the city. The gate has a large central aperture and two smaller openings at the sides, divided by four white stone pilasters supporting half-columns.

Above the main gate is a relief of St Chrysogonus on horseback and the lion of St Mark, symbol of Venetian rule. Beyond the gate are a few remains of the ancient walls, the former Venetian arsenal, and Liberation Square (Zoraničev trg or Trg Petra Zoranića) with a Roman column in the centre.

On one side of the square stands the medieval tower of Bablja kula. At the base are five fountains (Trg pet bunara), which once supplied water to the city of Zadar.

🏛 Church of St Simeon
Sv. Šime

Trg Petra Zoranića 7. **Tel** (023) 211 705. **Open** 8:30am–noon Mon–Sat.

Originally constructed in Romanesque style, the church was rebuilt after 1632 to house the remains of the saint, which are kept in a silver reliquary. This impressive work, nearly 2m (6 ft) long, was made between 1377 and 1380 by Francesco da Milano and bears reliefs showing scenes of St Simeon's life.

🏛 Museum of Ancient Glass
Muzej antičkog stakla

Poljana Zemaljskog odbora 1. **Tel** (023) 363 831. **Open** summer: 9am–9pm daily; winter: 9am–4pm Mon–Fri. 🅿 ♿ **mas-zadar.hr**

Housed in the restored Cosmacendi Palace, this museum displays a large number of ancient Roman glass objects found on archaeological sites in Zadar and its surroundings.

🏛 People's Square
Narodni trg

The Town Hall, which was built in 1934, faces the square, as does the Renaissance City Loggia (Gradska loža) built by Michele Sanmicheli in 1565 as the city courts. It is now used for exhibitions.

Nearby, the 16th-century Town Guard Palace houses the Ethnographic Museum, with collections of costumes and objects from the entire county.

🏛 Sea Gate
Vrata sv. Krševana

This complex construction is the result of rebuilding work carried out by Michele Sanmicheli in 1573 on a Roman arch dedicated to the Sergi family. On the seaward side is the lion of St Mark and a memorial stone recalling the Battle of Lepanto (1571). On the inner side of the gate is a stone commemorating Pope Alexander III's visit in 1177.

🏛 Church of St Chrysogonus
Sv. Krševan

Poljana pape Aleksandra III. **Closed** for restoration.

Prior to AD 1000 a church and monastery were built by Benedictines on the site of the Roman market. While the church, rebuilt in 1175, has survived with few alterations, the monastery was destroyed in World War II. At the height of the monastery's splendour it possessed a rich library and a *scriptorium*, famous for its transcribed and illuminated works. The three-aisle church,

The Church of St Chrysogonus

divided by columns (salvaged from a previous building), has a simple Romanesque appearance, except for the Baroque main altar with statues of Zadar's four patron saints: Chrysogonus, Zoilus, Simeon and Anastasia. The apse is the best-preserved part, with some 13th-century frescoes and a Romanesque crucifix on the altar.

🏛 Archaeological Museum
Arheološki muzej

Trg opatice Čike 1. **Tel** (023) 250 516. **Open** Jan–Mar: 9am–1pm Mon–Sat; Apr, May & Oct: 9am–3pm Mon–Sat; Jun–Sep: 9am–9pm daily; Nov & Dec: 9am–2pm Mon–Sat. 🐾 🎫 by appt. 🏠

This museum is housed in a building near the old Roman Forum. Its collection contains objects that date from pre-history all the way to recent times, and that come from the entire Zadar area and the islands. Of particular interest is glass from the Roman period, and the early Christian and medieval liturgical objects.

The Renaissance façade of the Church of St Mary

🏠 Church of St Mary and Museum of Sacred Art
Sv. Marija i Zlato i srebro Zadra

Trg opatice Čike 1. **Tel** (023) 250 496. **Open** summer: 10am–1pm, 6–8pm Mon–Sat, 10am–noon Sun; winter: 10am–12.30pm, 5–6.30pm Mon–Sat. 🐾 🎫 ♿ 🏠

On one side of the square called Poljana pape Ivana Pavla II stands a tall, Romanesque bell tower, built for King Koloman in 1105, and the Church of St Mary.

Sculpture, Museum of Sacred Art

VISITORS' CHECKLIST

Practical Information

Map C4. 🏙 92,000. 🛈 City: Smiljanića 5, (023) 212 222; Regional: Sv. Leopolda Mandića (023) 315 316. 🎵 Musical evenings at St Donat (Jul & Aug), Summer theatre.
🌐 visitzadar.net

Transport

✈ Zemunik 8 km (5 miles), (023) 313 311. 🚌 (023) 212 555.
🚍 A Starčevica 6, (060) 305 305.
⚓ Jadrolinija: (023) 254 800.

The church, built in 1066, has undergone various alterations and now has a Renaissance façade. The three-aisle interior has a large women's gallery; the stuccowork is from 1744. The former monastery next door is now the Museum of Sacred Art: on the ground floor are gold pieces; on the upper floor are paintings and statues, including a fine polyptych by Vittore Carpaccio (1487).

Zadar Town Centre

0 metres 300
yards 300

square of the ancient
city of Jadera was built
en the 1st century BC
he 3rd century. The forum,
n (295 ft) long and 45 m
47 ft) wide, was
bordered on three sides
by porticoes with
marble columns. In the
present square, Poljana
pape Ivana Pavla II, are
the foundations of
public buildings,
including a meeting
hall, some of the original
paving, several *tabernae*
(rectangular-shaped trading
areas) and a monumental pillar,
used in the Middle Ages as a
"pillar of shame".

The Romanesque façade of the Cathedral
of St Anastasia

⛪ Cathedral of St Anastasia

Katedrala sv. Stošije
Forum. **Tel** (023) 251 708.
Open 8am–noon, 5–7pm daily.

The magnificent Cathedral of
St Anastasia also stands on
the site of the Forum. It
was founded by the
Byzantines in the
9th century and
rebuilt in the
Romanesque style in
the 12–13th centuries.
It has a rectangular
ground-plan with a
large semicircular apse. The
harmonious façade with three
doors, completed in 1324, is
divided in half horizontally with
the upper part characterized by
arches and columns and two
splendid rose windows. The
main window is Romanesque
and the other is Gothic.

Rose window,
St Anastasia

The three-aisle interior is
divided by two rows of columns
and pilasters which support the
high arcades. At the sides of the
raised presbytery are engraved
wooden choir stalls, the work of
the Venetian Matteo Moronzoni
(early 15th century). The ciborium
with four Corinthian columns is
decorated with different motifs
(1332). Underneath is a small
sarcophagus containing the
remains of St Anastasia, dating
from the 9th century.

The right-hand altar inside the Cathedral
of St Anastasia

The altars are mostly Baroque;
on one there is a lovely painting
by Palma il Giovane. In the right-
hand nave is an imposing
Baroque altar dedicated to the
Holy Sacrament; just beyond is
the hexagonal baptistry.

🎵 Sea Organ and Greeting to the Sun

Designed by architect Nikola
Basic, this musical instrument is
built into the quayside. Under
white stone steps are a set of
pipes which produce musical
chords naturally as waves push
air up through the pipes. Next
to it is another installation by
the same architect called
Greeting to the Sun, consisting of
300 glass plates that produce
interesting light effects.

Plan of the Cathedral of St Anastasia

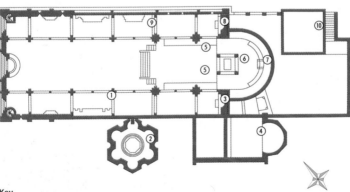

Key

① Altar of the Holy Sacrament
② Baptistry
③ Roman pilaster
④ Sacristy
⑤ Choir stalls
⑥ Main altar and ciborium
⑦ Bishop's chair
⑧ Chapel of St Anastasia
⑨ Souls of Purgatory altar
⑩ Bell tower

0 metres   15
0 yards   15

Zadar: Church of St Donat
Sv. Donat

The Church of the Holy Trinity, which later took the name of its founder Bishop Donat, is one of the finest examples of Byzantine architecture in Dalmatia. It was built in the early 9th century on the paving stones of the former Roman Forum and has a circular ground-plan with three circular apses. Inside is a women's gallery which goes all the way around the church and creates an upper storey. St Donat has not been used as a church since 1797, but because of the good acoustics, concerts are often held here.

VISITORS' CHECKLIST

Practical Information
Forum. *i* (023) 250 516.
Open Apr, May & Oct: 9am–5pm daily; Jun–Sep: 9am–9pm daily; Nov–Mar: by appt.

Exterior
The church is built of honey-coloured Dalmatian stone, much of which came from the old Roman Forum.

Dome
The cylindrical, conical dome rises in the centre of the church to a height of 27 m (88 ft).

Each of the three apses has blind arches. At one time the altar was situated in the central apse.

The Women's Gallery
The interior of the church has a matroneum, or women's gallery, supported by six pilasters and two Roman columns which border the circular nave and divide the structure into two floors.

The internal walls are completely bare. Probably the original decorations, frescoes or mosaics, have been lost.

Roman Fragments
Stones from the Roman Forum were used for the paving; other Roman material is visible in the walls, entrance and gallery.

❷ Zadar Archipelago

The Zadar Archipelago is made up of more than 300 islands surrounded by crystal-clear waters. The larger islands are covered in Mediterranean scrub and olive trees. The archipelago is what remains of a mountain chain which once ran parallel to the Velebit mountains, but which is now almost submerged. Only about a dozen of the islands are inhabited, and the small communities live by fishing, farming and rearing animals. There are a few hotels on the larger islands closer to Zadar, and private accommodation can be found on all the others. Daily ferry services link Zadar with the main islands.

Dugi Otok, the largest island in the Zadar archipelago

Dugi Otok

Covering an area of 124 sq km (48 sq miles), this is the largest island in the archipelago. The inhabitants live in about ten villages. Fishing and farming takes place in the northern part of the island and on the flatter areas of the island, while the southern, hillier terrain is given over to sheep farming. The western coast is steep and desolate but beaches and bays punctuate the eastern coast.

Proximity to Zadar means that since Roman times it has been a popular place for the city nobles to build holiday villas. In the Renaissance period more summer residences were built here, particularly in **Sali**. This is the largest town and port on the island and there are some houses in the flamboyant Gothic style. The Renaissance Church of St Mary has some paintings from the same period by Juraj Čulinović.

The fishing village of Božava, at the island's northernmost point, is also a popular yacht marina. It has a small church, dedicated to St Nicholas, which dates from the 10th century. Inside the church a sculpture depicts Arab saints.

The long bay of Telašćica, to the south, is a natural harbour and was once used by the Venetian fleet. One side ends in a sheer cliff and the other in thick pine woods. This area is being reforested after a disastrous fire in 1995. The southern part of the island has been designated the Telašćica Nature Park *(see p100)*.

Ugljan

This lush, green island is 22 km (13 miles) long and covers an area of 50 sq km (19 sq miles). It has a population of 7,600 and the small villages lie along the eastern coast of the island. In the main village, Ugljan, is the Franciscan monastery of St Jerome, built in the 15th century. It has a pretty cloister and the library contains numerous works written in Glagolitic script.

A more newly built village is **Preko**, where the wealthier citizens of Zadar own villas. There are also rooms in private houses available for renting. The village is dominated by the large Venetian fortress of St Michael which stands on a hill 265 m (869 ft) high. A bridge links the island to Pašman.

View from the fortress of St Michael, Preko

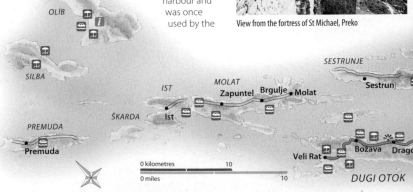

OLIB

SESTRUNJE

SILBA

Sestrun

IST

MOLAT
Zapuntel Brgulje Molat

ŠKARDA Ist

PREMUDA

Premuda

Veli Rat

Božava Drago

0 kilometres   10

0 miles   10

DUGI OTOK

The Monastery of SS. Cosmas and Damian in Pašman

Pašman

This wild, unspoilt island has a population of 3,500, who live in villages on the coast facing the mainland. There are fewer tourists than on Ugljan. The western side is given over to vineyards, while the eastern part has thick maquis right down to the coastline, where there are also some pebble beaches.

South of **Pašman**, a fishing village and the main centre on the island, is **Tkon**, an embarkation point for ferries. On Mount Čokovac, north of Tkon, is the Benedictine Monastery of SS. Cosmas and Damian (Sv. Kuzma i Damjan). Built in 1125, it became a centre of Glagolitic culture and has a well-stocked library with Glagolitic texts. In the 15th century the church and monastery were rebuilt in the Gothic style when they were taken over by the Franciscan order. The church (14th–15th century) has some good sculptures, including a painted crucifix.

Premuda

This island covers an area of 9 sq km (3 sq miles) and has fewer than 100 inhabitants, all of whom live in the village of Premuda. It is the most isolated of the islands in the archipelago. There are no hotels but visitors can find rooms in private houses.

In Italy, the island is remembered for a naval battle between Italy and Austria which took place on 10 June 1918 during World War I.

The island has beautiful beaches and thick pine woods, and as there are no private cars it is also very peaceful. There are several weekly connections to Zadar.

Molat

The three villages on Molat support several hundred people, who depend on fishing and farming. There are two ports: Zapuntel, the main ferry port, and Brgulje, which is used when the main port is inaccessible.

For centuries the island belonged to Venice, which fostered the establishment of a community of monks and local people, who set about re-establishing the woods which had disappeared with over-exploitation. An intense reforestation programme has been under way to aid with this.

The church of St Andrew is all that remains of the monastery. There are no hotels on the island but accommodation can be found in private houses in Molat, Zapuntel and Brgulje. There are many coves along the low, jagged coastline.

Olib

About 700 people live here in the village of Olib, where buildings include several 16th-century houses and a tower. The church of St Anastasia is from the same period and was once part of a monastery. In the parsonage are manuscripts and sacred books in Glagolitic script, as well as many stone remains, which confirm the presence of a community here in Roman times. The sea is delightful, and rocky cliffs alternate with coves and sandy beaches. Rooms can be found in private houses.

Goat on the peaceful island of Olib

Key
Minor road
Path

For keys to symbols see back flap

❸ Kornati National Park

Nacionalni park Kornati

In 1980 part of the Zadar Archipelago was declared a national park. The name Kornati derives from the name of the main island in the group, Kornat. The park was set up to protect the waters so that marine life might flourish. It measures 36 km (22 miles) in length and 6 km (4 miles) wide and is made up of 89 islands of white stone. Despite there not being any permanent inhabitants, and vegetation appearing to be sparse, flora and fauna are rich; there are some 19,000 olive trees in the park area. The islands are surrounded by clear blue sea, with jagged coastlines, hidden coves and underwater caves.

One of the few houses on the Kornati Islands

Exploring Kornati National Park

The Kornati Islands were the peaks of a mountain chain about 20,000 years ago. When this area was part of the Roman empire, the main islands were holiday resorts, popular with the prosperous inhabitants of Zadar. Beautiful Roman villas with mosaic floors as well as fishponds and baths were built.

During the long period under Venetian rule the islands, which were then covered with rich vegetation, were used as a base for the Venetian fleet. At present the Kornati Islands belong to the inhabitants of Murter, to the east, who bought them around the end of the 19th century to use as grazing for sheep and goats.

The bare and arid islands are characterized by steep cliffs, stony ground and sinkholes typical of a karst (limestone) landscape. Sheep farming has impoverished the flora of these islands. In fact, the vegetation disappeared when the shepherds of Murter cut down the trees and burned the scrub in order to grow grass for their livestock, which were left here to graze freely from spring to autumn. Dry-stone walls were built between the plots of land to form pens for the animals. On some of the islands near the coast are small cottages with stables and an outdoor hearth. Many also have a small jetty.

The Kornati Islands have become a popular destination for scuba divers and sailors. The marine life is varied with around 350 plant species and 300 animals. Fishing is prohibited throughout the entire Kornati National Park.

Besides dozens of rocky outcrops, the islands of Kornat, Levrnaka, Piškera, Lavsa, Kasela and Mana make up the park. West of Levrnaka lies the island of Mala Proversa, which, with the southern part of Dugi Otok *(see p98)*, forms another protected area, the **Telašćica Nature Park**. The best way to visit is by sailing boat, and there are organized day trips from Murter, Zadar, Biograd, Vodice, Primošten and Rogoznica.

Aerial view of the Kornati Islands

Map

DUGI OTOK
Sali
MALA PROVERSA
TELAŠĆICA
KATINA
SVRŠATA
KORNAT
Lučica
Vrulje
LEVRNAKA
MANA
PIŠK
KEY

Key

— Path
— Borders of the park

0 kilometres 10
0 miles 10

Olive trees on the slopes of Statival Bay, on the island of Kornat

Kornat

The island of Kornat is the largest island in the park. There is a small medieval church dedicated to the Virgin Mary here. There is also a look-out tower with the Venetian name of Toreta dating from the 6th century, an example of Byzantine military architecture. Near the old village of Vrulje, the main village in the archipelago, is **Vela Ploča**, where there is a spectacular chalk cliff leaning at a 40-degree angle over the sea, measuring 200 m (656 ft) long and 150 m (492 ft) high.

Levrnaka

The island of Levrnaka is one of the largest and highest islands of Kornati National Park, with two peaks, Veli Vrh and Svirac, which, at 117 m (380 ft) and 94 m (310 ft) respectively, afford stunning views of almost the entire Kornati archipelago. Also on Levrnaka is Lojena, the only sandy beach of the Kornati park, located in a lovely sheltered bay.

Lavsa

This island with its pretty bays and coves is a popular tourist destination. The ruins of a partly submerged wall are all that remain of an ancient Roman salt works.

Piškera

There are also traces of Roman presence in Piškera. Once there was a village here with about 50 houses, a warehouse for fish

VISITORS' CHECKLIST

Practical Information
Map C4.
i (022) 435 740.
w kornati.hr

Transport
from Biograd, Murter, Primošten, Rogoznica, Vodice, Zadar. (Organized trips only.)

and a tower for the tax collector. The houses and tower are now almost all in ruins. However, the church from 1560 is still standing.

Svršata

On the small island of Svršata there are two walls that go down to the sea and continue into the water, where they join up with another wall. It is thought that this square tank was a Roman construction for keeping fish fresh.

Mana

The island of Mana is famous for its semicircular cliffs. Spray from the waves breaking on the cliffs can reach up to a height of 40 m (131 ft). On top of the cliffs are the ruins of a Greek-style fishing village, built for the film *The Raging Sea* in 1961.

The Kornati Islands by Boat

The archipelago of the Kornati Islands is a real paradise for sailors. These are beautiful islands where the only sounds are those of the sea and the wind. There is only one small port, Piškera, which is open from Easter (March or April) to October; electricity and fresh water are rationed. The natural beauty of the area makes sailing here unforgettable.

A typical island of white rock, bare of vegetation

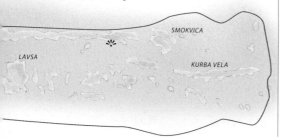

SMOKVICA

LAVSA

KURBA VELA

Kornati National Park, a paradise for sailing

❹ Nin

Map C4. 🏛 1,500. ✈ Zadar, 24 km (15 miles). 🚌 Zadar, 17 km (11 miles). 🚐 Zadar, 17 km (11 miles). 🛈 Trg braće Radić 3, (023) 264 280. 🖥 **nin.hr**

The ancient core of Nin lies within a natural lagoon, a sheltered position that made it an attractive choice for settlement. One of its oldest sources of income was salt-harvesting, and today its sandy beaches and warm, shallow waters for bathing make it a popular holiday destination.

Nin's many archaeological sites have enabled the town's past to be traced from prehistory through the Liburnian, Roman and early Christian times to its period of greatest glory, in the 9th–12th centuries, when it was both a bishopric and royal Croatian town. Nin's finest monuments date from this time.

Within the town walls is the small 9th-century Church of the **Holy Cross** (Sv. Križ), one of the finest examples of pre-Romanesque churches in typical Croatian style *(see p26)*. The church's harmony and beauty encapsulate the spirituality of the era. Its windows are positioned to act as a kind of calendar by which, according to the sun's rays, the exact date of the equinox and solstice can be determined.

Nearby is the former Cathedral of **St Anselm** (Sv. Anselm), where the kings of Croatia were crowned. The first cathedral in Croatia, it has a rich treasury with silver reliquaries from the 9th to 15th centuries. Near the church is a statue by Ivan Meštrović of

The small Romanesque Church of St Mary in Ljubač, near Nin

Bishop Gregory of Nin, promoter and defender of the Glagolitic script that enabled the use of the Croatian language in liturgy. The statue is said to grant wishes to those who rub its big toe. Also inside the walls is the 12th-century Church of **St Ambrose** (Sv. Ambroz), built in the Romanesque style with Gothic additions.

In Kraljevac Square is the small but interesting **Museum of Nin Antiquities**.

🏛 **Church of the Holy Cross, of St Anselm and of St Ambrose**
Open daily (St Anselm & St Ambrose for mass only).

🏛 **Museum of Nin Antiquities**
Trg Kraljevac 8. **Tel** (023) 264 160. **Open** May & Sep: 9am–noon, 5–8pm daily; Jun–Aug: 9am–10pm daily; Oct–Apr: 8am–2pm daily. 🖥 **amzd.hr**

Environs

A short way southwest of Nin stands the Church of St Nicholas (Sv. Nikola) in Prahulje. This unusual building, constructed on an Illyrian tumulus, has a dome with an octagonal watch tower from the 12th century on top of it, added during the Turkish invasion. The church is built on a trefoil plan and once held inscriptions and tombs of

Statue of Gregory of Nin, by Ivan Meštrović

members of the court of Princes Višeslav and Branimir, now in the archaeological museum in Zadar. The church is a fine example of primitive Croatian art.

Ljubač is 13 km (8 miles) northeast of Nin and the site of some ruins: the wall, central buildings and towers of the medieval Castrum Jubae, built by the Templar Knights. It fell into ruin after the order was dissolved. Still standing is the 12th-century Romanesque Church of **St Marcela**, noted for its three semicircular apses. Near the village is the small church of St John from the Middle Ages.

🏛 **Church of St Nicholas**
Open St Nicholas' Day and St Mark's Day only.

The Church of St Nicholas in Prahulje, not far from Nin

A Land of Salt Works

Salt trading was a very lucrative business in the Middle Ages. Three areas were suitable for its production in the upper Adriatic: the mouth of the River Dragonja, today the border between Slovenia and Croatia, the bay of Pag, and the lowlands around Nin. The salt works of Pag, of Roman origin, which were protected by two ranges of hills, were the largest and most profitable, and were once owned by Nin. The possession of these salt flats, still profitable today, has been the cause of various wars through history.

The salt works on Pag, of Roman origin, still in use today

❺ Paklenica National Park

Nacionalni park Paklenica

Map C4. 🛈 Starigrad Paklenica, (023) 369 202, 369 155. **Open** Apr–Oct: 6am–8:30pm daily; Nov–Mar: 7am–3pm daily. 🏵 🚾 **paklenica.hr**

Situated in the imposing Velebit massif, Paklenica National Park was founded in 1949. The entrance is in Starigrad Paklenica – look out for a road sign on the Magistrala coastal road (E65).

The park covers an area of 95 sq km (41 sq miles), and is formed by two gorges, Velika Paklenica (Big Paklenica) and Mala Paklenica (Small Paklenica), which cut into the limestone mountains. The gorges were eroded by two rivers and parts of the canyon walls are more than 400 m (1,312 ft) high.

Deep in the cliffs of Velika Paklenica Canyon there is an extensive system of underground tunnels built by the Yugoslav army. The tunnels are presently being renovated as the park administration intend to transform them into a multipurpose visitor centre.

The rock faces are pierced by numerous caves, but they are not easily accessible. Only the Manita cave can be visited, accompanied by a guide. The bare rock faces of Velika Paklenica are popular with rock

Rugged landscape of Paklenica National Park

climbers. High up, majestic birds of prey make their nests, in an ideal habitat for breeding. Golden eagles, hawks, and especially peregrine falcons can be seen here. In the forests there are bears, wild boar, foxes, roebucks and hares.

A path in the valley penetrates far into the interior of the park to a cliff edge where there is a magnificent view of the wooded Vaganski Vrh mountain, the highest in the Velebit chain.

One of many birds of prey in the park

The **Velebit** mountain chain is nearly 150 km (93 miles) long. The terrain is karst (limestone) with many sink holes and plateaux separated by deep fissures. In 1978 UNESCO listed Velebit as a

biological reserve for humanity with the aim of protecting this wild environment, with its 2,700 plant species and numerous colonies of large birds of prey. The *kukovi* – strange, impressive rock formations sculpted by wind and water – are also protected.

Hiking and mountain biking are other popular activities in the park and in summer visitors can stay overnight in the Mountain Hut, located on the banks of Velika Paklenica creek.

A good camp site is also situated next to a pebble beach. Along the creek there are seven disused water mills, still in good condition, which can be visited during the summer.

One of the paths leading into Paklenica National Park

➏ Pag

The island of Pag is 68 km (42 miles) long and has two mountain chains running parallel to the coast: at the southern end cliffs frame a deep bay with numerous inlets. The island was inhabited in the Neolithic Age, and was occupied by the Liburnians in around 1200 BC. When Dalmatia was conquered by Publius Cornelius Scipio in the 1st century AD, the Romans built the town of Cissa and the fortified port of Navalia here. In the Imperial period, villas were built and some mosaic floors and an aqueduct still survive. The Slavs settled in Pag in the 6th century and became sheep farmers. After 1000 AD Zadar and Rab fought over the island to gain control of the salt pans *(see p102)*. When Cissa was destroyed by the inhabitants of Zadar, the islanders chose a new location for a town, Stari Pag, which was fortified by the Venetians in 1192.

Sheep grazing on Pag

covered in maquis, olive groves and aromatic herbs, particularly sage. As well as the production of olive oil and a distinctive wine called Žutica, sheep farming is one of the main occupations on the island. Pag is famous for its sheep's cheese *(paški sir)*, which has a distinctive taste thanks to the aromatic herbs in the grazing. The cheeses are coated with olive oil, and undergo lengthy maturation.

Pag Town

The small main island town occupies a sheltered bay facing the mainland. It was granted the status of a free town by King Bela IV in 1244, but rivalry with Zadar brought about its destruction. The walls, the castle, a monastery and the Church of St Mary in the old town are in ruins. In 1409, Pag came definitively under the rule of Venice. In 1443 the Venetian rulers, with the assistance of local nobles, entrusted the

The dry, barren east-facing coast, swept by the bora wind

Exploring Pag

The island, connected by a bridge to the Magistrala coast road (E65) at its eastern tip, near Miškovići, is dry and barren, with only a few areas cultivated with vines and olive trees. The coastline facing the mainland, rocky and jagged and white in

colour, is exposed to the bora wind and bears little vegetation. The typical dry-stone walls were built to protect the land from the wind and to separate the flocks of sheep belonging to different farmers. The southwest coast is a little flatter with some small beaches. Here the land is

Key

━━ Major road

━━ Minor road

━━ Scenic route

0 kilometres   5

0 miles   5

For keys to symbols *see back flap*

Lace, Symbol of the Traditions of Pag

Typical pag lace

Pag is renowned for its clean waters and its delicious sheep's cheese, but it is also well-known for its lace. For centuries this lace has been created by the patient hands of the women of the island who, in warm weather, sit by their doorsteps intent on creating this intricate lace. Made using a special stitch, the lace is used to decorate blouses, bedlinen, altar cloths and table centrepieces. Some decades ago a school was established here to train new lacemakers. A collection of antique lace was left to the school by former lacemakers and the examples are used as models. Lace is sold here and some of the rooms are set up as a museum.

VISITORS' CHECKLIST

Map C4. 8,400. Pag: Od špitala 2, (023) 611 286; Novalja: Trg Briščić 1, (053) 661 404; Karlobag: Trg dr. Tuđmana 2, (053) 694 251. Lace exhibition (summer); Carnival of Pag (Feb & last weekend in Jul).

tzgpag.hr
tz-novalja.hr
tz-karlobag.hr

Transport
Prizna-Žigljen, Pag.

The Skrivanat Tower in the Old Town, Pag

design of a new town to the famous architect Juraj Dalmatinac (Giorgio Orsini). It took several decades to build what is now the present-day Pag.

Venetian rule brought a long period of peace and prosperity, bolstered by the income from the productive salt works. Between the 15th and 18th centuries, important public buildings and a parish church, locally called the cathedral, were built.

The town has preserved its original structure with two main roads intersecting in the main square, and minor roads running parallel. The high walls with eight towers and four gates were demolished at the end of the 19th century, but some traces (a gate and two bastions) still remain. The 15th-century Duke's Palace (Kneževa Palača), which has been altered, and the unfinished Bishop's Palace by Juraj Dalmatinac face the main square.

A monument to Dalmatinac by Ivan Meštrović and the Church of **St Mary of the Assumption** (1443–1448) stand in the same square. The church is a blend of Romanesque and Gothic, with three aisles divided by white stone columns with carved capitals. The façade has a rose window and there is a lunette above the door. Numerous precious works of art are preserved here, including a wooden 12th-century crucifix, a *Virgin of the Rosary* by Giovanni Battista Pittoni, an organ, and a treasury.

Novalja

Located at the beginning of the narrow peninsula of Lun, Novalja is the second town on the island. It makes its living entirely from tourism, thanks to its beach. In the centre of the town are the remains of an early Christian basilica and a pre-Romanesque church dating from the 9th–10th centuries.

A ferry service connects the island to the mainland, running from Novalja to Prizna.

Environs

Boat excursions to Pag leave from **Karlobag** on the mainland. Karlobag lies in a pretty bay and takes its name from the fortress that the Archduke of Austria, Charles of Habsburg, built in 1579 on the site of a village destroyed by the Turks.

The fortress lost its importance after the Turkish threat had passed and it was eventually abandoned. Its attractive stones were then salvaged and used to build the houses in the village. Still visible are some of the massive walls and a monastery, which has a famous library and a church.

The harsh landscape, characteristic of the island of Pag

❼ Krka National Park

Nacionalni park Krka

The park covers an area of 109 sq km (42 sq miles) and was established in 1985 to protect the middle and lower stretches of the River Krka, which flow into the bay of Šibenik. The source of the river is near Knin, and the river begins its journey of 75 km (47 miles) inside a canyon on the limestone plateau behind Šibenik. It finally spills over into the spectacular Roški slap and Skradinski buk waterfalls, forming a series of lakes and rapids surrounded by vegetation. The bird life in the park is very varied.

Monastery of Visovac
In the middle of the lake is the monastery of Visovac. It was founded by Franciscans in 1445 who were joined by Franciscans from Bosnia in 1576. They brought books, illuminated manuscripts and sacred vestments with them.

Skradin
Once a settlement of Illyrian and Liburnian tribes, then a Roman town, Skradin was a bishop's see from the 6th century. It is one of the main access points to the park; boats go upriver from here to the waterfalls.

KEY

① **The lower basin** becomes a pool of emerald-green water in the summer and is an attractive place to sunbathe or picnic.

② **Around the lake** families of egrets and night herons can be seen perched on the branches of the willows or hidden among the reeds. About 200 species of bird have been counted here.

③ **Krka monastery** was first mentioned in 1402.

④ **Lake Visovac** is at the heart of the park. After the waterfalls, the river flows through a narrow valley and then widens to form the lake. Some stretches of the banks are steep and others hilly with oak woods.

⑤ **Skradinski buk** is an impressive waterfall that cascades from a height of 45 m (147 ft) down 17 steps over a distance of 800 m (2,624 ft). Some of the park paths, sprayed by the falls, pass next to what is one of the most spectacular natural displays in Croatia.

Entrance 2

Bribirske Mostine

Bribirske Mostine

Đevrske

Smrdelje

56

Bratiškovci

②

Prukljan

311 **Dubravice**

Visov Je

Prukljansko Jezero

Skradin 🛈

Raslina

①

311

⑤ ★

🛈 **Lozovac**

Šibenik

8

Šibenik

Entrance 1

0 kilometres   5

0 miles   5

Roški slap
Here the river widens and deepens within the forest before finally cascading from between the trees, producing waterfalls of over 25 m (82 ft).

River Čikola
After Lake Visovac, the Krka is joined by the River Čikola and from here the river flows towards the Skradinski buk and then on to the sea.

Visiting the Park

The protected area begins at the Knin valley and continues to the bridge of Skradin. Road signs mark the entrances to the park; each has a parking area, a tourist information centre, and a ticket office. Cars can enter from Lozovac, while the Roški slap waterfalls can be reached from Miljevci or Skradin. About 15 km (9 miles) from Burnum, other road signs indicate the entrance to the area of the Roški slap waterfalls. Boats leave from Skradin for trips to the Skradinski buk waterfalls and from here it is possible to take a short cruise to the Roški slap falls, crossing the lake of Visovac and visiting the monastery on the island.

View of Krka Park

Key

▬ Major road
▬ Minor road
▬ Scenic route
★ Waterfall

❽ Šibenik

The town is first documented in 1066 as Castrum Sebenici, when King Petar Krešimir IV described it as a triangular fortified town. In the 12th century it came under Hungarian-Croat rule. Between 1412 and 1797 it was ruled by the Venetians, and the old centre acquired grand buildings and three large forts as well as bastions on the island of St Nicholas. It was a prosperous time and Šibenik became one of the liveliest cultural centres in Renaissance Croatia. Venetian rule gave way to a brief period of French occupation until Austria took over and ruled until 1917. The war during the 1990s brought about the collapse of local industry, and mass unemployment. The situation today is much improved.

Aerial view of the Cathedral of St James

🏛 Church of St Francis
Sv. Frane
Trg Nikole Tomaszea 1. **Tel** (022) 201 480. **Open** 7:30am–7:30pm daily.

Along the busy seafront, on the southern edge of the old town centre, once stood the Monastery and Church of St Francis, founded in 1229 and destroyed during a raid in 1321. Some capitals, a few statues, and parts of the arches in the cloister remain of the original structure. Towards the middle of the 15th century several new chapels were added on.

The buildings were completely rebuilt in the Baroque style around the middle of the 18th century. The church underwent complete renovation: the wooden ceiling and the sumptuous gilded carved wooden altars were remade, and every wall was decorated with paintings.

Inside, in the first chapel on the left, is a great organ from 1762, made by Petar Nakić. The large cloister has kept its

14th-century structure and there is a library with manuscripts and liturgical material in the monastery.

🏛 Church of St Barbara
Sv. Barbara
Kralja Tomislava. **Tel** (022) 214 899. Museum: **Open** May–Oct: 9am–1pm, 5–7pm; Nov–Apr: by appt.

The small Church of St Barbara, behind the Cathedral of St James, was built around the middle of the 15th century, and conserves parts of an older building. Irregular openings make the façade unusual: the lunette on the main door has a statue of St Nicholas from the workshop of Bonino of Milan (1430). Inside is an altar made by a youthful pupil of Juraj Dalmatinac, Giovanni da Pribislao, who was obliged to match another altar which had been saved from the previous church.

The church also houses a rich and interesting collection of religious art, with paintings, sculptures and illuminated texts dating from the 14th to the 16th centuries.

🏛 Count's Palace – Civic Museum
Muzej grada Šibenika
Gradska vrata 3. **Tel** (022) 213 880. **Open** 10am–9pm Tue–Sat.

This palace takes its name from the Venetian Count Niccolò Marcello who built it in the

12th–13th century. It was the Venetian governor's residence and is now a Civic Museum. This late-Renaissance building houses coin collections, archaeological finds from the Neolithic to Roman periods, tomb finds, early Croatian sculptures (7th–9th centuries), and a rich archive of historical documents about the town and its territory, many from the medieval period. There is a statue of the count (1609–11) on the façade by the entrance.

🏛 Cathedral of St James
Katedrala sv. Jakova
See pp110–11.

🏛 Old Loggia
Gradska loža
Trg Republike Hrvatske.
In front of the cathedral's Door of Lions stands the Old Loggia, formerly the seat of the town council, built between 1532 and 1543 to a design by Michele Sanmicheli, and restored after it was damaged during World War II.

This is a two-storey structure: the ground floor is an open portico with nine large arches, the upper floor is a loggia, with a balustrade.

The 16th-century Old Loggia, designed by Michele Sanmicheli

🏛 Foscolo Palace
Palača Foscolo
Andrije Kačića.
Venetian governor Leonardo Foscolo built this palace in the Venetian Gothic style in around 1450. The façade was decorated with Renaissance reliefs by Juraj Dalmatinac's pupils (15th century), and another relief, attributed to the master, has two putti supporting the coats of arms of the noble family, at the side of the entrance door.

View of Šibenik from the medieval Fort of St Michael

Fort of St Michael
Tvrđava sv. Mihovila

(022) 213 880 (Civic Museum).

The restored fort is of medieval origins and the oldest defensive structure in Šibenik. It was destroyed after lightning struck the powder magazine. When it was rebuilt, account was taken of the town's altered defence needs, and the towers were omitted. Its present appearance dates from the 16th–17th centuries. Formerly known as St Anne, it offers magnificent views over the islands.

Fort of St John
Tvrđava sv. Ivan

(022) 212 075.

Standing on a hill 115 m (410 ft) high, the fort was built in 1646 in a star shape after the town was attacked by the Turks in 1649.

Šubićevac Fort
Tvrđava Šubićevac

(022) 212 075.

The third large fort, called Šubićevac, or Baron's Fort, was constructed rapidly in 1646, in the face of an imminent Turkish attack. The fort, in fact, greatly contributed to the defeat of the Turks in 1647. After a long siege, large parts of it had to be rebuilt. The present structure dates from the middle of the 17th century and a pretty garden is laid out in front of the bastions.

Fort of St Nicholas
Tvrđava sv. Nikola

(022) 212 075.

The fort was planned by the Italian architect Michele Sanmicheli, and built between 1540 and 1547 on a cliff overlooking the city. It is a fine example of military architecture, both for its strength and for the beauty of the decorations above the entrance gate, in the apertures, in the rooms, and along the corridors. The fort was often used as a prison.

VISITORS' CHECKLIST

Practical Information

Map D5. 37,000. Local: Ulica Fausta Vrančića 18, (022) 212 075; Regional: Fra N. Ružića bb, (022) 219 072.

sibenik-tourism.hr

Transport

Split, 97 km (60 miles). (022) 333 699. Draga 44, (060) 368 368, (022) 216 066. Dr. F. Tuđmana 7, (022) 213 468.

The Fort of St Nicholas, outside the entrance to Šibenik harbour

Šibenik Town Centre

① Church of St Francis
② Church of St Barbara
③ Count's Palace – Civic Museum
④ *Cathedral of St James* *pp110–11*
⑤ Old Loggia
⑥ Foscolo Palace
⑦ Fort of St Michael

0 metres 200

0 yards 200

For keys to symbols *see back flap*

Šibenik: Cathedral of St James
Katedrala sv. Jakova

It took Croatian and international experts several years to restore Šibenik's cathedral after its shelling in 1991. Its original construction by renowned Dalmatian and Italian artists began in 1432 and was completed in 1555. The original project was entrusted to the Venetian Antonio Dalle Masegne, who built the lower Gothic level. His successor, Juraj Dalmatinac *(see p24)*, designed the upper Renaissance part of the sculptures by the doors, the 72 faces on the outside of the apse, many of the capitals, the tomb of Juraj Šižgorić and, along with Andrija Aleši, the beautiful baptistry. On Dalmatinac's death in 1475, the work was continued by Nikola Firentinac, who built the splendid presbytery with the choir, the dome, the galleries and vaulted roof. The Adam and Eve by the Door of Lions are by Bonino of Milan.

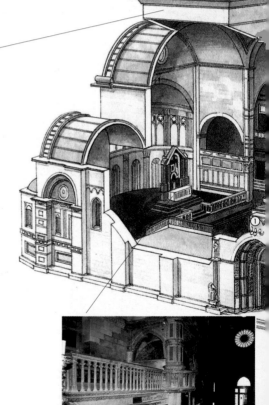

Transept
The transept is surmounted with a square structure below the dome; on three sides is an arch bearing a statue. The stones were worked in such a way that they fitted together without the need for mortar.

KEY

① **The exterior** is decorated with 72 sculpted human faces on the cornice, the work of Juraj Dalmatinac and his assistants.

② **The Dome**, a unique structure built of interlocking slabs of stone, was badly damaged in 1991.

③ **The barrelled roof**, built, like the rest of the cathedral, entirely in local stone, is a tribute to the great technical skill of the stone-cutters.

④ **The Gothic doorway** is decorated with groups of sculptures of saints ascending the arch, which is framed by two spires.

★ **Presbytery**
The finely worked stone stalls were made by Juraj Dalmatinac and Nikola Firentinac. Other sculpted reliefs adorn the upper parts.

★ Baptistry

At the end of the right aisle is an impressive baptistry with many statues and reliefs sculpted by Juraj Dalmatinac, Nikola Firentinac and Andrija Aleši. The fine baptismal font is supported by three putti.

VISITORS' CHECKLIST

Practical Information
Trg Republike Hrvatske 1.
Tel (022) 214 418.
Open daily. 🚻 📷
🌐 sibenik.hr/vodic-eng/
sibenik/kulturno_povijesna_
bastina2.asp

Façade

The symmetrical façade has an arched tympanum in the centre. The taller central section has a rose window in the centre and a smaller one above on the tympanum. The façade is framed by two pilasters and has only one door.

Interior

The three-aisle interior is divided by columns with carved capitals supporting pointed arches. The tall central nave has a frieze and women's gallery.

❾ Drniš

Map D4. 🏘 3,400. 🚌 Šibenik, 25 km (15 miles), (022) 333 699. 🚆 Šibenik, (022) 216 066. ℹ️ Domovinskog rata 5, (022) 888 619. 🌐 **www.tz-drnis.hr**

The town of Drniš first appears in documents towards the end of the 15th century, as the site of a fort built to stop a Turkish invasion, at the point where the River Čikola cuts into the valley and flows down towards Šibenik.

In 1526 the fort was captured and enlarged by the Turks, who made it one of their outposts. A village with a mosque and baths developed around the fort, but during the wars between Venice and the Ottoman empire, from 1640 to 1650, the fort and the village were almost entirely destroyed by the Venetians. In the reconstruction that followed the mosque was remodelled and became the Church of St Anthony. The minaret became the bell tower of the church of St Roch. Serbs populated the town and it became part of the Krajina territory.

Along the road from Drniš to Šibenik, the ruins of defence structures with high walls and a tower can be seen.

Environs
Some 9 km (5 miles) east of Drniš is the village of **Otavice**, the birthplace of Ivan Meštrović's parents. The great sculptor *(see p163)* built the Church of the Most Holy Redeemer here for himself and his family. It is simply designed in the form of a stone cube with a shallow dome.

Church of the Most Holy Redeemer in Otavice, near Drniš

❿ Knin

Map D4. 🏘 12,000. 🚌 (022) 663 722. ℹ️ Dr. Franje Tuđmana 24, (022) 664 822. 🌐 **tz-knin.hr**

A town on the main road from Zagreb to Split, Knin has long played an important role in Dalmatia's history. It occupies a strategic position on the plateau, and there have been defences of some kind here since prehistoric times. In the 10th century, when the town was known as Ad Tenen, the **Fort of Knin** was built here on Mount Spas. It was used by reigning Croat monarchs, who often stayed in the nearby town of Biskupija and held coronations here.

Early in the 11th century Knin became a bishopric and the residence of several aristocratic Croatian families. Occupied by the Turks in the early 16th century, in 1688 Knin fell to the Venetians.

The Morlachs, in the pay of Venice, distinguished themselves in the battle to retake the fort by scaling the walls. Afterwards they rebuilt the fort and settled in the town.

In 1991, the Serbian army used the fort when most of the inhabitants of Croat origin were forced out. It became a focus for the Serb rebellion and the Republic of the Serb Krajina, of which Knin was the capital, was created. In August 1995 the territory was returned to the Croats.

Environs
About 5 km (3 miles) away is **Biskupija**, once known as the "Field of five churches", for its religious buildings (9th–11th centuries) attended by the Croat kings. King Zvonimir was killed here by Croat nobles who did not accept his allegiance to the pope. By the main building is a church designed by Ivan Meštrović and frescoed by Jozo Kljaković.

The imposing Fort of Knin, on Mount Spas

⑪ Sinj

Map D5. 🏔 11,500. 🚉 Split. 🚌
Split. 🛈 Put Petrovca 12, (021) 826
352. 🎭 Madonna of Sinj Festival (Aug);
Sinjska alka jousting tournament
(1st Sun Aug). 🌐 **visitsinj.com**

On the Cetina plateau the
Romans founded Aequum, the
present-day Čitluk, on the road
towards Bosnia, but the
unhealthy area and malaria
forced the inhabitants to
abandon the town and move
to a nearby hill called Castrum
Zyn which, once fortified, was
safer and easier to defend.

At the end of the 1400s
some Franciscan monks fleeing
Bosnia came here, bringing with
them an image of the Virgin
believed to be miraculous; they
built a **Franciscan Monastery**
(Franjevački samostan) and a
church to house the image.

The town, by now called
Sinj, was captured
by the Turks
in 1513 and
remained in their
possession until
1699 when it was
liberated by the
Venetians. The star-
shaped **Kamičak Fort**,
was built with a tall
observation tower,
enabling Sinj
horsemen to mount
a surprise attack
on Ottoman troops
attempting to recapture the
town, in 1715. In gratitude to
the Miraculous Madonna for
their victory, the townspeople
gave her image a golden crown.

This historical event is
commemorated every year on
the first Sunday in August with
a jousting tournament (Sinjska
alka), when expert riders take
part in a competition to capture
a shield, the symbol of victory.

The Franciscan church, which
has been rebuilt at various
times, is a popular pilgrimage
site. The monastery has been
renovated and some of the
rooms house archaeological
finds from ancient Aequum.

🏛 **Franciscan Monastery**
A Stepinca 1. **Tel** (021) 707 010.
Open by appt only.

Primošten, once an island but now linked to the mainland

Sculpture of the
jousting tournament,
Sinj

⑫ Klis

Map D5. 🏔 2,300. 🚉 Split. 🚌 Split.
🛈 Megdan 57, (021) 240 578.
🌐 **tzo-klis.htnet.hr**

The little village of Klis is
dominated by an imposing
Fort which consists of three
concentric walls. It was founded
by the Romans on a hill
above a mountain pass
which led from the
plateau onto the plain.
The Venetians strength-
ened the fort and
enlisted the Uskoks to
help fight off the Turks,
who however finally
captured it in 1537.
The Turks enlarged the fort,
building a mosque and
a minaret and from
here they menaced the
city of Split until 1648
when they were driven
off by Venetian troops.
The fort was in use until the
Austrians took over. The mosque
was turned into a church and
the minaret was demolished.

The town's restaurants are
particularly known for their
excellent spit-roasted lamb.

The Fort of Klis, the scene of many
bloody battles

⑬ Primošten

Map D5. 🏔 1,800. 🚉 Split. 🚌 Split
(021) 329 180. 🚢 Marina (022) 570
068. 🛈 Trg biskupa J. Arnerića 2, (022)
571 111. 🎭 Gospe od Loreta (May).
🌐 **tz-primosten.hr**

Originally an isolated island,
Primošten is now connected to
the mainland by a bridge and a
causeway. The name Primošten
means "brought closer by a
bridge". The island was inhabited
in prehistoric times, and was
settled by Bosnian refugees
fleeing from the Turks. Under
Venetian rule, walls were built
around the town. The top of
the town is dominated by the C
hurch of **St George**, built in the
late 15th century and enlarged
around 1760. Inside is an icon of
the Virgin on a silver panel, and a
Baroque altar.

A popular resort with pebbly
beaches and good bike trails,
Primošten is also famous for its
vineyards (see p135) and a rich
red wine called Babić.

⑭ Marina

Map D5. 🏔 1,000. 🛈 Trg Stjepana
Radića 1, (021) 889 015.

This small holiday resort lies in a
sheltered bay and has a marina
and a pretty beach. The village,
surrounded by top-quality olive
groves, has been inhabited
since the 15th century. In 1495
the Bishop of Trogir built a mas
sive tower in the port, now the
Hotel Kaštil. Two notable
churches, St Luke and St John,
were built in the 15th century
and restructured at various
times by the Sobota family, the
feudal lords of the village.

⑮ Trogir

Set on a small island just off the mainland, Trogir is one of the jewels of the Dalmatian coast, with many splendid monuments. The Greeks of Issa (now Vis) first settled here in the 3rd century BC, when they founded the fortified town of Tragyrion (island of goats) which became Tragurium under the Romans in 48 BC. In the Middle Ages Trogir was protected by the Byzantine fleet, but in 1123 it was attacked and destroyed by the Saracens, and abandoned by the few surviving inhabitants. It revived again 70 years later and a period of artistic growth ensued, first under the kings of Hungary and, from 1420, under Venetian rule. In 1997 Trogir was listed as a UNESCO World Heritage Site.

The seafront of Trogir, with Kamerlengo Castle in the distance

Most of the old historic centre of the town is on an island and is encircled by a wall with two gates. A bridge now joins the island to the mainland and another links it to the island of Čiovo. Tourism is important to the town: ice-cream parlours, restaurants and pizzerias line the small squares. The main public and religious monuments, and other important buildings, have been the subject of restoration work.

🏛 Land Gate
Sjeverna vrata

Rebuilt in the 17th century, this gate was made from a tall doorway in pale rusticated stone, with grooves which once supported a drawbridge. On the cornice above the arch once stood the lion of St Mark and, above that, on a pedestal, stands a statue of the Blessed John of Trogir (Sv. Ivan Trogirski), one of the town's patron saints.

🏛 Civic Museum
Muzej grada Trogira

Gradska vrata 4. **Tel** (021) 881 406.
Open Jul–Aug: 9am–1pm, 5–10pm;
May, Jun, Sep & Oct: 9am–1pm,
5–10pm; Nov–Apr: 9am–2pm by appt.
🏛 ⬛ ⬛

On the other side of the Land Gate is the Baroque Garagnin Fanfogna Palace, now the Civic Museum, with 18th-century furnishings. There are archaeological collections, documents and antique clothes linked to the town's history.

🏛 Stafileo Palace
Palača Stafileo

Matije Gupca 20. **Closed** to the public.

Stafileo Palace was built in the late 15th century. A series of five windows in Venetian Gothic style punctuates each of the two floors, the openings framed by pillars, capitals and carved arches. Around the arches are reliefs of flowers and leaves. The design is attributed to the school of Juraj Dalmatinac, who worked for many years in Trogir.

🏛 Cathedral of St Lawrence
Sv. Lovre

Trg Ivana Pavla II. **Tel** (091) 531 4754.
Open mid-May–Oct: 9am–8pm; Nov–mid-May: by appt.

The cathedral stands on the site of an ancient church destroyed by the Saracens. Construction started in 1193, but was prolonged for decades and involved dozens of artists. The three-aisle building has three semicircular apses: the central nave is higher than the side aisles from which it is divided by eight columns.

There are two entrances. The side door, known as "the count's", is very simple, and dated 1213. The other entrance is a magnificent Romanesque door under an atrium, to the right of which stands a beautiful Gothic bell tower, built between the late 14th century and the beginning of the 17th century. This door was carved in around 1240 by the Dalmatian sculptor Master Radovan (see p24), and is the finest expression of Romanesque sculpture to be found in Dalmatia. Two stone lions support statues of Adam and Eve either side of the door. Next to them are pilasters depicting saints in Byzantine style. Scenes of the different months of the year are carved on the middle pilasters.

Above the door, in the large lunette, is a relief of the Nativity and in the semicircles are episodes from the life of Jesus. The door is enclosed under a sloping roof with a corbel at the top with a statue of St Lawrence. In the atrium is a baptistry designed by Andrija Aleši in around 1460 with a relief of the Baptism of Christ.

The intricate Romanesque door of the Cathedral of St Lawrence

Aerial view of the square and the cathedral

The church interior contains an octagonal stone pulpit from the 13th century built and sculpted by Mauro, a choir with wooden stalls inlaid by Ivan Budislavić towards the mid-15th century, and a ciborium on the main altar with sculptures depicting the Annunciation. On the altars are paintings by Palma il Giovane and Padovanino.

Along the left aisle is the chapel of the Blessed Orsini, a masterpiece by Nikola Firentinac and Andrija Aleši made in 1468–72, with 12 statues of the apostles in shell-shaped niches and, in the centre, the sarcophagus of the Blessed Orsini, the first bishop of Trogir. The sculptures are by Nikola Firentinac, Andrija Aleši and Ivan Duknović.

In the sacristy are paintings by Salvator Rosa and Gentile Bellini, cabinets carved by Grgur Vidov, and a Treasury with many gold pieces, reliquaries and paintings dating from the 17th century.

The tall bell tower was built in the 14th century, but was partly destroyed during the wars early in the following century and only the ground floor remains of the original building. When Trogir became part of Venetian territory, the bell tower was rebuilt. The first floor, with a balustrade by Matej Gojković (1422), is in the Gothic style, with two narrow mullioned windows with a trefoil, surmounted by blind arches. The second level has two tall windows on each side: the north and south walls have mullioned windows with four trefoil eyes, those on the east and west walls are surmounted by fretwork grilles, with columns and capitals at the centre and corners, giving a feeling of lightness to the entire floor. Recent studies attribute this work to the Italian sculptor Lorenzo Pincino, who worked in Trogir and Dalmatia for many years, with the assistance of local craftsmen.

The third storey, from the late 16th century, was built by the sculptor Trifun Bokanić and has large arched openings.

VISITORS' CHECKLIST

Practical Information
Map D5. 🏠 10,500. 🛈 Trg Ivana Pavla II 1, (021) 885 628.
Ⓦ tztrogir.hr

Transport
✈ Split Airport, 7 km (5 miles).
🚉 Split, 30 km (18 miles). 🚌 (021) 881 405. ⛴ (021) 881 508.

Trogir Town Centre

Exploring Trogir

A good time to visit Trogir is the late spring or early autumn, when the narrow streets, flanked by ancient stone houses, are not so busy with summer visitors, and there is space to stop and admire the ingenious architectural details that make this island so fascinating. A carved doorway, a coat of arms or a mullioned window may decorate the façade of a building; the entrance to a courtyard may offer glimpses of scented gardens. These are all indications of a once widespread prosperity and also evidence of Trogir's cultural past, when it was an important centre for the arts. After many years of hardship and neglect, the town has been restored to its former glory.

A Renaissance well in the courtyard of Čipiko Palace

🏛 Čipiko Palace
Palača Čipiko
Gradska ulica. **Closed** to the public, except courtyard.

An inscription indicates 1457 as the year of completion of the beautiful Čipiko Palace, built for Trogir's most illustrious family. Over a Renaissance doorway, distinguished by its columns with capitals, is a shell decoration above a finely worked cornice.

The first floor has a mullioned window with a balustrade in light-coloured stone. In the centre, two columns with capitals support pointed arches and at the ends of the window are two thin pilasters surmounted by capitals with spiral decorations. Between the arches are four sculptures of angels. Two

central ones hold a scroll with the coats of arms of the Čipiko family. The second floor lacks a balustrade, and is similar in style to the lower floor, although its decorations are less ornate.

A second door, opening on to a side street, has a complex structure. Two fluted door jambs support capitals with carved foliage decoration and a stone cornice with two sculpted lions holding a coat of arms. These are flanked by two sculptures of angels in medallions.

🏛 Town Hall
Gradska vijećnica
Trg Ivana Pavla II.

On the eastern side of the square is the Town Hall. This building originates from the 15th century and has three storeys with open arches and a beautiful mullioned window with a balustrade on the upper floor, which was restored in the 19th century.

Numerous coats of arms decorate the façade which has three Renaissance doors framed by projecting stone. The pretty porticoed courtyard is open to the public. However, the interior, which has been altered at various times, has nothing of significant interest.

🏛 Loggia and Clock Tower
Gradska loža
Trg Ivana Pavla II. **Open** daily.

The Loggia and the Clock Tower face John Paul II Square (Trg

Ivana Pavla II). The Loggia has a roof supported by six columns with Roman capitals and dates from the 14th century. On the wall are two reliefs, one from 1471 sculpted by Nikola Firentinac *(Justice)*, and one from 1950 by Ivan Meštrović *(Ban Berislavić)*. The Clock Tower stands to the left of the Loggia. It supports a pavilion dome, salvaged in 1447 from the Chapel of the Oratory of St Sebastian. The saint's statue on the façade was sculpted by Nikola Firentinac.

⬆ Church of St John the Baptist
Sv. Ivan Krstitelj
Open ask at tourist office for timings.

This small Romanesque church, built in the 13th century, is the pantheon of the powerful Čipiko family. The church housed an Art Gallery (Pinacoteca) with collections of medieval illuminated manuscripts, ornaments, paintings and precious gold pieces from various churches, but this is now in the **Museum of Sacred Art** near the cathedral of St Lawrence. The collection also includes a sculpture *(Deposition)* by Nikola Firentinac, organ panels by Gentile Bellini *(St Jerome and St John the Baptist)* and two polyptychs by Blaise of Trogir.

The doorway of the Romanesque church of St John the Baptist

The Fish Market, housed in a 16th-century loggia

🏛 Sea Gate and Fish Market
Južna vrata
Obala bana Berislavića.

The Sea Gate was built at the end of the 16th century and has two beautiful columns made of blocks of light-coloured stone which frame the opening and support a projecting block on which stands the lion of St Mark.

Nearby is the Fish Market which is held in an open loggia with nine columns supporting the roof. It was built in 1527 and was formerly the customs house.

Ceremonial costumes made by the tailor Boris Burić Gena

Boris Burić Gena

Trogir can boast a unique present-day success story: Boris Burić Gena, a tailor who specializes in making traditional Croatian suits. His signature jackets are made without lapels and have antique-style brocade buttonholes. They are often worn in ceremonies and parades. The careful choice of fabrics, meticulous design and matching of accessories have made this talented craftsman's name. His workshop, the Burić Palace, now draws wealthy and famous clients from all over Europe.

🏠 Church of St Nicholas
Sv. Nikola
Gradska ulica 2. **Tel** (021) 881 631.

The church and Benedictine convent date from the 11th century, but were rebuilt in the 16th century. The convent rooms now house the **Zbirka Umjetnina Kairos**, an art collection which includes the *Kairos*, a relief of Greek origins (1st century BC) depicting the god of opportunity, a Gothic Crucifix, and a Romanesque statue (*The Virgin with Child*).

Relief depicting Kairos, St Nicholas

🏠 Church of St Dominic
Sv. Dominik
Obala bana Berislavića. **Open** summer: 8am–noon, 4–7pm daily.

The Church and Monastery of St Dominic are Romanesque-Gothic buildings constructed in the 14th century. They were renovated by Nikola Firentinac in the Renaissance style. The single-nave church contains the tomb of Giovanni Sobota, a lawyer, attributed to Nikola Firentinac (1469), and a splendid painting by Palma il Giovane (*Circumcision of Christ*).

🏛 Kamerlengo Castle and St Mark's Tower
Kaštel Kamerlengo

In the southwest corner of the island stands Kamerlengo Castle, which was at one time the residence of the Venetian governor. It was built by the Venetians in about 1430, and is a four-sided structure with a hexagonal base. Facing the sea, its high walls connect the three towers and the bastion. This imposing structure was once connected to St Mark's Tower (Kula svetog Marka). The large open space inside the castle is used for outdoor theatre performances and concerts during the summer months.

St Mark's Tower was built by the Venetians after the construction of the castle and has the typical structure of defences built in the Renaissance period. A circular tower stands on a truncated cone base and there is a long series of embrasures on the roof. Artillery was installed on the top level in readiness to defend the strip of water that separates the island from the mainland.

What was once the parade ground, between the castle and St Mark's Tower, is now the town's sports field.

The imposing St Mark's Tower, built for defence in 1470

⑯ Salona

The ancient town of Salona, 5 km (3 miles) from Split, is famous for its Roman ruins. The name Salona (or Salonae) derives from the salt (*sal* in Latin) works in the area. Originally an Illyrian settlement, it was then Greek, but did not become an important centre until the Romans built a town next to the Greek city. During the rule of Augustus it became a Roman colony called Martia Julia Salonae and later it was the capital of the province of Dalmatia. In the 1st century AD the Romans built an amphitheatre, theatres, temples, baths, a Forum and town walls reinforced with towers, and Salona became the richest and most populated city in the mid-Adriatic. In 614 the Avars and the Slavs destroyed it and it fell into disuse. The buildings and the churches were stripped and the stone was used for new buildings.

Salona's main road

Ruins of the walls and triangular tower

Exploring Salona

At the end of the 19th century excavations began to bring to light the buried remains of this ancient settlement. The work has clearly shown that the town had two districts dating from different periods: the original, old centre *(Urbs vetus)* and a later part which dates from the Augustan era *(Urbs nova occidentalis* and *Urbs nova orientalis)*. The excavations have uncovered only a part of the layout of the **outer walls**, which were frequently reinforced over the centuries. However, the foundations and the remains of towers with triangular or rectangular bases are visible.

A good place to begin a tour is the **Necropolis of Manastirine**, the burial area just outside the walls, north of the city (near the parking area). In the 4th century a religious building was constructed here to house the relics of the Salonian saints, victims of Diocletian's persecution of Christians. The ruins of the necropolis and the basilica are well preserved.

From Manastirine, after the entrance, you reach the **Tusculum**, a villa built in the last century for the distinguished archaeologist Frane Bulić, to enable him to study Salona. A scholar and director of the Archaeological Museum in Split *(see p125)*, he devoted much of his life to researching the ancient ruins of this city. The building is now a small museum. However, the most interesting material is now in the Archaeological Museum in Split.

Further on is the richest area of ruins with the foundations of early Christian basilicas, baths and the Caesarea Gate. The **Baths** were built in the 1st century when the city became the capital of the province of Dalmatia. In the early Christian period the buildings were probably transformed into religious buildings: the **Bishop's Complex** in the northeastern sector of Salona comprised basilicas, a baptistry and the bishop's residence. Before Christianity became widespread, early Christian martyrs were slayed here, including St Domnius (the patron saint of Split), Venantius and Anastasius.

The foundations of two basilicas have been excavated. One is known as the Urban Basilica, the other, called Honorius' Basilica, had a Greek cross plan. This is also the site of what remains of the **Caesarea Gate**: arches flanked by two octagonal towers, showing the

The Necropolis of Manastirine, just outside the walls

Basilica Urbana in the Bishop's Complex

building techniques used by the Romans in the Imperial era.

Going west along the walls you reach the **Necropolis of Kapljuč**, another early Christian burial site, and then the imposing ruins of the **Amphitheatre**, in the easternmost part of the city.

The amphitheatre, in brick, was probably covered in stone and stood in the newer part of the city on the northwest edge of *Urbs vetus* (Old Town) close to the walls.

According to historians, the amphitheatre could seat 18,000–20,000 people. The foundations and a part of the lower tribune have been excavated and the discovery of a network of underground channels has led to the theory that simulated naval battles were held in the arena.

The amphitheatre's construction date was debated over for a long time, but has now been established as having taken place in the second half of the 2nd century AD.

From the amphitheatre, another path leads to the at the edge of the old city. This was built in the first half of the 1st century AD and part of the stage and the foundations of the stalls have been excavated. Next to the theatre is the **Forum**, the political and commercial heart of the city. Unlike the Forum in Zadar (*see pp94–7*), the paving was dismantled and only the foundations remain. In the Roman era some of the most important buildings stood around the Forum, which was begun in the 1st century AD and subsequently modified.

The best-preserved Roman construction in ancient Salona is the **Aqueduct**, built to bring water from the River Jadro to the city and extended in the time of Emperor Diocletian to reach his palace in Split (*see*

pp122–3). Repair work was carried out at the end of the 19th century and the southern part of the aqueduct is still in use. Alongside the walls it is possible to see some parts of the aqueduct above the surface.

From the theatre you return to the Manastirine necropolis. North of this site is the **Necropolis of Marusinac**, built outside the city around the tomb of St Anastasius. In this area a few traces of a basilica dating from the 5th century are still visible.

The Amphitheatre, of which only a part of the lower tribune remains

The Ruins of Salona

① Necropolis of Manastirine
② Tusculum
③ Baths
④ Bishop's Complex
⑤ Caesarea Gate
⑥ Necropolis of Kapljuć
⑦ Amphitheatre
⑧ Theatre
⑨ Forum
⑩ Necropolis of Marusinac

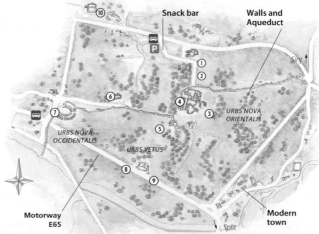

Snack bar

Walls and Aqueduct

Sinj

URBS NOVA ORIENTALIS

URBS NOVA OCCIDENTALIS

URBS VETUS

Motorway E65

Split

Modern town

0 metres   500
0 yards   500

For keys to symbols *see back flap*

⑰ Split

Shipyards, factories and a busy port present the modern face of Split, which expanded unchecked after World War II. The old town centre is still full of charm however; it grew up in and around the Emperor Diocletian's vast Roman palace, one of the largest and best-preserved left from the Roman world. In 614, the palace took in refugees from Salona (see pp118–19), which had been razed by the Avars, and these newcomers began to use the Roman structure as housing. Among the refugees were the bishop and other religious dignitaries, who breathed new life into the bishopric of Split. After two centuries of Byzantine rule and the establishment of Croat communities, Split became part of the Venetian territories in 1409. Under the Venetians, fortifications were built, including new walls, and the arts flourished.

Baptismal font in the Baptistry of St John, former Temple of Jupiter

View of the port and the seafront of Split

🔲 Golden Gate
Zlatna vrata
This was the main entrance to Diocletian's Palace (see p122) and was the most impressive of the gates, with towers and decorative elements above the arches. In the 11th century, the corridor between the gate and the gate was closed and turned into the Church of **St Martin** (Sv. Martin). An inscription commemorates Father Dominic, the founder.

🏛 Split City Museum
Muzej grada Splita
Papalićeva 1. **Tel** (021) 360 171.
Open May–Oct: 9am–9pm Tue–Fri, 9am–4pm Sat–Mon; Nov–Apr: 9am–5pm Tue–Fri, 9am–1pm Sat, 10am–1pm Sun. 🖼

The Gothic Papalić Palace, housing the Split City Museum, is one of the most interesting of the 15th–16th-century buildings constructed in the abandoned parts of the Diocletian complex. It houses an exhibition with various artistic finds, paintings and books illustrating the city's celebrated history from the 12th to the 18th centuries.

🔲 Peristyle
The peristyle, the interior courtyard, of Diocletian's Palace is an impressive part of the complex where the layers of centuries of building can clearly be seen. The slim columns bordering three sides rest on a high plinth and have finely worked capitals. The access to the former private quarters of Diocletian has a tall arched tympanum and relief decorations.

🔼 Baptistry of St John
Sv. Ivan Krstitelj
Tel (021) 345 602.
Open 9am–7pm daily.
This small, beautiful building, consecrated in the 6th century, was the Palace's Temple of Jupiter. Inside, the baptismal font incorporates a pre-Romanesque panel of King Zvonimir and other dignitaries. The statue of St John on the end wall is by Ivan Meštrović and was added before World War II. The tomb of Bishop John is from the 8th century and the one in front of it, that of Bishop Lawrence, dates from the 11th century.

🔼 Cathedral of St Domnius
Katedrala sv. Duje
See p123.

🔲 Silver Gate and Church of St Dominic
Srebrna vrata i Sv. Dominik
Hrvojeva ulica. Church of St Dominic: **Open** am.
Near the Silver Gate there is a market, a wonderful chaos of seasonal fruit and vegetables, homemade cheeses, hams and dried herbs. Because of the open space, this also provides the best view of the Palace of Diocletian. It is still possible to distinguish the different structures of the complex, and part of the guards' corridor, on the walls, can be walked along.

In front of the gate is the Oratory of St Catherine, built in the Middle Ages. It was used by the Dominicans while they built their own monastery (1217). The oratory was almost entirely rebuilt in the 17th century and became the Church of **St Dominic** (Sv. Dominik). Inside the church, which was enlarged in 1930, are a *Miracle in Surian* by Palma il Giovane and an *Apparition in the Temple*, attributed to his school.

🔲 Brass Gate
Mjedena vrata
Ethnographic Museum: Severova 1. **Tel** (021) 344 164. **Open** Jun–Sep: 9:30am–7pm Mon–Sat, 10am–1pm Sun; Oct–May: 9am–4pm Mon–Fri, 9am–1pm Sat. 🖼 ♿

Although the Brass Gate is plain and faces the sea and port, it opens on to the richest façade of the palace. The upper floor had a portico which was later enclosed for living quarters. The vast cellars have been excavated to reveal impressive arched vaults and skilful masonry. Shops occupy some of these while others house an exhibition about the palace and temporary local displays.

Close to the Brass Gate, on Severova, is the **Ethnographic Museum** (Etnografski muzej), displaying an array of skilled Dalmatian folk crafts.

🔲 Iron Gate
Željezna vrata

The church of **Our Lady of the Belfry** (Gospa od Zvonika) has the city's oldest early Romanesque bell tower (1081) and was constructed in the outer passageway above this Palace entrance.

🔲 People's Square
Narodni trg (Pjaca)

This was the centre of business and administration from the

VISITORS' CHECKLIST

Practical Information
Map D5. 🔼 175,000. *i* Peristil bb, (021) 345 606. 🎭 St Domnius Feast (7 May); Split Summer (mid-Jul–mid-Aug).
🔲 visitsplit.com

Transport
✈ Split Airport: Kaštel Štafilić, (021) 203 506. 🚌 Obala kneza Domagoja, (060) 333 444.
🚌 Obala kneza Domagoja, (060) 327 777. ⛴ Jadrolinija: (021) 338 333.

15th century and so the nobility erected prestigious buildings here. Examples are the Venetian-Gothic **Cambi Palace** and the Renaissance **Town Hall** (Vijećnica), built in the first half of the 15th century, with a loggia with three arches on the ground floor and a Gothic window on the upper floor.

The Renaissance Town Hall on People's Square in the centre of Split

---

Split Town Centre

Key

▧ Area of illustration, p122

0 metres 100
0 yards 100

Palace of Diocletian

Diocletian, probably a native of Salona, became emperor in 284. He made Maximian joint Augustus, senior co-emperor, in 285, and then in 293 he appointed Galerius and Constantius as Caesars, junior co-emperors (the Tetrarchy). After governing for 20 years, Diocletian retired from public life and in 305 moved to the palace which he had commissioned from the architects Filotas and Zotikos in the bay of Split. After Diocletian's death in 316, the palace was used as administrative offices and the governor's residence. In 615, refugees from Salona found shelter here after the destruction of their city by the Avars. The richest settled in the emperor's apartments, the poorer in the towers and above the gates. The corners of the palace were marked by four square towers, and four towers along the north, east and south sides, while the side facing the sea had a loggia with arches.

Iron Gate and the Clock Tower
This is the best-preserved gate: beyond is the church of Our Lady of the Belfry with a 12th-century tower next to it.

Temple of Jupiter
This had an atrium with six columns. The body of the building had a coffered vault and rested on an underground crypt. In the early Middle Ages it was turned into the Baptistry of St John.

The Temples of Venus and Cybele were circular outside and had a hexagonal ground-plan inside. A colonnaded corridor ran around the outside.

The Mausoleum of Diocletian, now the Cathedral of St Domnius

Peristyle
Near the crossroads where the *Cardo* and *Decumanus* intersected, the peristyle gave access to the sacred area. On one side were the temples of Venus and Cybele and, further back, that of Jupiter (now the Baptistry of St John); on the other side, the Mausoleum, now the cathedral.

For hotels and restaurants see pp226–31 and pp238–49

Portrait of Diocletian
After reorganizing the empire, the emperor sought the spiritual unification of its citizens. The state religion, personified by the emperor, gained in importance, and temples were constructed bearing his image. Christians were subject to extremely violent persecution.

The Golden Gate, facing Salona, was the main entrance to the palace. This was the most imposing of the gates with two towers and many decorations.

The Silver Gate, or eastern gate, was a simpler copy of the Golden Gate.

Reconstruction of Diocletian's Palace

The palace, shown here in its original form, was like a typical Roman military camp. It was 215 m (705 ft) long and 180 m (590 ft) wide and was enclosed by very thick walls, at times 28 m (92 ft) high. The four-sided stronghold was reinforced with towers on the north, east and west sides. There is a gate on each side, connected by two roads corresponding to the Roman Cardo and Decumanus.

⌂ Cathedral of St Domnius
Katedrala sv. Duje
Kraj sv. Duje 5. **Tel** (021) 345 602.
Open Jun–Aug: 8am–sunset daily; Sep–May: 9am–noon, 4:30–7:30pm daily.

Originally the mausoleum of the emperor Diocletian, the cathedral was consecrated in the 7th century when the sarcophagus containing the body of Diocletian was removed and replaced, with a certain poetic justice, by the remains of St Domnius (locally St Duje), a 3rd-century bishop martyred as part of Diocletian's persecution of the early Christians. It was the archbishop of Split at the time who transformed the mausoleum into a Christian church, and St Domnius became the city's patron saint.

The structure is widely regarded as the oldest Catholic cathedral in the world that has not been substantially rebuilt at any time. Since being first built it has remained practically unaltered except for the construction of a Romanesque bell tower (12th–16th centuries) and the addition of the 13th-century choir inside.

An ancient sphinx in black granite rests at the foot of the bell tower. The entrance doorway has wooden panels from 1214, with scenes from the Gospel in floral frames. The cathedral, built on an octagonal ground-plan, has a double order of Corinthian

Detail of the Altar of St Anastasius, Cathedral of St Domnius

The 13th-century hexagonal pulpit, Cathedral of St Domnius

columns, most of them the Roman originals; above these is a frieze decorated with scenes of Eros hunting, supporting medallions with portraits of Diocletian and his wife Prisca. In the second niche on the right, with frescoes dating from 1428, is the **Altar of St Domnius**, the work of Bonino of Milan (1427). The wooden choir stalls in the 17th-century presbytery are an example of Romanesque carving from the beginning of the 13th century.

To the side is a chapel housing the **Altar of St Anastasius**, designed in 1448 by Juraj Dalmatinac. The niche after this was altered in the 18th century to create the Baroque chapel of St Domnius. The 13th-century hexagonal **pulpit** is supported by thin columns with carved capitals. The 14th-century building behind the cathedral houses the sacristy and the name of one of the architects, Filotas, is inscribed by the entrance. In the sacristy, now the **Cathedral Museum**, are many works of art, including objects in gold and silver, ancient manuscripts, medieval icons and vestments.

Of particular importance are the *Historia Saloniana* written by Archdeacon Toma in the 13th century and a 7th-century Gospel.

Exploring Split

As well as Diocletian's palace, Split has much in the way of historical and artistic interest to offer. In the medieval period, villages were built near the walls. When the city became a free town, settlements became physically linked. The present-day Braće Radić Square and the People's Square were built, along with the Cambi Palace and the Town Hall. After 1420, construction of the external defences began and town walls were built. Between Split and Trogir, castles built for defence against the Turks still survive.

Distant Accords by Ivan Meštrović, Meštrović Gallery

The 15th-century Marina Tower, built by the Venetians

🚌 Braće Radić Square
Trg braće Radić

This medieval square is at the southwest corner of Diocletian's Palace. The tall **Marina Tower** (Hrvojeva kula) is the only evidence of the imposing castle built by the Venetians in the second half of the 15th century after the final defeat of Split. Built on an octagonal ground-plan, it stands on the southern side of the square.

On the northern side is the Baroque **Milesi Palace**, which dates from the 17th century. There is also a work by Ivan Meštrović in the centre of the square: the great monument to Marko Marulić, the writer and scholar (1450–1524) who was the founder of literature in the Croatian language. The imposing bronze statue dedicated to the writer has an inscription with some verses by the poet Tin Ujević.

Monument to Marko Marulić

⛪ Church of St Francis
Sv. Frane

Trg Republike. ℹ (021) 348 600 (tourist office). **Open** by appt.

The church has been rebuilt in recent times but the small Romanesque-Gothic cloister, with thin columns enclosing a flower garden, is original.

The church, with mainly Baroque furnishings, has a 15th-century crucifix by Blaž Juriev Trogiranin. It also houses the tombs of the city's illustrious citizens, including that of Archdeacon Toma (the first Dalmatian historian), writer Marko Marulić and the well-known composer Ivan Lukačić.

🏛 Museum of Croatian Archaeological Monuments
Muzej hrvatskih arheoloških spomenika

Stjepana Gunjace bb. **Tel** (021) 323 901. **Open** Jul & Aug: 9am–1pm, 5–8pm Mon–Fri, 9am–2pm Sat; Sep–Jun: 9am–4pm Mon–Fri, 9am–2pm Sat. **Closed** Sun, public hols. 🅿 ♿ ✉ 🌐 mhas-split.hr

Set up in 1975, this museum houses finds from the area around Split dating from the early Middle Ages. The collection also includes the works of early Croat sculptors, dating from 800. The stone fragments, salvaged from churches and castles, consist mainly of tombs, capitals, altar fronts, ciboria and windows. Highlights include Prince Višeslav's hexagonal baptismal font in marble, dating from the beginning of the 9th century, and the sarcophagus of Queen Jelena (10th century), discovered in the ancient Roman city of Salona.

🏛 Meštrović Gallery
Galerija Meštrović

Šetalište Ivana Meštrovića 46. **Tel** (021) 340 800. **Open** May–Sep: 9am–7pm Tue–Sun; Oct–Apr: 9am–4pm Tue–Sat, 10am–3pm Sun. ♿

The building housing this gallery was the residence of Ivan Meštrović in the early 1930s (*see p163*). The sculptor himself designed the building to be his family house, studio and gallery. His sculptures, including *Distant Accords* and *Persephone*, decorate the garden and the interior. Among statues in marble, wood and bronze are *The Contemplation*, *The Vow* and *Psyche*. Part of the building still preserves the artist's apartments.

The **Kaštilac**, further down the road at No. 39, can be visited with the same ticket. This 16th-century residence once belonged to the Capogrosso-Kavanjin family and was bought by Meštrović in 1939 to set up an exhibition hall. The artist also built a small church here to exhibit a series of reliefs called *New Testament*, now replaced by a different work, the *Author of the Apocalypse*.

🏛 National Art Gallery
Galerija umjetnina

Ulica kralja Tomislava 15. **Tel** (021) 350 110. **Open** May–Sep: 11am–4pm Mon, 11am–7pm Tue–Fri, 11am–3pm Sat; Oct–Apr: 9am–2pm Mon, 9am–5pm Tue–Fri, 9am–1pm Sat. **Closed** Sun, public hols. 🅿 📷 ♿

The gallery offers a broad overview of art in Split and the rest of Croatia from the 16th to the 20th centuries. As well as the Venetian masters there are also important icons from the so-called school of Bocche di Cattaro (18th–19th centuries) and more contemporary work, including works by Ivan Meštrović and Vlaho Bukovac. Temporary exhibitions are also held here.

🏛 Archaeological Museum
Arheološki muzej

Zrinsko Frankopanska 25. **Tel** (021) 329 340. **Open** Jun–Sep: 9am–2pm, 4–8pm Mon–Sat; Oct–May: 9am–2pm, 4–8pm Mon–Fri, 9am–2pm Sat. 🐾 🗹 ♿

The museum was founded in 1820 and has been on its present site since 1914. It contains a considerable number of finds from the Roman, early Christian and medieval periods which are exhibited in rotation. Of great interest are the finds from Roman Salona, including sculptures, capitals, sarcophagi (those from the 4th–5th century still have pagan reliefs), jewellery, coins, small objects in glazed terracotta and ceramics. There are also finds from the Roman town of Narona (see p136).

Polyptych by Girolamo da Santacroce, Our Lady of Grace

marsh (poljud). In the 1400s, the Franciscans built a fortified monastery here with large lateral towers, and a church with a trussed roof.

A polyptych by Girolamo da Santacroce from 1549 stands on the main altar, depicting the *Virgin and Saints*: the figure holding a model of the city is St Domnius, patron saint of Split.

Sarcophagus, Archaeological Museum

Many works of art are on display, including a *Portrait of Bishop Tommaso Nigris* by Lorenzo Lotto (1527) and miniatures by Bone Razmilović.

Not far from the monastery is the stadium of the famous Hajduk Split football team, built in 1979 in the suburb of Poljud and designed by Boris Magaš.

🏛 Our Lady of Grace in Poljud
Gospa od Poljuda

Poljudsko šetalište 17. 🛈 (021) 381 011. **Open** by appt.

Towards Zrinsko-Frankopanska in the direction of the suburbs lies an area once called the

🏞 Marjan Peninsula

This protected nature reserve is on the west side of town, and is reached by a winding flight of steps. On the way is the 13th-century church of St Nicholas (Sv. Nikola). A path leads out to the wooded peninsula, from where there

are fine views out to sea, with the islands of Šolta, Brač and Hvar clearly visible. You can also find the best beaches in Split in this pleasant area.

Environs

Seven Castles (Kaštela) is the name given to a series of fortifications built by the Venetian governor and local nobles to defend the town against the Turks between the end of the 15th century and the 16th century, between Split and Trogir. The village of Kaštela grew up around the complex. Five of the original castles are still preserved, as are the fortified villas which rose from their reconstruction.

St George's Castle (Kaštel Sućurac), the summer residence of the bishop of Split, was built at the end of the 14th century and strengthened the following century by building a wall, of which some traces remain.

Abbess Castle (Kaštel Gomilica) was built on an island which is now linked to the mainland.

Vitturi Castle (Kaštel Lukšić) was transformed into a large villa, keeping only the old external structure. It was built by the Vitturi family, who donated a sculpture by Juraj Dalmatinac to the church of St Raynerius (Sv. Arnir). **Old Castle** (Kaštel Stari) has kept its original aspect; the sea-facing side looks like a palace with Gothic windows.

All that remains of the **New Castle** (Kaštel Novi) are the tower and St Roch church, built by the Čipiko family.

The stadium of the Hajduk football team, built in 1979 in the suburb of Poljud

⑱ Šolta

Map D5. ⛰ 1,400. 🚢 from Split.
ℹ️ Rogač, (021) 654 657.
🌐 **visitsolta.com**

This long island, indented with bays and coves, covers an area of 57 sq km (22 sq miles). The economy is based on agriculture thanks to reasonably fertile soil and, over recent years, tourism has also become important. The Romans called the island Solenta and it was a holiday resort for the nobility of Salona. The ruins of many villas can be found in lovely locations on the island.

After the attack on Salona in 614, some of the refugees fled here and villages were built. Some still have small churches dating from the early Middle Ages. The island was later abandoned in favour of Split, due to constant Turkish raids – though some refugees from the mainland did settle here.

Today, many people from Split have holiday homes on Šolta. The fishing ports of Stomorska, at the eastern end of the island, and Maslinica, at the west, both lie in beautiful bays with plenty of nearby opportunities for swimming. There are many pretty inlets near Maslinica that make ideal moorings for yachts and motor-boats. But it is worth venturing inland, too: the main inland villages of Grohote and Donje Selo are characteristically atmospheric Adriatic settlements of well-preserved stone houses and narrow streets.

View of the mainland from Supetar on Brač island

⑲ Brač

Map D5. ⛰14,000. ✈ (021) 559 711.
🚢 to Supetar from Split. 🚌 (060) 393 060. Supetar: ℹ️ Porat 1, (021) 630 551. 🌐 **supetar.hr** Bol: ℹ️ Porat bolskih pomoraca bb, (021) 635 638.
🌐 **bol.hr**

The third largest island in the Adriatic at 40 km (25 miles) long and 15 km (9 miles) wide, Brač has an interesting geological structure. In some areas the ranges of limestone hills have sinkholes and are cut by ravines and gorges. In other areas a white, hard stone prevails. The stone has been quarried since ancient times (*see p140*) and is still much sought after. The island is covered with a mixture of woodland, Mediterranean scrub, and olive groves.

Although Brač has always been inhabited, it was first subject to Salona (the rich Salonians built villas and also sought refuge here when their town was attacked by the

Avars), and then to Split. Both Split and Brač came under Byzantine and then Venetian rule. Under the Venetians (1420–1797), villages were built in the interior but no defences were built to prevent the pirates and Turks landing.

Ferries from Split on the mainland dock at the old town of **Supetar**, which has some good pebble beaches and shallow bays popular with families. Supetar's graveyard is the site of the impressive Petrinović Mausoleum, a richly decorated rotunda designed by sculptor Toma Rosandić.

To the southwest lies the town of **Milna**, which was founded at the beginning of

The marina at Maslinica on Šolta

Key

▬ Major road

▬ Minor road

For keys to symbols *see back flap*

0 kilometres   10
0 miles   10

the 18th century and faces a sheltered bay. The exterior of the church of the Annunciation of Mary (Gospa od Blagovijestl) is Baroque and the interior is decorated in the Rococo style.

Nerežišća, in the centre of the island, was for a long period its main town. The Governor's Palace, the Loggia and a pedestal with the lion of St Mark are signs of its former status. Also inland is **Škrip**, probably the site of the first settlement on the island and the presumed birthplace of Helen, mother of Emperor Constantine. The church and a painting by Palma il Giovane on the main altar are dedicated to Helen. A fortified building houses **Brač Museum** and exhibits archaeological finds, evidence of humankind's ancient presence on the island.

The major attraction at **Bol**, on the southern coast, is the long beach on the western side of town (Zlatni rat, meaning Golden Horn), a triangular spit of shingle which reaches out into the sea and changes shape with the seasonal tides. Zlatni rat gets extremely busy in summer, with excursion boats bringing tourists here from resorts all over Brač and from nearby Hvar island too. It is also a popular spot for windsurfing.

Bol itself is an attractive town, arranged around a picturesque harbour. Occupying a water-front building, the **Branislav Dešković Gallery** displays paintings and sculpture by some of Croatia's leading 20th-century artists.

A **Dominican Monastery**, founded in 1475, stands on a headland at the edge of the town. The beautiful church is decorated with paintings, including a Virgin with Saints attributed to Tintoretto. A rich treasury includes liturgical objects.

From Bol you can climb up **Mount St Vitus** (Vidova Gora), a two-hour walk to one of the highest peaks in the Dalmatian islands, at 778 m (2,552 ft). Hidden in a ravine west of Mount St Vitus is Blaca Hermitage (Pustinja Blaca), a 16th-century fortified monastery clinging to the rocky slopes. Now a museum, the hermitage contains an absorbing collection of religious relics together with astronomical and other scientific equipment left behind by former monks. Walking to Blaca is a popular excursion. If a somewhat hot and dry trek in summer – it can be approached from the north via Nerezišća or from the southeast from Bol.

There are further attractions along the northern coast and to the east of the island. Along the coast from Supetar, quiet Lovrečina Bay is over-looked by the ruins of the 5th–6th century Basilica of St Lawrence, a pilgrimage site. Lying at the end of a long sea inlet, **Pučišća** is the centre of the island's stone quarrying industry, active since at least Roman times. The blocks were loaded onto ships at the port. **Povlja**, further east still, is one

Pleasure boats and swimmers on the southern coast of Brač

of the island's most charming former fishing ports, with stone houses straggling along the sides of a deep bay.

The quaint port of **Sumartin**, on the southeastern corner of the island, is where ferries from the mainland resort of Makarska arrive. It was founded by refugees from the Makarska region fleeing the Turks in 1645. There is a fine Franciscan monastery, the foundations of which were laid by the poet Andrija Kačić Miošić.

Brač Museum
Škrip. (021) 637 092. **Open** summer: 8am–8pm daily; winter: by appt.

Branislav Dešković Gallery
Put bolskih pomoraca bb, Bol. (021) 637 092. **Open** Jun–Oct: 9am–noon, 6–10pm Tue–Sun; Nov–May: 9am–2pm Mon–Fri.

Dominican Monastery
Anđelka Rabadana 4, Bol. (021) 778 000. **Open** 10am–noon, 5–8pm daily.

Bol's famous golden beach, changing shape with the tides

⑳ Vis

Further out in the Adriatic than the other Dalmatian islands, Vis was until 1989 a closed military base. Now gradually being rediscovered by intrepid travellers, it has a jagged coastline with beaches, and an inland mountain chain with Mount Hum reaching a height of 587 m (1,925 ft). The island was chosen by Dionysios of Syracuse as a base for Greek domination of the Adriatic. The Greeks founded the town of Issa – now Vis town – here. Later the island was ruled by the Romans, then the Byzantines and, from 1420, the Venetians. The island played a key role during World War II – in 1944 Marshal Tito used it as a base for co-ordinating partisan military operations. Crucial meetings between partisans, the Yugoslav government in exile and the Allies were also held on Vis.

Aerial view of the town of Komiža and its sheltered harbour

Vis Town

The main town of **Vis** is ranged along the shores of a deep, broad bay. On a hillside behind a group of tennis courts are the remains of an ancient Greek cemetery, where you can see the remains of tombstones left by the town's first inhabitants. Further along the north side of the bay are remnants of Roman mosaics, once part of a 2nd-century baths complex. Just beyond, the Franciscan Monastery Church sits on a small peninsula bordered by pebble beaches. Also on the peninsula is the town's graveyard, where a

monument in the form of a lion recalls the great sea battle that took place near here between the Austrian and Italian navies in 1866.

On the southern side of Vis town's bay is the Renaissance church of Our Lady of Spilica (Gospa od Spilica), with a painting by Girolamo di Santacroce. Occupying a former Austrian gun battery is the **Town Museum**, with a rich collection of Greek and Roman vases and amphorae. Further north, the suburb of Kut is a charming warren of alleyways and piazzas. Beyond Kut lies the British Cemetery,

a small walled enclosure honouring those who died while stationed here during both the Napoleonic Wars and World War II. A short walk uphill to the north of the town lie reminders of the early-19th-century British occupation of Vis – the King George III Fortress and the Bentich Tower. Both are empty shells today, but are set in beautiful countryside with good views.

🏛 Town Museum
Gospina batarija. ℹ️ (021) 711 729. **Open** Jun–Sep: 9am–1pm, 5–9pm Mon–Fri, 9am–1pm Sat; Oct–May: by appt for groups only.

Key

▬ Minor road

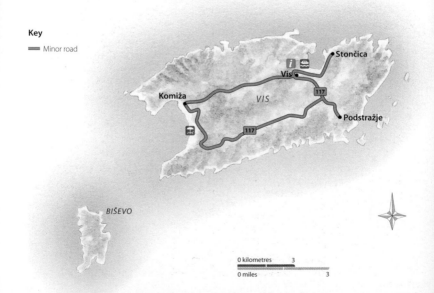

0 kilometres 3
0 miles 3

Komiža

On the western side of the island lies **Komiža**, a quaint port long associated with the anchovy-fishing industry. Lined with handsome stone houses, Komiža harbour is one of the most attractive in the Adriatic. Right on the quayside. A defensive tower, built by the Venetians and known as the Kaštel, is righ on the quayside. It now houses the **Fishing Museum**, which commemorates the swift Falkuša sailing boats unique to this town that were once used to bring in the local catch. On the north side of the bay is the 16th-century Church of Our Lady of the Pirates (Gospa Gusarica), so- called because, legend has it, a band of pirates who had stolen its wooden image of the Madonna were swiftly killed in a shipwreck, while the statue floated safely back to shore. It has an unusual triple-nave layout. Just inland from the town centre, the Benedictine Monastery sits on a small hill, fortified by defensive bastions and flanked by vineyards. Komiža's best beaches lie south, where there is a series of coves.

🏛 Fishing Museum

Riva svetog Mikule. **Open** Jun–Sep: 11am–noon, 7–10pm Mon-Sat, 7–10pm Sun.

Mount Hum

Looming above Komiža is Vis's highest point, Mount Hum (587 m/1,925 ft), which can be

The Kaštel, a fortified lookout tower built by the Venetians at Vis

reached either by road or by hiking path from Komiža. Superb views can be enjoyed from the summit, and adventure-sports enthusiasts use it as a base for hang-gliding. On the eastern side of the summit is Tito's Cave (Titova spilja) where the World War II partisan leader Josip Broz Tito based his HQ for several months in mid-1944. It was here that Tito's army planned the re-conquest of German-occupied Dalmatia. The cave is frequently open to visitors over the summer, although you should check with Komiža tourist office to make sure.

Plisko Polje

Plisko Polje is the main inland village on the south side of the island, where fertile fields yield some of the Adriatic's best Plavac wine, a dry red. The fields

outside Plisko Polje were used to create a landing strip during World War II so that Allied planes could supply Tito's partisans, although the site is now largely covered by vineyards. One part of the former landing strip is occupied by Croatia's only cricket pitch – built by enthusiastic locals who emigrated to Australia and returned home with a love of the sport. South of Plisko Polje, tracks lead to the enchanting coves of Stiniva and Mala Travna, both hugely popular with bathers despite being quite hard to reach – many trippers come on excursion boats from Vis town or Komiža.

Environs

The starkly beautiful **island of Biševo**, to the southwest of Vis, is sparsely inhabited and cannot be reached by regular ferry transport. It is a popular destination for boat excursions because of its Blue Grotto (Modra špilja), a cave where the water takes on beautiful colours. This mesmerising effect is produced by sunlight shining into the cave through a slightly submerged aperture. The grotto can only be reached by boat: day trips depart from Komiža in the morning (contact the tourist office or any of the private tourist agencies near Komiža harbour).

Many boat trips to the grotto also allow visitors a few free hours on the island of Biševo itself. A monastery was built here in around 1000 AD, which resisted raids by pirates and Saracens for 200 years. The ruins remain, along with a 12th-century church.

A small boat from a Komiža hotel, taking visitors to Biševo island

㉑ Hvar

Art treasures, a mild climate, good beaches and fields of scented lavender make this island one of the treasures of the Adriatic. Limestone hills form the central ridge. Hvar's story begins in the 4th century BC when the Greeks from Paros founded Pharos (the present-day Stari Grad) and Dimos (Hvar town). Traces have been left by the Romans, the Byzantines, the medieval Croatian kings and the Venetians, who ruled from 1278 until 1797. After 1420, defences were built, and the capital was moved from Pharos to Hvar town. In 1886, under Austria-Hungary, the Hvar Hygienic Society began to promote the town as a health resort. Hvar was an important centre of Croatian culture during the Renaissance, when local-born poets Hanibal Lucić and Petar Hektorović both wrote lyrically about the people and landscapes of the Adriatic.

Main square of Hvar, with the Cathedral of St Stephen

Narrow street between traditional stone houses in Stari Grad

Hvar Town
See pp132–3.

Stari Grad
Founded by the Syracusans in the 4th century BC and originally called Pharos, Stari Grad (literally, the Old Town) is still Hvar's main ferry port, despite having lost its political and cultural importance to Hvar town. Stari Grad lies at the end of a long bay and the main sights are scattered throughout

a picturesque old quarter of low stone houses and tiny streets. The 17th-century parish Church of **St Stephen** (Sv. Stjepan), with its free-standing Venetian-style bell tower, is the principal landmark. At the western end of the old quarter is the **Tvrdalj**, the fortified residence of Renaissance poet Petar Hektorović. Hektorović is best known as the author of *Ribanje i ribarsko prigovaranje (Fishing and Fishermen's*

Conversation) in which he vividly describes a fishing trip around the islands of Hvar, Brač and Šolta. He began building the Tvrdalj in 1514, intending for it to be both a palatial private house and a fortified sanctuary into which the local population could retreat should there be an attack by pirates. The Tvrdalj was intended to be a self-sustaining unit, with a garden, a dovecote and a seawater fishpond were included within its walls. Hektorović placed philosophical inscriptions in Latin on the walls of the Tvrdalj, turning his home into a unique monument to Renaissance humanist thought.

Nearby is Stari Grad's **Town Museum**, housed in the Renaissance Biankini Palace. It contains a stunning collection of Greek amphorae, some beautifully restored period rooms, and a picture gallery devoted to local artists, including the gifted, Paris-trained Juraj Plančić (1899–1930). The Moira Gallery at Vagonj 1 shows contemporary art and contains fragments of

Part of the tranquil canal system, Vrboska

Roman mosaic in the floor. On the edge of the old quarter is the **Dominican Monastery** (Dominikanski samostan), founded by Brother Germano of Piacenza in 1482 and rebuilt and fortified after destruction by Uluz Ali, the Ottoman corsair who raided the Adriatic islands in 1571. The most feared sea captain of his time, Uluz Ali was driven away by the stubborn defenders of Korčula, and came to pillage the less well-defended island of Hvar instead. As well as a beautiful cloister, the monastery has a library rich in medieval incunabula, and a collection of paintings including a *Deposition* by Tintoretto. The monastery church contains the grave of Petar Hektorović.

Immediately east of Stari Grad, the **Ager** is a fertile plain that still preserves the field plan established by the island's ancient Greek inhabitants. Archaeologists have revealed that the Greeks cultivated wine, figs and olives, much as their modern counterparts do today, but also grew wheat. Added to the UNESCO World Heritage list in 2008, the Ager can be explored on foot or by bike. There are splendid views from the 16th-century Španjola fort and the Napoleon fort (1811).

🏛 Tvrdalj
Priko bb. **Open** May, Jun & Sep: 10am–1pm daily; July & Aug: 10am–1pm, 5pm–8pm daily.

🏛 Town Museum
Ulaz braće Biankini 2. ℹ️ (021) 766 324. **Open** May, Jun & Sep: 10am–1pm Mon–Sat; Jul & Aug: 10am–noon, 7–9pm Mon–Sat, 7–9pm Sun; Oct–Apr: by appt.

🏛 Dominican Monastery
Trg sv. Petra bb. **Tel** (021) 765 442. **Open** Jun–Sep: 10am–noon, 6–8pm daily; Oct–May: by appt.

Jelsa
A traditional Dalmatian stone-built settlement around a small harbour, Jelsa is a popular base for family holidays, with several beaches on the outer fringes of town. For much of its history Jelsa was a prosperous port, exporting the wines produced in the villages just inland. Steps from Jelsa's café-filled main square ascend to the Gothic parish Church of St Mary (Sv. Marija). Hidden in the narrow alleys of the historic centre is Trg svetog Ivana, a Renaissance piazza grouped around a unique octagonal chapel. The palm-shaded park behind Jelsa's harbour contains a statue of 19th-century sea captain Nika Duboković by the prominent Dalmatian sculptor Ivan Rendić.

VISITORS' CHECKLIST

Practical Information
Map D–E5. 🚗 11,500. ℹ️ Hvar town: Trg svetog Stjepana bb, (021) 741 059. Stari Grad: Obala dr. Franje Tuđmana 1, (021) 765 763. Sucuraj: (021) 717 288. 🌐 **tzhvar.hr**

Transport
🚢 Split, Drvenik. Hvar town: (021) 741 007; Jadrolinija: (021) 741 132. Stari Grad: (021) 765 060; Jadrolinija: (021) 765 048. Sućuraj: (021) 773 228.

Vrboska
Vrboska is a pretty village huddled around a succession of stone bridges spanning a narrow canal connected to the open sea. Dominating the village is the 16th-century Church of St Mary (Sv. Marija), fortified with huge buttresses to provide shelter for villagers in times of siege. The Baroque Church of St Lawrence (Sv. Lovro) has a poly-ptych on the main altar by Paolo Veronese (c.1570) and a Virgin of the Rosary by Leandro da Bassano. A short walk north is the Glavica peninsula, with rocky beaches and pebbly coves. The seaside path from Vrboska to Jelsa is perfect for a relaxed stroll.

Zavala
Zavala is the principal village of Hvar's peaceful southern coast, where quiet hamlets lie below slopes covered with vineyards. The road here from Jelsa runs through a famously low and narrow single-lane tunnel. There is a long stretch of pebbly beach running along Zavala's shoreline. Boat captains here offer trips to the islet of Šćedro just to the south, with even quieter beaches, pine trees and maquis vegetation.

Sućuraj
Lying in a sheltered bay at the eastern tip of the island, Sućuraj is where the ferry from Drvenik on the mainland arrives. Its pretty harbour boasts the remains of a fortress built by the Venetians in 1630. Nearby, Mlaska Bay and Perna Bay are two of Hvar's best beaches, with clear shallow water over fine sand. 🏊

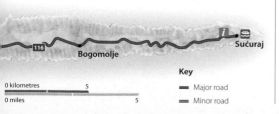

116 **Bogomolje** ℹ️ 🚢 **Sućuraj**

Key

— Major road
— Minor road

0 kilometres — 5
0 miles — 5

For keys to symbols *see back flap*

Exploring Hvar Town

Thanks to its wonderfully preserved Renaissance centre, Hvar town is one of the most visited on the Dalmatian coast. It has long been popular with Croatian artists and celebrities, lending it a chic ambience reflected in the growing number of stylish restaurants, bars and hotels. Much frequented by luxury yachts and boats in summer, Hvar's harbourside is one of the most glamorous in the Adriatic. Hvar town did not become the main town on the island until the 15th century, when Venetian governors decided that the harbour was easier to defend than the one at Stari Grad, and ordered all the island's noble families to move here. Hvar town became one of the most important ports for Venetian fleets going to and from the Orient, bringing an upsurge in trade and wealth. Cultural life and monastic orders also flourished.

Cafés on the main square, with the cathedral in the background

⛪ Cathedral of St Stephen
Katedrala sv. Stjepana
Trg svetog Stjepana. **Tel** (021) 743 107. Cathedral Treasury: **Open** summer: 9am–noon, 5–7pm daily; winter: by appt.

Dominating Hvar's harbourside main square, Trg svetog Stjepana, the Renaissance cathedral has a trefoil pediment and a 17th-century bell tower standing to one side. The interior houses many works of art: a *Virgin and Saints* by Palma il Giovane (1544–1628), a *Pietà* by Juan Boschetus, *Virgin with Saints* by Domenico Uberti and a fine 16th-century wooden choir. The cathedral treasury boasts a rich collection of reliquaries and silverware.

🏛 Arsenal
Trg svetog Stjepana. **Open** summer: 9am–1pm, 5–11pm daily; winter: by appt.

On the south side of the square, the Arsenal was built in the late 16th century as a dry dock for Venetian war galleys. A theatre built on the first floor in 1612 is one of the oldest in Europe. The theatre was open to people of all classes in a

Open to the sky, the Gothic windows of the Hektorović Palace, never completed

deliberate attempt to lessen social conflict between aristocrats and plebeians. The plush interior has been well preserved and art exhibitions are held in the foyer. There are fine views of town from the theatre's balustraded terrace.

Diagonally opposite the Arsenal, the Renaissance clock tower and loggia are all that remains of the **Rector's Palace**, where the administrator appointed by the Venetian Republic once held sway. The rest of the palace was demolished in 1900 to make way for the Hotel Elisabeth, since renamed Hotel Palace *(see p228)*.

🏛 Hektorović Palace
Hektorovićeva palača
North of the main square is a very ancient quarter of the town called Groda, consisting of stone houses and narrow alleys clinging to a sharply rising hillside. The most prominent landmark here is the **Hektorović Palace**, an unfinished building project by the15th-century poet Petar Hektorović *(see pp130–31)*. It is easily recognized by its beautiful Venetian-Gothic mullioned windows.

🏛 Benedictine Convent
Benediktini samostan
Groda bb. **Tel** (021) 741 052. **Open** 10am–noon, 5–7pm Mon–Sat.

Just behind the Hektorović Palace is a Benedictine convent founded in 1664 that houses a secluded community of nuns who still make, display and sell traditional Hvar lace, made by weaving fibres extracted from the spiky agave plants that can be seen all over the island.

🏰 Citadel
Open Apr & May: 10am–4pm daily; Jun–Sep: 10am–10pm daily
Paths ascend from the Groda district to the 16th-century Citadel on the hill above town, known locally as Španjola because it was built by Spanish architects who specialized in fortification work. Superb views of the surrounding coast are offered by the citadel's ramparts.

🏛 Church of St Mark
Crkva svetog Marka

Visible all over town is the belfry of the former Dominican monastery's Church of St Mark, west of the main square. The monastery was an important centre of culture during the Renaissance. It was here that friar Vinko Pribojević gave a famous speech on the Origins of the Slavs in 1525, proposing not only that the Slav peoples of Europe were ethnically related but also that they all originally came from the Croatian Adriatic.

🏛 Franciscan Monastery
Franjevački samostan

Križa bb. **Tel** (021) 741 193.
Open May–Oct: 9am–noon daily;
Nov–Apr: 11am–noon daily.

The monastery, dating from 1461, is located along the coastal path south of the Old Town. The monastery's Church of **Our Lady of Charity** (Gospa od Milosti), with a relief on the façade by Nikola Firentinac, also contains two paintings by Palma il Giovane (of St Francis Receiving the Stigmata and St Diego), three polyptychs by Francesco da Santacroce, a Christ on the Cross by Leandro

Popular with locals, Mlini beach on the Pakleni Islands

da Bassano, and six scenes inspired by the Passion of Christ by Martin Benetović.

The grave of Renaissance poet Hanibal Lucić can be seen on the floor of the nave. There are also many works of art in the rooms facing the cloister. The Mannerist painting of the Last Supper in the refectory is of uncertain attribution – possibly the work of Matteo Ingoli, Matteo Ponzone or the school of Palma il Giovane.

Environs

The sparsely inhabited **Pakleni Islands**, just off the coast from Hvar town, are popular bathing, walking and sailing destinations throughout the summer season. Their name derives from the resin (paklina) that was at one time extracted from the pines and used to waterproof fishing boats.

During the summer boat trips to the islands depart regularly from Hvar. Sveti Klement is the largest of the islands and has most to offer in terms of beaches, walking trails and restaurants. Marinkovac also has good beaches and a popular yachting marina. Be aware that the nearest island, Jerolim, is given over to naturism.

Hvar

① Cathedral of St Stephen
② Arsenal
③ Hektorović Palace
④ Benedictine Convent
⑤ Citadel
⑥ Church of St Mark
⑦ Franciscan Monastery

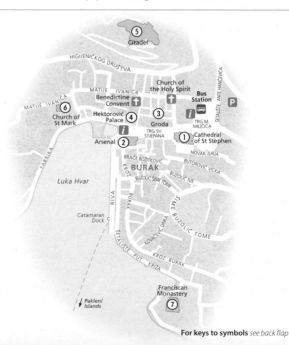

0 metres 300
0 yards 300

For keys to symbols *see back flap*

Boating on the river in the Cetina Valley Nature Park

㉒ Omiš

Map D5. ⚑ 6,000. 🚌 (021) 864 210.
🚢 (021) 861 025. ℹ Trg kneza
Miroslava bb, (021) 861 350.
🎭 Festival klapa (Jul). 🆆 **tz-omis.hr**

In the late Middle Ages Omiš
was known as the residence of
the terrifying corsairs who
fought fiercely against
Venetian rule from the
12th century until
1444, when the
town fell to Venice.
Today it is a peaceful
holiday resort with
some light industry
along the coast,
and the starting
point for visits to
the valley of the
River Cetina.

The church of St Peter in
Priko, a district of Omiš

In July, the Dalamatinksa
Klapa festival attracts many
visitors who come to hear
Klapa, a kind of plainsong
traditional to Dalmatia. It is
still very popular, even among
the young.

Only a few traces of the
Roman *municipium* of Onaeum
remain but many of the
medieval defences built by
the counts of Kačić and Bribir
are still visible on a hill, once
the site of the Old Town, or Stari
grad. These consist of the walls
going down to the River Cetina
and also the ruins of a large fort
(Fortica) with its distinctive high
tower. From the fort, built
between the 16th and the 17th
centuries, there is a splendid
view of Omiš and the central
Dalmatian islands.

There are three interesting
religious buildings in the town.
One is the Renaissance Church
of **St Michael** (Sv. Mihovil) with
a pointed bell tower, originally a
defensive structure. Inside is a
16th-century wooden altar, a
large 13th-century wooden
cross and two paintings by
Matteo Ingoli of Ravenna
(1587–1631). At
the end of the
main road is the
16th-century **Oratory
of the Holy Spirit**
(Sv. Duh) with
*Descent of the Holy
Spirit* by Palma il
Giovane (1544–
1628). However, the
most fascinating
monument here is in Priko, on
the opposite bank of the River
Cetina. This is the 10th-century
Church of **St Peter** (Sv. Petar),

one of the most appealing
pre-Romanesque churches
in Dalmatia. It has a single
nave, a dome, and remains
from the early Christian period
incorporated into the walls.

Environs
The **Cetina Valley Nature
Park**, immediately behind
Omiš, shelters a river which
flows into the artificial lake of
Peruča. The river runs out of
the lake and parallel to the
coast for some distance and
then, near Zadvarje, abruptly
turns and cascades down
before flowing into a narrow
gorge. This beautiful natural
environment, with its myriad
bird species, can be explored
on foot or by bicycle, but the
most popular way to see it is
to take one of the many boats
through the park.

㉓ Makarska

Map E5. ⚑ 14,000. 🚌 Ulica Ante
Starčevića, (021) 612 333. 🚢 (021) 611
977. ℹ Obala kralja Tomislava bb,
(021) 612 002. 🆆 **makarska-info.hr**

The Makarska coast extends
from Brela to Gradac and
includes a long stretch of shore
with lush vegetation sheltered
by the Biokovo massif.
Makarska, one of Dalmatia's
most popular mainland resorts,
lies within a bay sheltered by
the peninsula of St Peter's.
The town was the site of the
Roman Mucurum, which was

The Makarska coast, with white beaches and a mountainous backdrop

The Vineyards of Dalmatia

Vines are grown all along the coast of Dalmatia, and on many of the islands. Vineyards first start appearing around Primošten, near Trogir (see p113), where the

Vines protected by dry-stone walls

good quality red wine Babić is made, and become part of the landscape along the Makarska coast. Built on stony hillsides, these vineyards are often "fortified" with low dry-stone walls, painstakingly constructed with geometrical precision by peasant farmers. Low-growing vines cultivated inside the walls are protected from the cold north winds and kept cool in the hot summer months. A monument to human toil, the result of immense patience and effort, without these walls it would not be possible to cultivate this difficult ground.

The beach at Gradac, one of the longest in the eastern Adriatic

The Franciscan monastery, Makarska, now a museum

destroyed by the Goths in 548, and rebuilt at a later date. It belonged to the Kingdom of Croatia until 1499, when it was conquered by the Turks, for whom it was a port and trading centre until 1646, the beginning of Venetian rule.

There are two ancient monasteries in Makarska. St Philip Neri (Sv. Filipa Nerija) was built in 1757, and has medieval and Roman-era fragments in the cloister. The Franciscan monastery (Franjevački Samostan), built in 1614 on the foundations of a 15th-century monastery, houses the **Malacological Museum** (Malakološki muzej), with a collection of mollusc shells.

The centre of the modern town is the square called Brother Andrija Kačić Miošić, dedicated to the 18th-century Dalmatian scholar and author of theological and philosophical works. Two seafront promenades extend towards the wide beaches and Kalelarga, where there are 18th-century buildings.

🏛 **Malacological Museum**
Franjevački put 1. **Tel** (021) 611 256.

㉔ Gradac

Map E5. 🚐 1,200.
ℹ️ (021) 697 375 (high season only).
🌐 **gradac.hr**

This town's fame and popularity are due to the fact that it has one of the longest beaches in the eastern Adriatic. Over 6 km (4 miles) long, the beach is lined with hotels and campsites.

In the town itself there are two large 17th-century towers while nearby, in Crkvine, the remains of a Roman staging post between Mucurum (the present-day Makarska) and Narona (see p136) have been found. Gradac gets its name from the fort (grad) built in the 17th century to defend against the Turks.

Environs

west of Gradac, is a Franciscan monastery (Franjevački samostan) founded in the 16th century and completed a century later. The façade of the church has an inscription written in Cyrillic script. In the rooms around the beautiful cloister there is a fascinating folklore collection, an art gallery, and a library and archive where documents about the period of Turkish occupation are kept. The Dalmatian scholar Andrija Kačić Miošić (1704–60) lived and died in the monastery.

Around 20 km (12 miles) from Gradac, towards Makarska, is **Živogošće**, one of the oldest settlements on the Makarska coast. Today it is a busy tourist resort, but it was once famous for a spring which flowed from the rocks.

A Franciscan monastery was founded near this spring in 1616, and its beautiful church boasts an ornate Baroque altar. The monastery is famous for its well-stocked library and archives, which are the main source for the study of the area around the Biokovo massif.

Franciscan monastery, Zaostrog

The delta of the River Neretva in Opuzen, drained and turned into fertile fields

㉕ Opuzen

Map E6. 🏔 3,250. 🚌 Metković, (060) 365 365. 🛈 Trg kralja Tomislava 1, (020) 671 139. 🔲 **opuzen.hr**

At the edges of the delta of the River Neretva, where the road leaves the Magistrala coast road (E65) and climbs the river valley, stands Opuzen. For centuries it was fortified and has always been considered something of a border town.

Towards the end of the 15th century, the Hungarian-Croat king, Matthias Corvinus, built the fort of Koš here. It was captured by the Turks in 1490 who ruled until 1686, when it came under Venetian rule. There are also traces of a 13th-century castle built by the Republic of Dubrovnik and the remains of a fort (Fort Opus), built by the Venetians to defend the border of their territories. The town takes its name from this fort and the ruins can be seen on the eastern side of town.

In the entrance hall of the former Town Hall are some fragments discovered in the ancient town of Narona.

㉖ Narona

Map E6. 🚌 Metković, (060) 365 365. 🛈 (020) 691 596. 🔲 **a-m-narona.hr**

The ancient Roman town of Colonia Julia Narona was founded by the Romans in the 2nd century BC. It was an important road junction and a trading centre with the Pannonian hinterland, and had temples, baths, a theatre and other buildings grouped around the Forum. A walled town, it was one of the first dioceses in the Balkans and flourished until the 7th century when it was occupied and destroyed by the Avars. It fell into disuse afterwards.

At the end of the 19th century, after a few chance discoveries, the Austrian archaeologist Karl Patsch began to carry out excavations. Work continued after World War II and uncovered numerous finds from pagan and Christian temples, houses and public works. In 1995, a particularly fine temple was discovered. Large parts of the area have still to be explored, but it is possible to get an idea of the importance of the town

Head of Emperor Vespasian, now in Vid's Museum

by visiting the Archaeological Museum in **Vid**. This village stands on much of the site of ancient Narona, 3 km (2 miles) from Metković. In the museum are statues of gods and emperors, as well as weapons and jewels that were found in Narona. Other finds are in Split's Archaeological Museum *(see p125)*.

The 16th-century Church of St Vitus (Sv. Vid) stands just outside the town on the site of an old church, of which only parts of the apse remain.

㉗ Neum

Bosnia-Herzegovina. **Map** E6. 🏔 2,500. 🚌 Metković, (060) 365 365. 🔲 **neum.ba**

All the buses running along the coastal road between Split and Dubrovnik pass through the 9-km (5-mile) stretch of coast that is part of Bosnia-Herzegovina. The main town in this area is Neum, which is a holiday resort and Bosnia's only coastal town. Prices are cheaper here than in Croatia, and as a result it is a popular place for Croatians to stop off and go shopping.

Neum is a border town, and visitors should carry passports. There are several hotels and tourist facilities.

㉘ Pelješac Peninsula

Map E6. 🚌 Metković, (060) 365 365.
Ston: 🏛 580. 🚌 (020) 754 026.
ℹ️ Pelješka cesta 2, (020) 754 452.
🌐 **ston.hr** Orebić: 🏛 2,500.
🚌 (020) 743 542 (Trpanj). ℹ️ Zrinsko
Frankopanska 2, (020) 713 718.
🌐 visitorebic-croatia.hr

The peninsula of Pelješac juts
out 65 km (40 miles) from the
mainland, but it is only 7 km
(4 miles) wide at its broadest
point. A mountain chain forms
its backbone, which peaks at
Mount St Elijah (961 m/3,152 ft).
The slopes and plain are
covered with vineyards and
fruit trees, and the shallow
coastal waters are given over
to oyster farming.

The peninsula was first
colonized by the Greeks, then
by the Romans and later by the
Byzantines. From 1333 to 1808 it
belonged to Dubrovnik.

The Pelješac coast, a centre for
oyster farming

Ston

The town closest to the
mainland, Ston was formerly
called Stagnum because of its
shallow waters. There have
been salt pans here since the
time of the Romans, who built
a *castrum* on the site. It was
enclosed by walls prior to
1000 AD.

The present defensive
walls, still impressive above
the town, were begun in the
14th century and completed
in the 15th century on orders
from Dubrovnik. There are
more than 5 km (3 miles) of
walls climbing from Veliki
Ston, the main heart of the
town, to St Michael's Mount

and descending the opposite
slope until they reach Mali
Ston. The 41 towers, seven
bastions and two forts make
this one of the largest and
most interesting defensive
structures in the Adriatic and
indeed the world. Some of
the best military architects,
such as Michelozzo Michelozzi,
Župan Bunić, Bernardino of
Parma, Juraj Dalmatinac and
Paskoje Miličević, contributed
to its design and construction.
The walls are still in good
condition despite being
bombed in 1991 and struck
by an earthquake in 1996.

The main structures are at
Veliki Ston, which is built on an
irregular pentagonal ground
plan. The buildings include the
largest fort (Veliki Kaštio); the
Neo-Gothic Church of St Blaise
(Sv. Vlaho), built in 1870 to
replace a cathedral from the
14th century which was
destroyed by the earthquake of
1850; the Governor's Palace
(Knežev dvor), enlarged in the
same century, and the Bishop's
Palace (1573). The **Church and
Franciscan Monastery of St
Nicholas** (Sv. Nikola) was built
between the end of the 14th
century and the 16th century.

Mali Ston, the other focus
of the town, is dominated by
Fort Koruna, which dates
from 1347, with two arsenals
and a fortified warehouse
for storing salt. There are
wonderful views across the
peninsula to the north of the
town from here.

The Franciscan monastery between Orebić
and Lovište

Orebić

Towards the tip of the peninsula,
Orebić is the boarding point for
ferries to Korčula. It has a
Maritime Museum (Pomorski
muzej), which illustrates the
history of its inhabitants, who
were the most sought-after sea
captains in the Mediterranean.
At the end of their careers these
seamen invested in villas along
the coast or in the hills.

Just outside the village,
towards Lovište, is a massive
Franciscan Monastery
(Franjevački samostan), founded
in the 15th century. In the
church alongside are two reliefs:
one is a *Virgin with Child* by
Nikola Firentinac (1501), who
was a pupil of Donatello.

🏛 **Maritime Museum**
Trg Mimbelli bb. **Tel** (020) 713 009.
Open Jun–Sep: 9am–noon, 5–8pm
daily; Oct–May: 7am–2:30pm
Mon–Fri. 📷

Overlooking the circle of walls connecting the two parts of Ston

㉙ Korčula

Dense forests of Aleppo pine, cypress and oak are found all over this island, one of the largest in the Adriatic at 47 km (29 miles) long. Mountains run the length of the island, reaching 560 m (1,837 ft) at their peak. Inhabited since prehistoric times, the Greeks named the island Korkyra Melaina (Black Corfu). After 1000 AD, it was fought over by Venice and the Croat kings and later by the Genoese and the Turks (in the 1298 naval battle between Genoa and Venice, the Genoese captured Marco Polo, said to be a native of the island). Today it is a popular holiday spot for its cliffs and sandy beaches, its villages and Korčula, its main town.

VISITORS' CHECKLIST

Practical Information
Map E6. 🚹 17,000. 🚹 Obala dr. Tuđmana 4, Korčula, (020) 715 701. 🚹 Moreška, 9pm Mon & Thu in summer. Lumbarda: 🚹 (020) 712 005. Blato: 🚹 Trg dr. Franje Tuđmana 4, (020) 851 850. 📅 St Vincenca's Day (28 Apr). 🚹 Obala 3 br 19, (020) 813 619. 🆆 **visitkorcula.eu** 🆆 **tzvelaluka.hr**

Transport
🚢 from Orebić, Split and Rijeka. Korčula: 🚌 (020) 711 216. 🚢 Vela Luka: (020) 715 410. 🚢 (020) 812 023.

The Land Gate, main entrance to the old town of Korčula

Korčula Town

The town sits atop a peninsula, surrounded by strong 13th-century walls, reinforced with towers and bastions by the Venetians after 1420. The whole town is enchanting. The **Land Gate** (Kopnena vrata) was fortified by a huge tower, the Revelin, which overlooked a canal dug by the Venetians to isolate the town. There are now steps in this area. Narrow streets branching off the main road are designed to lessen the impact of the bora wind.

Facing **Strossmayerov trg**, the central square, is the town's main monument: the 13th-century Cathedral of St Mark (Katedrala Sv. Marka), built in pale, honey-coloured stone. Most of it dates from the end of the 15th century. The skill of Korčula's sculptors and stone masons is evident in the door, where two lions guard the entrance, decorated with thin spiral columns and a lunette with the figure of St Mark, attributed to Bonino of Milan. Two further doors open onto side aisles. On the left stands an imposing, 30-m (100-ft) bell tower, which visitors may climb.

Inside are large columns with elaborately decorated capitals and several important sculptural works: a 15th-century holy water stoup, a font from the 17th century, and the tomb of Bishop Toma Malumbra, attributed to the workshop of Marko Andrijić, who also made the ciborium in the presbytery in 1481. There is also a statue of St Blaise by Ivan Meštrović. The paintings include *St Mark with St Jerome and St Bartholomew* by Tintoretto. On a wall are trophies recalling the Battle of Lepanto of 1571.

Next to the cathedral, in the Bishop's Palace, now the Abbot's House, is the **Abbey Treasury** (Opatska riznica), which is particularly known for its Dalmatian and Venetian art, including a polyptych by Blaž of

Impressive entrance to the Gothic Cathedral of St Mark, Korčula

PROIZD

Prigradica

Vela Luka

Blato

Potirna

Prižba

Brna

Key

━━ Major road

━━ Minor road

Korčula, the main town on the island, on an isthmus on the northeast coast

Trogir, two altar paintings by Pellegrino of San Daniele, a *Sacred Conversation* by Titian, a *Portrait of a Man* by Vittore Carpaccio and an *Annunciation* by Titian. A door by Bonino of Milan decorates the Gothic Church of **St Peter** (Sv. Petar) to the left of the cathedral. Facing St Peter are the Gothic **Arneri Palace** and the Renaissance Gabriellis Palace (16th century). The latter has been the **Town Museum** (Gradski muzej) since 1957 and contains documents on Korčula's seafaring history, an interesting archaeological section covering the period from prehistoric to Roman times and other works of art.

Along the seafront is **All Saints' Church** (Svi Sveti), built in 1301 and remodelled in the Baroque style, which belongs to the oldest confraternity on the island. Inside is an 18th-century carved wooden *Pietà*, by the Austrian artist George Raphael Donner, and a 15th-century polyptych by Blaž of Trogir.

In the nearby quarters of the confraternity is the **Icon Collection** (Kolekcija Ikona), which is famous for its rich collection of Byzantine icons from the 13th to 15th centuries, many from Crete.

Outside the walls are the **Church and Monastery of St Nicholas** (Sv. Nikola), from the 15th century, with many paintings by Dalmatian and Italian artists.

Abbey Treasury
Trg sv. Marka. (020) 711 049.
Open call for information.

Town Museum
Trg sv. Marka. **Tel** (020) 711 420.
Open Apr–Jun: 10am–2pm Mon–Sat; Jul–Sep: 9am–9pm Mon–Sat; Oct–Mar: 10am–1pm; by appt Sun.

Icon Collection
Trg Svih Svetih. (020) 711 306 or (091) 593 1281. **Open** summer: 10am–2pm, 5–8pm Mon–Sat; Sun & winter: by appt.

Ancient Dances and Festivals

The Moreška and the Kumpanjija are Korčula's two most noted folk festivals. Officially, the Moreška sword dance takes place in Korčula on 29 July, the patron saint's day (St Theodore). However, it is repeated on Mondays and Thursdays during the summer for tourists. It commemorates the clash between Christians and Moors in the attempt to free a girl kidnapped by the infidels. In Blato, the Kumpanija dance is dedicated to the patron saint, St Vincenca, and is celebrated with drum music. At the end of the battle, girls in bright costumes appear, accompanied by pipes and drums. The dance takes place in front of the church on 28 April and is performed once a week for tourists who visit Blato.

Two Moreškants– actors performing the ancient Moreška sword dance

Račišće •

ORČULA Pupnat

118 Žrnovo

• Pupnatska Luka Lumbarda

118

avalatica

Korčula

0 kilometres 5
0 miles 5

For keys to symbols *see back flap*

The rocky coastline of Korčula

Lumbarda

Lumbarda is a village 6 km (4 miles) southeast of the town of Korčula and is thought to have been founded by Greeks from Vis. It was called Eraclea by the Romans. In the 16th century it became a holiday resort for the nobles of Korčula. Some inscriptions from the Greek period are now in the Archaeological Museum of Zagreb *(see pp168–9)*.

Today this village is one of the centres of production for the liqueur-like white wine called Grk, which is made from grapes of the same name grown in the sand. The nearby small beaches are havens of tranquillity.

Blato

In the central square of Blato, a town where the festival of the Kumpanija *(see p139)* is held every April, are an 18th-century Baroque loggia, the Renaissance **Arneri Castle**, where the Civic Museum documenting local history is being set up, and **All Saints' Church** (Svi Sveti), of medieval origin. This church was enlarged and rebuilt in the 17th century and has an altarpiece of the *Virgin with Child and Saints* on the main altar by Girolamo di Santacroce (1540)

and, in the chapel, the relics of the martyr St Vincenca, the object of veneration in the local community. The cemetery church of the **Holy Cross** and that of **St Jerome** date from the 14th century.

Vela Luka

Situated about 45 km (28 miles) west of Korčula is Vela Luka, called "the oldest and the newest town", because it was built at the beginning of the 19th century on the Neolithic site of Vela Spilja. It is one of the largest towns on the island and industries coexist with attractive bays and numerous islands.

The hills surrounding the town shelter this area from the winds from the north and south. Vela Luka is also the main port on the island and there are regular ferry services to Split and Lastovo.

Lumbarda on the island of Korčula, one of the greenest in the Adriatic

The Stone of Dalmatia

The excellent quality of the stone in the Dalmatian islands was known to the Romans, who used it to build the monuments of Salona and Diocletian's Palace in Split. On Brač, the old Roman quarries are still visible in Pučišća. Brač stone was used for the cathedral in Šibenik *(see pp110–11)*, for which Juraj Dalmatinac devised a method of cutting the stone so that blocks interlocked without mortar. Most of the palaces and churches in Venice are also made of Dalmatian stone. Further afield, part of the White House in Washington and the Royal Palace in Stockholm were faced with stone from Brač. In Korčula, quarrying ceased long ago, and stone cutting skills have largely died out. However, the quarries on the small island of Vrnik, facing Korčula, are still active and stone from here was used in the church of St Sophia in Istanbul, the Duke's Palace in Dubrovnik and the United Nations building in New York.

The ancient Roman quarries, Brač

The Franciscan church and monastery on the island of Badija

⑳ Badija

Map E6. 🚤 taxi-boats from Korčula.
W badija.com

This is the largest of the small islands, 1 sq km (0.4 sq m), in the archipelago surrounding the island of Korčula, and is covered with pines and cypress trees. It takes its name from the Franciscan monastery built here in 1392 for a community of monks who had fled from Bosnia. The monastery and church were enlarged in the following century and remained the property of the religious community until 1950, when it became a sports resort.

The church, whose furnishings have been transferred to the Civic Museum and the cathedral in Korčula, has a façade in pale-coloured stone and a large central rose window. The cloister is a good example of Gothic architecture at its most charming, with columns and arches.

The Loggia in the main square in Lastovo, a venue for festivals

㉛ Lastovo

Map E6. 🏔 800. 🚤 from Vela Luka (island of Korčula), Dubrovnik during summer and from Split. Harbour Master: (020) 805 006. 🅸 Pjevor bb, (020) 801 018. **W** lastovo.hr

The island of Lastovo, surrounded by about 40 small islands and rocky outcrops, was a military area and thus closed to tourists. The island is 9 km (5 miles) long and about 6 km (4 miles) wide. Although it is mostly mountainous terrain (Mount Hum reaches a height of 417 m/1,368 ft), vines, olives and fruit are cultivated on the terraced slopes. The coast is rocky apart from the bay close to the town of Lastovo.

Traces of the long period of rule by Dubrovnik (1252–1808) are visible in the upper part of the town and in the fort, built by the French in 1819 on the site of an earlier castle destroyed by Dubrovnik in 1606.

A church from the 14th century and a 16th-century loggia stand in the main square. Religious festivals are celebrated here.

Mention of the small Church of **St Blaise** (Sv. Vlaho), situated at the entrance to the village, is found in 12th-century documents. Also of ancient origins, in the cemetery, is the Romanesque **Oratory of Our Lady in the Field** (Gospa od Polja) from the 15th century. Some remnants of buildings and rustic villas testify to the presence of the Romans on the island. The lack of tourism has helped to preserve the old buildings.

Religious holidays are very popular and celebrated with traditional dances with antique musical instruments. The locals wear brightly coloured traditional costumes.

Some of the many uninhabited, unspoilt islands in the sea around the island of Lastovo

㉜ Mljet National Park

Nacionalni park Mljet

The island of Mljet, called Melita by the Romans and Meleda by the Venetians, covers an area of 98 sq km (37 sq miles). It is mountainous, with two limestone depressions in which there are two saltwater lakes linked by a channel. In Roman times Mljet was the holiday resort of the wealthy of Salona, who built villas here. Some ruins can still be seen. In 1151, Duke Desa gave the island to the Benedictines of Pulsano in Gargano (Italy), who founded a monastery here. Two centuries later Stjepan, the Ban (governor) of Bosnia, gave it to Dubrovnik, to which it belonged until 1815. In 1960 the western part was declared a national park to save the forest of Aleppo pine and holm oak.

Roman Palatium
In Polače lie the ruins of a Roman settlement named Palatium, including the remains of a large villa and an early Christian basilica and thermae.

Monastery of St Mary
In the centre of Big Lake (Veliko Jezero) is a small island with a 12th-century Benedictine monastery, remodelled in the 1500s. Although currently being restored, it can still be visited.

Big Lake (Veliko jezero)
The lake covers an area of 1.45 sq km (320 acres) and reaches a depth of 46 m (150 ft). A channel links the lake to the sea, and another channel links it to a smaller lake, Malo jezero.

National Park
The area of 31 sq km (12 sq miles) is almost entirely forested. The park is home to wild boar, deer, hares, lizards and many bird species.

| 0 kilometres | 3 |
| 0 miles | 3 |

Marine Life
Dozens of species of fish, including grouper, inhabit the underwater ravines and caves along the coast. The most valued creature is the endangered monk seal, protected in these waters.

The village of Babino Polje
was founded in around the middle of the 10th century by a group of refugees from the mainland. The governor's residence was built in 1554 when the island became part of the territory of the Republic of Ragusa (now Dubrovnik).

Saplunara
Saplunara lies at the southernmost point of the island and boasts the most beautiful beach in the area. It has been declared a nature reserve for its lush vegetation.

MLJET

Sobra — Prožura — Okuklje — Korita
Maranovići — 120
Saplunara

Uninhabited Islands
Nature is left undisturbed on these islands, with woods of pine, holm oak and oak going right down to the rocky shore.

Key
━━ Minor road
═══ Path
── Park border

Fishing Villages
The island's ancient stone villages are inhabited mainly by farmers and fishermen. These villages and the delightful bays and coves around the island are lovely places in which to spend time.

㉝ Street-by-Street: Dubrovnik

Set in the limpid waters of the Adriatic, Dubrovnik had been, until war broke out in 1991, one of the top international tourist destinations of Dalmatia, renowned for the beauty of its monuments, its magnificent walls and welcoming atmosphere. According to Emperor Constantine Porphyrogenitus it was founded by fugitives from Roman Epidaurum (now Cavtat) in the 7th century. It came under Byzantine and Venetian (1205–1358) rule, and attained formal independence after 1382, when it became the Republic of Ragusa. In the 15th and 16th centuries its fleet numbered over 500 ships. Artistically it flourished and its wealth was greatly influenced by the discovery of America and new trade routes. Much of the old town centre dates from the rebuilding that took place after the earthquake of 1667.

★ Rector's Palace
The highest level of city government met here. The rector lived here during his period of office, which was limited to one month.

★ Cathedral Treasury
The provenance of the objects here clearly demonstrates how the Dubrovnik merchants developed trading relations with the principal cities of the Mediterranean. The Treasury has works from the Byzantine, Middle Eastern, Apulian and Venetian schools. There are gold and enamel objects and also paintings by great artists.

LUCARICA   GUNDULIĆEVA POLJANA

PRED. DVORO

POLJANA MARINA DRŽIĆA

KNEZA DAMJANA JUDE

Key

— Suggested route

View of Dubrovnik
Lovely views of Dubrovnik can be seen from the coast about 2 km (1 mile) to the south, where there is an elevated terrace. From here you can look over the entire city and its walls.

Church of St Blaise
This 16th-century church was rebuilt in the following century. At the beginning of the 18th century, it was redesigned by Marino Groppelli.

For hotels and restaurants see pp228–30 and pp240–45

Sponza Palace
Originating in the 16th century, today the palace houses the State Archives. On the lintel is a Latin inscription: "Falsifying and cheating with the weights is forbidden. While I am weighing the goods, God is measuring me".

VISITORS' CHECKLIST

Practical Information
Map F6. 43,000.
Local: Brsalje 5 (020) 323 887;
Regional: Vukovarska 17 (020) 324 999. Dubrovnik Summer Festival (Jul–Aug).

Transport
Čilipi, (020) 773 377.
Obala pape Ivana Pavla 11, 44A, (060) 305 070. Harbour Master: (020) 418 988; Jadrolinija: (020) 418 000.

Franciscan Monastery and the Big Fountain of Onofrio

PRIJEKO

PLACA

ZLATARSKA

SVETOG DOMINIKA

The outer city walls

★ **Dominican Monastery**
Since its foundation in 1315, the monastery has played a leading role in cultural activities in the city. Important sculptors and architects played a part in its construction.

Ploče Gate
Next to the Dominican monastery is the Ploče Gate, which leads to the port. Goods arrived from, and were sent to, every port in the Mediterranean.

Fort of St John
To make the city impregnable, the governors employed the most important European architects of the time. This fortress was one of many bulwarks.

| 0 metres | | 50 |
| 0 yards | | 50 |

Exploring Dubrovnik

From the autumn of 1991 until May 1992, Dubrovnik was the target of relentless, heavy bombing by Yugoslav troops. During this period over 2,000 bombs and guided missiles fell on Dubrovnik, damaging some of the most significant symbols of Dalmatian culture. Over half the houses and all the monuments were shelled. The war also hit the city's economic activity, especially tourism, which suffered a dramatic decline for four years. Only after the Erdut Agreement of 1995 did life begin to return to normal. UNESCO and the European Union set up a special commission for the reconstruction of the city, and in a remarkably short space of time much of the damage has been repaired. Dubrovnik has now regained much of its former splendour and tourism is once again flourishing.

The solid Minčeta Tower, part of the wall defences

The splendid view from the impressive city walls

🏰 Walls
Gradske zidine

🛈 (020) 324 641. **Open** Jun & Jul: 8am–7:30pm; Apr, May, Aug & Sep: 8am–6:30pm; Oct: 8am–5:30pm; Nov–Mar: 10am–3pm. Access to the walls near the Franciscan monastery in Poljana Paška Miličevića, the large square behind Pile Gate near the Dominican monastery. 🎟

A symbol of Dubrovnik, the walls offer splendid views from the guards' walkway. They were built in the 10th century, with modifications in the 13th century. They were then reinforced at various times by great architects such as Michelozzo Michelozzi and Antonio Ferramolino.

The walls and ramparts are 1,940 m (6,363 ft) long and reach a height of 25 m (82 ft) in some parts. Those facing inland are up to 6 m (20 ft) wide and strengthened by an outer wall with ten semicircular bastions. Other towers and the Fort of St John defend the part facing

the Adriatic and the port. Completing the defences to the east and west of the city are two fortresses: the Revelin and the fortress of Lovrijenac.

🏰 Pile Gate
Gradska vrata Pile

This is the main entrance to the old fortified centre. The stone bridge leading to Pile Gate is

Pile Gate, leading to the old town

from 1537. The bridge crosses a moat which is now a garden. The gate is a strong defensive structure built on different levels. In a niche above the ogival arch stands a small statue of St Blaise, the patron saint of Dubrovnik, by Ivan Meštrović. In the ramparts between the inner and outer walls is a Gothic door dating from 1460.

🏰 Minčeta Tower
Tvrđava Minčeta

This is the most visited of the walls' defensive structures. It was designed by Michelozzo Michelozzi in 1461 and completed by Juraj Dalmatinac three years later. The semicircular tower is crowned by a second tower with embrasures at the top.

🏰 Ploče Gate
Vrata od Ploča

The gate faces a small port and is preceded by the polygonal **Asimov Tower**. Dating from the 1300s, the gate is reached by an imposing stone bridge. A moat separates the gate and **Revelin Fort** (Tvrđava Revelin), designed in 1538 by Antonio Ferramolino. It was the last of the defences to be built. The city's art treasures were brought here for safety in times of difficulty because of the fort's strength. The Lazareti served as a quarantine from the late 14th century, separating goods from ailing travellers. Today they are occupied by shops and entertainment facilities.

🏛 Fort of St John
Tvrđava sv. Ivana
Aquarium: **Tel** (020) 323 978. **Open**
Jun–Sep: 9am–9pm daily; Oct–May:
9am–1pm Mon–Sat. 🕮 Maritime
Museum: **Tel** (020) 323 904. **Open**
summer: 9am–6pm Tue–Sun; winter:
9am–2pm Tue–Sun. 🕮

A chain once helped to defend
the harbour, stretching from this
fort to the island in front and then
across to the Tower of St Luke
(Kula sv. Luke) along the walls.

The upper areas of the fort
house the **Maritime Museum**
(Pomorski muzej), where the
seafaring history of Dubrovnik
is told through model ships,
standards, prints, diaries
and portraits.

On the lower level is an
aquarium (akvarij) with an
assortment of Mediterranean
marine life, including sea horses,
symbol of the institution. At the
top is the circular **Bokar Fort**
(Tvrđava Bokar), built by
Michelozzo Michelozzi.

🏛 Big Fountain of Onofrio
Velika Onofrijeva fontana
This is one of the best-known
monuments in the city.
It stands in the square

The Big Fountain of Onofrio (1438–44)

which opens out immediately
after the Pile gate. It was
built in 1438–44 by the
Neapolitan architect Onofrio
de la Cava, who was also
responsible for
designing the city's
water supply system.
He decided to draw
the water from the
River Dubrovačka for
this purpose. The
imposing fountain
once had two storeys,
but the upper level
was destroyed in the
earthquake of 1667.

Tucked between
the city walls and the
Franciscan monastery
is the Church of St
Saviour (Sv. Spas). The
façade of the church is
an example of Venetian-
Dalmatian Renaissance
architecture, a style
dating from after the
earthquake of 1520.

Dubrovnik Town Centre

① Walls
② Pile Gate
③ Minčeta Tower
④ Ploče Gate
⑤ Fort of St John
⑥ Big Fountain of Onofrio
⑦ Franciscan Monastery
⑧ Stradun (Placa)
⑨ Square of the Loggia
⑩ Sponza Palace

⑪ Church of St Blaise
⑫ Rector's Palace
⑬ Cathedral and Treasury
⑭ Dominican Monastery
⑮ Dubrovnik Cable Car

Key

🔲 Street-by-Street
pp146–7

0 metres   150
0 yards   150

The lovely late Romanesque cloister, Franciscan monastery

⊡ Franciscan Monastery
Franjevački samostan

Placa 2. **Tel** (020) 321 410. **Open**
summer: 9am–6pm daily; winter:
9am–5pm daily. Franciscan Museum:
Open Apr–Oct: 9am–6pm daily; Nov–
Mar: 9am–5pm daily. ⊠

Construction of the monastery
began in 1317 and was
completed in the following
century. It was almost entirely
rebuilt after the earthquake in
1667, but the south door (1499),
in Venetian Gothic decorated
with a Pietà in the lunette, and
a 15th-century marble pulpit
escaped damage. The cloister,
which was completely undamaged by the earthquake, reveals
elements of the Romanesque
and the Gothic style and has a
fountain from the 15th century
in the centre.

One side of the cloister
leads to the **pharmacy** (Stara
ljekarna), in use since 1317,
where alembics, mortars,
measuring apparatus and
beautifully decorated jars are
displayed on the old shelves.

The capitular room of the
monastery houses the
Franciscan Museum (Muzej
Franjevačkog samostana),

which has religious works of art
and objects belonging to the
order. Instruments from the
pharmaceutical laboratory are
kept here.

⊡ Stradun (Placa)

The wide street that crosses the
city from east to west between
two city gates is known as
Stradun or Placa. It was
constructed in the 12th century

Stradun, the main street of Dubrovnik

by draining and filling in the
marshy channel that separated
the island of Ragusa from the
mainland. The street was paved
in 1468 and a series of stone
houses was built after the
earthquake of 1667. Today the
street is lined with busy bars
and cafés, and is a popular place
for locals and visitors to gather
in the evening.

⊡ Square of the Loggia
Luža

This square, the political and
economic heart of Dubrovnik,
is situated at the eastern end
of Stradun and surrounded
by important buildings. Today
it is still a popular meeting
place, in particular around
Orlando's Column, which
was built by the sculptor
Antonio Ragusino (1418).

On the eastern side of the
square is a **Clock Tower** (Gradski
zvonik). Repair work carried out
in 1929 restored a 15th-century
look to the Clock Tower. The
nearby **Loggia of the Bell**, with
four bells, dates from 1463. The
bells were rung to call the
citizens to gather whenever
danger threatened.

Next to this stands the **Main
Guard House**, rebuilt in 1706
after the earthquake of 1667.
It has a large Baroque doorway,
similar to a city gate, and is
enlivened on the first floor by
the Gothic mullioned windows,
reminiscent of the earlier
building which was built in
the late 15th century.

The **Small Fountain of
Onofrio** (Mala Onofrijeva
česma), dating from 1438,
stands alongside the
Guard House.

⊡ Sponza Palace
Palača Sponza

Tel (020) 321 032. **Open** May–Oct:
9am–10pm daily; Nov–Apr:
10am–3pm daily.

To the left of the square is
Sponza Palace. Remodelled in
1516–22, it has an elegantly
sculpted Renaissance loggia
on the ground floor and a
beautiful Venetian Gothic
three-mullioned window on
the first floor, evidence of its
14th-century origins, and a

statue of St Blaise on the upper floor. It was the Mint in the 14th century and now houses the State Archives.

⌂ Church of St Blaise
Crkva sv. Vlaha

Loža. **Tel** (020) 323 887.
Open 8am–noon, 4:30–7pm daily.

St Blaise was rebuilt in the early decades of the 18th century according to a 17th-century design and contains many Baroque works of art.

On the main altar stands a statue of the patron saint, Blaise. Produced in the 15th century in gold-plated silver, it depicts the saint holding a model of the city in the Middle Ages.

Baroque façade of the church of St Blaise

⊞ Rector's Palace
Knežev dvor

Pred Dvorom 1. **Tel** (020) 321 422.
Open Apr–Oct: 9am–6pm daily; Nov–Mar: 9am–4pm daily. 🖼 🏠 📷

The Rector's Palace was for centuries the seat of the most important government institutions of the Dubrovnik Republic. It housed the Upper and Lower Council, as well as the rector's quarters and rooms for meetings and audiences. The building was constructed in the early 15th century on the site of a medieval fortress, and designed by the Italian architect Onofrio de la Cava. In 1465 the portico by Petar Martinov from Milan was added. The Gothic works are by Juraj Dalmatinac.

The rooms of the palace house the interesting **Cultural Historical Museum**

The Rector's Palace, built in the 15th century as the administrative seat

(Kulturno-povijesni muzej), which contains 15 collections of historic items created in art and craft workshops throughout Europe between the 16th and 20th centuries. On the ground floor an authentic jail space, court, notary and archives have been preserved and presented. Coins, medals, stamps and measures, ancient weapons and numerous other works of art as well as an inventory of the state pharmacy "Domus Christi" are on display on the mezzanine floor. On the first floor, rooms contain valuable objects from the 16th–18th centuries.

Also of great interest are the portraits of illustrious personalities who were born or lived in Dubrovnik, whose history is told through their heraldic coats of arms. During the Festival of Dubrovnik concerts are held in the atmospheric internal courtyard.

Next door is the 1863 Neo-Renaissance **Town Hall** (Vijećnica), designed by Emilio Vecchietti. It is also the home of the café Gradska Kavana *(see p241)* and the Civic Theatre.

⌂ Cathedral and Treasury
Velika Gospa

Kneza Damjana Jude 1. **Open** Apr–Oct: 8am–5pm Mon–Sat, 11am–5pm Sun; Nov–Mar: 8am–noon, 3–5pm Mon–Sat, 11am–noon, 3–5pm Sun. Cathedral Treasury: **Tel** (020) 323 459.
Open same times as the cathedral. 📷

The cathedral was built after the earthquake of 1667 by the Roman architects Andrea Buffalini and Paolo Andreotti. Inside are three aisles enclosed by three apses. Paintings by

Italian and Dalmatian artists from the 16th–18th centuries decorate the side altars, while an *Assumption* by Titian (c.1552) dominates the main altar.

Alongside the church is the **Cathedral Treasury** (Riznica Katedrale), famous for its collection of about 200 reliquaries. It includes the arm of St Blaise which dates from the 13th century, and a Holy Cross which contains a fragment of the cross on which Jesus was said to have been crucified. The tondo *Virgin of the Chair* is thought to have been painted by Raphael himself, and is a copy of the masterpiece which is now in Florence.

The treasury also has an extraordinary collection of sacred objects in gold, including a pitcher and basin in gold and silver with decoration that illustrates the flora and fauna of the area around Dubrovnik.

The great dome of Dubrovnik's Baroque cathedral

The church of St Dominic, inside the monastery

⬆ Dominican Monastery
Dominikanski samostan Bijeli fratri
Od sv. Dominika 4. **Tel** (020) 321 423.
Open May–Oct: 9am–6pm; Nov–Apr: 9am–5pm. 🚫

Building began in 1315 and it soon became clear that because of the size of the complex, the city walls would have to be enlarged. The monastery was later rebuilt after the earthquake of 1667.

A long flight of steps with a stone balustrade leads up to the church. The door, the work of Bonino of Milan, is decorated with a Romanesque statue of St Dominic. The interior has a wide single nave and, hanging from the central arch, a splendid gilded panel *(Crucifix and Symbols of the Evangelists)* by Paolo Veneziano (14th century).

The various rooms of the monastery, arranged around the Gothic cloister by Maso di Bartolomeo (15th century), house the **Dominican Museum** (Muzej Dominikanskog samostana). It contains an extraordinary collection of works from the so-called "Dubrovnik school", including a triptych and an *Annunciation* by Niccolò Ragusino, from the 16th century, and works from the Venetian school, including *St Blaise, St Mary Magdalene, the Angel Tobias and the Purchaser* by Titian, as well as precious reliquaries and objects in gold and silver.

Dubrovnik Cable Car
Dubrovačka žičara
Frana Supila 35a. **Tel** (020) 311 577.
Open 9am–9pm daily. 🚫
w dubrovnikcablecar.com

Destroyed in 1991, the cable car that connects Dubrovnik City Walls and Mount Srđ is in operation again. The route takes three and a half minutes to complete, and offers wonderful views.

Environs
The island of **Lokrum**, 700 m (2,296 ft) across the water from Dubrovnik, is a nature reserve.

The first people to settle on the island were the Benedictines, who founded an abbey here in 1023. This was rebuilt in the 14th century, but later destroyed by the earthquake of 1667. In 1859, Archduke Maximilian of Habsburg built a palace here and renovated the cloister which later became the Natural History Museum.

In **Trsteno**, 20 km (12 miles) northwest of Dubrovnik, is an Arboretum. This was begun in 1502 in the park surrounding a villa built by Ivan Gučetić. The park has the layout of a Renaissance garden with grottoes and ancient ruins.

There are several Renaissance summer houses around Dubrovnik, including the **Villa Stay** in Rijeka Dubrovačka.

A statue in the Arboretum in Trsteno

❸ Elaphite Islands
Map F6. 🏔 2,000. 🚢 from Dubrovnik. ℹ Dubrovnik regional tourist office (020) 324 999.

Lying to the north of Dubrovnik, the Elaphite Islands (Elafitski otoci) can be reached from Dubrovnik by motorboat. There are several daily crossings. The islands were described by the natural historian Pliny the Elder, who named them after the fallow deer then found here. Only three of the islands are inhabited: Šipan, Lopud and Koločep, while Jakljan is devoted to farming. Characteristics common to the islands are the woods of maritime pines and cypresses in the uncultivated areas and beautiful beaches and bays frequented by pleasure boats. The islands have long been popular with the aristocracy of Dubrovnik, who built villas here. Some islands had monasteries which were suppressed with the arrival of French troops in 1808. Many of the churches date from the pre-Romanesque period, but few, however, are still intact.

Koločep
This is the nearest island to Dubrovnik and for this reason has been a summer retreat since the 16th century for its

The island of Lokrum in front of Dubrovnik, a protected nature reserve

Šunj beach on the southeast coast of Lopud, one of the Elaphite islands

citizens. Most of the island is covered in maritime pines and subtropical undergrowth.

The churches of **St Anthony** and **St Nicholas** have pre-Romanesque origins, while the **Parish Church** dates from the 15th century.

Lopud

The island, measuring 4.6 sq km (1.7 sq miles), has a fertile valley sheltered from the cold winds by two ranges of hills. Most of the inhabitants live in **Lopud**, a village in a bay. The two forts, now in ruins, date from the 16th century and the Franciscan monastery is from 1483. The monastery church, **St Mary of Spilica** (Sv. Marija od Špilica), contains a polyptych by Pietro di Giovanni (1520), a triptych by Nikola Božidarević, a painting by Leandro da Bassano, a triptych by Gerolamo di Santacroce and a carved choir from the 15th century.

Šunj, in the southeast, draws visitors because of its sandy beach, but the church is also worth visiting for its many works of art, including a painting by Palma il Giovane and a polyptych (1452) by Matej Junčić.

Šipan

This is the largest of the Elaphite Islands (15.5 sq km/ 6 sq miles) and there are two towns. In **Šipanska Luka** stands the pre-Romanesque church of St Michael and the ruins of a Benedictine monastery. In **Suđurađ** there is a castle and the ruins of a bishop's palace.

㉟ Cavtat

Map F6. 🏔 2,500. 🚢 from Dubrovnik, (020) 478 065. 🚌 from Dubrovnik. *i* Zidine 6, (020) 478 025. 🎭 Summer in Cavtat, Epidaurus Festival.
w visit.cavtat-konavle.com

Cavtat is the Croatian name for Civitas Vetus, the site of the Roman town of Epidaurum, destroyed by the Avars in the 7th century (occasional excavations have revealed the remains of a theatre, several tombs and parts of a road). The beauty of the area, the beaches, the luxuriant vegetation and the interesting monuments attract many visitors to the present-day village.

The **Baltazar Bogišić Collection**, assembled and donated by the scholar and jurist of the 19th century, whose birthplace this is, is housed in the 16th-century

Rector's Palace. The works of the painter Vlaho Bukovac are especially fine.

At the end of the seafront is the church of **Our Lady of Snow** (Gospa Snježna) and a Franciscan monastery, both from the end of the 15th century. On the hilltop stands the **Račić Mausoleum** built by Ivan Meštrović *(see p163)* in 1922.

㊱ Konavle

Map F6. *i* Zidine 6, Cavtat, (020) 478 025. **w** visit.cavtat-konavle.com

The area southeast of Cavtat occupies a narrow piece of land between the sea and the mountains of Bosnia-Herzegovina. Its name derives from the channels *(canalis)* which collected the water to supply the aqueduct – of which some traces remain – for the Roman town of Epidaurus.

The hilly areas are covered in vineyards and olive groves. The small villages maintain the old customs and traditional costumes are still worn by the inhabitants. Konavle was heavily damaged by bombing in 1991. This area is also renowned for its excellent cuisine and there are numerous restaurants. One of the best known is **Konavoski Dvori**, housed in a watermill near the waterfalls of the River Ljuta.

Traditional dress of Konavle, still used for festivities

The pretty seafront and port of Cavtat

ZAGREB

The capital of Croatia, Zagreb is also the heart of the political, economic and cultural life of the country. Surrounded by woods and parks, the city lies between the slopes of Mount Medvednica to the north and the River Sava to the south. Located at the centre of continental Croatia, this Central European city constitutes a meeting point between eastern and western Europe.

The political scientist Max Weber once declared that the quality of life in a city could be measured by the number of its cultural institutions. Zagreb has over 20 museums, 10 theatres, 350 libraries, a university, and lively programmes of artistic and cultural events. This is not just because Zagreb is the capital (it has only been the capital since 1991), but is also due to the leading cultural and political role that Zagreb has played over the centuries.

Zagreb was originally two separate medieval towns. Two settlements were built on two adjacent hilltops: Kaptol, the centre of religious power and a bishopric from 1094, and Gradec (now part of Gornji grad). In 1242, with the proclamation of a "Golden Bull", Gradec was given the title of royal free city by

the Croat-Hungarian King Bela IV. This granted various economic and administrative privileges to the inhabitants. From the 16th century onwards Gradec was also where the Ban – the governor of Croatia delegated by the Hungarian kingdom – and the Croat parliament carried out their business and where Croat nobles met to govern this turbulent territory. The two towns were both fortified with ramparts, towers, moats and gates, and separated by the Medveščak stream. The stream was often the site of violent clashes between Gradec and Kaptol, and that time is vividly recalled by the street called the Bridge of Blood (Krvavi most).

In 1880, a terrible earthquake struck the city and many of the major monuments date from after this time.

Colourful Dolac market, held in the square of the same name

◀ The famous polychromatic tiled roof of the Church of St Mark

Exploring Zagreb

The city is divided into two large sectors; the old town (Gornji grad or Upper Town), which includes the two districts of Gradec and Kaptol, situated in the hills, and the modern area (Donji grad or Lower Town) on the plain. The large square dedicated to the Croat governor Jelačić (Trg bana Jelačića) is where the upper and lower towns meet. The old town is home to the main centres of religious, political and administrative power. The more modern part developed after 1830 around a U-shaped series of parks and open spaces (known as the "green horseshoe"). The major museums, including the Ethnographic Museum, Mimara Museum, Gallery of Old Masters and Modern Gallery, are all located here, as well as the National Theatre. To the south of a series of gardens with sculptures lies the Botanical Garden. Around Jelačić Square there are plenty of cafés with summer terraces.

Sights at a Glance

Museums and Galleries

6 City Museum
7 Croatian Natural History Museum
8 Meštrović Atelier
12 Croatian History Museum
13 Croatian Museum of Naive Art
18 Museum of Arts and Crafts
19 Mimara Museum
20 Ethnographic Museum
22 Art Pavilion
23 Gallery of Old Masters pp170–71
24 Modern Gallery
25 Archaeological Museum
26 Museum of Contemporary Art

Churches

1 Cathedral of the Assumption of the Blessed Virgin Mary
3 Church of St Francis
4 Church of St Mary

9 Church of St Mark
14 Church of SS. Cyril and Methodius
16 Church of St Catherine

Palaces and Other Buildings

2 Archbishop's Palace
5 Stone Gate
10 Parliament Building
11 Viceroy's Palace
15 Tower of Lotrščak
17 Croatian National Theatre
22 Art Pavilion

Parks and Gardens

21 Botanical Garden of the Faculty of Science
27 Maksimir Park
28 Mirogoj Cemetery

0 metres 200
0 yards 200

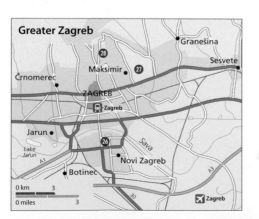

Greater Zagreb

Granešina
Sesvete
Maksimir
Črnomerec
ZAGREB
Zagreb
Jarun
Lake Jarun
Botinec
Novi Zagreb
Sava
Zagreb

0 km 3
0 miles 3

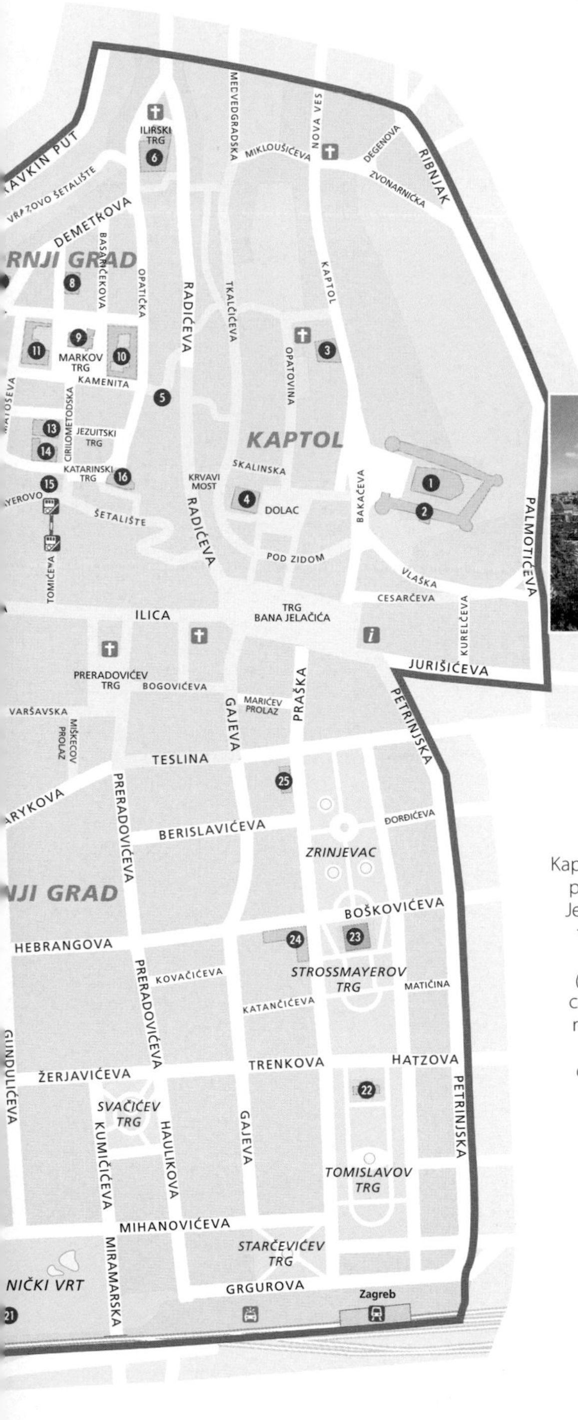

VISITORS' CHECKLIST

Practical Information
Map D2. 🔼 780,000.
ℹ️ Trg bana Jelačića 11, (01) 481
40 51. 🎭 Smotra folklora, Folklore
Festival (Jul); Zagrebačke ljetne v
ečeri, Zagreb Summer Festival.
🆆 **akz.hr**
🆆 **zagreb-touristinfo.hr**

Transport
✈️ at Velika Gorica, Pleso, (01) 626
52 22, 17 km (10 miles) SE.
🚉 Glavni Kolodvor, (060) 333 444.
🚌 Avenija Marina Držića 4, (060)
313 333.

Zagreb skyline

Getting Around
The districts of the old town,
Kaptol and Gronji Grad, are mostly
pedestrian areas, as is the central
Jelačić square, which is served by
tram routes joining the eastern
and western parts of the city
(see pp280–81). The Jarun sailing
centre, near the river, can also be
reached by tram. Buses going to
Novi Zagreb, on the other side
of the River Sava (where there is
a racetrack, exhibition area and
the Museum of Contemporary
Art) leave from the main
rail station.

Key
▪ Major sight
▪ Places of interest
▪ Pedestrian zone
▪ Funicular line

For keys to symbols see back flap

❶ Cathedral of the Assumption of the Blessed Virgin Mary

Katedrala Marijina Uznesenja

Kaptol. **Tel** (01) 481 47 27. **Open** 10am–5pm Mon–Sat, 1–5pm Sun.

Dedicated to the Assumption and St Stephen, this is the most famous monument in the city. Its present appearance dates from renovations carried out by Friedrich von Schmidt and Hermann Bollé after the earthquake of 1880, which destroyed the dome, the bell tower and some of the walls. The rebuilding, which retained the medieval plan of the cathedral, was just the latest in a series of alterations the building had undergone in its long history.

The building was already in existence in 1094 when King Ladislaus transferred the bishopric here from Sisak. Destroyed by the Mongols in 1242, the cathedral was rebuilt by Bishop Timotej a few years later. In the centuries that followed, the side aisles were added and the church was decorated with statues and reliefs.

The new Neo-Gothic façade (1880) is flanked by twin spires. The façade has a large ornate doorway with sculpted

Decorative detail of one of the cathedral spires

decorations, a rose window and three high windows, the whole crowned by a tympanum.

The interior has three aisles and a polygonal apse. During a late 19th-century reorganization, the Baroque and Rococo altars were transferred to other churches in the diocese, and as a result only a few Gothic and Renaissance works remain. These works include a statue of St Paul (13th century), wooden statues of the saints Peter and Paul from the 15th century, a triptych entitled *Golgotha* (1495) by Albrecht Dürer and a 14th-century *Crucifixion* by Giovanni da Udine. The cathedral also contains the tombs and votive chapels of bishops and important personalities in Croatian history, such as Petar Zrinski, Krsto Frankopan and blessed Cardinal Alojzije Stepinac, whose tomb behind the main altar is by Ivan Meštrović.

Of great interest are the frescoes from the Giotto-esque school in the sacristy: the oldest (12th century) in inland Croatia. In the basement of the bishop's sacristy, the **Cathedral Treasury** preserves a rich collection of religious

The central nave in the Neo-Gothic Cathedral of the Assumption

objects. These include illuminated manuscripts, finely crafted church ornaments from the 11th to the 20th centuries, and objects of veneration such as the Cloak of King Ladislaus (11th century), a bishop's veil from the 14th century and the so-called Sepulchre of God. This last piece was made by the embroiderers of the village of Vugrovec, where Bishop Petar Petretić founded an embroidery school in around 1650. Among the oldest works are a 10th-century ivory diptych and a bronze crucifix from the 11th–12th centuries.

❷ Archbishop's Palace

Nadbiskupska palača

Kaptol. **Closed** to the public.

The enormous Baroque buildings comprising the Archbishop's Palace enclose the other three sides of the cathedral square. The building incorporates three of the five round towers and one square tower, which were part of the fortifications built from 1469 as defence against Turkish attacks. The present palace dates from 1730, when several buildings were linked and united by an imposing Baroque façade.

Inside the complex is the Romanesque chapel of St Stephen Protomartyr (13th century). This is the oldest building in Zagreb to have

The elaborate twin spires of the Cathedral of the Assumption of the Blessed Virgin Mary

survived in its original form: the frescoes are from the 14th century.

In the square in front of the palace stands a fountain with a column crowned by a statue of Mary with four angels, the work of the Viennese artist Anton Dominik Fernkorn (1813–78) in around 1850.

The moats that once surrounded the walls have been filled in and turned into the **Ribnjak Public Gardens**, with various statues including one called *Modesty* by Antun Augustinčić (1900–79). The defences were partially demolished in the 19th century, however. At No. 18 ulica Kaptol, opposite the cathedral, is the **Northeast Tower**, which is now a residence. At No. 15 stands the **Northwest Tower** (Prišlinova kula), now part of a 15th-century building.

The Archbishop's Palace by the Cathedral of the Assumption

❸ Church of St Francis

Sv. Franjo

Kaptol 9. **Tel** (01) 481 11 25.
Open 7am–noon, 3–7pm daily.

Founded, according to legend, after St Francis's return from the East, this church dates from the 13th century. After the earthquake of 1880, the church was rebuilt in the Neo-Gothic style. It was at this time that the Baroque altars were removed. Some of the side altars are Neo-Gothic,

Stained-glass windows by Ivo Dulčić in the Church of St Francis

while on the main altar there is a fine painting of St Francis by Celestin Medović (1857–1920). The brightly coloured stained-glass windows were designed by Ivo Dulčić in the 1960s.

In the adjacent 17th-century **monastery**, where the saint supposedly stayed, is the much-visited chapel of St Francis (1683), with ornate stucco decorations and Baroque paintings.

❹ Church of St Mary

Sv. Marija

Dolac 2. **Tel** (01) 481 49 59.
Open for Mass.

Opatovina is a narrow street where some of the houses were built using parts of the late-15th-century fortifications. The street leads into the ancient district of Dolac, at the end of which stands the Church of St Mary, which dates from the 14th century. It was rearranged in 1740 when several Baroque altars were built by Franjo Rottman, but its present appearance dates back to rebuilding after the earthquake in 1880. Near the church

stands a statue by Vanja Radauš of the legendary wanderer and minstrel Petrica Kerempuh, playing to the figure of a hanged man.

The large, picturesque **Dolac Market**, which was first held in 1930, takes place around the church. This is a characteristic district of the city where Baroque houses face narrow streets and lanes. A historic pharmacy is at No. 19 Kaptol and an ancient house at No. 7.

❺ Stone Gate

Kamenita vrata

Kamenita.

In the walls around Gradec, the part of Upper Town built on a neighbouring hill to Kaptol, there were once five gates. Stone Gate the only one of these remaining. It was built in the 13th century, and stands beside a square tower from 1266. In 1731 a fire destroyed all the nearby houses, but a painting of Mary with Child on the gate was left undamaged. A chapel was established around this painting and a Baroque wrought-iron grille now protects the work, attributed to a local master from the 16th century.

On the west façade of the church is a statue of a woman, a character from a famous Croation novel and the work of the sculptor Ivo Kerdić in 1929.

On the other side of the gate, on the corner of Kamenita and Habdelićeva, stands an 18th-century building. On the ground floor of this building is a **pharmacy** (Alighieri ljekarna) which has been in existence since 1350 and which, from 1399 onwards, belonged to Nicolò Alighieri, the great-grandson of the great Italian writer Dante.

The monument to Petrica Kerempuh, Dolac

Street-by-Street: the Upper Town (Gornji grad)

In the Upper Town there are various institutions which have played a significant part in the history of the city and of Croatia. They now house the political and cultural centres of the country: the presidency of the Republic, Parliament, the State Audit Court and several government ministries. All of these buildings were restored, repaired or rebuilt after the terrible earthquake of 1880. Some of the ancient noble palaces have been converted into museums. There are also three interesting churches: the ancient church of St Mark, the Baroque church of St Catherine built by the Jesuits, and the church of Saints Cyril and Methodius. The daily signal to close the city gates was rung from the medieval tower of Lotrščak (Turris Latruncolorum).

❼ Croatian Natural History Museum
Created from three collections, the museum houses most of the finds from Krapina, which date human presence in Croatia back to the Palaeolithic era.

⓫ Viceroy's Palace
The building dates from the 17th century and was built after the city became the seat of the Ban (governor of Croatia) in 1621. It now houses the presidency of the Republic.

⓬ Croatian History Museum
This museum, housed in the Vojković-Oršić-Kalmer-Rauch palace, has works of art and documents collected since 1959.

⓭ ★ Croatian Museum of Naive Art
Over 1,500 works of Naïve art by the founders and followers of the Hlebine School are held here.

⓮ Church of SS. Cyril and Methodius
Built by Orthodox Christians in the first half of the 19th century, the church, designed by Bartol Felbinger, has a fine iconostasis.

⓯ Tower of Lotrščak
At noon every day a cannon is fired from this tower, which dates from the 12th century.

Key

— Suggested route

❽ ★ Meštrović Atelier
The great Croatian sculptor Ivan Meštrović lived in this 18th-century building from 1922 to 1941. About ten years before his death he donated his home and all the works of art in it to the state.

Locator Map

❿ Parliament Building
This building dates from 1910, when the provincial administration offices were enlarged. The independence of Croatia was proclaimed from the central window of the building in 1918.

❾ ★ Church of St Mark
The coloured tiles on the roof of this fine Gothic church form the coats of arms of Croatia, Dalmatia, Slavonia and Zagreb.

❺ The Stone Gate is all that remains of the five original gates constructed around the Gradec area in the 13th century.

The Klovićevi Dvori, an important temporary exhibition site, has been housed since 1982 in a 17th-century Jesuit monastery.

| 0 metres | 50 |
| 0 yards | 50 |

⑯ Church of St Catherine
Built on the site of an ancient Dominican church, this is the city's most fascinating Baroque building.

❻ City Museum
Muzej grada Zagreba

Opatička ulica 20. **Tel** (01) 485 13 61.
Open 10am–6pm Tue–Fri; 11am–7pm
Sat, 10am–2pm Sun. 🕐 by appt. ♿
👍 ✉ Kovačić residence: Masarykova
21. **Open** 10am–5pm Thu. Krleža
residence: Krležin Gvozd 23. **Open**
11am–5pm Tue. Dujšin-Ribar
residence: Demetrova 3/II. **Open**
11am–5pm Tue. 🌐 **mgz.hr**

Three historic buildings (the
convent of the nuns of St Clare
from around 1650, a 12th-century
tower, and a granary from the
17th century) have been linked
to form the City Museum. Its
vast collection of historic,
cultural, military and domestic
artifacts, many donated by
prominent townspeople, are
arranged in themed displays
illustrating every facet of the
city's development, from
prehistory to the present day.

Across the city, the museum
also maintains the former
residences of some of Croatia's
most celebrated recent figures;
that of the architect Viktor
Kovačić (1878–1924); the writer
Miroslav Krleža (1893–1981) and
his wife Bela; plus the poet and
painter Cata Dujšin-Ribar (1897–
1994) and her two husbands, the
actor/theatre director Dubravko
Dujšin and the politician Dr Ivan
Ribar. The period furnishings,
decor and works of art in each
are perfectly preserved, making
fascinating short tours.

Partial reconstruction of a late Iron Age
workshop, Zagreb City Museum

Sculptures in the garden of the Meštrović Atelier

❼ Croatian Natural History Museum
Hrvatski prirodoslovni muzej

Demetrova 1. **Tel** (01) 485 17 00.
Open 10am–5pm Tue–Fri (to 8pm
Thu), 10am–7pm Sat, 10am–1pm Sun.
🌐 **hpm.hr**

The 18th-century Amadeo
Palace, a theatre from 1797 to
1834, has been the Natural
History Museum since 1868,
when collections from the
Department of Natural Science
at the National Museum were
transferred here. At the end of
the 19th century there were
three museums
of natural history:
Mineralogy and
Petrography, Geology
and Palaeontology,
and Zoology. These
three merged in
1986 to form the
present museum.

A mineral in the
Croatian Natural
History Museum

There are over
2,500,000 exhibits,
including minerals from all over
the world and palaeontology
collections containing some of
the material found in Krapina.
The zoological collection
documents every species of
animal found in Croatia.

❽ Meštrović Atelier
Atelje Meštrović

Mletačka 8. **Tel** (01) 485 11 23.
Open 10am–6pm Tue–Fri,
10am–2pm Sat & Sun. ♿ 🕐 📷
🌐 **mdc.hr/mestrovic**

The atelier building dates
from the 17th century; the
sculptor Ivan Meštrović himself
modernized it to live in from
1922 to 1942. It now houses a
collection of his work. It is part
of The Museums of Ivan
Meštrović, together with
the Gallery and the Kaštilac
in Split, as well as the burial
chapel in Otavice *(see p112)*.

There are almost 100
works on display,
including exhibits
in the courtyard –
*History of Croatia,
Laookon of our Days*
and *Woman in Agony*.
The drawings, models
and sculptures in
wood, stone and
bronze testify to the
expressive ability and great
skills of the sculptor. His
personal archives are also
here, as well as photographic
records and works by other
artists associated with
the master.

Ivan Meštrović

Regarded as one of the most important sculptors of the 20th century, Ivan Meštrović was born in 1883 in Vrpolje where his parents had gone for the harvest from their native village of Otavice in the Dalmatian hinterland. As a young boy he delighted in making figures out of wood, and his work was noticed by the village mayor and by Lujo Marun, an archaeologist, who sent him to Split when he was 17 to study sculpture. Thanks to donors, he was able to attend the Academy of Fine Arts in Vienna, where he designed works for later production. Here he met and became friends with the great French sculptor, Auguste Rodin. In 1908 he moved to Paris and his first exhibition established his reputation. He worked in various cities, including Split – creating many of the works now on show in the Meštrović gallery there – and Zagreb. He also took up politics: during World War II he was imprisoned by the Nazi regime and freed on the Vatican's intervention. He then moved to Rome where he sculpted the *Pietà Romana*, now in the Vatican Museum. After the war he taught at universities in the US, where he died in 1962. He was buried in the burial chapel in Otavice *(see p112)* that he designed for himself and his family.

Meštrović, intent on his work

Detail of the *Resurrection of Lazarus* (1940)

Woman by the Sea is a splendid female figure in marble (1926) which seems to twist around on itself. The form of the body is vigorous and yet the hands are delicate and slender.

The Sculptor at Work

The speed at which Meštrović executed his works was proverbial, although the preparation time was lengthy. To satisfy demand, he replicated his works in wood, marble and bronze. Three copies, not quite identical, exist of the statue of the Bishop of Nin, in Nin, Split and Varaždin.

Mother and Child is a wooden sculpture from 1942 which demonstrates the artist's great expressive talent. The figure of the child is almost insignificant, leaving the face of the mother to play the main role.

History of Croatia is a work from 1932. There are four originals; one in bronze is in the Meštrović Atelier in Zagreb. The woman's thoughtful gaze looks to the future, symbolizing expectations and hopes.

The Church of St Mark, with its colourful glazed tile roof

❾ Church of St Mark

Sv. Marko

Markov trg. **Tel** (01) 485 16 11. **Open** check opening times (01) 481 40 51.

Today this is the Upper Town's parish church. St Mark's was first mentioned in 1256 when King Bela IV granted the town of Gradec permission to hold a market fair in front of the church. The fair lasted for two weeks and was held to celebrate the saint's day.

The church has undergone various alterations over the centuries. All that is left from the original construction is a Romanesque window and a splendid Gothic doorway, created by the sculptor Ivan Parler between 1364 and 1377. The 15 niches on the door contain statues of Jesus, Mary, St Mark and the 12 apostles. Some of these were replaced by wooden copies in the Baroque era.

On various occasions fires and earthquakes have been responsible for changes in the church's appearance. Its present look dates from 1882, when the coloured glazed tiles on the roof were

Mary with Child by Meštrović, St Mark's

added. The tiles bear the coats of arms of Croatia, Dalmatia, Slavonia and the city of Zagreb. The church has been refurbished with several statues by the sculptor Ivan Meštrović. On the high altar is a large *Christ on the Cross*, a *Pietà* stands on the altar of the Holy Cross and a bronze statue of *Mary with Child* adorns an altar dedicated to the Virgin Mary. The modern frescoes depicting Croat kings in action were painted by Jozo Kljaković.

❿ Parliament Building

Sabor

Markov trg. *i* (01) 456 96 07. **Open** groups only by appt.

Built in Neo-Classical style in 1908 after several 17th- and 18th-century Baroque buildings were razed, this building holds an important place in the story of Croatia. Historic proclamations have been issued from the balcony: the seceding of the nation from the Austro-Hungarian kingdom (29 October 1918) and independence from Yugoslavia after a referendum in 1991. Today the Sabor is still the centre of 21st-century Croat politics.

⓫ Viceroy's Palace

Banski dvori

Markov trg. *i* (01) 456 92 22. **Open** by appt.

The parliament chamber, the central archives, the law courts, the President of the Republic's residence and government offices are all housed in this building in front of St Mark's, which was badly damaged in an airstrike in 1991. The palace is similar in design to the parliament building and is made up of two long 18th-century structures. In the 19th century two two-storey wings were added.

⓬ Croatian History Museum

Hrvatski povijesni muzej

Matoševa ulica 9. **Tel** (01) 485 19 00. **Open** 10am–6pm Mon–Fri,10am–1pm Sat & Sun. **Closed** public hols. 🖼 🎦 📷 📧 🔲 **hismus.hr**

The museum, founded in 1846, has been housed here since 1959. It illustrates the history of Croatia from the Middle Ages to the present day by means of all kinds of historical mementoes and literature. These include documents and paintings of political, military and cultural events, as well as items such as firearms, flags and medals. The exhibitions are not permanent but change frequently due to limited space.

The museum is housed in the Baroque Vojković-Oršić-Kulmer-Rauch Palace, which dates from the second half of the 18th century.

The Parliament Building (Sabor), built in Neo-Classical style in 1908

My Homeland by Ivan Rabuzin (1961), Croatian Museum of Naive Art

⑬ Croatian Museum of Naive Art

Hrvatski muzej naivne umjetnosti

Ćirilometodska ulica 3. **Tel** (01) 485 19 11. **Open** 10am–6pm Tue–Fri, 10am–1pm Sat & Sun. **Closed** public hols. 🖼 📷 📷 **w** hmnu.org

Since 1967, this 19th-century building with its beautiful Neo-Baroque façade has housed works from an exhibition of Naive painters which opened in Zagreb in 1952. The paintings are characterized by the use of vivid colour and a strong feeling for narrative. There are paintings by the founders of the Naive trend, Ivan Generalić and Mirko Virius, as well as by the Hlebine School *(see p25)*, where works by Ivan Večenaj and Mijo Kovačić stand out, and artists from other regions (Ivan Rabuzin, Slavko Stolnik and Matija Skurjeni). Among the sculptures are several by Petar Smajić.

⑭ Church of SS. Cyril and Methodius

Sv. Ćiril i Metod

Ćirilometodska ulica. **Tel** (01) 48517 73.

First built in around 1830 in Neo-Classical style by the architect Bartol Felbinger (1785–1871), the church was rebuilt after the earthquake of 1880 in a Neo-Byzantine style designed by Hermann Bollé.

The interior contains a large iconostasis that was painted by the Ukrainian Epaminondas Bučevski, and four large paintings by Ivan Tišov.

The adjacent Greek-Catholic seminary was built in 1774 and enlarged at the beginning of the 20th century.

⑮ Tower of Lotrščak

Kula Lotrščak

Strossmayerovo šetalište. **Tel** (01) 485 17 68. **Open** Apr–Oct: 9am–9pm Mon–Fri, 10am–9pm Sat & Sun. 🖼 📷

Since the middle of the 19th century, the inhabitants of Zagreb have set their clocks at noon by the cannons fired from this tower. Dating from the 13th century, it is one of the oldest buildings in the city.

At one time this square tower had a bell, which announced the closing of the city gates each evening. Its name comes from the latin *campana latruncolorum* – bell of thieves – anyone left outside at night ran the risk of being robbed.

The tower originally stood alongside the southern side of the walls of Gradec. Even at that time, the walls, nearly 2 m (6 ft) thick, were built with chains inside them as an anti-earthquake measure.

The tower now houses a gallery. It is worth climbing to the top for spectacular views over the city.

⑯ Church of St Catherine

Sv. Katarina

Katarinin trg. **Tel** (01) 485 19 50. **Open** 8am–8pm daily.

The Jesuits built this church in around 1630 on the site of a Dominican building. The church is considered to be one of the most beautiful religious buildings in Zagreb. The white façade has a doorway and four niches with statues and six prominent pilasters. Above is a niche with a statue of Mary.

The single-nave church is home to numerous Baroque works of art. Of particular interest are the stucco reliefs (1721–3) by Antonio Quadrio, the *Scenes of the Life of St Catherine* by the Slovenian artist Franc Jelovšek (1700–64) in the medallion on the ceiling, a beautiful *Altar of St Ignatius* by the Venetian sculptor Francesco Robba (1698–1757) and, on the main altar (1762), *St Catherine among the Alexandrian Philosophers* by Kristof Andrej Jelovšek (1729–76).

In the nearby square called Jezuitski trg, there is a fountain with a statue of a *Fisherman with a Serpent* by Simeon Roksandić (1908). Facing this is a Jesuit monastery (17th century) and a large building from the same period which was the Jesuit seminary and, later, a boarding school for boys of noble parentage.

The rich Baroque interior of the Church of St Catherine

The Neo-Baroque building housing the Croatian National Theatre

⓱ Croatian National Theatre

Hrvatsko narodno kazalište

Trg maršala Tita 15. **Tel** (01) 488 84 18. **Open** for performances only. **Closed** public hols. 🆆 hnk.hr

The Croatian National Theatre stands in the square marking the beginning of a U-shaped series of parks and squares forming a "green horseshoe", the design of the engineer Milan Lenuci (1849–1924). The theatre, one of a number of imposing buildings in the square, was completed in 1895 and is a blend of Neo-Baroque and Rococo. It was designed by the Viennese architects Hermann Helmer and Ferdinand Fellner. The roof has two small domes at the front and a higher dome further back. The exterior is ornamented with two orders of columns running along its entire length.

A 19th-century clock, Museum of Arts and Crafts

The interior is richly decorated with works by Croatian and Viennese artists. Five stage backcloths include one called *The Croatian Renewal*, a splendid work by Vlaho Bukovac.

In the area in front of the theatre stands a masterpiece by Ivan Meštrović, *The Well of Life*, which consists of a group of bronze figures huddled around a well.

⓲ Museum of Arts and Crafts

Muzej za umjetnost i obrt

Trg maršala Tita 10. **Tel** (01) 488 21 11. **Open** 10am–7pm Tue–Sat, 10am–2pm Sun. 🅰 🅲 by appt. 🄵 🄿 🄼 🆆 muo.hr

This museum was first established in 1880 to house collections of artworks by craftsmen and artists. The building was designed by Hermann Bollé and was built between 1887 and 1892. More than 3,000 objects of applied arts from the Gothic period to the present provide an overview of Croatia's cultural history and its close ties to the rest of Europe.

The collections offer an insight into the Croatian and European production of arts and crafts, spanning from late Medieval times to Art Deco and right up to the more contemporary era. The collections housed at the museum include religious art, Judaica, and items including clocks and watches, ivories, metalworks, glass, ceramics, textiles and fashion. As the museum is supported by international backing, impressive temporary exhibitions from abroad occasionally take place here. The adjacent library has a total of 65,000 books on arts and crafts.

⓳ Mimara Museum

Muzej Mimara

Rooseveltov trg 5. **Tel** (01) 482 81 00. **Open** Oct–Jun: 10am–5pm Tue, Wed, Fri & Sat, 10am–7pm Thu, 10am–2pm Sun; Jul–Sep: 10am–7pm Tue–Fri, 10am–5pm Sat, 10am–2pm Sun. **Closed** Mon. 🅰 🅲 🄵 🆆 mimara.hr

In 1972, Ante Topić Mimara, a businessman who was also a collector, painter and restorer, donated his extensive collections to the city of Zagreb, and the Mimara Museum was set up for their display. The museum is housed in an enormous Neo-Renaissance building built in 1895 by the German architects Ludwig and Hülsner.

The works are displayed chronologically from the prehistoric era to the present day. The archaeological section is particularly fascinating, with important finds from ancient Egypt, Mesopotamia, Persia and Pre-Columbian America, as well as the Middle and Far East (Japan, Cambodia, Indonesia and India are represented).

The icon collection not only contains Russian pieces, but also has icons from Palestine, Antioch and Asia Minor dating from the 6th to the 13th centuries. There are ancient Persian, Turkish and Moroccan carpets, and about 300 exhibits cover over 3,500 years of the development of Chinese art, from the Shang to the Qing dynasties.

The 550 glassware exhibits come from Europe, as well as Persia, Turkey and Morocco.

The Bather by Renoir (1868), Mimara Museum

About 1,000 objects and pieces of furniture give a good overall picture of European craftsmanship from the Middle Ages to the 19th century.

There is also a wide-ranging collection of 200 sculptures, which date from ancient Greece to the time of the Impressionists. They include works by the Italian sculptors Giambologna, the Della Robbias and Verrocchio, and the Frenchmen Jean-Antoine Houdon and Auguste Rodin. Italian painting is represented by, among others, Veronese, Paolo Veneziano, Pietro Lorenzetti, Raphael, Canaletto, Giorgione and Caravaggio.

Dutch Baroque painting is represented by Rembrandt, Jacob Van Ruisdael and Jan Van Goyen. Flemish masters here include Rogier van der Weyden, Hieronymus Bosch, Van Dyck and Rubens. Diego Velázquez, Bartolomé Esteban Murillo and Francisco Goya represent the Spanish painters.

The museum also has paintings by the English artists John Constable and JMW Turner and the French painters Edouard Manet, Pierre-Auguste Renoir and Camille Pissarro.

Traditional Croatian costumes on display, Ethnographic Museum

pieces) of the 80,000 exhibits which the museum possesses are on display. Croatian culture is illustrated through exhibits of gold and silver jewellery, musical instruments, splendid embroidery, furnishings, kitchen utensils, tools, beautiful traditional women's costumes embroidered in gold and men's ceremonial dress. A reconstruction of a farmhouse room illustrates the customs and way of life of Croat farmers and fishermen.

Putto by Verrocchio, Mimara Museum

There is also a fascinating collection of dolls dressed in traditional costumes, called the Ljeposav Perinić collection.

The valuable collection of pieces from non-European civilizations, including Latin America, Africa, the Far East, Melanesia and Australia, was assembled from donations made by scholars and explorers, among them Dragutin Lerman and brothers Mirko and Stevo Seljan.

㉑ Botanical Garden of the Faculty of Science

Botanički vrt Prirodoslovno matematičkog fakulteta

Marulićev trg 9a. **i** (01) 489 80 60. **Open** Apr–Oct: 9am–2:30pm Mon & Tue; 9am–7pm Wed–Sun. **W** hirc.botanic.hr/vrt

Part of the "green horseshoe" designed by Milan Lenuci is a large, English-style garden created in 1890 by Antun Heinz, a professor of botany, and entrusted to the faculty of Mathematics and Natural Sciences at Zagreb University.

The garden, covering an area of 50,000 sq m (540,000 sq ft), is an oasis of tranquillity and for this reason it is a popular place in which to stroll. There are about 10,000 plant species here, including around 1,800 tropical plants from all over the world, with Asia particularly well represented.

Paths link the conifer woods, artificial ponds, the exhibition pavilions, rock gardens and glasshouses. A wonderful display is provided by the different varieties of trees, shrubs and flowers that are grown here. Aquatic plants are cultivated in special ponds.

⑳ Ethnographic Museum

Etnografski muzej

Mažuranićev trg 14. **Tel** (01) 482 62 20. **Open** 10am–6pm Tue–Thu, 10am–1pm Fri–Sun. **Closed** Mon, public hols. ▨ ▨ ▨ ▨ ▨ (flash). **W** emz.hr

This is the most important museum of its kind in Croatia. It was founded in 1919 and set up in this harmonious domed building, constructed in 1902 in the Art Nouveau style by the architect Vjekoslav Bastl, for exhibitions held by the Chamber of Commerce. The statues decorating the central part of the façade are by the sculptor Rudolf Valdec and the frescoes on the dome inside were painted by Oton Iveković. Only a small proportion (2,800

A pond in the Botanical Gardens

The Art Pavilion, a historic venue for major exhibitions

㉒ Art Pavilion
Umjetnički paviljon

Trg kralja Tomislava 22. **Tel** (01) 484 10 70. **Open** 11am–7pm Tue–Sun. 🖼 **W** **umjetnicki-paviljon.hr**

In 1896 the Art Pavilion represented Croatia at the international exhibition in Budapest. Its iron skeleton was then transported to Zagreb and rebuilt on this site in 1898 to fit the designs of Ferdinand Fellner and Hermann Helmer. Since then it has been used for large-scale, diverse art exhibitions. A work by Ivan Meštrović, a monument to the Renaissance painter Andrija Medulić, stands in front of the Pavilion.

The Pavilion faces onto a square, Trg Kralja Tomislava, dedicated to the first Croatian king, Tomislav. An equestrian statue by the sculptor Robert Frangeš-Mihanović stands here in commemoration.

㉓ Gallery of Old Masters
Galerija starih majstora

See pp170–71.

㉔ Modern Gallery
Moderna galerija

Andrije Hebranga 1. **Tel** (01) 604 10 55. **Open** 11am–7pm Tue–Fri; 11am–2pm Sat & Sun. **Closed** Mon, public hols. 🖼 🖼 🖼 🖼 🖼 **W** **moderna. galerija.hr**

The museum, housed in the Vranyczany Palace (1882), holds works by the most eminent Croatian painters and sculptors of the 19th–21st centuries. The collection dates from 1905 when the first works of Ivan Meštrović, Mirko Rački and others were acquired. Later purchases and donations brought the current total to some 9,800 paintings, sculptures, watercolours, drawings and prints.

The permanent display of 750 works includes modern classics from painters Vlaho Bukovac, Mato C Medović, Miroslav Kraljević and Josip Račić, the sculptors Ivan Meštrović, Frano Kršinić and Branislav Dešković, along with contemporary artists working in photography, video and other new media. The innovative, multisensory MG Tactile Gallery is aimed particularly at the blind and visually impaired.

㉕ Archaeological Museum
Arheološki muzej

Trg Nikole Šubića Zrinskog 19. **Tel** (01) 487 30 00. **Open** 10am–6pm Tue–Sat (to 8pm Thu), 10am–1pm Sun. 🖼 🖼 by appt. 🖼 **W** **amz.hr**

A large 19th-century building, the Vranyczany-Hafner Palace, has housed the Archaeological Museum since 1945. The institution itself, however, was founded in 1846.

Around 400,000 pieces from all over Croatia, and particularly the area around Zagreb, are on display here. The museum has five main sections: prehistoric, Egyptian, ancient and medieval, and a part devoted to coins and medals.

The first section covers the period from the Neolithic to the late Iron Age and includes the famous Vučedol Dove, a pouring vessel shaped like a bird. Despite the rustic materials used, it nonetheless reveals the technical skills that the pre-Illyrian civilizations had acquired.

Another important exhibit is the bandage used to bind the Mummy of Zagreb. This bandage has mysterious origins and bears text in the Etruscan language, which has not yet been completely deciphered.

The museum's ancient collection is the most important of all and includes the

Gundulić Imagining Osman by Vlaho Bukovac, founder of modern Croat painting, Modern Gallery

An avenue in Maksimir Park, home of the zoo

Lapidarium, which can be found in the courtyard. It is a collection of stone monuments dating from the Roman period (it is open every day except for Monday). The valuable exhibit of the *Head of Plautilla*, from the Roman town of Salona (*see pp118–19*), is the emblem of the museum.

An archaeological conservation laboratory dedicated to preserving the exhibits is also part of the museum. In addition the museum has developed several educational projects aimed at school children. The archaeological library next door houses over 45,000 volumes, some of which are very rare.

Head of Plautilla, Archaeological Museum

🅰 Museum of Contemporary Art

Muzej suvremene umjetnosti

Avenija Dubrovnik 17. **Tel** (01) 605 27 00. **Open** 11am–6pm Tue–Sun, 11am–8pm Sat. **W** msu.hr 🎨 🎭 ♿ 📷

This superb exhibition space displays more than 4,000 works by 900 artists. Highlights include the experimental films of Ivan Ladislav Galeta and Tomislav Gotovac, and conceptual pieces from Goran Trbuljak, Sanja Iveković and Atelier Kožarić. Works such as Miroslav Balka's *Eyes of Purification* and Carsten Höller's slides, also shown in Tate Modern's Turbine Hall in London, add to the museum's heavyweight credentials.

🅰 Maksimir Park

Maksimirski perivoj

Maksimirski perivoj bb. **Open** daily. 📷 **W** park-maksimir.hr

The largest park in the city (covering over 3 sq km/ 1 sq mile) is considered one of Croatia's living monuments. It is named after Bishop Maksimilijan Vrhovac, who initiated the project in 1794. The park was finally completed in 1843.

The park is land-scaped in the English style with wide lawns and flower beds, small woods and lakes. The **zoo** (Zoološki vrt) has hundreds of different animals. Among the follies scattered around the park, the **Vidikovac** (Belvedere) offers great views and has a small café.

🅰 Mirogoj Cemetery

Groblje Mirogoj

Mirogoj. **Open** Oct–Mar: 7:30am–6pm daily, Apr–Sep: 6am–8pm daily.

At the foot of Mount Medvednica, 4 km (2 miles) from the centre of the city, is the Mirogoj Cemetery, built in 1876 by Hermann Bollé. This great architect had already demonstrated his ability and talent with the building of the new city district. The cemetery covers an area of 28,000 sq m (6.91 acres) and the tombs of the most illustrious figures in the political, cultural and artistic life of Croatia lie here.

An imposing façade covered in ivy forms the entrance to the Catholic and Orthodox chapels. From here branch two long Neo-Renaissance arcades which house the burial rooms of the most important families.

A long tree-lined avenue divides the area into two sections which in turn are divided into squares of trees and bushes. Among the areas of greenery stand funeral monuments by leading Croatian sculptors and engravers. There are works by Ivan Meštrović, Jozo Kljaković, Ivan Rendić, Antun Filipović, Antun Augustinčić, Edo Murtić, Ivan Kerdić and Robert Frangeš-Mihanović.

As well as the tombs of notable personalities there is also a monument dedicated to the memory of the soldiers who died during World War I, by Juri Turkalj and V Radauš, and a monument dedicated to the Jews who died in World War II, by Antun Augustinčić. On one of the cemetery lawns there is a monument dedicated to the German soldiers killed in the war.

The well-preserved cemetery is a real open-air museum and is often visited by the local inhabitants, who regularly put fresh flowers and candles on the tombs of great Croats of the past.

Arcade in the Mirogoj Cemetery, one of the most beautiful in Europe

㉓ Gallery of Old Masters
Galerija starih majstora

In 1880 Josip Juraj Strossmayer, the rich and powerful Bishop of Đakovo and one of the leading proponents of a pan-Slav movement, had this gallery built to house the Academy of Arts and Sciences and the Gallery of Old Masters, to which he donated his own impressive collection of about 250 works of art.

The Neo-Renaissance building has a large internal porticoed courtyard. Nine rooms on the upper floor house around 200 works from the major European schools from the 14th to the 19th century. Behind the building is a large statue of Bishop Strossmayer sculpted by Ivan Meštrović in 1926.

Virgin with Child and St Francis and St Bernardine of Siena
This painting is one of the few works by Bartolomeo Caporali (c.1420–1505) to be found outside Perugia in Italy.

Susanna and the Elders
The three figures depicted in the painting stand out against the landscape in the background. The faces of the two old men are very expressive; it is as though they are revived by gazing at the beautiful Susanna. The artist, Master of the Prodigal Son, demonstrates great technical skill and vivid use of colour.

Second floor

Gallery Guide
The gallery is on the second floor of the building. Exhibits include works by important Italian, German, Flemish and French masters, representing schools and artistic trends from the 14th to the 19th century. Before visiting the gallery, note, in the entrance hall, the Baška Tablet, one of the oldest documents of Croat culture (11th century), written in Glagolitic script.

Madame Recamier
This portrait by Antoine Jean Gros (1771–1835) was probably painted around 1825. Madame Recamier was a leading figure of some notoriety in Parisian high society of that time.

Virgin Mary with Jesus, John and an Angel
This tondo by Jacopo del Sellaio uses exuberant colour. The Tuscan artist belonged to the circle of Filippo Lippi and Sandro Botticelli.

Adam and Eve
This lively oil on panel painting is by Mariotto Albertinelli (1474–1515), a Florentine painter. It shows Adam and Eve being expelled from Earthly Paradise.

Key

- ☐ Italian School 14th–16th century
- ☐ Italian School 16th–18th century
- ☐ Flemish and Dutch Masters and European School 15th–17th century
- ☐ French Masters 18th–19th century
- ☐ Non-exhibition space

★ **St Augustine and St Benedict**
The work reveals the expressive skill of the great Venetian master, Giovanni Bellini (1430–1516). The figures of the saints occupy simple niches.

Main entrance

★ **St Sebastian**
This delicate image of the saint by Vittore Carpaccio (1465–1525) was part of a polyptych. In this painting with its vivid colouring, the Venetian master expresses the drama of the martyrdom through the smile of the young man at the moment of his death.

CENTRAL CROATIA

Central Croatia is bordered to the west by the vine-covered hills of Samobor, which continue on towards Karlovac and Ogulin, and to the south by the Bosnia-Herzegovina border as far as Jasenovac. To the northeast is a stretch of fertile valley formed by the Sava river, which runs from Zagreb to the Lonjsko Polje Nature Park. These wetlands, south of Sisak, are home to all kinds of birds.

This region of Croatia has long been a meeting point for different civilizations. Until the 12th century BC, this area was inhabited by the Illyrians, who were joined by Celts in the 4th century BC. The first Illyrian cities became Roman towns after the 1st century AD. The most important was Siscia (now called Sisak), which was sacked by the Huns in 441 and raided by the Avars in the 6th century.

The southern border with Bosnia, which dates back to 271 AD, was confirmed at the time of the division between the Western and Eastern Churches in 1054, and later re-confirmed when the Turks occupied the Balkans. To stop the continuous Turkish raids, in 1578 the Austrian Emperor established a *Vojna krajina* (Military Frontier) in areas which had mostly been abandoned by the Croats, who had fled to the coastal cities for refuge. To help guard the borders,

Serbian refugees were brought in, along with minorities of Vlachs, Albanians, Montenegrin and German-speaking groups. Villages sprang up which were inhabited by Catholics, Muslims and people of the Orthodox faith. These diverse communities lived together without any serious tension until the mid-19th century, when feelings of nationalism swept across Europe. The most recent war, fought in the name of nationalism, not only created widespread destruction but also "ethnic cleansing", resulting in the exodus of thousands of Serbs.

This part of Croatia is the area least visited by tourists, although it offers magnificent scenery with rivers and wood-covered hills and good Croatian cuisine. There is plenty to see, with ancient castles, churches, museums and nature reserves.

Horses grazing in the Lonjsko Polje Nature Park

◄ Gentle slopes planted with vines near Samobor

Exploring Central Croatia

Three distinct areas make up this part of the country: the lowlands around the capital, Zagreb, with numerous 18th-century buildings constructed on the sites of ancient castles; the hilly area between Samobor and Karlovac, renowned for its wine production; and the strip of border with Bosnia-Herzegovina, south of Sisak. The landscape of Central Croatia is varied, with areas of rolling plains alternating with vine-covered hills. Higher areas are covered in thick woods and there is also an area of wetlands that comprise Lonjsko Polje Nature Park. In the cities and larger towns there are Baroque churches, monasteries, castles, fortresses and museums. Most suffered damage in the 1991–95 war, but some have been repaired since.

Roman piece, Civic Museum, Sisak

Interior of the Church of St Mary in Jastrebarsko

Getting Around

The road network which crosses central Croatia is good. Recently roads have been improved and the motorways extended. From Zagreb the A3 motorway goes to Samobor and the Lonjsko Polje Nature Park. State road number 30 serves Sisak, while a secondary road network connects the other towns. All the main towns and cities are served by the Croatian railway system, except for the city of Samobor. Buses go to all villages, however small.

For hotels and restaurants see p231 and pp247

0 kilometres 20

0 miles 20

Sights at a Glance

1. Samobor
2. Okić
3. Jastrebarsko
4. Ozalj
5. Karlovac
6. Ogulin
7. Topusko Toplice
8. Sisak
9. Hrvatska Kostajnica
10. Jasenovac
11. Novska
12. Lonjsko Polje Nature Park
13. Kutina
14. Garić

Locator Map

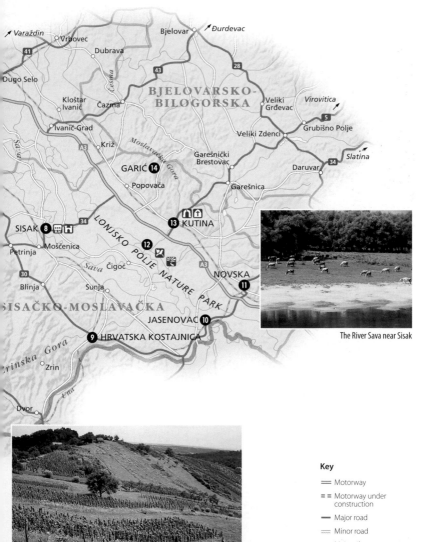

The River Sava near Sisak

The vine-covered hills around Okić

Key

= Motorway

= = Motorway under construction

— Major road

= Minor road

⌇ Main railway

▬ County border

▬ International border

For keys to symbols *see back flap*

The main altar in the Church of St Mary, Samobor

❶ Samobor

Map C2. 🏔 15,000. 🚌 (01) 336 72 76. 🛈 Trg kralja Tomislava 5, (01) 336 00 44. 🎭 Carnival (Feb); Day of the city (3rd Sat in Oct). 🔲 **tz–samobor.hr**

Samobor is built below the ruins of what was once a large fort (Stari Grad). In 1242 it was granted the status of a royal free town, and became an important trading centre. Today it is one of the capitals of Croatian gastronomy, priding itself on its traditional local dishes.

In the oldest area (Taborec) is the Gothic Church of **St Michael** (Sv. Mihalj), which was remodelled in the Baroque period. Dating from the same time is the Church of **St Anastasia** (Sv. Anastazija) and a Franciscan monastery with the Church of St Mary (Sv. Marija): the *Assumption* behind the main altar was frescoed by Franc Jelovšek in 1752, while the altar on the left

was decorated by Valentin Metzinger (1734). The adjacent monastery is laid out around a beautiful quadrangular cloister and has Baroque frescoes in the refectory and library.

The history of the city and local area is well documented in the **Civic Museum** (Muzej grada Samobora), housed in the 18th-century Livadić Palace. The section dedicated to the history of Croatian mountaineering is especially interesting.

🏛 **St Anastasia**
Ulica sv. Ane 2. **Tel** (01) 336 00 82. **Open** by appt.

🏛 **Civic Museum**
Livadićeva 7. **Tel** (01) 336 10 14. **Open** 9am–3pm Tue–Fri, 9am–1pm Sat, 10am–4pm Sun. 🖼 🎫 🖼 🖼

❷ Okić

Map C2. 🛈 County: Preradovićeva 42, Zagreb, (01) 487 36 65.

High on an isolated hilltop, towering above the fields and woodland surrounding the village of Okić, stand the ruins of a fortified town. These consist of the remains of a wall with round towers, an entrance gate and a Gothic chapel. The town, mentioned in documents from 1183, belonged to the counts of Okić, Zrinski, Frankopan and Erdödy. It was destroyed by the Turks and eventually abandoned in 1616. The steep, rocky approaches leading up to the ruins are popular with climbers, who are rewarded with fantastic views from the summit.

In the village around the foot of the hill is the Church of **St Mary** (Sv. Marija). It was rebuilt in 1893 incorporating a decorated doorway from 1691 and survived survived landslips in 1911 that engulfed much of the village. Inside are some Baroque altars, a splendid pulpit and a font. In front of the church is an octagonal bell tower with a vestibule.

A painting by Metzinger in the Church of St Mary in Jastrebarsko

❸ Jastrebarsko

Map C2. 🏔 5,500. 🚉 from Zagreb. 🚌 from Zagreb. 🛈 Strossmayerov trg 4, (01) 627 29 40. 🔲 **tzgj.hr**

At the foot of the Plešivica mountain chain, between Samobor and Karlovac, stands Jastrebarsko. The town appears in documents of 1249. It assumed greater importance in 1257 when it was declared a royal free town by Bela IV and became a trading centre for timber, livestock and the wine which is still produced locally.

In the 15th century the town was a feudal holding of the Erdödy family, who built an imposing **castle** on a square ground-plan with round towers at the corners and an internal porticoed courtyard. Two centuries later it was altered and turned into a residential building which is now closed to the public.

The Baroque Church of **St Nicholas** (Sv. Nikola; 1772– 75) contains a fresco by Rašica and the tomb of Petar Erdödy (1567).

The ruins of the fortified town of Okić, perched on a hilltop

In theChurch of **St Mary** (Sv. Marija; 1740), originally Dominican and later Franciscan, the altars are all Baroque. The painting on the altar dedicated to Mary is by Valentin Metzinger and dates from 1735.

❹ Ozalj

Map C2. 🏔 1,200. 🚍 (047) 731 158. 🚌 Karlovac, (060) 338 833, Ozalj, (047) 731107. ℹ️ Kurilovac 1, (047) 731 196. 🎉 Day of the city (30 Apr); Summer evenings in Ozalj (15–20 Aug). 🌐 **ozalj-tz.hr**

A castle (Stari grad) which belonged to royalty once stood on this rocky spur. It was built in the 13th century to monitor the roads and the traffic on the river Kupa which flows below it. The castle was strengthened by the Babonić counts and was also the property of the Frankopan family and, in the late 16th century, of Juraj Zrinski. After the Ottoman threat had passed, a village grew up around the castle which had become a residential manor.

Parts of the fortress remain visible: two encircling walls with five semicircular towers. Next to these are some more recent buildings: the granary *(palas)* (16th century) and a Gothic family chapel. The main building, on several levels, was renovated in 1928 by the Thurn und Taxis family who

Coat of arms, Civic Museum, Karlovac

Ozalj Castle, once owned by the Frankopans and Juraj Zrinski

had inherited it. For a time the building was abandoned but in 1971 it became a **museum**. Exhibits explain the history of the fort and local area and there are some Glagolitic inscriptions.

🏰 **Castle and Museum**
Ulica Zrinskih i Frankopana. ℹ️ (047) 732 271. **Open** 8am–8pm Mon–Fri, 10am–8pm Sat & Sun. 🎨

❺ Karlovac

Map C2. 🏔 55,000. 🚍 (060) 333 444. 🚌 (060) 338 833. ℹ️ Local: Ulica Petra Zrinskog 3, (047) 615 115; Regional: A Vraniczanya 6, (047) 615 320. 🌐 **karlovac-touristinfo.hr** 🎉 Spring Promenades (May); St John's Bonfires (Jun); International folk festival (Jul); Beer festival (Aug).

Today Karlovac is an industrial city and an important junction for roads to Slovenia. It originated as a bulwark against Turkish raids, but was actually founded in 1579 by the Archduke of Austria, Charles of Habsburg, from whom the town gets its name.

The town was planned by the Italian N Angelini as a city-fort at the confluence of the rivers Korana and Kupa. The layout was based on a six-pointed star with bastions and moats which have now been transformed into public gardens. The interior contained 24 buildings, all similar, all of which are still preserved today – although they are used for different purposes.

The heart of the city is Strossmayer Square with the Baroque Frankopan Palace which houses the **Civic Museum** (Gradski m uzej). The archaeological and ethnographic collections document the city's history. In the square Trg Bana Jelačića is a Franciscan monastery. The **Vjekoslav Karas Gallery** was built in 1975 in the New Centre. It uses its attractive display space for both visual art and museum exhibitions.

Clock tower of the Church of the Holy Trinity in Karlovac

The Catholic Church of the **Holy Trinity** (Presvetoga Trojstvo) dates mainly from 1683–92 with an 18th-century clock tower (1795). The church has an elaborate black marble altar made by Michele Cussa in 1698. The Orthodox Church of St Nicholas (Sv. Nikola) dates from 1786.

To the east the city now extends as far as **Dubovac Castle**, a medieval construction. Once used as a hotel, it is being restored to its original design.

🏛 **Civic Museum**
Strossmayerov trg 7. **Tel** (047) 615 980. **Open** 8am–4pm Tue, Thu & Fri, 8am–7pm Wed, 10am–noon Sat & Sun. 🎨 🎬 by appt. 🌐 **gmk.hr**

🏛 **The Vjekoslav Karas Gallery**
Ljudevita Šestića 3. **Tel** (047) 412 381. **Open** during exhibitions: 8am–4pm Mon–Fri (Sep–Jun also 5–7pm Wed & Fri), 10am–noon Sat & Sun.

⛪ **Holy Trinity**
Trg bana Jelačića 7. **Tel** (047) 615 950/1. **Open** before Mass. Other times by appt.

The 15th-century castle of the Frankopan counts in Ogulin

❻ Ogulin

Map C2. 🚠 9,000. 🚉 (047) 525 001. 🛈 Kardinala A. Stepinca 1, (047) 532 278. 🌐 tz-grada-ogulina.hr

When Marshal Tito was imprisoned here in 1927 and 1933 *(see p44)* this town became well known throughout Croatia. The prison was part of a castle built by the Frankopan counts in the 15th century. The castle walls enclosed a large building with two tall towers at the ends, a Gothic chapel and several houses which were built when Ogulin became a staging post on the *Vojna krajina* (Military Frontier, *see p41*) in 1627. Part of the structure is given over to the **Regional Museum** which has sections on archaeology, folklore and mountaineering.

A short distance from the fortified town is the Old Castle (Zulumgrad) situated near the Đula abyss, a chasm formed by the Dobra river.

❼ Topusko Toplice

Map D2. 🚠 800. 🚌 from Zagreb, Sisak, Karlovac. 🛈 Trg bana Jelačića 4, (044) 885 203. 🎿 Days of Honey (Feb); Folklore Day (Jun); Half Marathon (Aug).
🌐 turizam-topusko.com

The presence of a Cistercian abbey made this a centre for spreading Christianity in the Banovina area (a region of green valleys south of Sisak, between the Sava and Glina rivers). The abbey was founded in 1204 by King Andrew II and a village grew up around it in the Middle Ages. The remains can be found in Opatovina Park.

The nearby hot water springs (up to 78°C/172°F) were used in Roman times and in the first half of the 19th century a thermal spa was established, which was frequented by the Emperor Franz Joseph and other court dignitaries. Today the spa treats rheumatic and neurological problems, and the after-effects of incapacitating injuries. The spa has three main thermal sources and the water comes from a depth of 1,500 m (4,920 ft). The quality of the water has not changed in the last 200 years. There are two hotels in Topusko and a number of private accommodations also on offer.

❽ Sisak

Map D2. 🚠 37,000. 🚉 (044) 524 724. 🚌 (060) 330 060. 🛈 Rimska ulica bb, (044) 522 655. 🌐 sisakturist.com

The city of Sisak, at the point where the rivers Kupa and Odra flow into the Sava, has always played an important role in Croatian history. Its name has changed a number of times over the course of its 2,000 years of existence. It originated as the Illyrian-Celtic Segestica, becoming Siscia with the Romans, and later Colonia Flavia Siscia. Rome conquered the

Hercules (1st century AD), Sisak museum

town after a bloody battle in which Emperor Augustus was wounded. After the conquest of the Balkans, the emperor made it the capital of the Pannonia Savia province and it became a trading centre.

It was destroyed by Attila in 441, and in the 6th century it was raided by the Avars and Slavs. The town was finally rebuilt by the Croats and became Sisak. It was from here that Prince Ljudevit began the conquest of Croatia in the 8th century. Sisak was destroyed again by the Hungarians in the 10th century, and was also abandoned by the bishop, who transferred the see to Zagreb, but built a fort here. In 1593 this fort was the site of a battle which resulted in the first Turkish defeat in the Balkans.

The town rose again nearby and began to enjoy a long period of prosperity, thanks to tolls on river traffic. It still has some Baroque buildings, including the old and new town halls.

A park surrounds the **fortress** (Stari grad) on the River Kupa, south of the city. The fortress was built in the middle of the 16th century at the time of the Turkish invasions. It has a triangular ground plan, with three large round brick towers (1544–55), connected by a high wall with openings for firearms. In the park is a beautiful traditional farmhouse. The **Civic Museum** (Gradski muzej) has material from the Roman settlement.

🏰 Fortress
Tome Bakača Erdödyja. 🛈 (044) 811 811. **Open** contact for info.

🏛 Civic Museum
Kralja Tomislava 10. **Tel** (044) 811 811. **Open** Apr–Sep: 10am–6pm Tue–Fri, 9am–noon Sat & Sun; Oct–Mar: 7:30am–3:30pm Tue–Fri. 🚫 📷
🌐 muzej-sisak.hr

Environs
About 20 km (12 miles) south-west is **Gora** which, in the Middle Ages, was the centre of a Županija (county) of the same name. The county seat was a

Fortress of Sisak next to the Kupa river, built in the 13th century castle which appears in documents in 1242, but which was destroyed by the Turks in 1578. The Gothic Church of the **Assumption of the Blessed Virgin Mary** (Uznesenja Blažene Djevice Marije) was also badly damaged and was restored in the 18th century in the Baroque style. The church has chapels on all corners and resembles a castle, with a marble altar and pulpit inside.

❾ Hrvatska Kostajnica

Map D2. 🁢 2,000. 🚌 from Zagreb, Sisak. 🚌 from Zagreb, Sisak. 🅸 Vladimira Nazora 17, (044) 851 800.

Standing on the left bank of the River Una which, for much of its length, marks the border between Croatia and Bosnia-Herzegovina, this town still bears the signs of damage from the war in the 1990s. By the river, near a bridge, is a renovated castle built in the Middle Ages but frequently razed. Only three towers connected by a high wall remain in the wake of the last war. The Church and Monastery of **St Anthony of Padua**, built after the Turks left at the end of the 17th century, have been restored and are discreetly furnished (some of the Baroque altars were famous for their beauty).

Environs
Around 14 km (9 miles) to the southwest is **Zrin**, where the ruins of a castle built in the 14th century by the Babonić family stand on a hill. In 1347 it passed

The tulip-shaped monument by Bogdanović in Jasenovac Memorial Site

to the Bribir princes of Šubić. A branch of the family took the name of Zrinski after the village around the castle. It was occupied by the Turks from 1577 until the end of the 17th century when they destroyed it.

The Zrinskis played a key role in Croatia's history: as fierce defenders against the Turks; then as the authors of the failed attempt to free the territory from Habsburg rule *(see p181)*.

❿ Jasenovac

Map E2. 🁢 800. 🚌 from Sisak. 🚌 from Sisak. 🅸 Trg kralja Petra Svačića 3, (044) 672 490. 🆆 tzg-hrvatska-kostajnica.hr

This town is notorious as the place where, during World War II, tens of thousands of prisoners of war, Jews, Gypsies, Serbs and Croats, perished in the concentration camp which was located here. In memory of this terrible genocide, a large tulip-

shaped monument by the artist Bogdan Bogdanović now stands in what was formerly the camp's centre. The monument and the Memorial Museum are part of Jasenovac Memorial Site.

The Church of St Luke in Novska

⓫ Novska

Map E2. 🁢 7,500. 🚌 from Zagreb, Sisak, (044) 892 421. 🚌 from Zagreb, Sisak. 🅸 Ulica kralja Tomislava 2, (044) 601 305.

The town of Novska is the starting point for visiting the Lonjsko Polje Nature Park *(see p180)* and for excursions to the Psunj mountains. A number of recreational sports can be enjoyed here too.

The Church of **St Luke** (Sv. Luka) is a Baroque church dating from 1775. It has a fine altar and a painting by the modern painter Z Šulentić. In the **Bauer Gallery** there are many works by Naive and contemporary artists.

Novska's economy is based on industry and trade, and rail and road links are good.

The castle of medieval origins in Kostajnica, on the banks of the Una

Nesting storks in the Lonjsko Polje Nature Park

⑫ Lonjsko Polje Nature Park

Map D2. Park office (Krapje): 🛈 (044) 672 080. Entrance at Čigoć: 🛈 (044) 715 115. **Open** Apr–Oct: 8am–4pm daily; Nov–Mar: by appt. 🏠 **W** pp-lonjsko-polje.hr

The wide bend in the River Sava between Sisak and Stara Gradiška has been a special ornithological reserve since 1963. It became a nature reserve in 1990 to protect an area of 506 sq km (195 sq miles). This vast area was regularly flooded by the river and its tributaries (Lonja, Ilova, Pakra and Čazma) during the thaw, and in the summer and early autumn the waters would recede. Since the 1960s parts of the wetlands have been drained, but they still remain some of Europe's most important marshland.

Woods of oak, poplar, ash and willow trees grow along the banks of the river and on the higher ground, while the dry fields are used as grazing for sheep in the summer months. Wild boar live here, as well as deer, and there are also Turopolje pigs and Posavina horses, both of which are protected species.

The park is an important stopping place for black storks, which arrive in spring and leave in autumn after nesting, for numerous species of heron, for egrets and a variety of birds of prey, including the rare harrier and white-tailed eagles.

⑬ Kutina

Map D2. 🏔 15,000. 🚍 (060) 333 444. 🚍 (060) 355 060. 🛈 Tržna 8, (044) 681 004. **W** turizam-kutina.hr

Kutina, in the Moslavina region, was built over the ruins of a Roman *castrum* (a Roman military camp or fort) and numerous archaeological finds have been discovered. The town is linked to two castles; Kutinjac Grad, documented in 1256, and the fortress of Plovdin; however, only ruins and parts of the walls remain.

Kutina flourished again in the 17th century, developing on the plain south of the fortress. It is here that the Church of **Our Lady of the Snow** (Marija Snježna) was built by Count Karl Erdödy in around 1770. The church is surrounded by a covered portico and is decorated inside with stucco and *trompe-l'oeil* paintings by Josip Görner. The sculpture and the inlaid wooden furnishings which enclose the altar of the Holy Sepulchre are a unique example of Baroque composition.

Erdödy Castle, which was rebuilt in 1895, houses the **Museum of Moslavina** (Muzej Moslavine), which tells the history and folklore of Moslavina through an extensive collection of documents, objects and traditional costumes.

🏛 Museum of Moslavina
Trg kralja Tomislava 13. **Tel** (044) 683 548. **Open** 8am–1pm Tue–Fri.

Interior of the Church of Our Lady of the Snow in Kutina

Environs
Around 50 km (31 miles) north-west of Kutina is **Ivanić-Grad** and the nearby towns of **Kloštar Ivanić** and **Križ**. In Ivanić-Grad there are workshops making pretty flax and linen products, keeping local traditions alive.

In Kloštar Ivanić there is a Franciscan monastery founded in 1508 and the church of St Mary (Sv. Marija), with collections of silver, paintings and richly illustrated music codices.

In Križ, the parish church of the Cross was founded by the Knights Templar in the 11th century. The church has a decorative Baroque interior and a magnificent 1787 organ.

Some remains of the old fortifications around Garić

⑭ Garić

Map D2. 🏔 76 (Podgarić). 🛈 Regional: Trg Eugena Kvaternika 2, Bjelovar, (043) 243 944.

On a hill in the Moslavačka chain (Moslavačka Gora) near Podgarić stand the ruins of the fortified town of Garić, noted as a *castrum* in 1256. In 1277, it was granted by the king to Timotej, Bishop of Zagreb, who entrusted its defence to the counts of Gardun, and later to the counts of Celje. Nearby, below Garić, the Pauline order founded the monastery of St Mary in 1295. In 1544 the town and the monastery were destroyed by the Turks.

The fortified town was protected by high walls and was an irregular shape. There was a moat with towers, and further towers inside the walls.

The Zrinski and Frankopan Dynasties

Dujam, count of Krk, died in 1163 and his descendants took the name of Frankopan *(Frangere Panem)* after Venice confirmed the family's rule over Krk. They were allied with Venice until 1480 when they were forced to surrender the island. However, they still had vast estates given to them by the Hungarian kings. The Šubić family became counts of Bribir when they were granted the town by King Andrew II in 1290, and counts of Zrinski in 1347 when they were obliged to move to Zrin *(see p179)*. The execution of the Ban of Croatia, Petar Zrinski, and his brother-in-law Fran Krsto Frankopan in 1671 ended the two most powerful Croatian dynasties. The Habsburgs confiscated their property and the Zrinski line died out. A branch of the Frankopan family still survives in Friuli, Italy.

Fran Krsto Frankopan (1643–1671), great-grandson of Krsto Frankopan and Mario Frangipane's heir (the Roman branch of the family), was publicly executed in Wiener Neustadt in 1671, for his part in a plot against the Empire.

Krsto Frankopan, (1480?–1527), son of Bernard, Ban of Croatia, and Louise of Aragon, was Emperor Maximilian's general in the war against Venice in the early 16th century. He was imprisoned in Milan and died fighting for the independence of Hungary, of which Croatia was part.

Fran Krsto Frankopan awaiting execution

Petar Zrinski

Execution of the Rebels

On 30 April 1671, in the town square in Wiener Neustadt, the Ban of Croatia, Petar Zrinski, and his brother-in-law, Krsto Frankopan, were beheaded on charges of high treason on the orders of Emperor Leopold I. The two brothers-in-law had attempted to form a coalition of the Croatian feudal lords in order to limit Austro-Hungarian influence.

Petar Zrinski was the Ban (governor) from 1664, and the leader of the movement which sought to limit Habsburg activity in Croatia. The attempted revolt was foiled by betrayals and the promise of a possible agreement. The two leaders went to Vienna to negotiate with the Emperor. When they reached the capital they were imprisoned, and a few months later were beheaded.

Nikola Zrinski fought against the Turks and was a defender of Christianity. He died in the Battle of Siget in 1566, after he refused the sultan's offer to make him Governor of Croatia if he abandoned the Emperor.

SLAVONIA AND BARANJA

The easternmost part of northern Croatia, between Hungary, Serbia and Bosnia-Herzegovina, is one of the most fertile areas of Europe, known as the "granary of Croatia". The landscape of Slavonia and Baranja is characterized by expanses of wheat and maize fields and hills covered with vineyards or ancient woods. The main city, Osijek, is famous for its fortified centre.

First inhabited by the Illyrians, present-day Slavonia and Baranja came into contact with the Roman world in the 2nd century BC. It took the Romans more than 200 years to subdue the inhabitants of this region, which they referred to as Pannonia. From 402 Pannonia was invaded, first by the Goths, then the Huns, Visigoths, Burgundians, Gepids, Longobards, Sarmatians and finally the Avars. When the Slavs arrived, very little remained of Roman rule, and the land, ever since then called Slavonia, was practically uninhabited.

In 925 the Kingdom of the Croat Sovereigns was set up and this lasted until 1097, when King Koloman came to rule Slavonia and created the Hungarian-Croat kingdom. Following the Battle of Mohács in 1526, Slavonia became part of the Ottoman Empire, and remained so until 1689. To confront the constant disputes between the Turks and the Holy Roman Empire, the Habsburgs set up a Military Frontier (*Vojna krajina*), which lasted until 1881, when Austria-Hungary took Bosnia-Herzegovina from the Turks. The frontier was abolished and absorbed into Croatia.

When war broke out in 1991, the presence of Serb villages was a pretext for the Serbian occupation of Slavonia. In 1995, under the auspices of the United Nations, control of Slavonia reverted back to the Croatians. Although war damage is still visible along the border, particularly in Vukovar, great efforts are being made with rebuilding and Slavonia is once again well worth visiting for its historical treasures. It is also an area of great natural beauty and includes the nature reserve of Kopački rit, a wetlands sanctuary for wildfowl.

Local people in the typical traditional costumes of the region

◀ Fresco in the 18th-century church of St Francis in Požega

Exploring Slavonia and Baranja

Slavonia, the region between the rivers Sava, Drava and Danube, is made up of a vast rolling alluvial plain with chains of hills at its edges which are covered in woods and vineyards. At one time the rivers turned the area into an enormous swamp for many months of the year. Baranja is a triangular area of land in the far northeast, bordered at the extreme tip by the rivers Drava and Danube and the Hungarian border.

The plains are covered in fields of maize and the hills are given over to viticulture. In the southern corner, the Drava river regularly overflows from spring to autumn to create a broad area of marshland, now the Kopački Rit Nature Park. The park is an important wildlife sanctuary, a refuge for hundreds of different species of bird, including the rare black stork.

On the right bank of the Drava river is Slavonia's main city, Osijek. It has wide avenues, parks, and 19th-century, Viennese-style buildings, as well as a Neo-Gothic cathedral.

The Baroque belfry of St Roch in Virovitica

The countryside around Slavonski Brod

Sights at a Glance

1. Daruvar
2. Lipik
3. Nova Gradiška
4. Požega
5. Kutjevo
6. Slavonski Brod
7. Vrpolje
8. Đakovo
9. Novi Mikanovci
10. Županja
11. Vinkovci
12. Ilok
13. Šarengrad
14. Vukovar
15. Erdut
16. Osijek pp194–7
17. Ernestinovo
18. Kopački Rit Nature Park pp198–9
19. Topolje
20. Darda
21. Bizovac
22. Valpovo
23. Donji Miholjac
24. Našice
25. Orahovica
26. Virovitica

Getting Around

For many years Osijek was a rail, road and river junction of some importance. Since the war in the 1990s, rail and river traffic has become less significant. However, Osijek is still the centre of the road system in the area and, thanks to a good network, the city can easily be reached from Slavonia and Baranja using state road number 2 heading south from Varaždin, or the same number 2 road north from Vukovar and the E73 from Hungary. There is also an efficient public bus service. About 7 km (4 miles) from Osijek there is a domestic airport with daily connections to Zagreb. Osijek itself has an excellent tram service which makes it easy to get around the city.

Locator Map

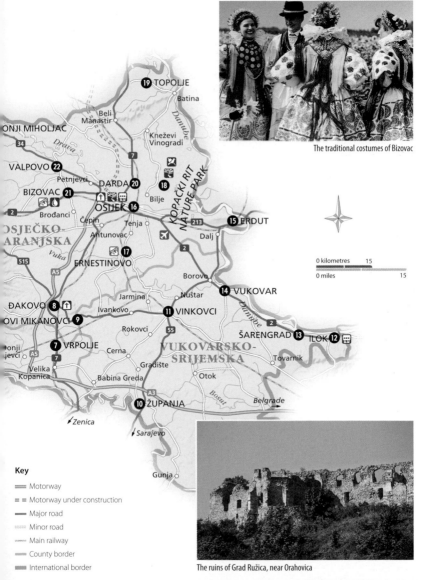

The traditional costumes of Bizovac

0 kilometres — 15
0 miles — 15

Key

▬▬▬ Motorway
= = Motorway under construction
▬▬ Major road
===== Minor road
━·━·━ Main railway
▬▬▬ County border
▬▬▬ International border

The ruins of Grad Ružica, near Orahovica

For keys to symbols *see back flap*

❶ Daruvar

Map E2. ⛰ 10,000. ✈ Osijek, 130 km (81 miles); Zagreb, 150 km (93 miles). 🚌 ⛴ 𝒊 Trg kralja Tomislava 12, (043) 331 382. ⛲ Wine exhibition (May/June). 🌐 **visitdaruvar.hr**

This spa town was known as Aquae Balissae in the time of the Roman Empire for the quality of its hot water spring, the source of which is at the foot of the Papuk mountains.

The town developed from three medieval settlements. In 1760 the area was bought by a Hungarian count, Antun Janković, who built a Baroque castle he named Daruvar, and the first **spa**. Today, Daruvar (meaning "city of the crane") has hotels, a **medical centre** (Daruvarske toplice) offering the spa waters, the Daruvar wine road and a thermal water park, Aquae Balissae.

There are two 18th-century churches in the town, one Catholic and one Orthodox. Daruvar is also a centre for the Czech people in Croatia, who maintain the Czech language and customs.

🌊 **Spa**
Julijev Park. **Tel** (043) 623 620.

❷ Lipik

Map E2. ⛰ 2,300. ✈ Osijek, 93 km (58 miles); Zagreb, 155 km (96 miles). 🚌 ⛴ from Zagreb. 𝒊 Trg kralja Tomislava 3, (034) 421 600. ⛲ June in Lipik (Jun). 🌐 **tz-lipik.hr**

The spa area (Aquae Balissae) was known in Roman times for its waters. In the late 18th century a hot water spring, rich in minerals, was rediscovered and Lipik became one of the most famous spas in Croatia. It was especially popular between the two World Wars. Lipik was damaged in the 1991 war, but a new **spa** has been built and the hotels and medical centres restored. Lipik is also known for breeding the famous Lipizzaner horses; its horse-riding and cycle trails are popular with visitors.

🌊 **Spa (Toplice)**
Marije Terezije 13. **Tel** (034) 440 700.

Baroque building in Požega's main square

❸ Nova Gradiška

Map E2. ⛰ 13,300. ✈ Osijek, 93 km (58 miles); Zagreb, 155 km (96 miles). 🚌 (035) 361 610. ⛴ (035) 361 219. 𝒊 Slavonskih graničara 7, (035) 361 494. 🌐 **tzgng.hr**

In 1748 this town was first founded as Fredrichsdorf by the Viennese, who planned to build a fortress here. The town, situated at the foot of Mount Psunj, is built on a fertile plain. An agricultural market is regularly held in the main square, which is lined with Baroque buildings.

The Neo-Classical Church of St Stephen of Hungary (Sv. Stjepan Kralj) is now the **Immaculate Conception**. The Baroque **Sanctuary of St Theresa** (Sv. Terezija) dates from 1756.

⛪ **Immaculate Conception**
Aloizija Stepinca 1. **Tel** (035) 362 203. **Open** 8am–6pm daily.

The Baroque Sanctuary of St Theresa in Nova Gradiška

❹ Požega

Map E2. ⛰ 21,000. ✈ Osijek, 67 km (42 miles); Zagreb, 175 km (109 miles). 🚌 (034) 273 911. ⛴ (034) 273 133. 𝒊 Antuna Kanižlića 3, (034) 274 900. ⛲ Feast of St Gregory (12 Mar), Music Festival Aurea Fest (early Sep). 🌐 **pozega-tz.hr**

The Romans first founded this town, a halfway settlement between the towns now called Sisak and Osijek, with the name of Incerum. In the 11th century it was one of the centres from which the heretical movement of the Bogomili spread; after their repression in the 12th century, properties in the environs of the city were granted to the Templars by King Bela IV.

In 1285 the Franciscans founded a monastery, the church of which was used as a mosque during the Turkish occupation. In the 18th and 19th centuries the town was called the "Athens of Slavonia" for the cultural events held to commemorate the expulsion of the Turks in 1691. The city took on a new look during this period: in the main square, Trg Sv. Trojstva, buildings with stucco and Baroque porticoes were built.

In the square stands a column, a memorial to plague victims made in 1749 by Gabrijel Granicije. To one side of the square is the renovated 18th-century Church of **St Francis** (Sv. Franjo). The monastery alongside still houses a community of Franciscan monks.

Interesting examples of Baroque architecture in the town include the Jesuit College (1711) and Gymnasium (1726), opened by the Jesuits who, in 1761, also founded the Požega Academy. Dating from 1763, the Church of **St Theresa** (Sv. Terezija Avilska) became a cathedral in 1997. The frescoed walls are by Celestin Medović and Oton Iveković.

The Church of **St Lawrence** (Sv. Lovro, 14th century) was renovated in Baroque style in the early 18th century. It still has some 14th-century frescoes. There are also tombstones testifying to the city's glory; one is for the poet Antun Kanižlić (1699–1777). In the square between the Church of St Francis and the Gymnasium is a statue of Luka Ibrišimović, a Franciscan who distinguished himself in the battles against the Turks.

14th-century fresco in the church of St Lawrence, Požega

The **Civic Museum** (Gradski muzej) contains an assortment of archaeological finds, Romanesque reliefs and Baroque paintings.

Every year on 12 March Požega holds an event called Grgurevo, to commemorate a local victory over the Turks won in 1688.

🏠 St Theresa
Trg sv. Terezije 13. **Tel** (034) 274 321. **Open** 8am–noon, 3–6pm daily.

🏛 Civic Museum
Matice hrvatske 1. **Tel** (034) 272 130. **Open** 9am–2pm Mon–Fri, by appt Sat & Sun.

❺ Kutjevo

Map F2. 🏠 2,800. ✈ Osijek 62 km (38 miles). 🚍 Našice, 27 km (17 miles). ℹ Trg graševine 1, (034) 255 288. 🎉 Feast of St Gregory (12 Mar). 🌐 tz-kutjevo.hr

An important wine-producing centre, the town is famous for a winery founded by the Cistercians. In 1232, the order built a monastery here and encouraged the cultivation of vines. After Turkish rule, at the end of the 17th century, Jesuits took over the monastery and wine-making resumed. The Cistercian cellars are still intact and wine is still an important industry. The Jesuits also built the Church of **St Mary** (Sv. Marija) in 1732, which houses a painting of the Madonna with Child by A Cebej (1759).

❻ Slavonski Brod

Map F3. 🏠 60,000. ✈ Osijek, 100 km (62 miles); Zagreb, 197 km (122 miles). 🚍 (060) 333 444. 🚆 Trg Hrvatskog proljeća, (060) 310 310. ℹ Local: Trg pobjede 30, (035) 448 594. Regional: Petra Krešimira IV 2, (035) 408 393. 🎉 Brodsko kolo: folk festival (mid-Jun). 🌐 tzgsb.hr

Built on the site of the Roman town Marsonia, this town was placed so as to monitor the traffic on the river Sava, the border with Bosnia-Herzegovina. The town

Baroque altar in Holy Trinity Church in Slavonski Brod

belonged to the counts Berislavić-Grabarski from the Middle Ages to 1526 when it was conquered by the Turks, who occupied it until 1691.

To defend the border, in 1741 the Viennese government built a fort with barracks, residences for governors and religious buildings. Damaged during World War II and again in the war in 1991, the buildings are under repair: some are used as schools and others house museums and galleries.

The town has grown beyond the original ramparts. Along the banks of the Sava is a **Franciscan Monastery**, dating from 1725, which has been renovated, and the Baroque Church of the **Holy Trinity** (Sv. Trojstvo) with many statues, paintings and altars.

The **Regional Civic Museum** (Muzej Brodskog Posavlja) contains historic documents and archaeological, geological and ethnological finds from the region.

The well-known Croatian writer Ivana Brlić-Mažuranić (1874–1938) spent much of her life in this town. She wrote fairytales for children: among her most famous works are *Fisherman Palunco, Jagor* and *The Forest of Stribor*. The town is also known for its folklore festival (Brodsko kolo) held in June.

🏛 Regional Civic Museum
Ulica Ante Starčevića 40. **Tel** (035) 447 415. **Open** 10am–1pm, 5–8pm Mon–Fri, 10am–1pm Sun. **Closed** Sat & 25 Dec, 1 Jan. 📷 (by appt). 📷 (without flash). 🌐 muzejbp.hr

The cloisters of the Franciscan monastery at Slavonski Brod

View of the 19th-century red-brick Cathedral of St Peter in Đakovo

❼ Vrpolje

Map F3. 🚹 2,200. ✈ Osijek, 39 km (24 miles). 🚌 from Osijek. 🛈 Regional: Petra Krešimira IV, 2, Slavonski Brod (035) 408 393.

A small country town, Vrpolje is known as the birthplace of the sculptor Ivan Meštrović (1883–1962) *(see p163)*. Many of the artist's works, donated to the town held in great affection, can be seen here. In the small parish Church of **St John the Baptist** (Sveti Ivan Krstitelj, 1774) is his statue of St John the Baptist, a relief and a crucifix, while outside is a striking *Bust of a Woman*. The **Ivan Meštrović Gallery** (Spomen galerija) has 30 of his works on display: casts, bronzes and wooden sculptures.

Bust of a Woman by Meštrović, Vrpolje

❽ Đakovo

Map F2. 🚹 21,000. ✈ Osijek, 48 km (22 miles). 🚌 (031) 811 360. 🚌 (060) 302 030. 🛈 Kralja Tomislava 3, (031) 812 319. 🎭 Đakovo embroidery, Đakovački vezovi (first week in Jul). 🌐 tzdjakovo.eu

In medieval times this town was known by the name of Civitas Dyaco, and later as Castrum Dyaco. Late in the 13th century it became a bishopric, and its influence extended over most of Slavonia and Bosnia. Conquered and destroyed by the Turks in 1536, it became a Muslim centre and a mosque was built. After Turkish rule, the city was renovated. Only the mosque, at the end of the central avenue, was retained. It was converted into the parish church of All Saints (Svi Sveti) in the 18th century. The central square is dominated by the Cathedral of St Peter (Sv. Petar), built between 1866 and 1882 by Bishop Josip Juraj Strossmayer; the project was the work of the Viennese architects Karl Rösner and Friedrich von Schmidt. The imposing façade is flanked by two 84-m (275-ft) belfries. The interior has frescoes by Maksimilijan and Ljudevit Seitz, sculptures by Ignazio Donegani and Tomas Vodcka, and decorations by Giuseppe Voltolini from the 19th century. The crypt houses the tombs of the bishops Strossmayer and Ivan de Zela. Next to the church is the 18th-century Bishop's Palace, which has an ornate Baroque doorway.

The Festival of Embroidery of Đakovo (Đakovački vezovi) is held at the beginning of July with displays of traditional local costumes, folk dancing and wine tasting.

🏛 Cathedral of St Peter
Strossmayerov trg. Tel (031) 802 200. **Open** 6:30am–noon, 3–7pm daily.

❾ Novi Mikanovci

Map F2. 🚹 700. ✈ Osijek, 50 km (31 miles). 🚊 Stari Mikanovci, 3 km (2 miles). 🛈 (032) 344 034.

The village is famous for the small Romanesque Church of **St Bartholomew** (Sveti Bartol), from the first half of the 13th century, a rare example of architecture from before Turkish rule. The church stands in a cemetery and is called the "Tower of Pisa of Slavonia" because of its leaning bell tower, which appears to be held up by the façade. At the cemetery entrance is a colourful statue of St Bartholomew.

❿ Županja

Map F3. 🚹 14,000. ✈ Osijek, 67 km (41 miles). 🚊 (032) 831 183. 🛈 Veliki kraj 66, (032) 832 711. 🎭 Folklore Festival, Šokačko sijelo (Feb). 🌐 tz-zupanja.hr

On the border with Bosnia-Herzegovina, Županja lies along a wide bend in the Sava River. The area has been inhabited since ancient times; Bronze Age finds have been discovered in a necropolis. One of the first Croat settlements was set up here. After Turkish rule this became one of the military staging posts on the *Vojna krajina* (Military Frontier) *(see p41)* and a trading centre.

The **Frontier House** is a wooden building originally from the early 19th century, used by tax collectors. Damaged during the bombings

Embroidered head-dress in the Ethnographic Museum, Županja

in the 1990s and now restored, it houses the **Ethnographic Museum** (Zavičajni muzej "Stjepan Gruber").

🏛 **Ethnographic Museum**

Savska 3. **Tel** (032) 837 101. **Open** 7am–7pm Mon–Fri, 5–7pm Sat & Sun. 📶 📷 (by appt).

⑪ Vinkovci

Map F2. 🗺 33,000. ✈ Osijek, 43 km (27 miles). 🚃 (032) 308 215. 🚌 (060) 332 233. ℹ Local: Trg bana Josipa Šokčevića 3, (032) 334 653; Regional: Glagoljaška 27, (032) 344 034. 🎭 Roman Days in Vinkovci (May); Autumn in Vinkovci, Vinkovačke jeseni (Sep). 🌐 **tz-vinkovci.hr**

A settlement existed here as far back as 6000 BC; the Romans named it Aurelia Cibalae. It was the birthplace of the Emperors Valens and Valentinian, and a bishop's see from the 4th century. In the Middle Ages it was called Zenthelye, because of the presence of the (now abandoned) Church of **St Elias** (Sv. Ilija). The 12th-century church is one of the oldest monuments in Slavonia.

The **Civic Museum** (Gradski muzej), situated in the former 18th-century Austrian barracks in the main square, holds finds from the Roman necropolis and has a folklore collection. Large Roman sarcophagi are displayed in the museum's lapidarium.

Exhibit in the Civic Museum, Vinkovci

Facing the garden is the church of SS Eusebius and Pollio (Sv. Euzebije i Polion) from 1775, and the Town Hall.

Each September a festival of music and popular traditions is held in the town and groups from all over the country take part. The streets are decorated, stallholders sell local produce, and artists perform.

🏛 **Civic Museum**

Trg bana Šokčevića 16. **Tel** (032) 332 504. **Open** Mar–Jul & Sep–Dec: 9am–3pm Tue & Wed, 9am–7pm Thu & Fri, 9am–1pm Sat; Jan, Feb & Aug: 8am–3pm Mon–Fri. 📷

The Church of St Ivan, next to the fortified walls in Ilok

⑫ Ilok

Map G2. 🗺 6,000. ✈ Osijek, 62 km (38 miles). 🚃 Vukovar, 39 km (24 miles). ℹ Trg Nikole Iločkog 2, (032) 590 020. 🎭 Grape harvest festival (first week in Sep). 🌐 **turizamilok.hr**

Overlooking a wide loop in the River Danube, Ilok is the easternmost city in Croatia and the centre of the region of Srijem, famous since Roman times for its wine. In the late Roman era the city grew in importance and took the name of Cuccium.

In the Middle Ages it was a *castrum* with high walls, towers and fortified buildings. The defences were reinforced in 1365, and the town was given to Nikola Kont, whose family later acquired the title of Counts of Ilok.

Around the middle of the 15th century, the Church and Monastery of **St Ivan Kapistran** (Sv. Ivan Kapistran) were built inside the fort. Ivan Kapistran was a Franciscan who was famous for uniting Christian forces against the Turks and who died here in 1456. When Ilok became a major Turkish administrative and military centre in the 16th century, mosques and baths were added to the fortress.

Both the church and the monastery have been renovated and between them, long stretches of the ancient walls can still be seen. Parts of one of the Turkish baths are still visible.

In 1683, after his role in winning the battle of Vienna, Commander Livio Odescalchi was given the town of Ilok by the Austrian Emperor. In this idyllic setting he built a U-shaped mansion, **Odescalchi Manor**. Today, the mansion houses a restaurant, public offices and the **Civic Museum** (Gradski muzej) with archaeological and ethnographic collections. The wines of Ilok are still produced here in the cellars, among them a dry white wine called Traminac.

⛪ **Church and Monastery of St Ivan Kapistran**

O M Barbarića 4. **Tel** (032) 590 073. **Open** by appt or before Mass.

🏛 **Odescalchi Manor and Civic Museum**

Šetalište oca Mladena Barbarića 5. **Tel** (032) 827 410. **Open** 8am–6pm daily, wine tastings only. Civic Museum: **Open** 9am–6pm Fri, 9am–3pm Tue–Thu, 11am–6pm Sat. 📶 📷 ♿ 🏛 🚭

The mansion built by Commander Livio Odescalchi in Ilok

Tabernacle in the Franciscan monastery in Šarengrad

⑬ Šarengrad

Map G2. 🏛 100. 🛧 Osijek, 53 km (33 miles). 🚍 Vukovar, 30 km (19 miles). 🅹 Regional: Vinkovci, (032) 344 034.

A medieval fort once controlled the heavy traffic along the river Danube at this spot. In the 15th century, Count Ivan Morović added a **Franciscan Monastery**. The fort, however, was destroyed during the war with the Turks and the area remained uninhabited until their departure late in the 17th century.

With the return of the inhabitants, the monks set up a school and collected archaeological items for a museum.

During the break-up of former Yugoslavia between 1991 and 1995, the area was heavily bombed. The church and monastery have since been restored and the statue of St Anthony of Padua has been put back in position. From the hill there are good views of the Danube.

⑭ Vukovar

Map G2. 🏛 28,000. 🛧 Osijek, 33 km (20 miles). 🚍 Priljevo 2. 🚌 from Vinkovci. 🅹 J J Strossmayera 15, (032) 442 889. 🎬 Vukovar Film Festival (end Aug). 🌐 **turizamvukovar.hr**

This Baroque city was once known for its churches, elegant 18th-century buildings, numerous museums and art galleries. However, Vukovar has come to symbolize the war which raged in Slavonia in 1991, when it was bombed by the Serbs and the JNA (Yugoslav People's Army). Many years have been spent restoring the historic Baroque nucleus from the damage it sustained, and work on the town is still ongoing.

Vukovar has a very long history, as evidenced by the famous Dove of Vučedol from 2000 BC. This vessel, found 5 km (3 miles) from Vukovar, is now in the Archaeological Museum in Zagreb (see pp168–9).

The city, at the confluence of the Danube and the river Vuka, was known as Volko, Walk or Wolkov (Vukovo in Croatian) in the Middle Ages. Later it was given to various families: the Horvat, the Gorjanski and the Talovci. Conquered by the Turks, Vukovar became a military garrison and a key trading centre. After liberation from the Turks in 1687, it resumed its role as an advance post of the Christian Catholic world against the Muslim and Orthodox religions.

In 1736, it was given to the Eltz counts, who called the town Vukovar. As the inhabitants were Catholics or of the Orthodox faith, churches were built for both religions, including a Franciscan monastery (1727).

The Dove of Vučedol, symbol of Vukovar

In 1751, the Eltz family built a huge Baroque mansion. It was nationalized after World War II and then housed the **Civic Museum** (Gradski muzej). Badly damaged in 1991, its contents were taken to Novi Sad and Belgrade. In 2001 the collections were returned, and gradually restored. The new permanent exhibits explore not only the rich archaeological history of the area and the development of the city, but also its ethnic heritage and, via a multimedia presentation, the chronology of the recent war. The Catholic Church of SS Philip and James (Sv. Filip i Jakov) and the Orthodox Church of St Nicholas (Sv. Nikolaj) were also badly damaged in 1991.

🏛 **Civic Museum**
Županijska 2. **Tel** (032) 441 270. **Open** 7am–3pm Mon–Fri, Sat & Sun by appt.

⑮ Erdut

Map G2. 🏛 1,500. 🛧 Osijek, 37 km (23 miles). 🚌 from Osijek. 🅹 Regional: Kapucinska 40, Osijek, (031) 214 852.

The town of Erdut gained a place in history when, on 12 November 1995, an agreement between Croatia and Yugoslavia was drawn up here, setting out the return of Slavonia and Baranja to Croatia after almost four years of Serb occupation.

The town occupies an important strategic position overlooking the Danube, and a fortification was erected in Roman times. In the medieval period a **castle** was built. It was damaged by the Turks, but then rebuilt by them. The castle was also used by the Habsburgs. Two towers, one circular and one square, survive from the old castle.

Erdut is also famous for its wine and, moreover, its winery's 75,000-litre, 150-year-old oak barrel, listed in the Guinness Book of Records. The 19th-century Adamović-Cseh Castle is next to the winery.

The circular tower of the medieval castle, Erdut

⑯ Osijek

See pp194–7.

Naive sculpture on show at Ernestinovo

⓱ Ernestinovo

Map F2. 🏔 1,200. ✈ Osijek, 20 km (12 miles). 🚌 from Osijek. ℹ Regional: Kapucinska 40, Osijek, (031) 214 852. 🎨 Open-air exhibition of sculpture (Aug).

For many years, well-known sculptors have been meeting in Ernestinovo to present their work in a summer show. This small village is now famous for its open-air exhibitions. The first exhibition was organized in 1976 by the sculptor Petar Smajić. It took place in exile from 1991 to 1996 and returned to Ernestinovo the following year. Many works of art are displayed and offered for sale in the village galleries. Ernestinovo was badly damaged during the war in the 1990s.

⓲ Kopački Rit Nature Park

See pp198–9.

⓳ Topolje

Map F2. 🏔 200. ✈ Osijek, 46 km (28 miles). 🚉 Beli Manastir, 16 km (10 miles). 🚌 from Osijek. ℹ Regional: Kapucinska 40, Osijek, (031) 214 852.

In 1687, after the victory in Vienna over the Turks, Prince Eugene of Savoy, commander of the Imperial forces, decided to build a church to commemorate the victory in the countryside surrounding Topolje. The location has particular charm as the church is set among trees standing alone among a patchwork of fields of maize and tobacco. The church was sacked, however, and nearly completely destroyed in the conflicts following the break-up of former Yugoslavia. The building is now undergoing extensive restoration although the splendid furnishings have sadly been lost.

Here, as in Darda *(right)*, there are several Hungarian communities, who, together with the Croats, are gradually returning after their exile during the Yugoslav occupation. The Hungarian-style houses with their overhanging roofs add a distinctive character to the area. In the autumn, long strings of chilli peppers can be seen hanging out to dry in the sun.

Environs

Around 10 km (6 miles) east of Topolje is the town of **Batina**. In Roman times this was the site of a fortress on the banks of the River Danube and was known by the name of Ad Militarae. Until the war of 1991, which depopulated this small town set among hills and vineyards, there was a bridge connecting Baranja with Hungary and Vojvodina, but since its destruction, both river and road traffic have stopped.

On one of the small hills near Topolje, a tall monument in

Hungarian-style houses with chilli peppers hanging to dry, Topolje

white stone with a female figure in bronze representing Victory commemorates the fallen of World War II. It is the work of one of the great Croatian artists of the 20th century, Antun Augustinčić *(see p24)*.

Mansion of the Esterházy barons, now the Town Hall of Darda

⓴ Darda

Map F2. 🏔 5,400. ✈ Osijek, 15km (9 miles). 🚌 from Osijek. ℹ Regional: Kapucinska 40, Osijek, (031) 214 852.

An elegant mansion built by the Esterházy barons in the second half of the 18th century, now renovated and used as the Town Hall, is the only evidence of Darda's history. Darda was once a fortified city, represented on 17th-century maps as a large fortress, connected to Osijek by the 8-km (5-mile) bridge of Solimano. Built in 1566 to cross marshland, the bridge was destroyed in 1664 by Nikola Zrinski *(see p181)* to block the Turkish army. On that occasion the city was subsequently devastated.

In the recent war in the 1990s, two 18th-century churches were destroyed: the Catholic church of St John the Baptist (Sv. Ivan Krstitelj) and the Orthodox church of St Michael (Sv. Mihajlo).

Environs

Bilje, 4 km (2 miles) south of Darda, is the site of the information office for the Kopački Rit Nature Park *(see pp198–9)*. It is housed in a palace built by Prince Eugene of Savoy, who was granted the small town of Bilje after the victory in Vienna over the Turks (1687).

⑯ Osijek

The capital of Slavonia sits in the middle of a fertile plain. It is a centre of industry, a university town, and a lively Central European city with wide roads linking three districts: the Fort (Tvrđa), Lower Town (Donji grad) and Upper Town (Gornji grad). The city developed in 1786 when the three areas merged. Due to its position on the River Drava, Osijek has always played a strategic role. In 1809 Emperor Francis I declared it a Royal Free Town (this document is now in the Museum of Slavonia). In 1991, after the declaration of independence by Croatia, the city was bombed for over a year by Yugoslav forces and much of the old centre (Upper Town) was damaged. Liberated in 1995, in 1998 Osijek became part of the Croat state again.

View of the main square in the heart of Tvrđa

Exploring Osijek

The Fort (Tvrđa) is the fortified centre of Osijek. It was constructed in the early 18th century after liberation from the Turks. Fortunately, Tvrđa did not suffer serious damage during the war in the 1990s. As a result it has preserved its Baroque architecture, which is characterized by simple, austere lines, unusual at this time. This lack of ornamentation was due to the fact that the buildings were intended for use by soldiers and office workers.

Facing Trg Sv. Trojstva, the central square of Tvrđa, named after the Holy Trinity, are various Baroque buildings, including the Building of the Guard, with an 18th-century clock tower, and the General Headquarters of Slavonia, which is now part of the university, and recognizable by its monumental Baroque entrance.

The heart of city life is the main square in the Upper Town, Trg Ante Starčevića, with its shops,

bars and restaurants. Facing the square is the County building, built in the early 20th century in the Renaissance style.

▥ Museum of Slavonia
Muzej Slavonije

Trg sv. Trojstva 6, Tvrđa. **Tel** (031) 250 730. **Open** 9am–7pm Tue–Fri (to 8pm Thu, to 10pm in summer), 10am–2pm Sat & Sun. 🅿️ ♿ 🎥 📷 🏛 **w** mso.hr

On Tvrđa central square, the old Town Hall has housed the Museum of Slavonia since 1946. Geological, prehistoric, Greek, Illyrian and Roman objects are on display here. One section is dedicated to ancient Roman Mursa with statues, tombstones, architectural pieces and a coin collection. Other sections are dedicated to folklore with exhibits of richly decorated costumes. Today these clothes provide models for a flourishing handicrafts industry making golden silk fabrics.

🏛 Church of the Holy Cross
Sv. Križ

Franjevačka ulica, Tvrđa. **Tel** (031) 208 177. **Open** 8am–noon, 3–8pm.

Northeast of the main square, on the site of a sacred medieval building, stands the Church of the Holy Cross, built by the Franciscans between 1709 and 1720. Next to this is the monastery (1699–1767) which housed the first printing press in Slavonia (1735), and from the mid-18th century also housed schools of philosophy and theology. In the church is a statue of the Virgin from the 15th century and some liturgical furnishings.

🏛 Church of St Michael
Sv. Mihovil

Trg Jurja Križanića, Tvrđa. **Tel** (031) 208 990. **Open** before Mass.

Standing a little way back from the square is the Church of St Michael, which was built by the Jesuits. The façade is flanked by two bell towers, and the monastery has a splendid doorway (1719). Below street level the foundations of the 16th-century Kasim-paša mosque are still visible.

War memorial in Kralja Držislava park

🚏 Europe Avenue
Europska avenija

This is the main road of Osijek, linking the Fort (Tvrđa) to the Upper Town (Gornji grad). It crosses some of the city's parks, one of which is Kralja Držislava park, site of a striking bronze memorial to the fallen of the 78th Infantry Regiment (Soldier in the Throes of Death), by Robert Frangeš-Mihanović (1894), which is regarded as the first modern sculpture in Croatia.

Interior of the Neo-Gothic Church of SS. Peter and Paul

🏛 Museum of Fine Arts
Muzej likovnih umjetnosti
Europska avenija 9. **Tel** (031) 251 280.
Open Jul & Aug: 10am–6pm Mon–Fri
(to 8pm Thu); Sep–Jun: 10am–6pm
Tue–Fri (to 8pm Thu); 10am–1pm Sat
& Sun. 🖼 🎫 by appt. 📷 📱
🌐 mlu.hr

The Museum of Fine Arts,
founded in 1954, is housed in
an elegant 19th-century house.
It has collections of paintings
from the 18th and 19th
centuries, as well as works by
contemporary Croatian artists.
There is also a section dedicated
to the Osijek School.

🏛 Church and Monastery of St James
Sv. Jakov
Kapucinska ulica 41, Gornji grad.
Tel (031) 201 182. **Open** 6:30am–
noon, 4–8pm & by appt.

The oldest building in Upper
Town is the Church of St James
(1702–27), with a Capuchin
monastery. In the sacristy are
mid-18th-century paintings
about the life of St Francis.

🏛 Church of SS Peter and Paul
Sv. Petar i Pavao
Trg Marina Držica, Gornji grad.
Tel (031) 310 020. **Open** 2–6:30pm
Mon, 9am–6:30pm Tue–Fri.

This imposing Neo-Gothic
church is dedicated to
St Peter and St Paul. The
church is known as "katedrala"
(cathedral) by the locals
because of its size: the façade
has towers 90 m (295 ft) high.
It was designed by Franz
Langenberg and built in the
late 19th century. The 40
stained-glass windows and
some of the sculptures are
by the Viennese artist Eduard
Hauser. Most of the windows
were bomb-damaged but
have been restored.

VISITORS' CHECKLIST

Practical Information
Map F2. 🗺 90,000. 🛈 Local:
Županijska 2, (031) 203 755;
Regional: Kapucinska 40 (031) 214
852. 🎉 City day (2 Dec), Summer
Nights of Osijek (Jun–Aug).
🌐 tzosijek.hr

Transport
✈ 20 km (12 miles) Vukovarska
67, (060) 339 339. 🚌 Bartola
Kašića, (060) 334 466. 🚆 Trg
Ružičke, (031) 205 155.

🎭 Croatian National Theatre
Hrvatsko narodno kazalište
Županijska ulica 9, Gornji grad.
Tel (031) 220 700.

The Croatian National Theatre
was built in the Moorish style in
the 19th century. Opera and
drama productions are put on
from September to June.

Interior of the Croatian National Theatre

Osijek City Centre
① Museum of Slavonia
② Church of the Holy Cross
③ Church of St Michael
④ Europe Avenue
⑤ Museum of Fine Arts
⑥ Church of St James
⑦ Church of SS Peter and Paul
⑧ Croatian National Theatre

Key

▨ Street-by-street pp196–7

0 metres   500
0 yards   500

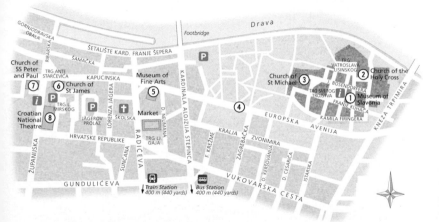

Street-by-Street: the Fort (Tvrđa)

The fortified centre of Osijek (Tvrđa) was built on the site of the Roman settlement of Mursa, which, in 131 AD, became the capital of Lower Pannonia with the name of Colonia Aelia Mursa. Destroyed by the Avars and rebuilt by the Croats, it remained a military and administrative centre until it was attacked and burned by the Turks in 1526. Making the most of the strategic position, the Turks rebuilt the fort and, under Suleyman II, also constructed a bridge across the Drava. After the expulsion of the Turks in 1687, the Austrian Emperor destroyed the mosques and other reminders of Turkish rule. He then built a fortified series of buildings, more like a city than a fort. Tvrđa now houses the Town Hall, the university faculties, and the Museum of Slavonia. The only remaining part of the ramparts is towards the river Drava and includes the Water Gate (Vodena Vrata).

★ Church of St Michael
Constructed by Jesuits in the first half of the 18th century, the church has a Baroque façade flanked by two towers.

Building of the Guard
On the western side of the square stands the Building of the Guard, with a clock tower from the 18th century. It now houses the Archaeological Museum.

Croatian Academy of Science and Arts

Key

 Suggested route

Plague Column
The centre of the square is dominated by the "column of the plague", erected in 1729 in thanks for the ending of an outbreak of the disease.

TRG J. KRIŽANIĆA

FRANJE KUHAČA

PINTEROVIĆ

KAMILA FIRINGERA

MARKOVIĆA

KAMILA FIRINGER

BOSKO

TR SVET TROJS

Church and Monastery of the Holy Cross
The church, erected by Franciscans between 1709 and 1720, is next to the monastery which housed the first printing press in Slavonia.

View of Osijek and the River Drava
Splendid views of the city can be enjoyed from the banks of the Drava. It was once important for river trading, but trade is now practically non-existent.

0 metres 100
0 yards 100

TRG VATROSLAVA LISINSKOG

TANČIĆA

BOSENDORFERA

FRANJEVAČKA

FRANJE KUHAČA

JEVAČKA

FAKULTETSKA

JAGIĆA

KNEZA TRPIMIRA

Darda
(see p193)

Đakovo
(see p190)

★ Museum of Slavonia
This museum contains interesting collections of geological, prehistoric, Greek, Illyrian and Roman material.

Headquarters of Slavonia
On the northern side of the main square of Tvrđa is the former Headquarters of Slavonia, now the University Rectorate, easily recognized by the imposing façade.

⓲ Kopački Rit Nature Park

Park prirode Kopački rit

This triangular piece of land is bordered by the final stretch of the river Drava before it meets the Danube. The landscape changes with the seasons and becomes flooded when the Danube overflows. The area covers 177 sq km (68 sq miles) and can turn into an immense wetland marsh. At other times it is a vast grassland plain with pools and ponds. There are also dry areas which support enormous willows and tall oak trees. A nature reserve since 1967, it has a rich and varied fauna and for many months of the year provides a sanctuary for hundreds of different species of bird, both migratory and domestic. A high embankment on the western side stops the further spread of the flood waters. On top is a road which allows cars to cross this part of the park.

White Storks
One of the park's symbols, the white stork is especially visible in the breeding season.

Park Entrance
The main entrance to the Kopački Rit Park is in the village of Bilje *(see p193)*.

Osijek

Sakadaš Canal

Sarvaška Pond

0 kilometres 2
0 miles 2

Black Storks are rare; only a few dozen pairs of the bird inhabit the park.

Drava

Drava

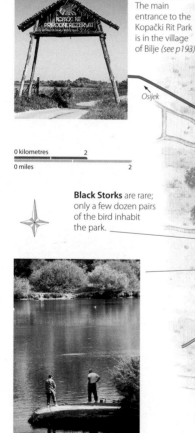

Lakes
Forty different species of fish live in the lakes and ponds which form in the park.

White-Tailed Eagle
The many birds of prey maintain a balance among the bird population. The white-tailed eagle is the rarest eagle in Europe.

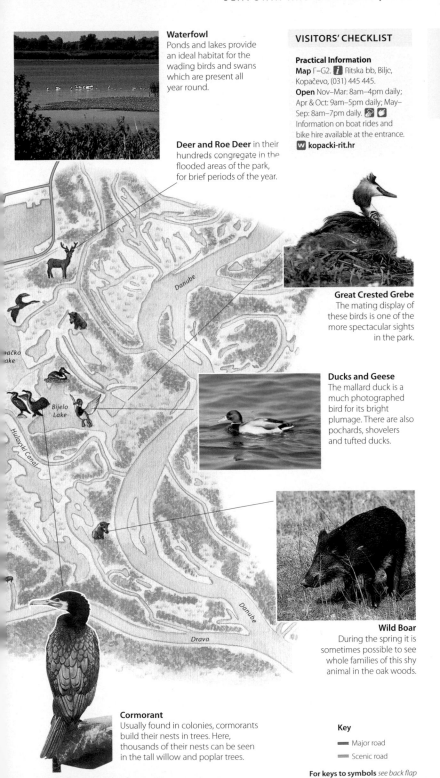

Waterfowl
Ponds and lakes provide an ideal habitat for the wading birds and swans which are present all year round.

Deer and Roe Deer in their hundreds congregate in the flooded areas of the park, for brief periods of the year.

VISITORS' CHECKLIST

Practical Information
Map Γ–G2. ℹ Ritska bb, Bilje, Kopačevo, (031) 445 445.
Open Nov–Mar: 8am–4pm daily; Apr & Oct: 9am–5pm daily; May–Sep: 8am–7pm daily. 🚲 📷
Information on boat rides and bike hire available at the entrance.
🌐 **kopacki-rit.hr**

Great Crested Grebe
The mating display of these birds is one of the more spectacular sights in the park.

Ducks and Geese
The mallard duck is a much photographed bird for its bright plumage. There are also pochards, shovelers and tufted ducks.

Wild Boar
During the spring it is sometimes possible to see whole families of this shy animal in the oak woods.

Cormorant
Usually found in colonies, cormorants build their nests in trees. Here, thousands of their nests can be seen in the tall willow and poplar trees.

Key

━ Major road

━ Scenic road

For keys to symbols *see back flap*

Thermal spa in the village of Bizovac

㉑ Bizovac

Map F2. 🏔 2,300. ✈ Osijek, 20 km (12 miles). 🚈 from Osijek. 🚌 from Osijek. ℹ Regional: Kapucinska 40, Osijek, (031) 214 852.
🆆 **tz-virovitica.hr**

During the search for oil in the middle of the 20th century, a hot water spring was discovered here. The water of the spring reaches a temperature of 90°C (194°F) and is rich in minerals. A few years later, the thermal spa of **Bizovačke toplice** was built. The spa proved to be extremely successful and it is now an enormous complex including a hotel, two large swimming pools, and cabins for thermal baths. Every day hundreds of guests come here to undergo thermal treatments which are helpful in treating rheumatic and respiratory illnesses, and in healing injuries.

The small centre of Bizovac is also well known in Slavonia for its exquisite gold and silver embroidery. The work is carried out by the young women of the area, usually to a commission.

🔵 **Bizovačke toplice**
Sunčana 39. **Tel** (031) 685 100.
🆆 **bizovacke-toplice.hr**

Environs
Around 9 km (5 miles) south of Bizovac is the village of **Brođanci**, famous for the Olympics of Ancient Sports, held here in August every year. During the competition, athletes take part in some of the sports once practised by the peasants of Slavonia,

such as tug-of-war, boulder-throwing, bare-back riding and other strenuous challenges and competitions.

A lively popular festival has developed around the event; musicians perform in the streets and there are displays of old crafts. Local handicrafts can be bought and regional food can be sampled.

㉒ Valpovo

Map F2. 🏔 8,000. ✈ Osijek, 30 km (18 miles). 🚌 (060) 390 060. ℹ Trg kralja Tomislava 2, (031) 650 306.
📅 Summer in Valpovo: dancing, folk music and theatrical shows (summer).
🆆 **tz-valpovo.hr**

The centre of Valpovo stands on the remains of the fort of Lovallia, one of many fortified settlements which the Romans established on the Pannonian plain. In the Middle Ages, a castle was erected to keep a look-out over the nearby Drava river. The castle was later granted to the Morović, Gorjanski and Norman families. After the Turkish conquest in 1526, the castle was used as a garrison.

In 1687, after the expulsion of the Turks, the area was handed over to the Hilleprand Prandau family. At the beginning of the 19th century the castle was destroyed by fire and was then extensively rebuilt as a larger building, which today houses the **Valpovo Museum** (Muzej Valpovštine). The museum contains period furniture and interesting archaeological finds. The complex stands in a large

The imposing castle at Valpovo, now a museum

park and a moat surrounds the medieval walls, the tower, the new building and the church. A town developed around the fort, and with it the splendid Baroque church of the **Immaculate Conception** (Začeće Marijino) of 1722.

🏛 **Valpovo Museum**
Dvorac Prandau-Normann. **Tel** (031) 650 639. **Open** 4–7pm (8pm in summer) Mon & Thu, 10am–noon Tue, Wed & Fri, 3–6pm Sat.

Majláth, a mock-medieval manor in the town of Donji Miholjac

㉓ Donji Miholjac

Map F2. 🏔 6,700. ✈ Osijek, 45 km (28 miles). 🚈 Valpovo, 20 km (12 miles); Našice, 30 km (18 miles). 🚌 (060) 357 060. ℹ Trg Ante Starčevića 2, (031) 633 103. 📅 Miholjačko sijelo: festival in costume (summer). 🆆 **tz-donjimiholjac.hr**

On the banks of the Drava river, this small town lies on the Hungarian border. All traces of the past have been erased, except for the Church of **St Michael** (Sv. Mihovil). The mock-medieval **Majláth Manor** was built at the beginning of the 20th century by the Majláth family. It has pinnacles and a tall tower on the façade. The manor is now the Town Hall.

🏛 **Majláth Manor**
Vukovarska 1. **Tel** Tourist office (031) 633 103. **Open** by appt. 📷

Environs
About 25 km (15 miles) west is the village of **Čađavica**. Traces from ancient Croatian settlements have been discovered near here. The Romanesque church of St Peter was used by the Turks as a mosque and was renovated in the 18th century.

❷❹ Našice

Map F2. ⛰ 8,500. ✈ Osijek, 42 km (26 miles). 🚃 (060) 333 444. 🚌 (060) 334 030. ℹ Pejačevićev trg 4, (031) 614 951. 🅦 **tznasice.hr**

A small plateau is the setting for the town of Našice, which is surrounded by vineyards and woods. Built on the site of an ancient settlement, it was referred to in the first half of the 13th century under the name of Nekche, as property of the Knights Templar. After the dissolution of this order in 1312, it passed to the Gorjanski nobles and, later, through marriage to the counts of Ilok, before falling into the hands of the Turkish forces in 1532.

After the expulsion of the Turks, Našice's fortunes changed. The Franciscans returned and restored the Church of **St Anthony of Padua** (Sv. Antun Padovanski). They also rebuilt their monastery, which had been founded here at the start of the 14th century. Both needed repairing after war damage suffered in 1991.

A short distance away is a large manor house, built at the beginning of the 19th century in Neo-Classical style by the Pejačević family, where the musician Dora Pejačević (1885–1923) lived. Situated in a large park, the two-storey building has been restored. This building is now the **Civic Museum**.

🏛 **Civic Museum**
Pejačevićev trg 5. **Tel** (031) 613 414. **Open** 8am–3pm Mon–Fri; 9am–noon Sat. 🅿 📷 (by appt). ✉ 🅦 **zmn.hr**

❷❺ Orahovica

Map F2. ⛰ 4,300. ✈ Osijek, 62 km (38 miles). 🚃 (033) 646 079. 🚌 (033) 673 231. ℹ Trg sv. Florijana bb, (033) 673 540. 🎭 Spring in Orahovica: folklore event (Jun). 🅦 **tzgorahovica.hr**

The town of Orahovica is well known in Croatia for its wines. It was a feudal estate in 1228, and later a Turkish garrison, acquiring its present-day look in the 18th century.

On one of the hills around the town stand the ruins of **Rosetta** (Ružica grad), one of the largest of Croatia's medieval forts. The walls were 9m (29 ft) thick and enclosed military buildings, a church, and the governor's residence. The complex was so large it was often referred to as a city.

The Turks burnt down the fort, then partially restored it and used it as a military garrison. Liberated in 1690, the fort was once again used for defence, and a village, inhabited by Serbs, developed around its base.

Environs
Along the road to Kutjevo, 5 km (3 miles) south of Orahovica, near the village of Duzluk, is the Orthodox Monastery of St Nicholas (Manastir Sv. Nikola), which has ancient frescoes and illuminated manuscripts. Some 30 km (18 miles) from Orahovica, following the road to Virovitica, then turning left for Čeralije, is **Voćin**, a small village where the destruction caused by the war in 1991 is still evident. The village lies at the foot of a large castle built in the second half of the 13th century by the Aba counts. Today, the houses in Voćin are in ruins. All that remains of the Church of **St Mary** (Sv. Marija), which was built by King John Corvinus in the first half of the 15th century, is part of the apse wall.

Ornate altar in the Baroque church of St Roch, Virovitica

❷❻ Virovitica

Map E2. ⛰ 16,000. ✈ Osijek, 89 km (55 miles). 🚃 Ulica Stjepana Radića, (033) 730 121. 🚌 Trg fra. B. Gerbera 1, (033) 721 113. ℹ Trg Kralja Tomislava 1, (033) 721 241. 🎭 Day of the City (16 Aug). 🅦 **tz-virovitica.hr**

Documents from the end of the first millennium give the town its Hungarian name of Wereuche. It was declared a free town by King Bela IV in 1234 and it developed into an agricultural and trading centre. Later occupied by the Turks, it remained under their rule until 1684. When it later flourished, all Ottoman traces were destroyed.

The Baroque Church of **St Roch** (Sv. Rok), decorated by the sculptor Holzinger and the painter Göbler, dates from the 18th century. On the site of the ancient Wasserburg Castle stands the imposing **Pejačević Manor** (1800–4), now the **Civic Museum** (Gradski muzej) with archaeological and folklore collections and an art gallery.

🏛 **Civic Museum**
Dvorac Pejačević, Trg bana Jelačića 23. **Tel** (033) 722 127. **Open** 8am–3pm Mon, Fri; 8am–7pm Tue–Thu; 10am–1pm Sat. 🅿 📷 (by appt). ✉ 🅦 **muzejvirovitica.hr**

The Church of St Anthony of Padua in Našice

THE NORTHERN COUNTIES

The landscape in this part of Croatia is made up of a variety of elements: the rolling hills of Zagorje with their therapeutic spring waters and thermal spas; the county of Međimurje, which is famous for its wines; the cities of Varaždin and Čakovec, which developed around ancient castles; Koprivnica, surrounded by lush countryside and vineyards, and Bjelovar and Križevci with their palaces.

The principal towns in the area have ancient origins and two, Varaždin and Križevci, were also at various times the seat of the Sabor, the Croatian Parliament. Bjelovar is the most recent and largest city-fortress in the country. Even before the 1991 war which affected the south of this area, the wars of the second half of the 18th century had already destroyed all evidence of the Middle Ages and Turkish occupation. However, there are many religious buildings in the area, including a number of Catholic Franciscan and Pauline monasteries in places once inhabited by Orthodox communities. Religious life is still very active here and church buildings are cherished.

The high hills of Zagorje are covered in forests, broken up only by the clearings created for imposing medieval castles, many of which have since been transformed into sumptuous Baroque residences. In Podravina, drained by the River Drava, which in some parts flows along the Hungarian border, the hills are lower and are characterized by vineyards and sparse woodland.

This part of Croatia has preserved all kinds of ancient customs and traditions, a source of inspiration for the Naive art movement. The home of Naive art is Hlebine, where artists such as Ivan Generalić encouraged and fostered the talent of local amateur painters.

Stacks of maize in the countryside between Belec and Marija Bistrica

◄ The Black Madonna of Marija Bistrica, visited by pilgrims in their thousands

Exploring the Northern Counties

This is an area of good, fertile agricultural land and the lush countryside produces an abundance of maize, tobacco and sunflowers. The hillsides are covered in vineyards as far as the eye can see and yield wines, good whites in particular, which can be bought along the Wine Road, from wineries or in the village shops. Despite these attractions, the region does not see a great deal of international tourism. This is particularly true of Međimurje, the valley crossed by the River Mura, granted to Croatia after World War I. Part of the population here is of Hungarian origin and the people have preserved their Hungarian customs and traditions.

A side chapel of St Mary of the Snows, Marija Bistrica

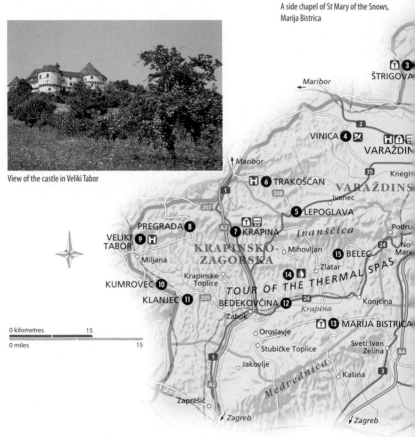

View of the castle in Veliki Tabor

0 kilometres 15
0 miles 15

Sights at a Glance

1. Varaždin pp206–7
2. Čakovec
3. Štrigova
4. Vinica
5. Lepoglava
6. Trakošćan
7. Krapina
8. Pregrada
9. Veliki Tabor
10. Kumrovec
11. Klanjec
12. Bedekovčina
13. Marija Bistrica
15. Belec
16. Varaždinske Toplice
17. Ludbreg
18. Koprivnica
19. Đurđevac
20. Bjelovar
21. Križevci

Tour

14. Tour of the Thermal Spas pp216–17

For hotels and restaurants see p231 and pp248–9

Getting Around

Motorways connect Zagreb to Maribor in Slovenia, passing through Krapina, and serve Varaždin en route for Hungary. Cars still use state roads which run more or less parallel to the two motorways. State road 2 goes from the Slovenian border, northwest of Varaždin, and continues on towards Osijek. A railway line runs alongside state road 3 and at Varaždin interconnects with railway lines from Zagreb, Slovenia and Hungary. There are also train connections to Slovenia and Hungary from Čakovec and Koprivnica stations.

Locator Map

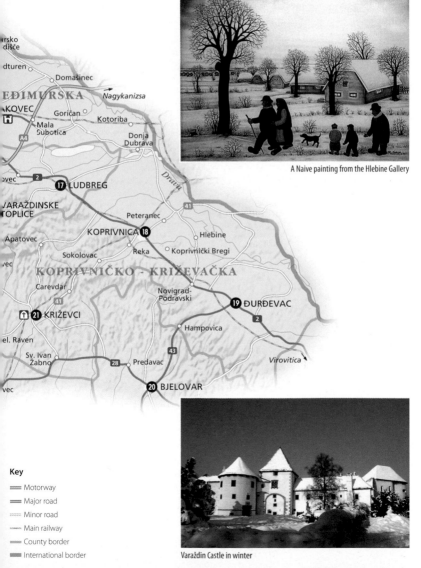

A Naive painting from the Hlebine Gallery

Key

═══ Motorway

─── Major road

⋯⋯ Minor road

⌐⌐ Main railway

━━━ County border

━━━ International border

Varaždin Castle in winter

For keys to symbols see back flap

❶ Varaždin

Traces of occupation from the Neolithic age, the La Tene civilization and the Roman period have been found around Varaždin castle. Despite this, the first mention of the town is found in a document from 1181, when King Bela III confirmed the rights of the Zagreb Curia to the thermal spas in the area. In 1209, it was declared a free town by King Andrew II and it began to develop as a trading centre. In the late 14th century it passed into the hands of the counts of Celjski, followed by the counts of Frankopan, Brandenburg and Erdödy. In 1446, it was destroyed in a fire and in 1527 the Turks attacked. In 1776 another fire destroyed the houses, but the Baroque buildings for which the town is famous were fortunately spared.

Aerial view of the castle, today home to the Civic Museum

🏛 Castle and Civic Museum
Stari grad & Gradski muzej
Strossmayerovo šetalište 7. **Tel** (042) 658 754. **Open** 9am–5pm Tue–Fri, 9am–1pm Sat & Sun. 🅿 📷 ✉

It is unknown when exactly this castle was built, though some documents suggest it dates back to the 12th century. It was built over the ruins of an observation tower and, in the 15th century, two round towers were added. The castle was rebuilt in 1560 by the Italian architect Domenico dell'Allio, who created a Renaissance structure on two floors with arcades and corridors facing courtyards.

The castle's present look dates from the time of the Erdödy counts, who added the bastions and a moat. It is now the Civic Museum, which has collections of weapons, porcelain, furniture, handicrafts, and a pharmacy from the 18th century. Remains of the wall and the Lisak tower, to the east of the castle, are the only evidence remaining of the ancient walls that existed at this site.

🖼 Gallery of Old and Modern Masters
Galerija starih i novih majstora
Stančićev trg 3. **Tel** (042) 214 172. **Open** 9am–5pm Tue–Fri, 9am–1pm Sat & Sun. 🅿 📷 by appt. ✉

The gallery has a large collection of works by artists from all over Europe, particularly landscapes by Flemish and Italian artists, and portraits by German and Dutch painters.

🏛 Tomislav Square
Trg kralja Tomislava
Town Hall (Gradska vijećnica): Trg kralja Tomislava 1. **Tel** (042) 402 508. **Open** by appt. Drašković Palace (Palača Drašković): Trg kralja Tomislava 3. **Closed** to the public.

This square is the heart of the town. Facing the square is the **Town Hall** (Gradska vijećnica), one of the oldest buildings in Varaždin. Built in the Gothic style in the 15th century, it has since been altered and a clock tower added. It has been the Town Hall since 1523, when Prince George of Brandenburg gave it to the city. It is guarded in summer by the Purgers, who

wear richly decorated blue uniforms and bearskin hats.

To the east of the square stands **Drašković Palace** (Palača Drašković), built in the late 17th century with a Rococo façade. The Croat Parliament met here in 1756–76. Opposite stands the Renaissance Ritz House, one of the oldest in the town, as evidenced by the date (1540) engraved on the doorway.

⛪ Cathedral of the Assumption
Uznesenja Marijina
Pavlinska ulica 4. **Tel** (042) 210 688. **Open** 9:30am–12:30pm, 4–7pm daily.

The Church of the Assumption became a cathedral in 1997. Both the church and the annexed monastery were built in the first half of the 17th century by the Jesuits. Later, the Pauline order moved in.

The cathedral's tall façade is enlivened by pillars. The interior is a triumph of the Baroque. The main altar occupies the width of the central nave and has gilded columns, stuccoes and engravings. At the centre of the altar is an *Assumption of the Virgin*, reminiscent of Titian's work in Venice. Evenings of Baroque music concerts are held here.

The rich Baroque altar in the Cathedral of the Assumption

🏛 Church of St John the Baptist
Sv. Ivan Krstitelj
Franjevački trg 8. **Tel** (042) 213 166. **Open** 8:30am–noon, 5:30–7pm daily.

The church was built in 1650 in the Baroque style on the site of a 13th-century church. The façade has a Renaissance doorway with a tympanum and

The bell tower of St John the Baptist in Tomislav Square

two statues of St Francis of Assisi and St Anthony of Padua. The interior has eight side chapels and an ornate gilded pulpit from the late 17th century. The bell tower is 54 m (177 ft) high.

In front of the church is one of the copies of the *Monument of Bishop Gregory of Nin* by Ivan Meštrović. The adjacent pharmacy has many works of art, among them some allegorical frescoes by Ivan Ranger *(see p210)*.

🏛 Hercer Palace
Palača Hercer

Franjevački trg 6. **Open** 9am–5pm Tue–Fri, 9am–1pm Sat & Sun. Entomological Museum: **Tel** (042) 658 760. **Open** same opening times as the palace. 🌀 🟢

Built at the end of the 18th century (the founders' coat of arms is on the door), the palace has housed the well-organized **Entomological Section of the Civic Museum** (Entomološki odjel Gradskog muzeja) since 1954. The museum was founded thanks to the entomologist Franjo Košćec (1882–1968), who, in 1959, donated his natural history collection to the city. From 1962 to 1980 his work was carried on by his daughter Ružica, a biologist. As well as thousands of insects, the museum also has a herbarium. From time to time, temporary exhibitions on a variety of themes are organized.

⛪ Church of the Holy Trinity
Sv. Trojstvo

Kapucinski trg 7. **Tel** (042) 213 550. **Open** 9am–noon, 6–7pm Mon–Sat, Sun before and after mass.

The church dates from the early 18th century and houses numerous Baroque paintings,

VISITORS' CHECKLIST

Practical Information
Map D1. 🗺 42,0 00. ℹ Local: Ivana Padovca 3, (042) 210 987; Regional: Uska 4, (042) 210 096. 🎭 Baroque evenings, Varaždin, (Sep–Oct); Gastrolov (Oct).
🌐 **tourism-varazdin.hr**

Transport
🚉 Frane Supila, (042) 210 444.
🚌 Kolodvorska 17, (060) 333 555.

furnishings by local masters, and an organ with figures of angels playing instruments.

The neighbouring monastery, from the same period, is famous for its library of parchments, incunabula and manuscripts, and some of the oldest documents in ancient Croatian *(kajkavski)*.

🏛 National Theatre
Narodno kazalište

Ulica Augusta Cesarca 1. **Tel** (042) 214 688. **Open** for performances only.

Built by Hermann Helmer in 1873, this is one of the main cultural centres in the city. During the summer and autumn, theatregoers from all over Europe come to attend performances.

Varaždin Town Centre

1. Castle and Civic Museum
2. Gallery of Old and Modern Masters
3. Tomislav Square
4. Cathedral of the Assumption
5. Church of St John the Baptist
6. Hercer Palace
7. Church of the Holy Trinity
8. National Theatre

0 metres 200
0 yards 200

Vineyards in the countryside around Čakovec

❷ Čakovec

Map D1. ⛰ 16,000. ☒ (040) 384 333. ☒ Masarykova ulica, (040) 313 947. ℹ Local: Kralja Tomislava 1, (040) 313 319. Regional: Ruđera Boškovića 2, (040) 374 064. 🎭 Carnival in Međimurje (Feb); The Town of Čakovec Day. 🆆 **tourism-cakovec.hr**

In the second half of the 13th century, on a site once inhabited by Romans, Count Demetrius Chaky, a magistrate at the court of King Bela IV, built a tower here which was called Chaktornya. In the following century, the main defensive structure in Međimurje was built around the tower. In 1547 Emperor Ferdinand gave it to the Ban (governor) of Croatia, Nikola Zrinski *(see p181)*, together with a large estate, as a reward for the victory against the Turks and to settle a debt. Nikola Zrinski died heroically

while fighting against the Ottomans in defending Siget, and became a national hero. On 29 May 1579, one of his successors, a member of the Zrinski family of Siget, guaranteed tax privileges to whoever went to live in the city that was developing around the fort. This date is considered the founding of the city and is celebrated with a festival. Bastions and a moat were added in this period as defence against cannon fire. Inside the walls, a four-storey palace was built around a square courtyard.

In 1671 Petar Zrinski led a plot to separate Croatia from the Kingdom of Hungary. The plot was discovered and Zrinski and his co-conspirator Fran Krsto Frankopan were beheaded on 30 April 1671. Čakovec then came under the direct rule of the Emperor.

The Renaissance **Old Castle**, of which only the first floor remains, and the Baroque **New Castle** with a rectangular plan, face each other inside the medieval walls. For a long time the Old Castle was used as a prison. It is now being restored and is to be used in future for cultural activities. The church has been reopened for worship.

The **Međimurje Civic Museum** of Čakovec has on display exhibits of prehistoric material, many Roman finds, and ethnographic collections. There is also an exhibition dedicated to the local composer, J Slavenski (1896–1955), who was known for his love of the traditional music of the region.

Čakovec is the main administrative centre of the Međimurje, a frontier region which borders Slovenia and Hungary. The land in the western part of the region is hilly with broad valleys, and is renowned for its wines, while the fertile plains of the eastern part produce cereal crops.

🏛 **Međimurje Civic Museum** Trg Republike 5. **Tel** (040) 313 499. **Open** 8am–3pm Mon–Fri; 10am–1pm Sat & Sun. 🅿 🖪 ♿ 🖼

Environs
In the village of Šenkovec, 2 km (1 mile) from Čakovec, stands the Church of **St Helen** (Sv. Jelena). What little remains of its

The Old and New Castles of Čakovec

original Gothic form has been integrated into an overall Baroque appearance. The church is all that survives of the monastery founded by the Paulines in 1376. It has been rebuilt at various times, firstly after a Protestant revolt, then because of a fire and finally after an earthquake.

Inside the church are the tombstones of the powerful Zrinski family, the lords of Čakovec: that of Nikola Zrinski and his wife Catherine Frankopan, and also that of Petar Zrinski.

The church also contains a number of tombs of members of the Knežević family, who became the successors to the Zrinskis.

Fresco on the door of the church of St Jerome, Štrigova

One of the frescoes decorating the church of St Helen, Čakovec

❸ Štrigova

Map D1. 🅼 450. 🚆 from Čakovec. 🚌 from Čakovec. 🚹 Štrigova 29, (040) 851 325. 🆆 **strigova.info**

Numerous finds of Roman origin have been discovered here, leading historians to believe that this village was built on the site of the Roman city of Stridon, the birthplace of St Jerome.

The counts of Štrigovčak lived here, but their castle was destroyed during a raid by the Turks. Nearby, the Bannfy counts also built a castle, which was transformed into a palace in the

17th century. At one time the palace was famous for its rich furnishings, its art collections, and for the fact that the Hungarian king, Matthias Corvinus, was often a guest here.

The Church of **St Jerome** (Sv. Jerolim) stands on a hill at the edge of the village. Restoration has uncovered the frescoes above the doorway and in the niches on the façade, which is flanked by two harmonious bell towers and culminates in a curvilinear tympanum.

In the church are numerous *trompe-l'œil* paintings by the Tyrolean artist Ivan Ranger *(see p210)*, depicting *Angels*, the *Evangelists* and the *Life of St Jerome*. There are also statues representing the fathers of the Church.

❹ Vinica

Map D1. 🅼 1,200. 🚌 from Varaždin. 🚹 Trg Matije Gupca 14, (042) 722 233.

This small town lies at the foot of vine-covered hills. It was first mentioned in documents of 1353 as the site of a medieval fortress. At one time it was known for the large palace built by the Patačić counts on the site of their old castle. The palace is now in ruins, as is that of the

The frescoed façade of the Church of St Jerome, Štrigova

Drašković counts, which was situated in the centre of a large park.

In the late 19th century, Count Marko Bombelles created **Opeka Park**, 2 km (1 mile) south of Vinica. This large arboretum was at that time the only one of its kind in Croatia. Here Bombelles planted exotic trees and plants from around the world, including the Americas, Japan, Tibet and the Caucasus, over an area of flat and hilly ground.

Next to this wonderful park, declared a protected nature reserve in 1961, a school of horticulture has been set up. This school has several glasshouses and a large garden of flowering plants.

🏠 **Opeka Park**
Open at all times.

Spring floral display in Opeka Park, near Vinica

Choir stalls in the Church of St Mary, frescoed by the artist Ivan Ranger

Along with the lace of Pag and of Hvar, it has been entered into UNESCO's list of Intangible Cultural Heritage.

🏠 **Church of St Mary**
Trg 1. hrvatskog sveučilišta 3.
Tel (042) 792 566. **Open** by appt.

❻ Trakošćan

Map D1. 🚌 for Trakošćan.
ℹ️ Trakošćan, (042) 796 281.
🅦 **trakoscan.hr**

The pretty surroundings of the **Castle of Trakošćan**, and its excellent state of conservation, make this one of the most visited tourist sights in Zagorje. The castle was built to guard the road which descends from Ptuj towards the valley of the River Sava. The castle was listed in 1434 as one of the properties granted by Sigismund of Austria to the Count of Celje. It was used for defence purposes until the end of Turkish rule. In 1568 it became the property of the Drašković counts.

❺ Lepoglava

Map D1. 🏛️ 8,500. 🚍 (042) 791 193.
🚌 for Ivanec. ℹ️ Local: Hrvatskih pavlina 7, (042) 494 317; Regional: Ivanec, (042) 784 284. 🎭 International Lace Festival (Sep).
🅦 **lepoglava-info.hr**

A pretty town on the Bednja river, nestled between the forested slopes of two mountain peaks, Lepoglava rose to prominence from 1400, when the Pauline order built a church and monastery here, which gradually became a prominent seat of learning and scholarship. By the mid-17th century the monastery had become one of Croatia's first universities; at around the same time the church, dedicated to **St Mary** (Sv. Marija), was enlarged and embellished. It is a Baroque Gothic building with a richly furnished interior, noted for an organ dating 1649, which still plays, and the magnificent series of frescoes by Ivan Ranger. Also of interest is the pulpit and the altar of St Anne by the Pauline monk and sculptor Aleksije Königer.

In 1854, after the dissolution of the Pauline order, Lepoglava's monastery entered a more notorious period of its history. It was converted into a prison, in which many major Croatian revolutionaries, dissidents and activists of the 20th century were incarcerated, including Josip Broz (Tito), Moša Pijade, Archbishop Alojzije Stepinac

and Franjo Tuđman. However, at the start of the 21st century, a modern penitentiary was built and the monastery buildings were returned to the church.

The Pauline brotherhood may also have been responsible for instigating Lepoglava's other claim to fame: the making of exquisite and intricate lace, a centuries-old tradition and its centuries old Lace School.

Typical lace from Lepoglava

Ivan Ranger (Johannes Baptiste Ranger)

Born in Götzens, near Innsbruck in Austria, in 1700, Ivan Ranger joined the Pauline order at a very early age. Not much is known of his years as an apprentice, but it is certain that he lived for a time in Italy, where he encountered the Baroque style in Venice, Rome, Bologna and Mantua. At the age of 30 he was invited to Lepoglava, then the headquarters of the order, to which he remained loyal until his death in 1753. He also worked in nearby towns and in Slovenia (at the monastery of Olimje and the castle-monastery of Sveti Jernej in Rogatec). In line with Pauline principles, he created a school of fresco painters. With these artists he produced colourful fresco cycles which were full of expression (the trompe-l'œil paintings also reveal great technical skill). His themes were always religious, and he was much imitated.

Fresco painted by the Pauline monk Ivan Ranger

The Castle of Trakošćan, now a museum

During the second half of the 19th century, it was transformed into a splendid Neo-Gothic residence by Juraj Drašković. He also added an artificial lake, a park and gardens, while at the same time preserving some of the military aspects of the castle. It stands on a wooded hilltop and is surrounded by a high wall with a tower, which encircles the imposing palace.

All 32 of the rooms of the castle are now a **museum** where furniture, armoury, vestments and paintings, as well as a rare series of portraits of the Drašković family, are on display.

🎠 Castle and Museum
Tel (042) 796 422. **Open** Apr–Oct: 9am–6pm daily; Nov–Mar: 9am–4pm daily. 🐾 🎫 🎦 🏠

❼ Krapina

Map D1. 🚠 4,500. 🚉 Frana Galovića bb, (049) 328 028. 🚌 A. Starčevića, (049) 315 018. 🛈 Magistratska 28, (049) 371 330. 🎭 Week of music and Kajkaviana culture (Sep).
W tzg-krapina.hr

This town is well known in the scientific field because of the remains of Krapina man, *Homo krapinensis*, who lived in the Palaeolithic age, that were found nearby. The Neanderthal skeleton, discovered in 1899 in a hillside cave, is now in the Archaeological Museum in Zagreb. The **Museum of Krapina Neanderthal Men** is one of the most modern museums in Croatia. Multimedia

presentations and exhibits explore the life and culture of Neanderthal man.

Krapina is first documented in 1193 as the site of a castle, now destroyed, built to guard the river of the same name. After the danger of Turkish attack had passed, it was conceded to the Keglević counts and became an important administrative town.

It also became a religious centre. In the mid-17th century, a Franciscan monastery and the Baroque Church of **St Catherine** were built. The sacristy and some of the monastery rooms are decorated with vivid frescoes by Ivan Ranger.

In one of the town squares is a monument to Ljudevit Gaj, born in Krapina in 1809. During

Bust of Ljudevit Gaj, Krapina

the first half of the 19th century he was a prominent figure in the movement which promoted the revival of Croatian politics and culture.

🏛 Museum of Krapina Neanderthal Men
Šetalište V Sluge bb. **Tel** (049) 371 491.
Open Mar & Oct: 9am–6pm Tue-Sun; Apr–Jun & Sep: 9am–7pm Tue–Sun; Jul & Aug: 9am–6pm Tue–Fri; Nov–Feb: 9am– 4pm Tue–Fri, 9am–5pm Sat & Sun. 🐾 🎫 by appt. 📷

Environs
Just northeast of Krapina is the sanctuary of the **Madonna of Jerusalem** in Trški Vrh, regarded as one of the most magnificent examples of Baroque art in Croatia. Built in 1750–61, on a square plan, the façade has a bell tower with an onion dome. Inside is an arched portico with rounded corners and four chapels similar to the tower. The walls, vaults, ceilings and dome of the church are covered with a cycle of frescoes of biblical subjects and scenes from Mary's life by the Styrian artist, Anton Lerchinger. The ornate main altar (with a statue of the Virgin brought from Jerusalem in 1669) is by sculptor Filip Jacob Straub of Graz, while the pulpit and the other three altars are the work of Anton Mersi.

Fresco in the Baroque Church of the Madonna of Jerusalem in Trški Vrh

❽ Pregrada

Map C1. 🏘 1,700. ℹ Trg Gospe Kunagorske 2, (049) 377 050. 🎭 Carnival (Feb), Branje grožđa, grape harvest (Sep). 🖥 **pregrada.hr**

The village church has ancient origins but now presents a 19th-century appearance, made distinctive by the façade flanked by two pointed bell towers. Inside, as well as the tombs of members of the Keglević and Gorup families, there is also a very large organ, which was at one time in Zagreb Cathedral.

On the site of a medieval castle, in the Hrvatsko Zagorje woods along the Wine Road, stands **Gorica Castle**, once owned by the Keglević family and the feudal manor of the area. Two round towers frame the structure of the elaborate façade. Other buildings behind the towers are now used as a winery.

Environs
On a vineyard-covered hill 7 km (4 miles) west of Pregrada, in **Vinagora**, stands an unusual sanctuary of ancient origins. This place of worship became the parish church in 1780. The church of St Mary of the Visitation (Sv. Marija od Pohoda) contains some Gothic statues and rich furnishings. The church is surrounded by walls which encircle the hill. Two round towers guard the

Inside the Church of St Mary of the Visitation, Vinagora

sanctuary entrance, which also once had a drawbridge. These towers are now used as chapels.

❾ Veliki Tabor

Map C1. 🚌 from Krapina or Zagreb for Desinić. ℹ Košnički Hum 1, Desinić, (049) 374 970. 🎭 Knights tournament (Sep). 🖥 **veliki-tabor.hr**

One of the most famous and best-preserved castles in Croatia, Veliki Tabor stands on a bare hilltop, making it visible from a great distance. It was royal property in the 14th century at the time of King Matthias Corvinus I (the

fact that it was royal property justified its imposing appearance). It was granted to the family of the Ratkaj counts, who in the 16th century transformed it into a sumptuous residential palace.

Walls with four semicircular towers encircle the main body of the castle, which is built on a pentagonal ground-plan. Two floors with porticoes face the central courtyard. The bastions (no longer extant) made Veliki Tabor a fortress to be feared. The castle is now a museum.

🏛 Castle
Košnički Hum 1, Desinić. **Tel** (049) 374 970. **Open** Apr–Sep: 9am–5pm Tue–Fri, 9am–7pm Sat & Sun; Mar & Oct: 9am–4pm Tue–Fri, 9am–5pm Sat & Sun; Nov–Feb: 9am–4pm Tue–Sun.

Environs
Miljana, just to the southwest of Veliki Tabor, is home to one of the most picturesque Baroque castles in Croatia. Construction began in the 17th century but was not completed until the mid-19th century. This time span resulted in a variety of styles; there are striking 18th-century Rococo frescoes in some rooms, and some delightful artworks.

❿ Kumrovec

Map C1. 🏘 300. 🚆 (049) 553 129. 🚌 from Zagreb. ℹ Ulica Josipa Broza 12, (049) 553 728. 🎭 Marriage of Zagorje (Sep). 🖥 **kumrovec.hr**

This was the birthplace of Marshal Tito, born Josip Broz in 1892. His house, which dates from 1860, was turned into a museum in 1953. On display are the furniture and household goods which belonged to his family.

In the square in front of the house is a monument to Tito, the work of Antun Augustinčić in 1948. Along with other village houses, Tito's birthplace is now part of a folk museum, the **Ethnological Museum – Staro Selo**, which means "old village". The preserved thatched houses are furnished with utensils and household goods of the time.

The Castle of Veliki Tabor, one of the best-preserved castles in Croatia

◀ The Castle of Trakošćan, built in around 1334 as part of Croatia's northwestern fortification system

Birthplace of Marshal Tito, part of the Staro Selo museum in Kumrovec

Reconstructed workshops have been set up to demonstrate crafts such as hemp- and flax-weaving.

Ethnological Museum – Staro Selo
Kumrovec bb. **Tel** (049) 225 830. **Open** Apr–Sep: 9am–7pm daily; Mar & Oct: 9am–4pm Mon–Fri, 9am–6pm Sat & Sun; Nov–Feb: 9am–4pm daily.

⓫ Klanjec

Map C1. ⚐ 600. 🚃 (049) 550404. 🚌 from Zagreb, Krapina, Zabok. ℹ Trg A Mihanovića 2, (049) 551 002. ⚑ Thanksgiving to Autumn (Oct). 🌐 **klanjec.hr**

Antun Augustinčić (1900–79) is one of the most important Croatian sculptors of the 20th century, and his works can be seen around the world. He was born here, and the **Antun Augustinčić Gallery** displays his work.

Also of interest are the Franciscan monastery and the annexed church of St Mary, both built in the 17th century by the powerful Erdödy family, whose tombs lie here. Tours can be arranged by the tourist office.

In the main square is a monument by Robert Frangeš-Mihanović, dedicated to the poet Antun Mihanović, who wrote the Croatian national anthem.

Another memorial dedicated to Antun Mihanović is the 9-m (29-ft) memorial stone which stands in Zelenjak, 3 km (2 miles) north of Klanjec, in the direction of Kumrovec.

Antun Augustinčić Gallery
Trg A Mihanovića 10. **Tel** (049) 550 343. **Open** Apr–Sep: 9am–5pm daily; Oct–Mar: 9am–3pm Tue–Sun.

⓬ Bedekovčina

Map D1. ⚐ 3,500. 🚃 Trg A Starčevića 12, (049) 213 106. 🚌 from Zagreb. ℹ Regional: D.G. Kramhergera 1, Krapina, (049) 233 653. ⚑ Wine fair (Jun).

This town is home to a particularly attractive castle and palace, one of many buildings erected over the ruins of ancient castles in the Zagorje hills. The majority of these were destroyed during the wars against the Turks. This particular castle was built in the early 18th century, and now houses public offices. The castle is built on a quadrangular plan, on two levels and with a sloping roof. Coats of arms are emblazoned above the two entrance doors.

Statue of Antun Mihanović, Klanjec

⓭ Marija Bistrica

Map D1. ⚐ 1,000. 🚃 Zlatar Bistrica, 5 km (3 miles). 🚌 from Zagreb. ℹ Zagrebačka bb, (049) 468 380. ⚑ Summer in Marija Bistrica (Jun–Aug). 🌐 **info-marija-bistrica.hr**

This small village lying on the northern side of the Medvednica mountain is home to the **Sanctuary of St Mary of Bistrica** (Majke Božje Bistričke), one of the best-known pilgrimage sites in Croatia. There has been a church on this site since 1334. In the mid-16th century, when a Turkish invasion seemed imminent, a wooden statue of the *Black Madonna with Child* was hidden in the church. Some decades later, it was miraculously rediscovered, to great joy and emotion. It still inspires tremendous devotion today.

The church has been enlarged several times and was the first to be declared a Sanctuary of Croatia by Parliament (1715). It was rebuilt in 1883 by the architect Hermann Bollé. He adopted an eclectic approach, combining Romanesque, Gothic and Baroque styles. The church also has a large frescoed portico.

The sanctuary possesses a rich store of beautiful religious objects: gold and silver pieces, furnishings and sacred vestments adorned with gold embroidery. Some objects are now on exhibit in the Diocesan Museum in Zagreb.

Sanctuary of St Mary of the Snows
Trg pape Ivana Pavla II 32. **Tel** (049) 469 156. **Open** by appt.

Sanctuary of St Mary of the Snows in Marija Bistrica, a place of pilgrimage

⓮ Tour of the Thermal Spas

Between Varaždin and Zagreb are six thermal spas (*toplice*), dating from different eras. Set in a pleasant hilly landscape of vineyards and woods, the spas are popular with Croatians and visitors from nearby European countries. As well as being attracted by the well-equipped thermal spas, visitors are also drawn by the cities and towns nearby. In addition there are numerous castles, sanctuaries, churches and museums, making this a very pleasant area to stay in.

Decorative detail from the Roman baths, Varaždinske Toplice

④ Krapinske Toplice

This thermal spa was built in the second half of the 19th century near a hot water spring rich in calcium, magnesium and carbonate. The hospital treats rheumatic, cardiovascular and neurological illnesses with bathing in its three indoor pools (the hotel also has outdoor pools and a whirlpool) and mud treatments.

⑤ Sutinske Toplice

Located 8 km (5 miles) northwest of Zlatar, at an altitude of 170 m (557 ft), this site has been famous since the 13th century for its curative waters, which are slightly radioactive and rich in minerals, particularly calcium and magnesium. Mud baths are particularly effective for the treatment of a variety of ailments. Outdoor pools only.

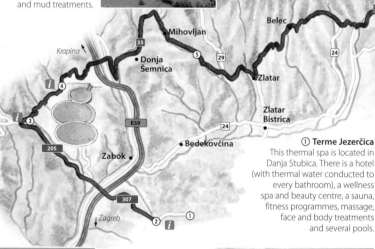

① Terme Jezerčica

This thermal spa is located in Danja Stubica. There is a hotel (with thermal water conducted to every bathroom), a wellness spa and beauty centre, a sauna, fitness programmes, massage, face and body treatments and several pools.

Key

▬ Tour route

▬ Motorway

▭ Other roads

③ Terme Tuhelj

This spa town is 40 km (25 miles) from Zagreb. At the hotel with its eight pools, rheumatic, respiratory, urological and gynaecological illnesses are treated.

② Stubičke Toplice

This spa is located at the foot of Mount Medvednica, 3 km (2 miles) from Donja Stubica. The spa dates from 1776. There is a hospital here that specializes in the treatment of degenerative diseases of the joints and spine. The hot spa waters emerge at 69°C (156°F).

The decorated interior of the church of St Mary of the Snows, Belec

ⓑ Belec

Map D1. 🏠 500. 🚌 from Zabok.
🛈 Regional: D G Krambergera 1,
Krapina, (049) 233 653.

Among the hills of Zagorje is the village of Belec, much loved by art historians, because on its outskirts is the small Church of **St George** (Sv. Jurja), one of the few Romanesque buildings preserved in inland Croatia. The bell tower takes up nearly all of the façade (it resembles a defensive tower rather than a campanile). On the right is a small portico with two thin columns. This leads to the interior, where there is an ornate Gothic altar and interesting frescoes dating from the year of its construction.

Lower down the hillside is the Church of **St Mary of the Snows** (Sv. Marija Snježna), constructed by the Keglević family in 1674. This church is considered a masterpiece of Croatian Baroque, because of its sumptuously decorated and ornamented interior. The monk and artist Ivan Ranger (*see p210*) painted some of his *trompe-l'œil* masterpieces here, including *Scenes from the Old Testament* and *Episodes of the Virgin Mary's Life*. The church also has a magnificent main altar, surrounded by cherubs and saints.

🏠 **Church of St Mary of the Snows**
Tel (049) 460 040. **Open** by appt.

⓰ Varaždinske Toplice

Map D1. 🏠 2,000. 🚊 from Zagreb and Novi Marof. 🚌 from Zagreb.
🛈 Trg slobode 16, (042) 633 133.
🌐 toplice-vz.hr

The waters that gush from a sulphurous spring at the foot of the hill south of Varaždin were known to the Jasi, an Illyrian tribe, in the 3rd century BC. The town was known as Aquae Jasae by the Romans, and the spa rapidly developed, as shown by the numerous archaeological finds discovered here. The baths were used until the area was invaded by the Goths. Later, a landslide buried the baths in mud and for centuries they were forgotten.

In the 12th century, under the rule of the bishop of Zagreb, a village was founded with the name of Toplissa and the inhabitants began to use the hot water from the spring once more. During the construction of the present-day resort, the Roman town was rediscovered.

Varaždinske Toplice also boasts a medieval district which includes a castle, part of which houses a **History Museum**. Inside a small fortress is the parish church with an organ from 1766 and two carved altars made by Francesco Robba.

In a nearby park is Seoska Kuća, an 18th-century rural house with furniture and objects from the same era.

Ludbreg

Novi Marof

E65
E71

ražbin →

ⓢ **Varaždinske Toplice**
The spa resort in Varaždinske Toplice is one of the oldest in Croatia. The first baths were set up at the end of the 18th century and the first public spa was opened to the public in 1829. The thermal waters are used to treat rheumatic and orthopaedic conditions.

0 km   5

0 miles   5

The sanctuary dedicated to the Trinity, Ludbreg

⑰ Ludbreg

Map D1. 🗻 3,800. 🚗 from Zagreb via Koprivnica or Varaždin. 🚌 from Zagreb. 🛈 Trg sv. Trojstva 14, (042) 810 690. 🎭 Celebration of Miraculous Blood (1st Sun in Sep).
🌐 **tz-ludbreg.hr**

Many traces from the Roman era, such as walls and baths, have been found in this area. In researching these finds, some historians have identified Ludbreg as being the Roman site of Jovia.

The town later became one of the first bishop's sees in inland Croatia. In 1411, during a mass, a priest saw the wine in the chalice turn to blood and the town chapel where this miracle took place became a destination for pilgrims. In 1513 Pope Leo X declared Ludbreg the only **Sanctuary of the Trinity** (Sv. Trojstvo) in Croatia.

The church, originally Gothic, was altered in 1829, and now features a Baroque altar and frescoes by M Rački (1937). The portico is typical of churches of pilgrimage and dates from 1779.

In 1739, Parliament voted to build a large chapel dedicated to the Precious Blood of Christ here, in order to preserve the miraculous chalice in an appropriate place. The chapel was not finally consecrated until 1994.

A manor house in Baroque and Classical style, built by the Battahyany family in 1745, today houses workshops belonging to the Croatian Restoration Institute.

⑱ Koprivnica

Map D1. 🗻 25,000. 🚗 Kolodvorska 31, (060) 305 040. 🚌 Zagrebačka ulica, (048) 621 282. 🛈 Local: Trg bana Jelačića 7, (048) 621 433; Regional: Nemčićeva 5, (048) 624 408. 🎭 Podravski motivi, Naive art exhibition (first week of Jul).
🌐 **koprivnicatourism.com**

Koprivnica (originally known as Kukaproncza), was founded by the powerful Ernust family, and was a key trading centre for the Podravina area as well as a royal city from 1356. It was burned down by the Turks in the 16th century, destroying one of Croatia's first free towns.

Slowly rebuilt in the 17th century, the town took on a Baroque appearance with a wide avenue flanked by the main buildings. At one end stands the 19th-century County Hall of Koprivnica and Križevci. There are many Serbian immigrants here, hence the Orthodox Church of the Holy Spirit (Sveti Duh), dating from the late 18th century.

A significant event for the city was the establishment in 1685 of a **Franciscan Monastery** and the church of St Anthony of Padua. The monastery was a source of culture and learning for the whole region and it has resumed this role in recent times.

Nearby is the **Civic Museum** (Gradski muzej) with archaeological, historical and cultural collections, and the **Koprivnica Gallery** with a collection of Naive works linked to the Hlebine School (see p25). Next door, in a former old brewery, is the beer hall Kraluš (see p249), much loved by the locals.

🏛 **Civic Museum**
Trg Leandera Brozovića 1. **Tel** (048) 622 307. **Open** 8am–3pm, 6–9pm Mon–Fri; 10am–1pm Sat.

🏛 **Koprivnica Gallery**
Zrinski trg 9/1. **Tel** (048) 622 564. **Open** 8am–3pm & 6–9pm Tue–Fri, 10am–1pm Sat & Sun. 🖼

Environs
Hlebine, 13 km (8 miles) east of Koprivnica, owes its fame to the peasant painters fostered by the artist Krsto Hegedušić. In the 1930s this group founded the so-called Hlebine School (see p25) of Naive art: the core of a trend in painting which represented the landscape and people of this region in a simple and original way. Their work is exhibited in both the **Hlebine Gallery** and the Koprivnica Gallery.

🏛 **Hlebine Gallery**
Trg Ivana Generalića 15. **Tel** (048) 836 075. **Open** 10am–4pm Tue–Fri, 10am–2pm Sat & Sun. 🖼

A work of Naive art of the Hlebine School in the Koprivnica Gallery

The medieval castle in Đurđevac, today housing a gallery

⑲ Đurđevac

Map E1. ⚊ 6,500. ⬚ Kolodvorska 21, (048) 813 089. ⬚ (048) 812 002. ℹ Vladimira Nazora 2, (048) 812 046. ⬚ Đurđevo, City Day (23 Apr); Legend of the Picoki, culture and folklore show (last week of Jun).

Although the town's name derives from an ancient religious building dedicated to St George (Sv. Jurai), the town is now known for the **Castle** (Stari grad), whose ancient name is mentioned as Wasserburg, meaning castle on the water. In the Middle Ages the structure was much larger (excavations reveal a rectangular plan with a drawbridge and tower). All that remains now is a roughly octagonal building with an internal courtyard. A gallery occupies the upper floor.

⑳ Bjelovar

Map D1. ⚊ 28,000. ⬚ Masarykova ulica, (043) 241 263. ⬚ Masarykova ulica, (043) 241 269. ℹ Local: Trg Eugena Kvaternika 2, (043) 243 944; Regional: Trg Eugena Kvaternika 4, (043) 243 944. ⬚ Terezijana, cultural display (Jun). ⬚ turizam-bilogorabjelovar.com.hr

In the Middle Ages this was a fort called Wellowar. It acquired greater status in 1756, when Maria Theresa of Austria built a fort here. It became a military town, and was built on an octagonal layout, centred around two intersecting roads. These are now home to the Cathedral of St Theresa, schools, the Orthodox church of the Holy Trinity and the barracks. The town's **Civic Museum** (Gradski muzej) has an extensive and varied collection.

⬚ Civic Museum
Trg Eugena Kvaternika 1. **Tel** (043) 244 207. **Open** 10am–7pm Tue–Fri, 10am–2pm Sat & Sun.

The iconostasis in the Church of the Holy Trinity, Križevci

㉑ Križevci

Map D1. ⚊ 12,000. ⬚ (048) 716 193. ℹ Nemčićev trg 6, (048) 681 199. ⬚ tz-krizevci.hr ⬚ Križevačko veliko spravišče, cultural and gastronomic event (mid-Jun).

References to this town are found in acts from the early 12th century. In 1252 it was declared a royal free town, and at various times it was chosen as the meeting place for the Croatian parliament. During a meeting in 1397 certain nobles considered traitors to King Sigismund were massacred. Of these, one was the Prince palatine, Stjepan Lacković.

The town was later fortified but after Turkish rule, only the towers' foundations and pieces of the wall remained. The town prospered with the arrival of the railway in 1871.

The oldest building is the medieval **Church of the Holy Cross** (Sv. Križ), but only the side doorway dates from this period. The church was restructured in the Baroque style in the second half of the 18th century. The altar of the Holy Cross was sculpted by Francesco Robba in 1756 for the cathedral in Zagreb.

The Greek Catholic Church of the Holy Trinity (Sv. Trojstvo) has an iconostasis, frescoes by Celestin Medović and Ivan Tišov from the early 19th century, and a magnificent main altar. It was restored durng the 19th century according to the drawings of the architect Herman Bollé.

The attached monastery became the **Bishop's Palace** (Biskupski dvor). It houses paintings, icons, manuscripts and holy objects. The **Civic Museum** (Gradski muzej) has interesting archaeological and art collections.

⬚ Church of the Holy Cross
Ivana Dijankovečkog 1. **Tel** (048) 711 711. **Open** by appt.

⬚ Bishop's Palace
Tel (048) 712 171. **Open** by appt.

⬚ Civic Museum
Sermageova 2. **Tel** (048) 711 210. **Open** 8am–3pm Mon, Wed & Fri, 8am–7pm Tue & Thu, 10am–noon Sat. ⬚ ⬚

Altar by Francesco Robba in the church of the Holy Cross, Križevci

TRAVELLERS' NEEDS

WHERE TO STAY

Croatia is one of the boom destinations of European tourism and accommodation facilities are going through a dynamic period of expansion and improvement. This means that there is a great deal of choice available to visitors. There are plenty of modern hotels, apartments and holiday villages, especially along the coast. Rooms and apartments rented privately by their owners represent a particularly inexpensive option. The number of B&Bs and boutique backpacker hostels is also on the rise, and there are plenty of well-equipped, idyllically situated campsites along the coast. Numerous tour operators and travel agencies offer package holidays to different resorts in Croatia, but it is not difficult to make your own travel arrangements. Accommodation is best booked in advance, and planning ahead is a good idea if you are intending to visit in the peak summer months of June, July and August.

"Birdcage" balcony, Lešić-Dimitri Palace hotel, Korčula *(see p229)*

Hotels

Tourism first boomed in Croatia in the 1970s and 1980s and most of the hotels, particularly those in the resorts along the coast, date from this period. Facilities are generally up to modern standards although decor and furnishings can seem rather anonymous. Recent years have seen many hotels renovated and upgraded, providing a growing stock of 4- and 5-star accommodation.

Grand hotels erected in the late 19th and early 20th century can be found in Zagreb, the capital, and in Opatija, in the Kvarner gulf. Opatija became a popular seaside resort at the time of the Austro-Hungarian Empire, when the Habsburg aristocracy were regular visitors, and it still has several hotels dating from this time. They offer a somewhat faded elegance not found in the more modern multistorey buildings along the coast. Both Zagreb and Dubrovnik also have a number of larger luxury hotels, including several belonging to well-known international hotel chains. There are also a growing number of boutique and design hotels in fashionable destinations such as Dubrovnik, Split and Hvar. The facilities and services offered by these hotels are of a very high standard, which is reflected in the prices.

Private Rooms and Apartments

A good-value alternative to staying in a hotel while in Croatia is to look for accommodation in privately rented rooms *(privatne sobe)* or apartments *(apartmani)*.

Private rooms are usually doubles (single travellers may be expected to pay the full double price), and come in all shapes and sizes – the most expensive ones will have en-suite bathrooms, but many will not. Apartments come in all sizes too, from 2-person studios to 6-person family flats, and represent an inexpensive alternative to hotel accommodation for those travelling as a family or as a group. Apartments usually have a well-equipped kitchen for those who want to self-cater and there is usually a local market or food shop nearby.

Fresh Sheets B&B, overlooking a pretty square in Dubrovnik *(see p228)*

Hotel Lone in Rovinj, Istria, a five-star option outside the major cities *(see p227)*

Private rooms and apartments are frequently rented out privately by their owners via international booking sites like **Booking** or **Airbnb**. They can also be booked through the various tourist agencies which can be found in all the tourist resorts. A tourist tax and commission are charged and in summer landlords may require stays of a minimum of four nights.

Landladies and landlords often congregate at ferry terminals and bus stations to offer rooms to arriving tourists. While this is a reasonably safe way to secure a room, it is essential to check the location and price before committing yourself in any way.

Otherwise you can seek out accommodation yourself in the areas you would like to stay in by looking out for signs reading *sobe* (Croatian for 'rooms'), *Zimmer* in German or *camere* in Italian, hanging outside the door. It is a good idea to begin looking fairly early in the day. If you find somewhere you like, you can ask to be shown the room and, if you are happy with what you see, you can arrange the terms and the price of your stay. It may even be possible to negotiate the price, especially out of season. Private rooms rarely come with breakfast, although you can always ask if it is available – an increasing number of renters are beginning to provide it.

B&Bs and Pensions

The concept of the bed-and-breakfast is relatively new in Croatia but there are an increasing number of them in Zagreb, on the coast, and in national park areas where rural tourism is on the increase. Usually these offer simply furnished rooms in family houses, although some B&Bs are swish affairs, almost on the level of boutique hotels. Pensions *(pansion)* are small family-run hotels that offer breakfast, and possibly half- or full board as well.

Hotel Grading

Croatia has adopted the standard star system for categorizing hotels common in other European countries, which ranges from one star, awarded to the simplest sort of accommodation, to five stars for a luxury hotel.

The five-star category indicates hotels offering a high standard and a wide range of services and facilities, usually including spa and fitness facilities, a swimming pool and at least one gourmet restaurant. There are not very many five-star hotels in Croatia, and most of them are in Dubrovnik and Zagreb.

Four-star hotels offer facilities and services similar to those in the five-star category, but the furnishings are less luxurious and more standardized and there are fewer facilities.

Most of the hotels in Croatia fall within the three-star category, which indicates hotels offering a good standard of comfort. Two-star hotels are generally cheaper and more spartan in their furnishings and offer fewer services.

It is common practice in resort areas for hotels to offer half-board *(polupansion)*, with the price including bed and breakfast as well as another meal (usually an evening meal). Prices for half-board can be very reasonable; often not much more than you would pay for just the room. However, hotel restaurant food tends often to be based on rather standardized "international" cooking, and may be lacking in local character.

Karmen's self-contained apartments within a historic residence, Dubrovnik *(see p228)*

Deluxe hotels such as the Esplanade, Zagreb, often more accessible for the disabled *(see p231)*

Camp Sites

There are plenty of camp sites in Croatia, ranging from small, family-run sites with a few pitches under the olive trees to large camps with facilities such as sports grounds, restaurants and shops. Many Croatian camp sites are located in woods by the sea, so you can keep cool under shady trees on summer days. While there is a wide choice of sites on the Adriatic coast and islands, there are far fewer camp sites inland. **Kamping Udruženje Hrvatske** (the Croatian Camping Union) has useful directories on its website.

All camp sites are open in the summer months of June, July, August and until the middle of September. However, it is best to check with the campground directly if you are planning on going during May or late September, as the opening periods can vary from year to year.

Some of the loveliest camp sites, situated as they are in hidden-away spots, are those marked "FKK" *(see p266)*, which are for naturists only.

Camping outside designated areas is prohibited in Croatia, so do not be tempted to stop overnight in the woods or forests, on the beaches or in any areas not specifically reserved for campers.

Hostels

There are a growing number of backpacker hostels in Croatia, most of which offer cheap, simple dorm accommodation

in fun, informal surroundings. A bed in a hostels can be booked via the hostel's own website or on specialist websites such as **Hostelworld**. Many hostels offer double rooms, triples and quads as well as dorms, and these are increasingly popular with couples and families who enjoy the social aspects of backpacker culture but who want their own room. Some hostels have invested a lot of money in contemporary design and comforts, and are similar in style to small boutique hotels. Breakfast is available at some, but not all, Croatian hostels – check when booking.

Prices

All accommodation prices in Croatia are seasonal, with the cheapest rates occurring in winter and the most expensive coinciding with the high summer season – which used to mean July and August, but which is now spreading to June and September as well.

During the high season accommodation in Croatia can be just as expensive as (if not more than) anywhere else in the Mediterranean – especially in fashionable destinations such as Dubrovnik, Hvar and Split. Bargains might be found in the shoulder seasons of April, May and October; and winter is in general a more inexpensive time to travel – although be aware that many hotels situated on the coast close their doors for at least a few months out of season.

Bookings

The prevalence of Internet booking sites means that it is nowadays fairly easy to organize hotel reservations in Croatia yourself. However places fill up quickly from June through to September, so you are advised to book well in advance in order to be sure of getting the accommodation you want.

The **Croatian National Tourist Board** *(see p267)* can supply information on accommodation ahead of your trip. Once you are in Croatia, local tourist offices (there is one in every town) will either help you find a room or direct you to an accommodation agency that can sort out your needs.

Disabled Travellers

Care for the disabled in Croatia is good, for the grim reason that the numbers of disabled people has risen here as a result of the 1991–95 war. However, despite renewed sympathy and consideration, it is taking time to improve disabled access to buildings such as hotels and restaurants. Many hotels can be unsuitable for persons with restricted mobility.

As a general rule, hotels of four stars or above will have facilities for the disabled; cheaper places will probably not. For further information, contact **Hrvatski Savez Udruga Tjelesnih Invalida**, the Association of Disabled Organizations of Croatia *(see p267)* or RADAR in the UK.

Lighthouses

A delightful and unusual accommodation option in Croatia is a stay in one of the lighthouses which stand on isolated points along the coast. Lighthouses, which usually contain one or two apartments, are often situated on uninhabited islets, and will suit those who require solitude, unspoilt nature and unimpeded sea views. Several agencies deal with lighthouse accommodation; they will supply you with boat transfer and provisions for the duration of your stay. For more information and bookings, contact **Lighthouses of Croatia** or **adriatica.net.**

Of the more famous lighthouses, **Savudrija** is 9 km (5 miles) from Umag, and is the oldest lighthouse in the Adriatic, built in an ideal spot for windsurfers. **Rt Zub** is on the Lanterna peninsula, 13 km (8 miles) from Poreč and Novigrad. Even though it is in a relatively isolated position, it is within reach of a number of tourist resorts.

Sveti Ivan na pučini is situated on an island which is part of the archipelago off Rovinj, which is 3.5 km (2 miles) away. It is ideal for those who love fishing or diving.

The **Porer** lighthouse, on the island of the same name, is 20 km (12 miles) from Pula. It offers truly spectacular views and is in a particularly isolated position. **Veli Rat** stands among pine trees on the northwestern promontory on the island of Dugi Otok, 35 km (22 miles) from Zadar, while at the entrance to the port of Makarska, near one of the most beautiful beaches in the Adriatic, stands the **Sveti Petar** lighthouse.

Pločica is situated on the island of the same name, which lies between the islands of Hvar and Korčula and the Pelješac peninsula.

View from the Hotel Mozart, Opatija, chosen for its historic ambience *(see p226)*

The lighthouse of **Sušac** was built in 1878 on the island of the same name, 40 km (25 miles) from Hvar. It stands 100 m (328 ft) above sea level and offers a wonderful view of the open sea. It is possible to scuba dive near the rocks at the southern end of the island.

The lighthouse of **Palagruža** is situated 68 km (42 miles) from Split, between the Italian and Croatian coasts, while on the island of Lastovo, 80 km (50 miles) from Split, is the **Struga** lighthouse, dating from 1839. This is a great location for those who love fishing.

The **Sveti Andrija** lighthouse stands on the island of the same name and is 10 km (6 miles) from Dubrovnik. Finally, there is **Prišnjak** lighthouse on the island of Murter, surrounded by a thick pine wood.

Recommended Hotels

The hotels listed on the following pages have been chosen for a wide range of reasons and criteria. All are representative of their context, be that bustling Split, fairy-tale Dubrovnik, the beach resorts of the Adriatic coast or the quaint ports of the Dalmatian islands. Each has earned a reputation for hospitality and charm.

The listings cover all kinds of accommodation, from simple farmhouses to spawling resorts, family B&Bs to contemporary design hotels and luxurious palaces. A warm welcome earns plenty of points, as do little extras like coffee- and tea-making facilities, and allowing guests use of the kitchen.

The DK Choice label means the hotel is in some way outstanding. It may be in beautiful surroundings, offer a spectacular outlook, occupy a landmark building, provide outstanding service, radiate romance or be particularly charming, have a great spa, or a noteworthy sustainable outlook. Whatever the reason, it is a guarantee of an especially memorable stay.

DIRECTORY

Internet Booking Sites

Booking
w booking.com

Airbnb
w airbnb.com

Hostelworld
w hostelworld.com

Camping Websites

Kamping Udruženje Hrvatske (Croatian Camping Union)
w camping.hr

Lighthouses

Lighthouses of Croatia
w lighthouses-croatia.com

Adriatica.net
w adriatica.net

Modern and minimalist, but set in a Roman palace: the Vestibul Palace, Split *(see p230)*

Where to Stay

Istria and the Kvarner Area

BUZET: Hotel Vela Vrata ⓦ
Boutique   **Road Map** B2
Šetalište Vladimira Gortana 7
Tel *052 494 750*
ⓦ velavrata.net
Lovely hotel at the gates of Buzet's hilltop Old Town, with snug rooms and modern fittings. Closed Jan & Feb.

BUZET: Kotli ⓦ
Historic   **Road Map** B2
Kotli
Tel *098 228 432*
ⓦ istra-kotli.com
A street of stone houses in the traditional village of Kotli, 13 km (8 miles) from Buzet, converted into atmospheric family-sized apartments with good facilities.

CRES: Kimen ⓦ
Resort   **Road Map** B3
Melin 1/16
Tel *051 573 305*
ⓦ hotel-kimen.com
A large but welcoming hotel, with lots of facilities and live music nightly. Closed Nov–Mar.

CRIKVENICA: Hotel Kaštel ⓦ
Resort   **Road Map** B2
Frankopanska 22
Tel *051 241 044*
ⓦ jadran-crikvenica.hr
Simple rooms in a former 14th-century monastery, right by the river and close to the beach.

KRK: Valamar Koralj ⓦⓦ
Resort   **Road Map** B3
V. Tomašića bb
Tel *052 465 120*
ⓦ valamar.com/hr/hoteli-krk
A large hotel close to a beautiful bay, with comfortable rooms and plenty of on-site facilities.

KRK: Marina ⓦⓦⓦ
Boutique   **Road Map** B3
Obala hrvatske mornarice 8
Tel *051 221 128*
ⓦ hotelmarina.hr
A charming well-run hotel on the pretty harbourfront, with a café-restaurant terrace that's perfect for people-watching.

LOŠINJ: Apoksiomen ⓦⓦ
Boutique   **Road Map** B3
Riva lošinjskih kapetana 1
Tel *051 520 820*
ⓦ apoksiomen.com
Delightful hotel on the harbour-front with an understated sense of style and attention to detail.

LOŠINJ: Aurora ⓦⓦ
Resort   **Road Map** B3
Sunčana uvala 4t, Mali Lošinj
Tel *051 667 200*
ⓦ losinj-hotels.com
Large, well-organized beach-front hotel with a range of facilities and beauty treatments.

DK Choice

LOŠINJ: Punta ⓦⓦ
Spa   **Road Map** B3
Šestavine, Veli Lošinj
Tel *051 662 000*
ⓦ losinj-hotels.com
Built on rocks overlooking the sea, and backed by fragrant pines, this is a well-equipped and soothing resort-hotel. The fishing harbour of Veli Lošinj lies 5 minutes' walk in one direction; the resort town of Mali Lošinj is 20 minutes away in the other. Punta's other main attribute is the on-site spa centre, which offers a pool, massage facilities and a variety of beauty treatments and exercise programmes.

LOŠINJ: Bellevue ⓦⓦⓦ
Resort   **Road Map** B3
Čikat 9, Mali Lošinj
Tel *051 231 268*
ⓦ losinj-hotels.com
A superbly equipped 5-star hotel offering excellent standards of service, and close proximity to the beaches of Čikat Bay.

LOVRAN: Bristol ⓦ
Historic   **Road Map** B2
Šetalište maršala Tita 27
Tel *051 710 444*
ⓦ remisens.com

Large and modern, with plenty of facilities: Hotel Aurora, Lošinj

Price Guide

Prices are based on one night's stay in high season for a standard double room, Iinclusive of service charges and taxes.

ⓦ	up to 800 kuna
ⓦⓦ	800–1300 kuna
ⓦⓦⓦ	over 1300 kuna

An attractive late 19th-century wedding-cake of a building on the promenade, with high-ceilinged rooms.

MOTOVUN: Hotel Kaštel ⓦ
Boutique   **Road Map** A2
Trg Andrea Antico 7
Tel *052 681 607*
ⓦ hotel-kastel-motovun.hr
Restored 17th-century town house in the heart of a beautiful hill-town, offering a warren of cosy rooms.

OPATIJA: Palace-Bellevue ⓦ
Historic   **Road Map** B2
Maršala Tita 144
Tel *051 710 444*
ⓦ remisens.com
Two impressive 19th-century buildings next to the main beach. The rooms are simple but the social areas – all marble columns and chandeliers – are wonderful.

OPATIJA: Galeb ⓦⓦ
Historic   **Road Map** B2
Maršala Tita 160
Tel *051 271 177*
ⓦ hotel-galeb.hr
A lovely little hotel in the centre of town offering clean, good-sized rooms with sea views. Closed Nov–Apr.

OPATIJA: Villa Ariston ⓦⓦ
Boutique   **Road Map** B2
Maršala Tita 179
Tel *051 271 379*
ⓦ villa-ariston.hr
Grand in architecture and cosy in atmosphere, this seaside villa is a relaxing upscale choice.

OPATIJA: Hotel Milenij ⓦⓦⓦ
Luxury   **Road Map** B2
Maršala Tita 109
Tel *051 278 007*
ⓦ milenijhoteli.hr
Set in impressive sea-front buildings, with spa facilities and a lovely ground-floor café.

OPATIJA: Hotel Mozart ⓦⓦⓦ
Luxury   **Road Map** B2
Maršala Tita 138
Tel *051 718 260*
ⓦ hotel-mozart.hr
Beautifully restored 19th-century building with replica period furnishings and elegant ambience.

PLITVICE: Plitvice ⓦⓦ
Resort **Road Map** C3
Plitvička jezera
Tel *053 751 200*
ⓦ np-plitvicka-jezera.hr
Smart and comfortable hotel set
in the middle of the Plitvice
National Park, with a good range
of on-site facilities.

POREČ: Laguna Parentium ⓦⓦⓦ
Resort **Road Map** A2
Zelena Laguna
Tel *052 410 102*
ⓦ lagunaporec.com
Large hotel on its own peninsula
amid shady pines, oriented
towards adults with a wealth of
spa, sport and relaxation options.

POREČ:
Valamar Club Tamaris ⓦⓦⓦ
Resort **Road Map** A2
Lanterna 6
Tel *052 401 000*
ⓦ valamar.com
Self-contained complex 10 km
(6 miles) out of Poreč with some
lovely pebble beaches.

PULA: Hotel Riviera ⓦ
Historic **Road Map** A3
Splitska 1
Tel *052 211 166*
ⓦ arenaturist.com
A glorious 19th-century building
that has been little altered inside
– the high-ceilinged rooms are
simple and inexpensive.

PULA: Hotel Scaletta ⓦ
Boutique **Road Map** A3
Flavijevska 26
Tel *052 541 599*
ⓦ hotel-scaletta.com
Tastefully decorated family-run
hotel, located just up the road
from Pula's famous amphitheatre.

PULA:
Hotel Park Plaza Histria ⓦⓦⓦ
Resort **Road Map** A3
Verudela 17
Tel *052 590 000*
ⓦ arenaturist.com
This large and well-equipped
resort hotel is surrounded by
charming pebble beaches.

PULA: Hotel Valsabbion ⓦⓦⓦ
Boutique **Road Map** A3
Pješčana uvala IX/26
Tel *052 218 033*
ⓦ valsabbion.hr
Smart, characterful, family-run
hotel with tasteful rooms and an
intimate spa centre on site.

RAB: Grand Hotel Imperial ⓦⓦ
Historic **Road Map** B3
Palit bb
Tel *051 667 788*
ⓦ imperialrab.com

Harbour views, Hotel Marina, Krk

Originally built by the Habsburgs,
this is a lovely but not too gaudy
hotel, surrounded by greenery.

RAB: Padova ⓦⓦ
Resort **Road Map** B3
Banjol bb
Tel *051 667 788*
ⓦ imperialrab.com
A large, modern hotel beside
Rab's marina, with a wide range
of facilities and excellent views of
the Old Town across the bay.

RABAC: Albona ⓦⓦ
Resort **Road Map** B3
Rabac bb
Tel *052 465 120*
ⓦ valamar.com
Rabac's most versatile resort
hotel, with plenty of children's
facilities and views out to sea.

RABAC: Villa Annette ⓦⓦⓦ
Boutique **Road Map** B3
Raška 24
Tel *052 884 222*
ⓦ villa-annette.com
A modernist villa set on a hillside
overlooking the shore, this friendly
place is an appealing alternative
to the huge resort hotels.

RIJEKA: Neboder ⓦ
Historic **Road Map** B3
J.J. Strossmayera 1
Tel *051 373 538*
ⓦ jadran-hoteli.hr
Built in the 1930s, this slender
grey slab is a modernist classic.
Rooms are masterpieces of
minimalist design.

RIJEKA: Best Western Jadran ⓦⓦ
Luxury **Road Map** B3
Šetalište XIII divizije 46
Tel *051 216 600*
ⓦ jadran-hoteli.hr
This elegant modernist
building is right on the sea.
Many of the large refurbished
rooms come with expansive
sea views.

RIJEKA: Grand Hotel Bonavia ⓦⓦ
Luxury **Road Map** B3
Dolac 4
Tel *051 357 100*
ⓦ bonavia.hr
An upmarket, business-oriented
hotel right in the centre of
town, offering top-notch service,
the usual facilities and an
excellent restaurant.

ROVINJ: Valdaliso ⓦ
Resort **Road Map** A3
Monsena bb
Tel *052 800 250*
ⓦ maistra.com/Valdaliso_Rovinj
Around the bay from Rovinj, this
hotel provides excellent sports
facilities and access to some
great pebble beaches.

ROVINJ: Hotel Adriatic ⓦⓦ
Historic **Road Map** A3
Trg maršala Tita 5
Tel *052 800 250*
ⓦ maistra.com/Adriatic_Rovinj
Occupying a 19th-century
building right by the harbour,
this is Rovinj's oldest hotel
and still makes for a charming,
town-centre pied-à-terre.

DK Choice

ROVINJ: Hotel Lone ⓦⓦⓦ
Luxury **Road Map** A3
Luje Adamovića 31
Tel *052 800 250*
ⓦ maistra.com/Lone_Rovinj
A design hotel that lives
up to its billing, this uber-
contemporary hotel lies above
Lone Bay. Every detail of
the interior is the work of
Croatian designers and artists,
from the abstract sculptures
and wall hangings right
down to the staff uniforms.
The rooms are well appointed
and the social areas,
grouped around a spiral
stairway, are a joy to use.

For more information on types of hotels *see pp222–5*

ROVINJ: Monte Mulini ⓦⓦⓦ
Luxury   Road Map A3
A. Smareglia 3
Tel *052 800 250*
W maistra.com/Monte_Mulini_Rovinj
Smart, well-appointed and
perfectly situated five-star, over-
looking the beaches of Lone Bay.

**UMAG: Kempinski
Hotel Adriatic** ⓦⓦⓦ
Luxury   Road Map A2
Alberi 300A, Savudrija
Tel *052 707 000*
W kempinski.com
Right beside the Slovene border,
this chic hotel comes with
superb facilities, and there is an
18-hole golf course nearby.

VRSAR: Petalon ⓦⓦ
Resort   Road Map A3
Petalon 5
Tel *052 800 250*
W maistra.com/Petalon_Vrsar
A self-contained hotel situated
on a peninsula with pebble
beaches, Petalon boasts an
impressive range of sport and
recreational facilities.

Dalmatia

**BRAČ:
Bluesun Hotel Elaphusa** ⓦⓦ
Resort   Road Map D5
Put Zlatnog rata 46, Bol
Tel *021 306 200*
W hotelelaphusabrac.com
Situated in a pine wood, not far
from the beaches and ten
minutes from town. Facilities
galore include sporting activities
and beauty treatments.

BRAČ: Villa Adriatica ⓦⓦ
Boutique   Road Map D5
Put Vele Luke 31, Supetar
Tel *021 755 010*
W villaadriatica.com
A chic family-run alternative
to the big resort hotels, with a
pool and hot tub, in a quiet
neighbourhood minutes from
the seafront. Closed Oct–Apr.

BRAČ: Bluesun Hotel Borak ⓦⓦⓦ
Resort   Road Map D5
Put Zlatnog rata 42, Bol
Tel *021 306 202*
W brachotelborak.com
One of the better, large resort
hotels on Brač, set among
cypresses near Bol's famous
beaches and windsurfing bases.

CAVTAT: Hotel Supetar ⓦⓦ
Historic   Road Map F6
Obala A. Starčevića 27
Tel *020 300 300*
W adriaticluxuryhotels.com

Cool rooms and sea views, Monte Mulini, Rovinj

In an old stone house right on
Cavtat's lovely harbourfront, this
is hard to beat for charm, setting
and value. Closed Nov–Mar.

DUBROVNIK: Adriatic ⓦ
Resort   Road Map F6
Masarykov put 9
Tel *020 433 609*
A good-value hotel just above
Lapad Bay with its pebble beach,
4 km (2 miles) from the Old Town.

DUBROVNIK: Karmen ⓦ
B&B   Road Map F6
Bandureva 1
Tel *020 323 433*
W karmendu.com
Comfortable apartments in
one of the Old Town's most
atmospheric corners, attractively
furnished with antiques.

DK Choice

**DUBROVNIK:
Fresh Sheets B&B** ⓦⓦ
B&B   Road Map F6
Bunićeva poljana 6
Tel *091 896 7509*
W freshsheetsbedandbreakfast.
com
Occupying a unique position
behind the cathedral, in a
historic church-owned building,
Fresh Sheets offers a mixture of
double rooms and apartments,
decorated in bright colours and
equipped with modern fittings.
Breakfast is brought to your
room on a tray: the experience
of waking up in the middle of
Dubrovnik before the tour groups
have arrived is wonderful.

DUBROVNIK: Excelsior ⓦⓦⓦ
Luxury   Road Map F6
Frana Supila 12
Tel *020 300 300*
W www.adriaticluxuryhotels.com
Top-of-the-market historic hotel
up on a cliff a short distance from
the Old Town, with a private
beach and magnificent views.

DUBROVNIK: Pucić Palace ⓦⓦⓦ
Luxury   Road Map F6
Od Puča 1
Tel *020 326 222*
W thepucicpalace.com
Set in a 17th-century palace
overlooking the Old Town's
market, this is Adriatic luxury and
atmosphere at its best.

DUBROVNIK: Stari Grad ⓦⓦⓦ
Boutique   Road Map F6
Od Sigurate 4
Tel *020 322 244*
W hotelstarigrad.com
Intimate (8-room) designer hotel
ideally situated in the Old Town;
stunning views from its rooftop
restaurant. Closed mid-Nov–Feb.

DUGI OTOK: Hotel Lavanda ⓦⓦⓦ
Resort   Road Map C4
Božava bb
Tel *023 291 291*
W hoteli-bozava.hr
Small complex overlooking the
sea, with excellent sports facilities
and lots of surrounding greenery.

HVAR: Adriatiq Resort Fontana ⓦ
Resort   Road Map D5
Vitarnja bb, Jelsa
Tel *021 761 810*
W resortfontana-adriatiq.com
On a hillside, this complex is
minutes away from pebbly
beaches and the town of Jelsa.

HVAR: Palace ⓦⓦ
Historic   Road Map D5
Trg svetog Stjepana 5
Tel *021 741 966*
W suncanihvar.com
The oldest hotel in Hvar, with
modernized rooms set behind
the town's colonnaded loggia.

HVAR: Amfora ⓦⓦⓦ
Resort   Road Map D5
Jurja Dubokovića 5
Tel *021 750 300*
W suncanihvar.com
Large resort hotel along the bay
from Hvar town, with chic rooms,
a pebble beach and all mod cons.

Key to Price Guide *see p226*

HVAR: Hotel Podstine 🅦🅦🅦
Boutique   **Road Map** D5
Put Podstina 11
Tel *021 740 400*
🆆 podstine.com
A contemporary hotel with charm
and a boutique feel, perched above
the sea some 1 km (half a mile)
round the bay from Hvar town.

KORČULA: Bon Repos 🅦
Resort   **Road Map** E6
Dubrovačka cesta 19
Tel *020 726 800*
🆆 korcula-hotels.com
Large hotel, some distance from
the Old Town but on the sea.
Rooms are simple but have been
newly refurbished, and the
surroundings are idyllic.

KORČULA: Korčula 🅦🅦
Historic   **Road Map** E6
Obala dr. Franje Tuđmana 5
Tel *020 711 078*
🆆 korcula-hotels.com
Elegant pre-World War I hotel
on the harbour-front. The
recently updated rooms are
comfortable, and the ground-
floor café has one of the best
terraces on the Adriatic.

DK Choice

KORČULA:
Lešić-Dimitri Palace 🅦🅦🅦
Boutique   **Road Map** E6
Don Pavla Poše 1–6
Tel *021 715 560*
🆆 lesic-dimitri.com
A handful of luxury apartments,
all different, occupying a row of
carefully restored houses in one
of central Korčula's atmospheric,
stepped alleyways. Each
apartment has a fully equipped
kitchen and contemporary
bathroom facilities. Breakfast is
served on the seafront a short
distance away. The friendly staff
attend to every detail.

MAKARSKA: Biokovo 🅦🅦
Historic   **Road Map** E5
Obala kralja Tomislava 14
Tel *021 615 244*
🆆 hotelbiokovo.hr
Comfy, intimate hotel in the
heart of Makarska, with some
rooms overlooking the lively
harbour-front.

MAKARSKA: Hotel Meteor 🅦🅦
Resort   **Road Map** E5
Kralja Petra Krešimira IV 19
Tel *021 564 200*
🆆 hoteli-makarska.hr
This ziggurat-like classic of
Adriatic modernism is right on
the seafront promenade, with a
wealth of on-site faciities.

METKOVIĆ: Villa Neretva 🅦
B&B   **Road Map** E6
Splitska 14, Krvavac
Tel *020 672 200*
🆆 hotel-villa-neretva.com
Set among the mandarin
orchards of the Neretva delta, this
family-run pension offers cosy
rooms above a famous restaurant.
Guests can join in with the harvest.

MLJET: Hotel Odisej 🅦
Resort   **Road Map** E6
Pomena bb
Tel *020 300 300*
🆆 adriaticluxuryhotels.com
Ideal for exploring the lakes and
forests of Mljet National Park, this
modern hotel has a beach and
good sports facilities too.

OREBIĆ: Grand Hotel Orebić 🅦🅦
RESORT   **Road Map** E6
Kralja Petra Krešimira IV 107
Tel *052 858 600*
🆆 grandhotel-orebic.com
Set on a woodland beach, this is
a large hotel with a wide range of
activities and sporting facilities.

OREBIĆ: Hotel Bellevue 🅦🅦
RESORT   **Road Map** E6
Obala pomoraca 36
Tel *020 797 500*
🆆 orebic-htp.hr
A stone's throw from a broad
pebble beach, Bellevue offers
unfussy, good-value rooms and
some excellent facilities.

PAG: Pagus 🅦🅦🅦
Resort   **Road Map** C4
Ante Starčevića 1
Tel *023 611 310*
🆆 hotel-pagus.hr
Stretching along a pebble beach,
this hotel has large rooms and
lovely sea views.

PRIMOŠTEN: Zora 🅦🅦
Resort   **Road Map** D5
Raduča bb
Tel *022 570 048*
🆆 www.hotelzora-adriatiq.com

Nestled in a thick blanket of
pines and cypresses, this resort-
style complex offers plenty of
amenities and is good for families.

ŠIBENIK: Solaris Hotel Jure 🅦🅦
Resort   **Road Map** D5
Solaris
Tel *022 361 001*
🆆 www.solarishotelsresort.com
Beachside hotel in the Solaris
resort set in park-like grounds
with an outdoor swimming-pool
complex.

ŠIBENIK:
Solaris Hotel Jakov 🅦🅦🅦
Resort   **Road Map** D5
Solaris
Tel *022 361 001*
🆆 www.solarishotelsresort.com
Family-oriented hotel in the Solaris
complex 6 km (3 miles) from town,
with ample facilities and a beach.

ŠOLTA: Martinis Marchi 🅦🅦🅦
Luxury   **Road Map** D5
Put svetog Nikole 51, Maslinica
Tel *021 572 768*
🆆 www.martinis-marchi.com
Pampered luxury in a restored
villa, with smart spacious rooms
grouped around a courtyard
swimming pool.

DK Choice

SPLIT: Goli&Bosi 🅦🅦
Hostel   **Road Map** D5
Morpurgova poljana 2
Tel *021 510 999*
🆆 www.gollybossy.com
A converted department store
is home to this innovative
design hostel, characterized by
its bold yellow, white and black
colour scheme. Dorm beds
take the form of semi-private
cubicles; en-suite doubles and
top-floor family rooms are also
on offer. The hostel's café-
restaurant spreads out into the
neighbouring piazza in summer.

View of the old walled city, Excelsior Hotel, Dubrovnik

For more information on types of hotels *see pp222–5*

A modern temple to wellbeing: Hotel ladera, on the coast just outside Zadar

SPLIT: Hotel Peristil ⓦⓦⓦ
Boutique   **Road Map** D5
Poljana kraljice Jelene 5
Tel *021 329 070*
Ⓦ www.hotelperistil.com
A wonderful location in the heart of Split's historical centre, boasting ancient stonework in some rooms.

SPLIT: Radisson Blu Resort ⓦⓦⓦ
Resort   **Road Map** D5
Put Trstenika 19
Tel *021 303 030*
Ⓦ radissonblu.com/resort-split
With a pebble beach and well-appointed rooms, Radisson Blu is 4 km (2 miles) east of the centre.

SPLIT: Vestibul Palace ⓦⓦⓦ
Boutique   **Road Map** D5
Iza Vestibula 4
Tel *021 329 329*
Ⓦ vestibulpalace.com
Spectacular hotel combining modern design with Roman stonework, in Diocletian's former palace.

STON: Hotel Ostrea ⓦⓦ
B&B   **Road Map** E6
Mali Ston
Tel *020 754 555*
Ⓦ ostrea.hr
Family-run hotel right on the harbour, with large rooms, great service and a fabulous restaurant.

TROGIR: Hotel Concordia ⓦ
B&B   **Road Map** D5
Obala bana Berislavića 22
Tel *021 885 400*
Ⓦ concordia-hotel.net
Impressive 18th-century town house offering snug rooms and attentive service.

TROGIR: Villa Sikaa ⓦⓦ
B&B   **Road Map** D5
Obala kralja Zvonimira 13
Tel *021 881 223*
Ⓦ vila-sikaa-r.com
Small hotel set on the waterfront opposite the Old Town, with spacious rooms and helpful staff.

VIS: Dionis ⓦ
B&B   **Road Map** D6
Matije Gubca 1
Tel *021 711 963*
Ⓦ dionis.hr
Family-run B&B above a pizzeria offering snug rooms, many of them with sloping attic ceilings.

VIS: Issa ⓦ
Resort   **Road Map** D6
Šetalište Apolonija Zanelle 5
Tel *021 711 124*
Ⓦ hotelsvis.com
Overlooking pebbly beaches on the fringes of Vis town, the Issa has a wealth of sporting facilities.

VIS: Hotel San Giorgio ⓦⓦ
Boutique   **Road Map** D6
Petra Hektorovića 2
Tel *021 711 362*
Ⓦ hotelsangiorgiovis.com
An old stone house in a narrow alley, with cosy modern rooms and a walled orchard garden. Closed Nov–Mar.

VIS: Hotel Tamaris ⓦ
Historic   **Road Map** D6
Obala sv. Jurja 20
Tel *021 711 350*
Ⓦ hotelsvis.com
Stately 19th-century villa right on the harbour, with high-ceilinged rooms and a lively first-floor café.

ZADAR: Boutique Hostel Forum ⓦⓦ
Hostel   **Road Map** C4
Široka 20
Tel *023 250 705*
Ⓦ en.hostelforumzadar.com
One of the new super-hostels, with designer interiors and a couple of private double rooms.

ZADAR: Club Funimation Borik ⓦⓦⓦ
Resort   **Road Map** C4
Majstora Radovana 7
Tel *023 555 600*
Ⓦ falkensteiner.com
Family-oriented hotel just west of the town, with sports facilities, crèches and a pebble beach.

DK Choice

ZADAR: ladera ⓦⓦⓦ
Spa   **Road Map** C4
Punta Skala, Petrčane
Tel *023 555 601*
Ⓦ falkensteiner.com
Located 10 km (6 miles) north of Zadar just outside the unspoiled seaside village of Petrčane, this luxury spa hotel offers the full range of state-of-the-art facilities, with indoor pools, numerous therapeutic programmes and plenty of beauty treatments. The hotel grounds include a pine forest and grassy lawns. A pebbly beach is a short walk away.

Zagreb

ZAGREB: Hostel Shappy ⓦ
Hostel   **Road Map** D2
Varšavska 8
Tel *01 483 04 83*
Ⓦ hostel-shappy.com
Smart and soothing hostel with dorms, double rooms and quads, right in the centre of town.

ZAGREB: Studio Kairos ⓦ
B&B   **Road Map** D2
Vlaška 92
Tel *01 464 06 80*
Ⓦ studio-kairos.com
Cosy B&B with small, simply furnished rooms, each themed around Zagreb's history.

ZAGREB: Hotel Palace ⓦⓦ
Historic   **Road Map** D2
Trg J J Strossmayera 10
Tel *01 489 96 00*
Ⓦ palace.hr
An elegant pre-World War I townhouse with retro furnishings and Art Deco design touches.

ZAGREB: Sheraton Zagreb ⓦⓦ
Luxury   **Road Map** D2
Kneza Borne 2
Tel *01 455 35 35*
Ⓦ hotel-sheratonzagreb.com
International chain hotel with the standards of comfort and service you would expect, ten minutes' walk from the main square.

ZAGREB: The Westin Zagreb ⓦⓦ
Luxury   **Road Map** D2
Izidora Kršnjavog 1
Tel 01 489 20 00
Ⓦ hotelwestinzagreb.com
Plush, well-equipped 5-star in a superb location, towering above an open plaza in the Lower Town.

DK Choice

ZAGREB: Esplanade 🆆🆆🆆
Historic   Road Map D2
Mihanovićeva 1
Tel *01 456 66 66*
🆆 esplanade.hr
Opened in 1925 as a haven
for passengers on the Orient
Express, the prestigious and
uber-stylish Esplanade Zagreb
is an architectural gem. Located
within easy reach of key
attractions such as the cathedral
and the Art Pavilion, the city's
most iconic hotel combines
Art Deco glamour with every
contemporary convenience.

Central Croatia

ČIGOĆ: Tradicije Čigoć 🆆
B&B   Road Map D2
Čigoć 7a
Tel *044 715 124*
🆆 tradicije-cigoc.hr
Traditional wooden house in the
heart of Lonjsko Polje Nature
Park, offering cosy rustic rooms
with mod cons.

KARLOVAC: Hotel Korana
Srakovčić   🆆🆆
Luxury   Map C2
Perivoj Josipa Vrbanića 8
Tel *047 609 090*
🆆 hotelkorana.hr
A grand villa set in a delightful
riverside location, the Korana
offers style, sophistication and
plenty of sports facilities.

KRAPJE: Ekoetno Selo Strug 🆆
B&B   Road Map D2
Plesmo 26
Tel *044 611 212*
🆆 ekoetno-selo-strug.hr

Hotel Vestibul Palace, Split, set in an
imperial Roman residence

Modern bungalows decked out
in traditional country style, in a
rustic Lonjsko Polje park village.

SAMOBOR: Hotel Livadić 🆆
Historic   Road Map C2
Trg kralja Tomislava 1
Tel *01 336 5850*
🆆 hotel-livadic.hr
A delightful small hotel on a
charming square, with antique
furnishings and a lovely café.

Slavonia and Baranja

DK Choice

BILJE: Crvendać 🆆
B&B   Road Map F2
Biljske satnije 5
Tel *031 750 264*
🆆 crvendac.com
Welcoming, family-run B&B in
the tranquil Baranja village of
Bilje, just north of Osijek. Set in
a well-tended garden, Crvendać
(Robin Redbreast) features a
charming red-white colour
scheme that runs throughout
the rooms and communal
areas. The owner rents out
bikes, perfect for exploring the
Kopački Rit Nature Park nearby.

DARUVAR: Balise 🆆
B&B   Road Map E2
Trg kralja Tomislava 22
Tel *043 440 220*
🆆 hotel-balise.hr
Small, centrally located hotel
with simply furnished but comfy
air-conditioned rooms.

ILOK: Villa Iva 🆆
B&B   Road Map G2
Stjepana Radića 23
Tel *032 591 011*
Neat, bright rooms grouped
around a lovely arcaded
courtyard, in the centre of this
small wine-producing town.

OSIJEK: Vienna Apartments 🆆
B&B   Road Map F2
Radićeva 26a
Tel *031 214 026*
🆆 vienna-smjestaj.com
Small but cosy, fully equipped
rooms, in a quiet courtyard just
off a lively café-lined street.

OSIJEK: Hotel Osijek 🆆🆆
Luxury   Road Map F2
Šamačka 4
Tel *031 230 333*
🆆 hotelosijek.hr
Large modern hotel towering
above the Drava waterfront, with
smart rooms and spa facilities.

OSIJEK: Hotel Waldinger 🆆🆆
Historic   Road Map F2
Županijska 8
Tel *031 250 450*
🆆 waldinger.hr
Nineteenth-century city-centre
building with burgundy-hued
rooms and modern bathrooms.

ŠPIŠIĆ BUKOVICA:
Hotel Mozart 🆆
B&B   Road Map E2
Kinkovo bb
Tel *033 801 000*
🆆 hotelmozart.hr
Country-house hotel in the
middle of the countryside,
offering a slice of luxury in idyllic,
unspoilt surroundings.

VUKOVAR: Hotel Lav 🆆🆆
Luxury   Road Map G2
J J Strossmayera 18
Tel *032 445 100*
🆆 hotel-lav.hr
Smart, modern hotel offering
4-star rooms, exceptional service
and a central, riverside location.

The Northern Counties

KRAPINSKE TOPLICE:
Villa Magdalena 🆆🆆
Spa   Road Map D1
Mirna ulica 1
Tel *049 233 333*
🆆 www.villa-magdalena.net
Award-winning, intimate
wellness hotel; both the Jacuzzis
in every room and the spa are fed
by thermal waters.

TRAKOŠĆAN: Trakošćan 🆆🆆
Resort   Road Map D1
Trakošćan bb
Tel *042 440 800*
🆆 hotel-trakoscan.hr
Located right next to Trakošćan
Castle and its lake, this modern
hotel comes with plenty of
sports facilities.

TUHELJSKE TOPLICE:
Hotel Well 🆆🆆
Spa   Road Map C1
Ljudevita Gaja 4
Tel *049 203 750*
🆆 terme-tuhelj.hr
Plush rooms and modern
architecture are on offer at this
welcoming hotel.

VARAŽDIN: Pansion Garestin 🆆
B&B   Road Map D1
Zagrebačka 34
Tel *042 214 314*
🆆 gastrocom-ugostiteljstvo.com
Simple but well-equipped rooms
above a restaurant ten minutes'
walk from the town centre.

For more information on types of hotels *see pp222–5*

WHERE TO EAT AND DRINK

Food in Croatia is very varied, from the fresh fish and seafood found along the coast to the Central European staples such as veal, pork and poultry offered in inland Croatia. Proximity to the Balkans ensures that grilled meats and savoury pastries are always to be found too. Croatia's coastal areas offer an extraordinarily rich and healthy Mediterranean cuisine, with fish, octopus and squid joining lamb, fresh vegetables and olive oil. In the east, paprika-

flavoured, goulash-style dishes predominate. Pasta dishes and pizza (with a thin base, in the Italian style) feature virtually everywhere. Wherever you eat, fresh produce and locally sourced ingredients are the rule. Croatian specialities include sheep's milk cheese (*paški sir*) from Pag, home-cured ham (*pršut*), and truffles from Istria. Prices are generally lower than elsewhere in western Europe, making eating out in Croatia even more appealing.

Modern dining in a glass pavilion at Bevanda, Opatija

Taverns and Restaurants

The Croatian word *restoran* is used almost in exactly the same, broad way as we use restaurant. It is used to refer to any place where you can eat that offers a perhaps more upmarket, more formal dining experience compared to a straightforward bar or café. This can range from expensive fine dining at a hotel *restoran* to low-key, family-run establishments offering traditional menus. Equally, prices may range from the very expensive to more budget-friendly options.

Less formal places to try out are the numerous *gostionica* or *konoba* (both are similar to a trattoria or taverna). These are often family-run businesses and they are good places to try good, traditional, local food. The usual dishes found in a *konoba* include risotto (*rižoto* or *rižot*, depending on the region), *lignje* (squid rings), *grah* or *fažol* (bean soup) and basic grills such as *ražnjići* (pork kebabs) and *čevapi* (minced meat rissoles in a bun). There are a growing number of

Asian restaurants (especially sushi outlets), and the number of stylish contemporary bistros offering international food is also on the rise.

Most of the *gostionica* and *konoba* fall within the mid-price range and some offer very good value for money. The average cost of a meal is from around 150 to 220 kuna (between about £16 and £24). This sum would include a starter, a main course (always served with a vegetable) and a dessert. Prices vary according to the standard of the place and its location. A *gostionica* or *konoba* along the coast will almost certainly be more expensive than those inland. Sometimes there is an extra charge for bread, but the service charge is usually included in the price of each individual dish.

Along the coast, fresh fish is plentiful though not inexpensive. On menus, the prices of fish and seafood are generally given by the kilo. A useful rule of thumb is that a good-sized portion of fish or seafood will usually

weigh about 300 grams (10 ounces) and so you should be able to predict roughly how much you will be spending. The choice of fish and seafood on offer will vary daily depending on the catch.

Wine is often drunk with restaurant meals in Croatia (for an overview of Croatia's wines, *see pp236–7*), but it is very common for restaurants to serve a drink called *bevanda*, a mixture of wine and water, or *gemišt*, a mix of sparkling mineral water and wine. The local wine and water will be brought to the table separately for you to mix.

Many Croatian cafés (*kafić* or *kavana*) don't serve food at all, although an increasing number are beginning to offer quality cakes and sandwiches. Ice-cream and pastry shops, called *slastičarnica*, are great places to enjoy something sweet.

Pizzerias

Pizzas are always a good choice for the visitor travelling on a budget. Croatian pizzas are very

Giaxa, set in a superb Renaissance mansion in Hvar town, Hvar island (*see p242*)

The clue is in the name at 360 Degrees in Dubrovnik, with its wraparound views *(see p241)*

good and can compete with the best Italian tradition. Pizzerias usually have a range of pasta dishes and salads too. The prices are always reasonable and are on average 30–40 per cent lower than similar meals in many other parts of Europe.

Picnics and Self-Catering

Picnic food can easily be bought from food shops, supermarkets or from one of the typical open-air markets where you can find a great variety of salami, cheeses, bread and olives, as well as fresh fruit and drinks.

Retail food prices are very reasonable and shopkeepers usually try to be helpful. Ready-made sandwiches are becoming more popular in Croatia, though some places still make them to order. You will also find simple ready-made snacks such as *burek*. This is a type of savoury pastry, filled with meat *(meso)*, cheese *(sir)*, spinach *(špinat)* or potato *(krumpir)* and baked in an oven. Bakeries selling *burek* and other pastries can be found on every Croatian high street.

Families or groups staying in self-catering apartments should also have no problem stocking up. Many hotel complexes with apartments also have mini-supermarkets.

Vegetarian Food

More and more restaurants now offer vegetarian dishes and there are a few that specialize in vegetarian food. Be aware that some dishes that appear meat-free, like *manistra* (vegetable soup), may contain meat stock. However, restaurants, pizzerias and cafés serving Italian-style food will provide options such as pizzas with vegetable toppings and pasta dishes. Otherwise several side orders of vegetables are usually an option and omelettes *(omlet)* may be available in some places. The choice increases in autumn with the fresh mushroom season, especially in the Istria region.

Paying

You will find that most Croatian restaurants now accept credit cards, although it is still possible to come across a few where the bill has to be paid in cash.

However, credit cards are often not accepted in cafés or in rural establishments, so make sure that you carry enough cash with you.

Opening Hours

Places serving food and drinks have very flexible opening hours, and it is possible to eat at more or less any time of the day, especially in tourist resorts. However, meal times for locals are broadly as in other Mediterranean countries. Lunch is generally served from about noon to 2pm and dinner from around 8pm to 10pm.

Recommended Restaurants and DK Choices

The restaurants listed in this guidebook have been chosen based on a wide range of criteria. All are representative of their setting, be that city streets, the Dalmatian islands or the inland plains of eastern Croatia. Each stands out and has earned a noteworthy reputation.

Listings cover a vast variety of eateries, from simple, family-run taverns to stylish bistros, formal white-tablecloth restaurants, and gourmet destinations. Particular attention is devoted to regional specialities, from the fresh fish and seafood of the Adriatic to the spicy paprika-flavoured fare of Slavonia.

The DK Choice label means the restaurant is outstanding and heartily recommended. It may serve stand-out dishes with local specialities, offer excellent value, located in beautiful surrounds or a historic building, or have a particularly romantic or charming atmosphere. Whatever the reason, it is an indication that you should have an especially memorable meal.

Deliciously fresh fish and seafood is served at Proto, Dubrovnik

The Flavours of Croatia

Croatia can be broadly divided into four main culinary regions: Istrian cuisine is proud of its Italian heritage and features elegant pasta, gnocchi and truffle dishes; Dalmatian cuisine is seafood-based and has Venetian echoes; the fertile farmlands of Slavonia have a more Hungarian influence of peppers and spice; while central Croatia retains Austrian predilections – schnitzel, desserts and cakes. However, there are some consistent characteristics – bread is key and is always freshly made either at home or in the local bakery *(pekara)*; fish is important all over the country given the length of the coastline and the many lakes and rivers; and grilling is the preferred cooking method.

Wild aparagus

Sardines and other seafood on sale at Split's busy fish market

Istria

With a noticeably Italianate cuisine, food is taken more seriously in Istria than anywhere else outside of Zagreb. Here the truffle, *tartufi,* is venerated. Although freshest in autumn, truffles are used dried all-year-round in risottos and pasta dishes such as *mare monti* (a "surf and turf" combination of mushrooms and shellfish). Many restaurant kitchens roast food in a *peka* – a lidded pot buried in hot ashes – to retain all the flavour and juices. Look out for *srnetina,* venison stew with gnocchi, or roasted, meadow-fed lamb. Other delights are the soft Istrian smoked ham *(pršut)* and don't miss the best oysters and mussels in Croatia, farmed in the clean waters of the Limski Channel.

Dalmatia

The Adriatic supplies Croatia with much of its fish. Gilthead bream, red mullet, sole and John Dory are common, as are clams, mussels, oysters, octopus, squid, prawns and even crab and lobster. The channels created by hundreds of islands are perfect for cultivating excellent quality shellfish. Produce is prepared with olive oil, garlic and herbs,

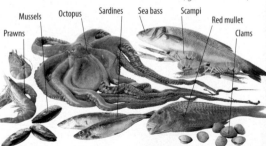
Mussels Octopus Sardines Sea bass Scampi
Prawns Red mullet Clams
Selection of typical seafood popular throughout Croatia

Croatian Dishes and Specialities

Pršut – smoked ham

Many of Croatia's religious and folk holiday festivals are traditionally associated with a particular dish. *Bakalar* (salt cod), for example, is eaten on Christmas Eve and Good Friday, *kulen* (spiced salami) is a Harvest Thanksgiving dish and *guska* (goose) served with chestnuts is a St Martin's Day treat. The Turkish occupation, over 200 years ago, has left behind a legacy of grilled meats and kebabs, *sarma* (cabbage leaf stuffed with rice and mince), *burek* (filo pastry tube filled with meat or curd cheese), and *baklava* (pastries filled with nuts and drenched in sweet syrup). Coastal specialities include *brudet* (fish stew with polenta), *crni rižot* (cuttlefish ink risotto) and *lignje* (squid), served lightly fried in breadcrumbs or *na žaru* (grilled whole).

Maneštra A filling soup made of smoked meat, beans, pasta and vegetables – an Istrian version of minestrone.

Fresh-baked bread and pastries for sale at a Croatian bakery *(pekara)*

Slavonia & Baranja

The Austro-Hungarian Empire has also affected Slavonian cooking but with a Hungarian flavour. Large portions of warming dishes insulate the mainly rural population from a cold, wet and often snowy climate. Expect meat or fish in rich sauces, spiced with paprika. The Drava river provides a good supply of freshwater fish like pike and carp. Do try a few slices of Slavonia's famous appetizer, *kulen*. This smoke-cured salami, flavoured with chilli and paprika, is often served with peppers, tomatoes, *turšija* (pickled vegetables) and sometimes curd cheese.

cooked quickly – fried, grilled or boiled – and served simply. Easy Italian cooking reigns here – risottos, pizza and pasta feature on menus as a result of history, proximity and the sheer number of Italian visitors. Try Dalmatian *pršut*, firmer than the Istrian version, or *janjetina* – lamb fed on lush island grass and herbs; it's great spit-roasted.

Central & Northern Croatia

Inland the food is much richer – olive oil is replaced by butter, lard or dripping. Menus are meat-driven with hearty, filling side dishes such as dumplings and noodles – legacies from Austrian rule. Zagreb has a sophisticated gastronomy but outside of the capital, rustic flavours and styles abound and there is a greater use of veal

and game. As well as being grilled, meat is often cooked in a rich stew or spit-roasted *(pečenje)* – goose, duck, lamb, wild boar and venison are favourites. But perhaps the most obvious Viennese influence is on the rich desserts – pancakes, strudels and rib-sticking *štrukli*.

Croatian cheese shop, with a variety of hard, soft and goat's cheeses

ON THE MENU

Fiš paprikaš: Fiery fish stew from Slavonia often made with carp and spiced with paprika.

Zagrebački odrezak: Veal, ham and cheese fried in breadcrumbs – a super-schnitzel.

Ajvar: A savoury red pepper sauce/relish – everyone has their own secret recipe.

Čevapčići: A Turkish legacy – spicy meat rissoles served with raw onion, flatbread and ajvar.

Blitva s krumpirom: Popular side dish of chard boiled with potatoes, olive oil and garlic.

Palačinke: One of Croatia's top desserts: jam-filled pancakes, with chocolate and walnuts.

Škampi na buzaru Scampi is gently simmered in wine, tomatoes, garlic and herbs; finished with breadcrumbs.

Pašticada A beef joint and seasonal vegetables are slowly pot-roasted in wine – prunes are also sometimes used.

Štrukli This northern Croatian dish of parcels of curd cheese, boiled and then baked, can be either sweet or savoury.

What to Drink in Croatia

A wide variety of locally made drinks is available throughout Croatia, from beers and wines to fiery fruit brandies. Croatian beer is usually of the lager type but dark beers can also be found. Foreign brands such as Stella Artois, Tuborg, Beck's and Carlsberg are brewed in Croatia under licence, and there are Irish pubs selling Guinness and other Irish beers. Croatia's vineyards yield all kinds of red and white wines, most of which are rarely seen outside the country. Spirits based on grapes are popular as aperitifs rather than as after-dinner drinks, as are other fruit brandies made from plums or pears. Brandies flavoured with herbs, walnuts or even honey are also popular. Tap water is safe to drink but if the taste does not appeal there is a wide range of bottled mineral waters, both sparkling and still.

Typical sign for a pub, *pivnica* in Croatian

Traditional utensils for the preparation of strong Turkish coffee

Coffee and Tea

Coffee (*kava*) is drunk throughout Croatia. All over the country it is served very strong and black, in little cups, like an *espresso* coffee. If it is too strong you can add a little milk or order a *cappuccino* (freshly ground coffee with frothy hot milk). Strong Turkish coffee is also available in some places. Herbal teas (*čaj*) are sold everywhere. Indian teas can also be found, usually served with lemon, but you can ask for milk.

Beer

Another very popular drink sold in cafés and pubs is beer (*pivo*), which is always served very cold.

Most bottled beers are of the lager type, but some darker beers can be found. The most well-known brands of lager beer are Ožujsko, made in Zagreb, and Karlovačko (Karlovac). Another common brand is Pan. Well-known international beers such as Stella Artois are also widely available (some brewed under licence in Croatia), but tend to be more expensive.

Karlovačko beer   Ožujsko beer

Spirits

A wide variety of spirits is available in Croatia, demonstrating the nation's fondness for strong alcoholic drinks, in particular fruit-based eaux-de-vie. One of the most popular spirits is a plum brandy originating in Slavonia called Šljivovica. It is found all over the country. Loza is a grape-based eau-de-vie with a high alcohol content, and Travarica is a herb-based spirit. Vinjak is a brandy, Pelinkovac is a herb liqueur, and Maraskino, a liqueur from Zadar, is flavoured with maraschino cherries.

Many spirits are drunk as aperitifs. A spirit called Bermet is produced in Samobor, near Zagreb, and is made according to an ancient, well-guarded recipe. It is drunk as an aperitif, served with ice and a slice of lemon.

Pelinkovac liqueur   Zrinski brandy

Šljivovica eau-de-vie

Some bottles of eau-de-vie with fruit, made at home all over the country

Mineral Water, Soft Drinks and Fruit Juices

All bars and cafés in Croatia will offer a wide range of fruit juices, as well as the usual internationally known brands of soft drinks and fizzy drinks like cola. Tap water is safe to drink everywhere in Croatia and bottled mineral waters *(mineralna voda)* are also widely available. The most common brands of mineral water in Croatia are Studena, Jamnica and Jana, but there are also many imported brands available as well. Ask for *gazirana* (carbonated) *voda* for sparkling water, or *negazirana* for still.

Mineral water

Orange juice

Pubs and bars with live music: a popular way to socialize

Drinking Customs in Croatia

Pubs, bars and cafés are not only places to stop at various times of the day for refreshment, but also places to meet friends and socialize. For visitors this can also be a good way of meeting and getting to know local people.

One tradition found in Croatia is that of mixing wine with other drinks such as mineral water or even cola. A *bevanda* is red or white wine with plain water, while *gemišt* is white wine mixed with sparkling mineral water. One of the most popular summer drinks is red wine and fizzy cola, a drink called *bambus*.

Croatians like a drink or two, as is demonstrated by the custom in the Slavonian region of wine drinking with friends. This traditional ritual should only be undertaken by people with a very strong head for alcohol. It begins with the first phase, which is before any wine is consumed, known as the *Dočekuša*. This is then followed by the *Razgovoruša*, during which you chat while sipping at least seven glasses of wine. The final phase is called the *Putnička*, reserved for the leave-taking, when yet more glasses are emptied before people say their final farewells.

Wines

Croatia is a land of vineyards, with vines growing on the slopes of rolling hills inland and in pockets of stony soil on the coast and islands. Production varies in quantity and quality but standards are improving and there are some very decent wines around. From the Kvarner area come the white wine Žlahtina (from Vrbnik on Krk), red Cabernet (from Poreč) and Teran (from Buzet), a light red. Dalmatia is known for Pošip and Grk from Korčula (both white wines), Dingač (one of the best Croatian reds) and Postup from the Pelješac peninsula. Plavac (red) comes from Brač and Malmsey from Dubrovnik. Finally, from Slavonia come Kutjevačka Graševina, Kutjevo Chardonnay and Riesling, and Krauthaker Graševina.

Zlahtina

Dingač   Postup

Where to Drink

There are various types of establishments which serve drinks and it is useful to know a few of the basic categories. A *kavana* or *kafić* is equivalent to a café, and serves both alcoholic and non-alcoholic drinks, while a *pivnica* serves mainly beer. Irish pubs can also be found, selling Guinness and other Irish beers. Wine is generally drunk in a *konoba* in coastal towns. In the larger towns you can have a snack with your drink in one of the *bife*, the Croatian equivalent of a snack bar. However, there are not really rigid distinctions between the types of drinks served in one or other of these places. Cafés open early and close late – usually around 11pm or later in the summer.

Drinks of various kinds (though rarely alcoholic) are also served in pastry shops – *slastičarnica*. The close links that Croatia's gastronomic tradition has with Austria, and in particular with Vienna, has influenced the production of delicious cakes and pastries as well as excellent *sladoled* (ice cream). Pastry shops close earlier than cafés in general.

A snack bar with outdoor tables in Fažana, a coastal resort

Where to Eat and Drink

Istria and the Kvarner Area

BUZET: Toklarija 🍷🍷🍷
Fine Dining   **Road Map** B2
Sovinjsko polje 11
Tel *091 926 6769*   **Closed** *Tue*
An acclaimed restaurant in a tiny village, the rustic Toklarija takes the best local ingredients, including asparagus, truffles and mushrooms in season, and transforms them into haute cuisine. Slow cooking, superb quality, high prices.

CRES: Gostionica Belona 🍷
Seafood   **Road Map** B3
Šetalište 23 travnja 24
Tel *051 571 203*   **Closed** *Dec–Feb*
A rustic place popular with locals and lively in the evenings, Belona serves seafood staples, usually including excellent squid alongside simple pasta and grilled-meat dishes.

CRES: Riva 🍷🍷
Seafood   **Road Map** B3
Riva creskih kapetana 13
Tel *051 571 107*   **Closed** *Nov–Mar*
Facing the town square on one side and the harbour on the other, Riva offers good, fresh fish – try sea bass, scampi or seafood risotto.

HUM: Humska konoba 🍷
Traditional   **Road Map** B2
Hum 2, Roč
Tel *052 660 005*   **Closed** *weekdays, Nov–Mar*
Tiny village tavern with a beautiful terrace and tasty inland-Istrian cuisine. Try local sausages with sauerkraut, or home-made pasta with truffles.

KASTAV: Kukuriku 🍷🍷🍷
Mediterranean   **Road Map** B2
Trg Lokvina 3
Tel *051 691 519*
Famous for presenting traditional Croatian and Mediterranean food in contemporary haute-cuisine style, Kukuriku offers seasonally changing five-course menus, each accompanied by appropriate wines.

KRK: Konoba Nono 🍷🍷
Traditional   **Road Map** B3
Krčkih iseljenika 8
Tel *051 222 221*   **Closed** *Nov–Mar*
A traditional restaurant specializing in local seafood and Krk specialities – try the *šurlice*, tubes of pasta basted in goulash or seafood sauce.

KRK: Konoba Šime 🍷🍷
Seafood   **Road Map** B3
Riva bb
Tel *051 220 042*
A trusty harbourside restaurant, quite dark inside but with a bright outdoor seating area, serving fresh local seafood (breaded squid and black risotto are among the favourites), as well as Balkan-style grilled meats.

LIMSKI CHANNEL: Viking 🍷🍷🍷
Regional   **Road Map** A3
Lim bb, Sveti Lovreč
Tel *052 448 223*
Breathtakingly situated on the shores of the Limski Channel marine reserve, Viking (named after a Hollywood movie that was shot here) serves locally raised mussels, oysters and other shellfish, alongside superb fresh-caught fish.

LOŠINJ: Marina 🍷🍷
Seafood   **Road Map** B3
Obala maršala Tita 38, Veli Lošinj
Tel *051 236 178*   **Closed** *Nov–Mar*
A superb location on Veli Lošinj's main harbour and an emphasis on freshly caught fish make this one of the best places to sample seafood on the island.

LOŠINJ: Bora Bar 🍷🍷🍷
Mediterranean   **Road Map** B3
Rovenska 3, Veli Lošinj
Tel *051 867 544*   **Closed** *Nov–Mar*
Run by a long-standing truffle enthusiast, Bora Bar specializes in dishes flavoured by the mighty fungus, although there are plenty of other pasta and seafood dishes on the menu.

Cheerful outdoor terrace and tables at Bora Bar, Lošinj

LOVRAN: Draga di Lovrana 🍷🍷
Mediterranean   **Road Map** B2
Lovranska draga 1
Tel *051 294 166*
On a verdant mountainside overlooking the Kvarner Gulf, Lovran specializes in bringing the freshest produce – from forest or seaboard – direct to the table.

MOŠĆENIČE DRAGA: Johnson 🍷🍷
Mediterranean   **Road Map** B2
Majčevo 29b, Mošćenika Draga
Tel *051 737 578*   **Closed** *Oct–May; Tue*
Family members are in charge of the kitchen, service and daily supplies of fresh fish which determine the menu for the day.

MOTOVUN: Mondo 🍷🍷🍷
Regional   **Road Map** A2
Barbacan 1
Tel *052 681 791*
Excellent-value restaurant with a romantic candlelit interior, an evocative outdoor terrace, and a menu rich in local Istrian truffles.

MOTOVUN: Zigante 🍷🍷🍷
Regional   **Road Map** A2
Livade 7
Tel *052 664 302*
Owned by a local truffle harvesting firm, this restaurant naturally focuses on inland Istria's favourite fungus. Truffle pastas, truffle omelettes and truffle-covered steaks dominate the menu.

NOVIGRAD: Damir i Ornella 🍷🍷🍷
Seafood   **Road Map** A2
Zidine 5
Tel *052 758 134*   **Closed** *Nov–Feb*
Something of a pilgrimage place for seafood lovers, this small and intimate restaurant serves superb fish, including some sashimi-influenced raw fish dishes.

NOVIGRAD: Marina 🍷🍷🍷
Seafood   **Road Map** A2
Sv Antona 38
Tel *052 726 691*
Situated beside the yachting marina, this dedicated seafood restaurant serves imaginative fish dishes accompanied by excellent local wines.

NOVIGRAD: Pepenero 🄦🄦🄦
Gourmet **Road Map** A2
Porporela
Tel *052 757 706*
Adriatic seafood is the main theme at this top-notch restaurant, though most dishes feature a measure of creative fusion; the seven-course tasting menu puts Pepenero to the test.

OPATIJA: Istranka 🄦
Traditional **Road Map** B2
Bože Milanoviça 2
Tel *051 271 835*
A folksy restaurant with checked tablecloths just uphill from the main street, serving filling soups, inexpensive seafood and tasty local sausages.

OPATIJA: Tramerka 🄦🄦
Seafood **Road Map** B2
Dr A. Mohorovičića 15
Tel *051 701 707*
Occupying a narrow alley just above Volosko harbour, Tramerka combines the cosy virtues of a traditional tavern with the finest seafood, with the accent on what's in season and fresh.

OPATIJA: Bevanda 🄦🄦🄦
Seafood **Road Map** B2
Zert 8
Tel *051 493 888*
A seafood restaurant offering high-quality cuisine and impeccable standards of service, Bevanda occupies a chic seafront pavilion with a glass-enclosed terrace.

OPATIJA: Le Mandrać 🄦🄦🄦
Fusion **Road Map** B2
Obala Frana Supila 10
Tel *051 701 357*
A sleek glass pavilion right on Volosko harbour, Le Mandrać is famous for matching Adriatic staples with modern creative kitchencraft. Look out for set lunches and multi-course tasting menus.

DK Choice

OPATIJA: Plavi podrum 🄦🄦🄦
Seafood **Road Map** B2
Obala Frana Supila 12
Tel *051 701 223*
A refined restaurant on Volosko's picturesque fishing harbour, Plavi podrum has a Croatia-wide reputation for its creative fish dishes. It's the perfect place to sample Kvarner scampi, prepared here in a variety of ways. The excellent cellar contains local and international wines by the bottle or the glass; the owner is also a highly regarded sommelier.

Waterside dining with expansive views, Bevanda restaurant, Opatija

POREČ: Nono 🄦
Pizza **Road Map** A2
Zagrebačka 4
Tel *052 453 088*
Nono serves some of the best and certainly the biggest pizzas in Istria, alongside good steaks, grilled squid and other Adriatic staples. It's small and often full, but worth the wait.

POREČ: Konoba Ulixes 🄦🄦
Traditional **Road Map** A2
Decumanus 2
Tel *052 451 132* **Closed** *Nov–Apr*
Rustic and maritime objects decorate the interior of this classy little restaurant, with reasonably priced seafood, pasta and truffle dishes dominating the menu.

POREČ: Sveti Nikola 🄦🄦🄦
Seafood **Road Map** A2
Obala maršala Tita 23
Tel *052 423 018*
Refined dining right on Poreč's harbour-front, with delicately prepared fish dishes and superb risottos backed up by a well-chosen selection of Croatian wines.

PULA: Amfiteatar 🄦
Mediterranean **Road Map** A3
Amfiteatarska 6
Tel *052 375 600*
Set in the chic modern interior of the Amfiteatar hotel, this restaurant takes the best of Mediterranean cuisine and presents it in both a creative and affordable way.

PULA: Jupiter 🄦
Pizza **Road Map** A3
Castropola 42
Tel *052 214 333*
A welcoming pizzeria in the middle of town, with an affordable range of big thin-crust pies, Jupiter also serves soups, salads and grilled-meat snacks.

PULA: Vodnjanka 🄦
Traditional **Road Map** A3
D. Vitezića 4
Tel *052 210 655* **Closed** *Sun*
A little way outside the centre of town but well worth the trip, the homely Vodnjanka serves home-made pasta, marinated fish dishes and roast meats, all at very reasonable prices.

PULA: Batelina 🄦🄦
Seafood **Road Map** A3
Čimulje 25
Tel *052 573 767*
Three kilometres (2 miles) south of Pula, this family-run restaurant is legendary for its superb, frequently creative, cooking, always involving freshly caught fish and shellfish. Reservations are essential.

PULA: Milan 🄦🄦🄦
Seafood **Road Map** A3
Stoja 4
Tel *052 300 200*
An elegant location in which to enjoy the best local seafood, Milan offers fresh fish either grilled or baked, plus a dessert trolley brimming with temptation.

PULA: Velanera 🄦🄦🄦
Mediterranean **Road Map** A3
Franje Mošnja 3b, Šišan
Tel *052 300 621*
Located in Šišan, 7 km (4 miles) from central Pula, this chic hotel restaurant serves up Mediterranean and international cuisine with a splash of local Istrian flavour.

RAB: Konoba Riva 🄦🄦
Traditional **Road Map** B3
Ulica biskupa Draga 3
Tel *051 725 887*
Appealingly decked out in fishing paraphernalia, wooden beams and exposed stone, Riva is a great place to enjoy quality Adriatic seafood at a reasonable price.

For more information on types of restaurants *see pp232–3*

RAB: Astoria ⓦⓦⓦ
Seafood **Road Map** B3
Trg Municipium Arba 2
Tel *051 774 844* **Closed** *mid-Oct–Apr*
A first-floor restaurant looking out over the main square, Astoria serves fresh fish and seafood with style and panache, followed by some terrific desserts.

RAB: Marco Polo ⓦⓦⓦ
Seafood **Road Map** B3
Banjol 486
Tel *051 725 846*
Located in the coastal suburb of Banjol, Marco Polo offers Adriatic seafood with an imaginative twist, served in an elegant dining room or on a garden terrace.

RIJEKA: Bracera ⓦ
Pizza **Road Map** B2
Kružna 12
Tel *051 322 498*
A popular and enjoyable pizzeria just off the main Korzo, with nautical decorations and a satisfying menu of inexpensive pastas, salads, pizzas and risottos, and meats grilled over charcoal.

RIJEKA: Konoba Tarsa ⓦ
Traditional **Road Map** B2
Josipa Kulfaneka 10
Tel *051 452 089*
Up the hill from the centre in Trsat, Tarsa offers a huge menu of pasta and meat dishes, a wide choice of Croatian wines, and an atmospherically rustic interior.

RIJEKA:
Kuća istarskog pršuta ⓦ
Bistro **Road Map** B2
Riva Boduli 3a
Right on the harbour, this informal bistro with a handful of tables and bar stools offers soups, cheeses, home-cured *pršut* (ham) and local wines from the barrel.

RIJEKA: Bistro La Rose ⓦⓦ
French **Road Map** B2
Andrije Medulića 8
Tel *051 315 504* **Closed** *Sun*
A welcoming restaurant decked out like a 19th-century living room, La Rose offers French-influenced soups, quiches and stews, alongside Adriatic seafood standards.

RIJEKA: Kamov ⓦⓦⓦ
Modern European **Road Map** B2
Dolac 4
Tel *051 357 980*
The restaurant of the Bonavia hotel provides chic modern decor, old-school service, and a menu of Croatian meat and seafood classics given a creative, contemporary European twist.

Contemporary cuisine in an upmarket setting at Monte, Rovinj

ROVINJ: Giannino ⓦⓦ
Seafood **Road Map** A3
Augusta Ferrija 38
Tel *052 813 402* **Closed** *Tue*
Located in a typically atmospheric alley, Giannino offers superb pasta and seafood in a dining room full of artworks or on a shaded terrace on the street.

ROVINJ: La Puntulina ⓦⓦ
Seafood **Road Map** A3
Svetog Križa 38
Tel *052 813 186*
Set in a cliff-hugging stone house decorated with arty objects, La Puntulina excels in imaginative fish dishes, seafood pastas and risottos. The adjoining cocktail bar offers seating on the rocks.

ROVINJ: Veli Jože ⓦⓦ
Traditional **Road Map** A3
Svetog Križa 1
Tel *052 816 337*
Wooden benches and a jumble of quasi-antiques characterize this enjoyable restaurant offering seafood, pastas and roast meats. Often crowded, but it's well worth the wait.

ROVINJ: Kantinon ⓦⓦⓦ
Regional **Road Map** A3
Obala Aldo Rismondo bb
Tel *052 816 075*
A high-ceilinged harbour-side former storehouse houses this Istrian speciality restaurant, serving the best local meats and fish with recipes taken from old-fashioned cookbooks.

ROVINJ: L ⓦⓦⓦ
Global Fusion **Road Map** A3
Luje Adamovića 31
Tel *052 632 000*
Housed in the futuristic Hotel Lone, L fuses Adriatic ingredients with global herbs and spices to create a light, healthy, exotic cuisine that looks as well-designed as the building itself.

ROVINJ: Monte ⓦⓦⓦ
Mediterranean **Road Map** A3
Montalbano 75
Tel *052 830 203* **Closed** *mid-Oct–mid-Apr*
A high-class dining experience with friendly, informal service, Monte offers sparkling fish and seafood alongside multi-course tasting menus showcasing creative Mediterranean cuisine.

ROVINJ: Wine Vault ⓦⓦⓦ
Gourmet **Road Map** A3
A. Smareglia 3
Tel *052 636 017*
Based in the Monte Mulini hotel, Wine Vault is renowned for its quality, French-influenced cuisine and multi-course tasting menus intended to last several hours.

UMAG: Badi ⓦⓦ
Seafood **Road Map** A2
Lovrečica, Umag
Tel *052 756 293* **Closed** *Nov–Mar; Wed*
A fine restaurant in the village of Lovrečica, ten minutes' drive from Umag. Great seafood and sublime desserts, in a leafy green setting.

Dalmatia

BRAČ: Bistro Palute ⓦ
Traditional **Road Map** D5
Porat 4, Supetar
Tel *021 631 730*
Sit right on Supetar's harbour to enjoy Palute's superbly fresh fish alongside inexpensive dishes such as pasta and grilled meats.

BRAČ: Taverna Riva ⓦ
Regional **Road Map** D5
Frane Radića 5, Bol
Tel *021 635 236*
Baked lamb, veal, octopus and Brač *vitalac* (sheep innards) are among the specialities at this tavern on the Bol seafront.

Key to Price Guide *see p238*

BRAČ: Konoba Mlin 👛👛
Regional   **Road Map** D5
Ante Starčevića 11, Bol
Tel *021 635 376*   **Closed** *Nov–Mar*
Situated in an old mill in a
beautiful part of Bol, this
restaurant serves traditional
Dalmatian seafood and meat
dishes on a terrace with lovely
sea views.

BRAČ: Ribarska kućica 👛👛
Seafood   **Road Map** D5
Ante Starčevića bb, Bol
Tel *021 635 033*
The bare stone interior and
shore-side terrrace of the
"Fishermen's Hut" provide an
ideal venue to enjoy fish soups,
shellfish, scampi, lobster and
other Adriatic treats.

CAVTAT: Kolona 👛👛
Seafood   **Road Map** F6
Put Tihe 2
Tel *020 478 787*   **Closed** *Nov–Mar*
A cosy and traditional restaurant
with a leafy terrace, Kolona offers
traditional seafood specialities
and genuinely friendly service.
The owner is a fisherman, so
freshness is guaranteed.

CAVTAT: Galija 👛👛👛
Seafood   **Road Map** F6
Vulićevićeva 1
Tel *020 478 566*
Baked fish with potatoes is
just one of the specialities at
Cavtat's leading seafood
restaurant, with outdoor seating
overlooking the seafront.

DUBROVNIK: Gradska kavana 👛
Café   **Road Map** F6
Pred dvorom 1
Tel *020 321 202*
The principal meeting point for
coffee-sipping locals, the "town
café" offers an appetizing selection
of traditional desserts, including
torta od makarule, a famously rich
pasta-and-walnut cake.

DUBROVNIK: Komarda 👛
Grill   **Road Map** F6
Frana Supila bb
Tel *020 311 393*
Hidden down steps just outside
the eastern entrance to the
Old Town, Komarda cooks meat
and fish on an open grill, with
tables set out on a shore terrace.

DUBROVNIK: Tabasco 👛
Italian   **Road Map** F6
Hvarska 48a
Tel *020 429 595*
Immediately below Dubrovnik's
cable-car station, Tabasco offers
thin-crust pizzas from a wood-
fired oven, served on a shady
secluded terrace.

DUBROVNIK: Dalmatino 👛👛
Seafood   **Road Map** F6
Miha Pracata 6
Tel *020 323 070*   **Closed** *Jan & Feb*
An evocatively decorated Old
Town restaurant, Dalmatino serves
exquisite fish and superb desserts,
alongside selected regional wines.

DUBROVNIK: Glorijet 👛👛
Seafood   **Road Map** F6
Obala Stjepana Radića 16
Tel *020 419 788*   **Closed** *Sun*
This comfortable restaurant next
to the fish market in Gruž is the
ideal place to try marinated
anchovies, grilled squid, seafood
risottos and other Adriatic treats.

DUBROVNIK: Kopun 👛👛
Regional   **Road Map** F6
Poljana Ruđera Boškovića 7
Tel *020 323 969*   **Closed** *Dec & Jan*
Roast capon and traditional
Dubrovnik dishes are the
specialities at this restaurant, with
shaded seating on a lovely piazza
beside the Jesuit church.

DUBROVNIK: Lady Pi Pi 👛👛
Grill   **Road Map** F6
Peline bb
Closed *Nov–Mar*
Nestling beneath the town walls,
the Lady serves up delicious cuts
of fish and meat, grilled expertly
and served in a walled-garden
terrace. No reservations; be
prepared to wait.

**DUBROVNIK:
Lokanda Peskarija** 👛👛
Seafood   **Road Map** F6
Na ponti bb
Tel *020 324 750*
With outdoor seating spread
along the Old Port quayside, this
is a reliable choice for grilled
squid, seafood risotto and other
Adriatic staples.

> ### DK Choice
>
> **DUBROVNIK: Nishta** 👛👛
> Vegetarian   **Road Map** F6
> *Prijeko bb*
> **Tel** *020 322 088*   **Closed** *Sun*
> Nishta kicked off something of
> a gastro-revolution in fish- and
> meat-obsessed Dalmatia by
> opening this strictly vegetarian
> restaurant right in the heart of
> Dubrovnik's Old Town. The menu
> combines Thai, Indian, Mexican
> and Mediterranean influences
> to produce a satisfying and
> varied cuisine (suitable for vegans
> and gluten-free diners too) that
> frequently surprises with its
> creativity and flavour. Only
> a few tables, so booking ahead
> is advisable.

DUBROVNIK: Orhan 👛👛
Seafood   **Road Map** F6
Od Tabakarije 1
Tel *020 411 918*
On a rocky section of coast
beneath Lovrijenac fortress,
Orhan is a romantic location off
the beaten tourist track in which
to enjoy grilled fish and steaks
accompanied by quality
Dalmatian wines.

DUBROVNIK: Taj Mahal 👛👛
Bosnian-Herzegovinian
    Road Map F6
Nikole Gučetića 2
Tel *020 323 221*
Don't be fooled by the name: this
is a place for delicious Bosnian-
style grilled meats, stews and
freshly baked pastries filled with
minced meats, tender spinach or
salty white cheese.

**DUBROVNIK:
360 Degrees** 👛👛👛
Modern European   **Road Map** F6
Svetog Dominika 1
Tel *020 322 222*   **Closed** *Jan–Mar*
Modern European cuisine, a huge
wine list and extravagant cocktails
are on offer at this romantically
situated restaurant, which
occupies a section of the Old
Town fortifications.

**DUBROVNIK: Bota Oyster
and Sushi Bar** 👛👛👛
Global Fusion   **Road Map** F6
Od Pustijerne bb
Tel *020 324 034*
Fresh on-the-shells from the
nearby oyster beds at Ston, and
imaginative sushi fashioned from
local ingredients, in evocative
Old Town surroundings.

Atmospheric dining on a section of the old
city walls at 360 Degrees on Dubrovnik

DUBROVNIK: Levanat ©©©
Seafood   Road Map F6
Nika i Meda Pucića 15
Tel *020 435 352*
Fresh fish is either grilled, baked
or served with imaginative
sauces at this beautifully situated
restaurant on the coastal path
between Lapad and Babin kuk.

DUBROVNIK: Nautika ©©©
Seafood   Road Map F6
Brsalje 3
Tel *020 442 526*   **Closed** *Nov–Mar*
Offering fine dining in elegant
surroundings, Nautika blends
local seafood with the finesse of
modern European cuisine,
backed up by impeccable
standards of service.

DK Choice

DUBROVNIK: Proto ©©©
Seafood   Road Map F6
Široka 1
Tel *020 323 234* **Closed** *Nov–Mar*
Traditional Dalmatian fish
and seafood dishes are served
with care and imagination at
this elegant restaurant just off
the Old Town's main street.
Affordable daily specials are
offered at lunchtime, and
there is an excellent list of
fine regional wines. Outdoor
seating on the first-floor
terrace makes Proto one of
the most evocative dining
spots in town.

DUGI OTOK: Tamaris ©
Traditional   Road Map C4
Sali 18, Sali
Tel *023 377 377*
A simple place, popular with
the locals as a bar, Tamaris
nevertheless serves excellent
fish, squid and shellfish from the
surrounding seas.

HVAR: Jurin podrum ©
Seafood   Road Map D5
Donja kola 11, Stari Grad
Tel *021 765 448*   **Closed** *Nov–Apr*
Occupying a stone building in
the centre of Stari Grad's Old
Town, "Jura's Cellar" mixes local
favourites such as octopus stew
or shellfish in wine sauce with a
more international selection of
grills, pastas and salads.

HVAR: Kod Kapetana ©
Seafood   Road Map D5
Fabrika 30, Hvar town
Tel *021 742 230*
Occupying a pleasant spot on
Hvar's harbour-front, "At The
Captain's" is popular among the
locals for its fresh fish and squid,
expertly grilled.

HVAR: Pizzeria Kogo ©
Pizza   Road Map D5
Trg svetog Stjepana 34, Hvar town
Tel *021 742 136*
Kogo is a main-square pizzeria
that serves up reliable and
well-priced thin-crust pies
throughout the year, alongside
inexpensive Dalmatian snacks
and daily specials.

HVAR: Turan ©
Regional   Road Map D5
Jelsa
Tel *021 761 441*
A handsome choice of perfectly
executed local dishes including
stewed octopus, grilled fish and
succulent fresh squid, fuelled by
first-rate house wine.

HVAR: Eremitaž ©©
Seafood   Road Map D5
Priko bb, Stari Grad
Tel *021 766 167*
Located in what was once a
hospital for quarantined sailors,
this family-run restaurant serves
up a wide range of excellent
fish specialities.

HVAR: Antika ©©©
Seafood   Road Map D5
Donja kola 24, Stari Grad
Tel *021 765 479*
In the pretty cobblestoned
centre of old Stari Grad is this
characterful café-restaurant,
serving everything from tuna
steaks and seafood risottos to
cakes and cocktails.

HVAR: Gariful ©©©
Seafood   Road Map D5
Obala Riva 33, Hvar town
Tel *021 742 999*   **Closed** *out
of season*
With fabulous views of the
Pakleni islands and a stunning

Fish restaurant Proto, Dubrovnik, with
outdoor seating on two levels

under-floor aquarium, family-run
Gariful serves local seafood with
real finesse – although prices are
on the special-treat side.

HVAR: Giaxa ©©©
International   Road Map D5
Petra Hektorovića 11, Hvar town
Tel *021 741 073*   **Closed** *Nov–
mid-Apr*
Although the ingredients are
sourced locally, the accent at
Giaxa is on inventive European
cuisine. The retaurant's setting, in
a restored Renaissance mansion,
is outstanding.

DK Choice

HVAR: Macondo ©©©
Seafood   Road Map D5
Groda bb, Hvar town
Tel *021 742 850*
This fine restaurant just uphill
from the main square has long
been regarded as one of the
best places on the island for
excellent seafood served in an
informal and friendly ambience.
The spaghetti with lobster or
the scampi in buzara sauce are
well worth trying; and the list
of local wines provides a good
introduction to the island's
developing viniculture. Outdoor
seating is in an atmospheric
narrow alley.

KORČULA: Arsenal ©
Regional   Road Map E6
Rampada 1
Tel *020 711 720*
Don't allow the deceptively
plain decor to take your attention
away from the first-class food
here, with the accent on regional
specialities such as *Žrnovski
makaruni* (local pasta) and
Dalmatian *pašticada* (marinated
meat stew).

KORČULA: Kanavelić ©©
Seafood   Road Map E6
Sveta Barbara 12
Tel *020 711 800*   **Closed** *Nov–Apr*
A walled courtyard shaded by
orange trees provides the venue
for this speciality seafood
restaurant, offering a range of
freshly caught fish either grilled,
baked or stewed.

KORČULA: LD ©©©
Gourmet   Road Map E6
Don Pavla Poše 1–6
Tel *020 715 560*
Local meat and fish dishes are
given an inventive twist at this
classy restaurant, with seating on
Korčula's waterfront promenade.
It's the ideal place to sample the
best of the local wines, too.

MAKARSKA: Jež
International   **Road Map** E5
Petra Krešimira IV 90
Tel *021 611 741*
Traditional Dalmatian cuisine is served in a modern, light and airy environment. The fish dishes are excellent; the desserts divine.

METKOVIĆ: Villa Neretva
Regional   **Road Map** E6
Splitska 14, Krvavac II
Tel *020 672 200*
This family-run hotel restaurant is famed for its Neretva Delta specialities: frogs legs prepared in a variety of ways, or mixed with chopped eel to make a delicious *brodet*, a spicy red soup.

OREBIĆ: Amfora
Traditonal   **Road Map** E6
Šetalište kneza Domagoja 6
Tel *020 713 779*
Local fish, squid and grilled meats fill the menu of this friendly family-run restaurant. The terrace offers sweeping views of Korčula across the water.

PAG: Konoba Bodulo
Traditional   **Road Map** C4
Vangrada 19
Tel *091 564 8212*   **Closed** *mid-Oct–mid-Apr*
Fresh and simple food is served in the welcome shade of a grapevine. The menu offers all kinds of seafood and pasta dishes; the soupy fish stew *(brodet)* is delicious.

PAG: Boškinac
Traditonal   **Road Map** C4
Novaljsko polje bb
Tel *053 663 500*
Local island produce, including Pag's excellent lamb, fresh fish and famous cheese, are served with style at this boutique hotel's restaurant in its pretty setting.

Tables under the ancient stone arcades at Giaxa, old Hvar town

Restaurant Nautika in Dubrovnik, on the western entrance to the Old Town

ŠIBENIK: Tinel
Traditional   **Road Map** D5
Trg pučkih kapetana 1
Tel *022 331 815*
Situated in a small square in the Old Town, this restaurant covers two floors and serves a range of Dalmatian classics – seafood, grilled meats and stews.

ŠIBENIK: Uzorita
Regional   **Road Map** D5
Bana Josipa Jelačića 58
Tel *022 213 660*
A sleek interior and modern patio give a contemporary feel |to this traditional restaurant, specializing in locally farmed mussels, fresh seafood and roast meats.

ŠIBENIK: Pelegrini
Mediterranean   **Road Map** D5
Jurja Dalmatinca 1
Tel *022 213 701*   **Closed** *Mon*
In a 700-year-old villa alongside the cathedral, Pelegrini gives a modern twist and exquisite, contemporary presentation to local produce and specialities, including an extensive list of the best Croatian wines. Attentive staff serve unmissable fare in a gorgeous setting.

SPLIT: Bobis
Café   **Road Map** D5
Riva 29
Bobis is something of a Split institution, serving coffee, cakes and pastries to generations of locals. It's a good place to try local specialities like *krostata* (fruit pie).

SPLIT: Bufet Fife
Traditional   **Road Map** D5
Trumbićeva obala 11
Tel *021 345 223*
Very much a legend of the local culinary scene, Fife offers large, inexpensive portions of Dalmatian seafood and stews, and remains totally unspoiled by its growing popularity with in-the-know tourists.

SPLIT: Galija
Pizza   **Road Map** D5
Kamila Tončića 12
Tel *021 347 932*
For years Galija has been a favourite among locals, offering inexpensive thin-crust pizzas In a cosy street-corner location a short walk from Diocletian's Palace.

SPLIT: Kod Joze
Traditional   **Road Map** D5
Sredmanuška 4
Tel *021 347 397*
The traditional decor featuring bare stone walls and fishing nets provides the ideal background for a reliable menu of good, inexpensive seafood.

SPLIT: Marjan
Traditional   **Road Map** D5
Senjska 1
Tel *098 934 6848*
A tiny, family-run tavern serving fresh fish, squid and traditional stews, Marjan is popular with locals and tourists – be prepared to wait for a table in summer.

SPLIT: UpCafé
Vegetarian   **Road Map** D5
Domovinskog rata 29a
A short walk away from the Old Town, this two-storey café is well worth seeking out for its wide range of vegan dishes and tasty desserts.

SPLIT: Varoš
Traditional   **Road Map** D5
Ban Mladenova 7
Tel *021 396 138*
A traditional restaurant popular with lunching locals, Varoš has an extensive menu of traditional Dalmatian seafood and grilled meat dishes, washed down with robust house wine.

For more information on types of restaurants *see pp232–237*

SPLIT: Bajamonti ⓦⓦ
Café/Restaurant   **Road Map** D5
Trg republike 1
Tel *021 341 033*
This elegant coffee-and-cakes
venue can also prepare you a
juicy steak or a lobster straight
from their tank. There is outdoor
seating on the Venetian-style
Prokurative square.

SPLIT: Noštromo ⓦⓦ
Seafood   **Road Map** D5
Kraj sv. Marije 10
Tel *091 405 6666*
Right next to the fish market,
Nostromo is a reliable place to
find fresh seafood, cooked with
flair and imagination. Formal
restaurant upstairs; casual bar
on the ground floor.

SPLIT: Stellon ⓦⓦ
International   **Road Map** D5
Uvala Bačvice bb
Tel *021 489 200*
Stellon is a modern-looking bar-
restaurant above Bačvice beach,
serving pastas and European
classics to a young and
fashionable clientele.

SPLIT: Boban ⓦⓦⓦ
European   **Road Map** D5
Hektorovićeva 49
Tel *021 543 300*
Tucked into a residential street,
Boban has a long-standing
reputation for its high-quality
menu of Adriatic and European
fare; the inexpensive daily specials
are popular with local lunchers.

SPLIT: Kadena ⓦⓦⓦ
Seafood   **Road Map** D5
Ivana pl. Zajca 4
Tel *021 389 400*
Occupying a terrace overlooking
the seafront path and yachting
marina, Kadena specializes in
local fish and shellfish, prepared
with haute-cuisine flair.

SPLIT: Oyster & Sushi Bar
Bota ⓦⓦⓦ
Seafood   **Road Map** D5
*Obala Hrvatskog narodnog
preporoda 6*
Tel *021 488 648*
Located in a striking modern
pavilion behind Bačvice beach,
this is the place to go for expertly
grilled fresh fish, sushi Dalmatian-
style, and sparkling-fresh oysters
from Ston just along the coast.

SPLIT: Uje Oil Bar ⓦⓦⓦ
Bistro   **Road Map** D5
Dominisova 3
Tel *095 200 8008*
Billed as an olive-oil bar, Uje
serves quality, tapas-style light
bites based on traditional

Dining area on a canopied stone jetty at Foša in Zadar

Dalmatian ingredients, backed
up with an impresssive wine list –
and a chance to sample
boutique Dalmatian olive oils.

STON: Konoba Bakus ⓦⓦ
Regional   **Road Map** E6
Angeli Radovani 5
Tel *020 754 270*
Traditional family-run restaurant
where the local seafood menu is
impeccably cooked and presented
– oysters from Mali Ston, and
traditional Dubrovnik-region
desserts are among the specialities.

STON: Kapetanova kuća ⓦⓦⓦ
Regional   **Road Map** E6
Mali Ston
Tel *020 754 555*
Mali Ston bay is famous for its
oysters, which are prepared in a
variety of ways at this elegant
restaurant near the waterfront.

TROGIR: Fontana ⓦⓦ
Seafood   **Road Map** D5
Obrov 1
Tel *021 844 811*
With an outdoor terrace right
on the harbour, Fontana
specializes in local seafood,
although you can also enjoy
pizzas and juicy grilled meats.

TROGIR: Kamerlengo ⓦⓦ
Seafood   **Road Map** D5
Vukovarska 2
Tel *021 884 772*
In the heart of the Old Town and
boasting a lovely walled garden,
Kamerlengo mostly serves
seafood – although the grilled
meats are also a speciality.

VIS: Karijola ⓦ
Pizza   **Road Map** D6
Šetalište viškog boja 4, Vis
Tel *021 711 358*   **Closed** *Oct–Apr*
A branch of the Karijola pizzeria
based in Zagreb, this place, with
a sea-facing terrace. serves
reliable thin-crust pies.

VIS: Jastožera ⓦⓦⓦ
Regional   **Road Map** D6
Gundulićeva bb, Komiža
Tel *021 713 859*
Local lobster is the focus at this
atmospheric restaurant, situated
in a wooden pavilion mounted
above the shoreline lobster pens.
A variety of fresh fish is also
available.

DK Choice

VIS: Pojoda ⓦⓦⓦ
Regional   **Road Map** D6
Don Cvjetka Marasovića 10, Vis
Tel *021 711 575*
Situated in a walled garden
shaded by orange trees in the
enchanting suburb of Kut,
Pojoda enjoys a Croatia-wide
reputation for cultivating
traditional Adriatic island
recipes. The lobster, squid and
shellfish dishes are first-class;
there are also a lot of home-
style dishes specific to Vis that
combine seafood with barley,
lentils and chick peas. It's a
popular place in summer, so
be sure to reserve.

VIS: Villa Kaliopa ⓦⓦⓦ
Seafood   **Road Map** D6
Vladimira Nazora 32, Vis
Tel *021 711 755*
Set in a palm-shaded walled
garden, Kaliopa is one of the
most romantic places to eat
on the Adriatic coast. The fresh
seafood is excellent, if a little
on the expensive side.

ZADAR: Na Po Ure ⓦ
Traditional   **Road Map** C4
Spire Brusine 8
Tel *023 312 004*
Dalmatian staples including fish,
squid and *pašticada* (beef stewed
in prunes) fill the menu of this
inexpensive and homely bistro in
the Old Town.

ZADAR: Šime
Pizza   Road Map C4 Ⓚ
Matije Gupca 15
Tel *023 334 848*
In the seaside suburb of Borik, the enjoyable Šime offers excellent pizzas and pastas on a large outdoor terrace crammed with wooden benches.

ZADAR: Pet bunara
Regional   Road Map C4 ⓀⓀ
Stratico bb
Tel *023 224 010*
Locally sourced ingredients, a modern-European sense of creativity, and traditional recipes forgotten elsewhere combine to make this one of the best places to enjoy Dalmatian cuisine.

ZADAR: Foša
Seafood   Road Map C4 ⓀⓀⓀ
Kralja Dmitra Zvonimira 2
Tel *023 314 421*
Situated in a stone house on a small harbour, Foša serves expertly prepared fresh fish, either simply grilled or served with imaginative sauces.

Zagreb

Chocolat 041
Café   Road Map D2 Ⓚ
Masarykova 25
Tel *01 485 53 82*
This centrally located café with a 1980s New Wave theme is noted for its excellent ice creams and a seriously dangerous array of chocolate cakes.

Ivica i Marica
Café   Road Map D2 Ⓚ
Tkalčićeva 70
Tel *01 482 89 99*
A bright, folksy café that seves beautiful cakes, all made with wholemeal flour. Try a slice of *Međimurska gibanica*, a rich layered cake.

Kaptolska klet
Central European   Road Map D2 Ⓚ
Kaptol 5
Tel *01 481 48 38*
In an attractive courtyard right opposite the cathedral, this restaurant excels in schnitzel-style meat dishes and freshwater fish.

Karijola
Pizza   Road Map D2 Ⓚ
Vlaška 63
Tel *01 553 10 16*
A long-standing favourite among locals, Karijola serves up thin-crust pizzas with a variety of traditional Italian and creative Croatian toppings.

Lari & Penati
Bistro   Road Map D2 Ⓚ
Petrinjska 42a
Tel *01 465 57 76*
High-quality but affordable bistro dishes based on what the chef finds fresh in the market, with traditional Croatian fare spiced up with global combinations.

Millennium
Café   Road Map D2 Ⓚ
Bogovićeva 7
Tel *01 481 08 50*
One of the most popular places on the Bogovićeva café strip, Millennium has a wide choice of hard-to-resist ice creams, plus tarts, puddings and cakes galore.

Nokturno
Italian   Road Map D2 Ⓚ
Skalinska 4
Tel *01 481 33 94*
With tables set out attractively in a sloping alleyway, Nokturno is a popular venue for good, inexpensive pizzas and large, substantial salads.

Oranž
Café   Road Map D2 Ⓚ
Ilica 7
Tel *01 778 73 00*
This smart, chic city-centre café boasts an impressive selection of cakes and some good savoury choices too, including quiches, sandwiches and salads.

Pauza
Bistro   Road Map D2 Ⓚ
Preradovićeva 34
Tel *01 485 45 98*   **Closed** *Sun*
Adriatic seafood and Asian spices are the hallmarks of Pauza's imaginative menu, although there's a lot more besides, with soups, pastas and salads serving the lunchtime crowds.

Ribice i tri točkice
Seafood   Road Map D2 Ⓚ
Preradovićeva 7/1
Tel *01 563 54 79*
This enjoyable restaurant decked out in maritime murals specializes in Adriatic seafood dishes that won't break the bank, with fillets of fish, squid and octopus stews and risottos filling an extensive menu.

Sofra
Bosnian   Road Map D2 Ⓚ
Radnička cesta 52
Tel *01 411 16 21*
In the Green Gold shopping centre, Sofra is one of the best places in the city to try traditional Balkan grilled-meat dishes and hearty savoury cheese, spinach or potato pies.

Torte i to
Café   Road Map D2 Ⓚ
Centar Kaptol, Nova ves 11
Tel *01 486 06 91*
Situated in a shopping centre ten minutes' walk from Zagreb's main square, this small café/pastry shop serves the most famous cheesecakes in town. Expect flavours both classic and creative – all are delicious.

Vallis Aurea
Central European   Road Map D2 Ⓚ
Tomićeva 4
Tel *01 483 13 05*   **Closed** *Sun*
Traditional Croatian fare is served in a wood-panelled interior. Slavonian dishes such as čobanac (paprika-rich stew) feature on a meat-heavy menu.

Vincek
Café   Road Map D2 Ⓚ
Ilica 18
Tel *01 483 36 12*   **Closed** *Sun*
Vincek is justifiably famous for its home-made ice cream, but this is by no means all that this popular café offers, with an array of delicious cakes and pastries filling the display counter.

Boban
Italian   Road Map D2 ⓀⓀ
Gajeva 9
Tel *01 481 15 49*
In a brick-lined basement below the café of the same name, Boban serves some of the best pasta dishes in the city, backed up by a good list of Italian wines.

Carpaccio
Italian   Road Map D2 ⓀⓀ
Teslina 14
Tel *01 482 23 31*
This is a chic but not too formal place to enjoy mainstream Italian food, with meat and fish carpaccios filling out the list of starters, veal cutlet mains, and some thrilling desserts.

Old and new combined in the decor and on the menu at Pet bunara, Zadar

Tables on the covered terrace at Vinodol, central Zagreb

Čiho ⓦⓦ
Seafood   Road Map D2
Pavla Hatza 15
Tel *01 481 70 60*
Popular seafood restaurant with an informal bar area at ground level and a plusher restaurant downstairs. Try the excellent seafood risottos or grilled fish.

Korčula ⓦⓦ
Seafood   Road Map D2
Nikole Tesle 17
Tel *01 487 21 59*   **Closed** *Sun*
A traditional Adriatic-themed restaurant specializing in fresh fish, simply but expertly grilled. Squid, octopus and shellfish are also on the menu; daily specials are chalked up on a board.

Kulinarijat ⓦⓦ
International   Road Map D2
Opatovina 35
Tel *01 488 02 09*
Classic European meat, fish and poultry dishes are prepared with a touch of Mediterranean flair at this bright, welcoming restaurant in Zagreb's pedestrianized nightlife quarter.

Mali Bar ⓦⓦ
Bistro   Road Map D2
Vlaška 63
Tel *01 553 10 14*
Through a courtyard and up some steps, this small, semi-hidden bistro serves quality Croatian-European fare in small but delicious portions.

Mostovi ⓦⓦ
Bosnian-Herzegovinian
        Road Map D2
Radnička cesta 1a
Tel *01 619 21 78*
A large, lively, popular restaurant in Zagreb's new business district, serving Balkan-style oven-roast meats, savoury pastries and delicious syrupy desserts.

Nishta ⓦⓦ
Vegetarian   Road Map D2
Masarykova 11/1
Tel *01 889 74 44*   **Closed** *Sun*
Quality, creative vegetarian cuisine, complete with vegan and gluten-free options, is served here in bright, relaxing surroundings. The drinks menu includes home-made lemonades and organic wines.

Pod gričkim topom ⓦⓦ
Central European   Road Map D2
Zakmardijeve stube 5
Tel *01 483 36 07*
Dishes from all over Croatia are served at this uniquely secluded venue, nestling in a walled garden just below the Upper Town's funicular station.

Vinodol ⓦⓦ
Central European   Road Map D2
Teslina 10
Tel *01 481 14 27*
Grilled meats and roast lamb are the specialities at this popular city-centre restaurant, boasting a large terrace in a covered courtyard.

5/4 ⓦⓦⓦ
Mediterranean   Road Map D2
Dukljaninova 1
Tel *01 461 66 54*   **Closed** *Sun*
With a Croatian-Sicilian chef at the helm, 5/4 serves delicious, imaginative, and visually arresting Croatian-Mediterranean food, with the menu changing daily according to what's in season at the market.

Baltazar ⓦⓦⓦ
Grill   Road Map D2
Nova ves 4
Tel *01 466 69 99*
Baltazar has long been a firm favourite among meat-eaters, with traditional cuts of pork and veal expertly grilled and served in an atmospheric courtyard.

DK Choice
Bistro Apetit
ⓦⓦⓦ
International   Road Map D2
Jurjevska 65a
Tel *01 467 73 35*
A short walk north of Zagreb's Upper Town, award-winning Apetit specializes in creative Mediterranean-European cuisine, with fresh, locally sourced ingredients forming the backbone of a seasonally changing menu that includes a good balance of meat and fish. There's a strong list of Croatian and international wines, and the desserts are sublime. In summer tables are set out in an attractive garden.

Dubravkin put ⓦⓦⓦ
Seafood   Road Map D2
Dubravkin put 2
Tel *01 483 49 75*
A culinary landmark that has had several facelifts over the years, Dubravkin put offers a mixture of classic and creative fish dishes in a relaxing woodland setting.

Mano ⓦⓦⓦ
Fusion   Road Map D2
Medvedgradska 2
Tel *01 466 94 32*   **Closed** *Sun*
Exposed brick walls lend post-industrial chic to this restaurant set in a former leather factory; the building also houses a sculpture museum. The menu takes its cue from seasonal availability at the Dolac market.

Okrugljak ⓦⓦⓦ
Gourmet   Road Map D2
Mlinovi 28
Tel *01 467 41 12*
Traditional Croatian a dishes are cooked with finesse at this Zagreb institution, which has just celebrated its centenary year.

Nishta, a haven for those seeking meat-free and gluten-free choices in Zagreb

Takenoko ⓦⓦ
Global Fusion **Road Map** D2
Nova ves 17
Tel *01 486 05 30*
Much more than just a sushi bar,
Japanese-themed Takenoko
serves some of the most inventive
fusion cuisine in the country,
including Adriatic seafood spiced
up with oriental ingredients.

Zinfandel's ⓦⓦⓦ
Gourmet **Road Map** D2
Mihanoviceva 1
Tel *01 456 66 44*
Modern European cuisine is the
name of the game at this elegant
but not over-formal hotel
restaurant, boasting an Art Deco-
styled interior and a long list of
international wines.

Tapas-style Croatian food at Mali Bar, Zagreb

Central Croatia

ČIGOĆ: Tradicije Čigoć ⓦ
Regional **Road Map** D2
Čigoć 7a
Tel *044 715 124*
This traditional-style wooden
house in a riverside Lonjsko Polje
village provides the perfect
ambience in which to feast on
freshwater fish and local game.

GRABERJE IVANIĆKO:
Kezele ⓦⓦ
Traditional **Road Map** D2
Vinogradska 6
Tel *01 282 04 96*
Superb country-cooked classics
on a working farm in a rural
setting: mouthwatering spit-
roasts and baked meats, delicious
baked dessert pastries and the
farm's own wines and liqueurs.

JASTREBARSKO: K Lojzeku ⓦ
Central European **Road Map** C2
Strossmayerov trg 12
Tel *01 628 11 29* **Closed** *Sun*
A well-respected restaurant that
provides traditional Croatian
cooking with a creative twist;
expect plenty of roast poultry
and grilled meats.

KARLOVAC: Žganjer ⓦⓦ
Central European **Road Map** C2
Turanj bb
Tel *047 641 304*
South of Karlovac towards
Plitvice, this roadside restaurant
prides itself on serving traditional
specialities such as spit-roast
lamb and suckling pig.

SAMOBOR: Samoborska klet ⓦ
Central European **Road Map** C2
Trg kralja Tomislava 7
Tel *01 332 65 36*
This family-run restaurant just

behind the town square serves
straightforward Croatian fare –
schnitzel-style cuts of meat, tasty
sausages, and the occasional
Adriatic seafood option.

SAMOBOR: U prolazu ⓦ
Café **Road Map** C2
Trg kralja Tomislava 5
Tel *01 336 64 20*
One of the specialities of
Samobor is a cream cake called
kremšnita, and this popular café,
with chairs spread across the
town square, is one of the best
places to try it.

SAMOBOR: Pri staroj vuri ⓦⓦ
Central European **Road Map** C2
Giznik 2
Tel *01 336 05 48* **Closed** *Tues*
In a charming cottage above the
town square, the "Old Clock"
bases its reputation on hearty
country cooking involving plenty
of veal, pork and fowl.

SAMOBOR:
Samoborski slapovi ⓦⓦ
Seafood **Road Map** C2
Hamor 16
Tel *01 338 42 34*
Just northwest of Samobor in a
wooded valley, Samoborski
slapovi is a fish farm with its own
excellent restaurant – try the
pan-fried trout.

SISAK: Cocktail ⓦⓦ
Central European **Road Map** D2
A. Starčevića 27
Tel *044 549 137*
Located in the centre of Sisak,
this popular restaurant opts for a
mixture of traditional Croatian
pork and veal dishes and
Mediterranean-influenced pastas
and salads.

ZVEČAJ: Zeleni kut ⓦ
Regional **Road Map** C2
Zvečaj 109
Tel *047 866 100*

Freshwater fish from their own
pond and local meats dominate
the menu in this plainly built but
idyllically situated restaurant, by
gently cascading river falls.

Slavonia and Baranja

BRODSKI STUPNIK:
Zdjelarević ⓦⓦⓦ
Traditional **Road Map** E2
Vinogradska 65
Tel *035 427 775*
Dine (almost) among the vines
at the restaurant of this restful
hotel and fine winery, in a
picturesque vine-growing village.
The helpful team are ready to
help you match their traditional
dishes – including wine soup –
with their own and other
Croatian vintages.

ĐAKOVO: Croatia Turist ⓦⓦ
Regional **Road Map** F2
Petra Preradovića 25
Tel *031 813 391*
This is a restaurant that serves
the whole gamut of Slavonian
cuisine, from spicy *kulen* salami
to freshwater fish and *čobanac*
(spicy meat stew).

DARUVAR: Terasa ⓦⓦ
Central European **Road Map** E2
Julijev park 8
Tel *043 331 705*
Located near Daruvar's main spa
buiding, this restaurant serves
Croatian, Hungarian and Italian
cuisine in an ambience of old-
fashioned elegance.

ILOK: Villa Iva ⓦ
Regional **Road Map** G2
Radićeva 23
Tel *032 591 011*
This popular guesthouse with a
well-stocked wine cellar serves
fish fresh from the Danube, pastas,
salads, and some superb desserts.

For more information on types of restaurants *see pp232–3*

ILOK: Dunav ⓦⓦ
Regional Road Map G2
Julija Benešića 62
Tel *032 596 500*
Set on lawns right beside the
Danube, this hotel restaurant is
renowned for its fresh fish,
serving the spicy stewed *fiš
paprikaš* in individual metal
cauldrons.

ILOK: Stari podrum ⓦⓦ
Central European Road Map G2
Šetalište O M Barbarića 4
Tel *032 590 088*
This award-winning wine
producer has a restaurant in the
medieval part of the town over
its cavernous cellars, offering
new wines and venerable
vintages to pair with traditional
freshwater fish and meat dishes.

DK Choice

KOPAČKI RIT: Kormoran ⓦⓦ
Traditional Road Map G2
Podunavlje bb
Tel *031 753 099*
A hearty freshwater fish stew
with home-made noodles,
spit-grilled carp and dishes
made with local game are just
some of the rural delights on
the menu at this rustic complex
set in the Kopački Rit Nature
Park. With a relaxed, country-
tavern vibe inside and large,
safe play areas outside, it's ideal
for a family pitstop.

KUTJEVO: Schön Blick ⓦⓦ
Regional Road Map F2
Zagrebačka 18, Vetovo
Tel *034 267 108*
Located in an idyllic rural setting,
Schön Blick serves freshwater
fish and grilled meats with
great finesse.

NAŠICE: Ribnjak ⓦ
Regional Road Map F2
Stjepana Radića 1
Tel *031 607 006*
Located in a charming rustic
location 10 km (6 miles) outside
Našice on the Osijek road, the
Ribnjak, or "Fishpond", is an
excellent place in which to
enjoy local dishes, including
freshwater fish.

NOVA GRADIŠKA:
Slavonski biser ⓦ
Central European Road Map E2
Teslina 2–4
Tel *035 363 259*
This simple but welcoming
restaurant serves a well-cooked
standard range of Central
European dishes and a few
local Slavonian staples.

Cosy rustic styling at Kod Ruže, Osijek

OSIJEK: Café Waldinger ⓦ
Café Road Map F2
Županijska 8
Tel *031 250 470*
Osijek's most elegant café is a
key meeting point for locals
and a lovely venue for people-
watching: it serves an irresistible
range of cakes, pastries, tarts and
ice cream.

OSIJEK: Rustika ⓦ
Pizza Road Map F2
Pavla Pejačevića 32
Tel *031 369 400*
Pizza is the main attraction at this
large, family-oriented restaurant,
although grilled meats, salads
and pasta dishes ensure that
there is something for everyone.

OSIJEK: Kod Ruže ⓦⓦ
Regional Road Map F2
Kuhačeva 25a
Tel *031 206 066*
Appropriately decked out
in agricultural implements,
Kod Ruže serves traditional
country food such as paprika-rich
stews featuring plenty of game
and fish.

OSIJEK: Slavonska kuća ⓦⓦ
Regional Road Map F2
Kamila Firingera 26
Tel *031 369 955*
Decorated to look like a country
kitchen, the Slavonska kuća or
"Slavonian House" is one of the
best places to sample freshwater
fish, either pan-fried, or stewed as
hot, spicy *fiš paprikaš*.

SLAVONSKI BROD: Onyx ⓦ
Pizza Road Map F3
Nikole Zrinskog 50
Tel *035 445 555*
Bright, welcoming Onyx is
primarily a pizzeria, although it
also serves a solid range of
traditional Croatian/European
fare, from grilled meats to fried
squid and Wiener Schnitzel.

VUKOVAR: Vrške ⓦ
Regional Road Map G2
Parobrodarska 3
Tel *032 441 788*
Set right beside the River
Danube, Vrške is the place for
freshwater carp, catfish or pike-
perch, pan-fried *au naturel* or in
breadcrumbs or batter.

DK Choice

ZMAJEVAC: Josić ⓦⓦ
Regional Road Map G2
Planina 194
Tel *031 734 410* **Closed** *Mon, Tue*
Located in an artfully renovated
surduk, or tunnel-like wine cellar
burrowed into a hill, Josić is one
of the trend-setters of Baranja
tourism, serving local specialities
such as *fiš paprikaš* (paprika-
stewed fish), and game, all in a
modern setting. The owner is a
leading winemaker and there is
an excellent choice of wines
from both Josić and other
Croatian vineyards.

The Northern
Counties

ČAKOVEC: Mala hiža ⓦⓦ
Traditional Road Map D1
Balogovec 1, Mačkovec
Tel *040 341 101*
A menu based firmly in the
indigenous, seasonal cuisine is
complemented by an extensive
wine list in this lovingly restored
traditional oak building.

ČAKOVEC: Lovački dvori ⓦⓦⓦ
Regional Road Map D1
Gajeva 35
Tel *040 391 053* **Closed** *Sun*
The centrally located "Hunters'
Lodge" specializes in a game-rich
cuisine, with dishes such as
bograč (a goulash-style stew).

KOPRIVNICA: Pivnica Kraluš
Central European   **Road Map** D1
Zrinski trg 10
Tel *048 622 302*
A 250-year-old beer hall on the main square, Kraluš serves up hearty and inexpensive dishes such as beer sausage, grilled pork chops and tasty *pečeni grah* (baked beans).

KOPRIVNICA: Podravska klet
Regional   **Road Map** D1
Prvomajska 46a, Stari grad
Tel *048 634 069*   **Closed** Mon
Rustic restaurant with a thatched roof and solid wooden tables, offering good local produce – home-made sausage, creamy cows' cheese, game stews and roast boar.

DK Choice

KRAPINA: Vuglec breg
Regional   **Road Map** D1
Škaričevo 151
Tel *049 345 015*
A rustic hilltop restaurant 7 km (4 miles) west of Krapina, Vuglec breg specializes in traditional Zagorje specialities such as roast turkey, goose, pork and veal knuckle – all of which are best enjoyed with home-made *mlinci* (pasta sheets soaked in meaty juices). The wine list features inland Croatia's best labels. The desserts are first-class and the views of the rolling Zagorje hills are worth savouring.

KRAPINSKE TOPLICE:
Zlatna Lisica
Central European   **Road Map** D1
Martinišče 29
Tel *049 236 627*
With a great view overlooking rolling hills, this simple restaurant serves great country food. Try the sausages, game stews, and locally caught roast boar.

DK Choice

KRAPINSKE TOPLICE:
Villa Magdalena
Gourmet   **Road Map** D1
Mirna ulica 1
Tel 049 233 333
Seasonal produce and local specialities are given a contemporary gastro-style makeover at award-winning Villa Magdalena, offering both à la carte and multi-course taster menus, with vegetarian and macrobiotic options for those immersing themselves in the ambience of this spa destination. The setting, amid the green slopes of the Zagorje hills, is beautiful.

KUMROVEC: Stara Vura
Central European   **Road Map** C1
Josipa Broza 13
Tel *049 553 157*
Right beside the Kumrovec museum complex, the "Old Clock" is a comfortable restaurant with a classic Croatian menu of grilled meats, roast poultry and the odd fish dish.

MARIJA BISTRICA:
Restoran Academia
Gourmet   **Road Map** D1
Zagrebačka bb
Tel *049 326 600*
Located in the Hotel Kaj, this smart restaurant injects some modern European creativity into the traditional Zagorje repertoire of poultry, grains and pasta.

SVETI KRIŽ ZAČRETJE:
Klet Kozjak
Regional   **Road Map** D1
Kozjak 18a, Sveti Križ Začretje
Tel *049 228 800*
In a restored hilltop farmhouse 10 km (6 miles) south of Krapina, this traditional restaurant offers

roast meats and poultry with home-made pastas, followed by a choice of fine strudel.

TRAKOŠĆAN: Trakošćan
Central European   **Road Map** D1
Trakošćan bb
Tel *042 440 800*
A hotel restaurant set in rural surroundings, the Trakošćan serves Croatian standards with a regional, Zagorje slant – substantial soups and meat dishes are the stand-outs.

VARAŽDIN:
Kavana Grofica Marica
Café   **Road Map** D1
Trg kralja Tomislava 2
Tel *042 320 077*
With outdoor seating that billows across the main square, Grofica Marica is an ideal spot for a mid-morning coffee, and also has a wide choice of pastries and cakes – including their own-brand Grofica Marica chocolate torte.

VARAŽDIN: Verglec
Regional   **Road Map** D1
Silvija Strahimira Kranjčevića 12
Tel *042 211 131*
The centrally located Verglec straddles two culinary cultures with a menu offering both excellent pizzas and filling northern Croatian fare. Roast duck and roast pork are among the specialities.

VARAŽDIN: Turist
Central European   **Road Map** D1
Aleja kralja Zvonimira 1
Tel *042 395 395*
This elegant hotel restaurant serves fine food from all of Croatia's regions, with game dishes, grilled meats and Adriatic seafood all well represented.

VELIKI TABOR:
Grešna Gorica
Regional   **Road Map** C1
Taborgradska 35, Desinić
Tel *049 343 001*
This hilltop farm (with a diverting petting zoo) offers generous cuts of grilled and roast meats, locally sourced poultry, and home-made pasta. Grab a table that enjoys the views of Veliki Tabor castle.

ZABOK: Dvorac Gjalski
Central European   **Road Map** D1
Gredice Zabočke 7
Tel *049 201 100*
This excellent hotel restaurant is based in a former castle and has a medieval theme. The extensive menu includes a wide variety of Croatian cuisine.

Newly built on old traditions: a family-friendly welcome at Vuglec breg, Krapina

For more information on types of restaurants *see pp232–3*

SHOPPING IN CROATIA

Croatia does its best to encourage its visitors to go shopping (indeed it is a significant factor in local economies) and there is a range of traditional and typical crafts that make excellent souvenirs. The prices are by and large very reasonable too. Shoppers can choose from a variety of products, from works of creative handicraft such as handmade lace or hand-painted ceramics to jewellery.

On the island of Pag, exquisite lace is made and in Osijek, where beautiful embroidery is a proud tradition, you can also buy pretty costume dolls. Ties and fountain pens, both of which originated in Croatia, also make good purchases. In some resorts, local artists make a living by selling their watercolours. Visitors can also buy all sorts of delicious Croatian comestibles, from honey to plum brandy.

Jars of various types of honey, a speciality on the island of Šolta

Opening Hours

Shops and department stores are usually open from 8am to 8pm from Monday to Friday (but some stores may open at 7am and close at 9pm) and from 8am to 2 or 3pm on Saturdays. However, remember that sometimes small shops in the smaller towns close at lunchtime, usually from noon to 4pm in summer. Shops are generally closed on Sundays and holidays but in the high season in the tourist resorts many shops stay open for business as usual.

Prices

The prices are fixed in the shops and it is not usual to haggle over prices. This is also the case in the markets and at the street stalls where prices are also fixed and it is not common practice to negotiate. The prices are often displayed in the markets, but it should be remembered that at times the prices displayed are not always the same as those applied to the local people. The spending power of foreign visitors is frequently much greater than that of the local Croats and can occasionally result in pricing variations for locals.

Paying

In department stores, shopping centres and the major chain stores, it is possible to pay using one of the main international credit cards. In the smaller shops and in places such as markets, payments should be made in cash, with kuna.

Vat Refunds

Tourists in Croatia who spend more than 740 kuna on a single item are entitled to a refund of the Value Added Tax (VAT), which is called PDV in Croatia. When making your purchase, you should ask the sales assistant for the appropriate form (PDV–P), which should be properly filled in and stamped, on the spot.

This document should be handed to the customs authorities on departure from Croatia, thus verifying that the item bought is genuinely destined for export.

A PDV refund in kuna can be obtained within three months, either at the same shop where the goods were purchased (in which case the tax is refunded immediately), or by posting the verified receipt back to the shop, together with the number of the bank account into which the refund should be paid. In this case the refund is dealt with within 15 days of receipt of the claim.

Markets

The street markets of Croatia are colourful, lively places to stroll around.

In Zagreb, the Dolac *(see p159)* is a daily market where food is sold under colourful red umbrellas. There is also an underground area here where other products such as meat, dairy products and food are sold.

In Split there is a morning market which is held every day on Pazar, just east of the palace walls. This market sells absolutely everything: fruit, vegetables, flowers, shoes,

Fruit and vegetables on sale at the Dolac market in Zagreb

clothes and a vast assortment of souvenirs. There is a local saying which has it that if you cannot find what you are looking for at this market, it probably does not exist (at least not in Split).

Shopping Centres

Large shopping centres can also be found in Croatia, mainly in the larger towns and cities. Here you will find a number of shops selling assorted merchandise under one roof, usually including a large department store or supermarket.

In Zagreb one of the busiest and best-known department stores is **Nama**, which is right in the centre of the city. Another useful shopping centre, also in the city centre, is **Importanne Centar**. The **Importanne Galerija** is open weekdays and Saturdays.

Avenue Mall is another huge shopping centre has over 130 shops, including international names such as Benetton, Adidas, Esprit and Marks & Spencer. **Westgate Shopping City** is a huge shopping centre just outside Zagreb.

Traditional Handicrafts

There are lots of opportunities for the visitor to buy a variety of typical Croatian handicrafts and produce, which make very tempting souvenirs.

The country has a long tradition of skilled production of a rich range of handicrafts and typical produce. Production of these crafts is encouraged and supported by the local authorities, who see it as a good way of preserving the cultural heritage and the ancient traditions and crafts of the country.

In Zagreb, you can buy clothes, handbags, fashion accessories, pillow cases and table linens embroidered with Glagolitic (ancient Slavic) letters and traditional motifs at **Etno butik Mara**. In Split you can find a large assortment of souvenirs, including objects

Decorated ceramic objects on display

clearly inspired by maritime themes. You can also buy good reproductions of objects from the era of Roman rule in the underground area of Diocletian's Palace (see p122).

In Osijek, many shops in the centre of the city sell typical locally made handicrafts. Here you can also find dolls dressed in beautifully made costumes, packages of special lace and in particular fabrics finely embroidered with gold and silver thread.

Embroidery and Lace

One important typical Croatian craft is the art of embroidery, which is carried out more or less everywhere. One very characteristic design is a red geometric pattern stitched onto

Gold thread embroidery produced in the town of Osijek

a white background. This design is used to decorate table linen, pillow cases and blouses.

In 2009 lace making in Croatia was inscribed on the UNESCO Intangible Cultural Heritage of Humanity list. This includes three different traditions of lace making, namely Pag needlepoint lace, Lepoglava bobbin lace and Hvar aloe lace.

The lace of Pag is justly famous and widely admired. The origins of the lace date back to the Renaissance period, when it was used to decorate the blouses of the ladies of the island of Pag.

However, it was not until the beginning of the 20th century that this particular handiwork assumed its well-deserved fame, thanks to a beautifully decorated blouse given by a noblewoman to the Archduchess of Austria Marie Josephine. This gift was so greatly appreciated and admired that the archduchess went to Pag in person to order more items of clothing. At that time, the Austrian court set trends for others to follow, and this was enough to guarantee the future success for the production of this lace.

The lace is made on a long cylindrical cushion by lacemakers of great skill and tremendous patience. The lace patterns produced are the lacemaker's interpretation of patterns and designs which have been passed down from generation to generation. In this

Lacemaker working on a piece of Pag lace

since that time it has become more lavish and elaborate, so much so that its production has become the preserve of goldsmiths. The body of the figure is traditionally glazed ceramic. On request, precious stones may be used to decorate this figure. The best place to buy a *morčić* in Rijeka is the **Mala Galerija**.

Curiosities

Croatia can claim to have invented one of the most well-known of men's accessories, the tie, or cravat. The tie actually originates from a type of scarf worn by Croatian cavalrymen to distinguish them from other soldiers during the bloody 30-year war which devastated Europe in the 17th century.

The French took to referring to this particular way of tying the scarf as *"à la cravate"*, meaning "in the Croatian way". Since that time the tie, or cravat, has become a standard symbol of smart, elegant dressing for hundreds of millions of men in the world.

An earring with the *morčić* of Rijeka

The production of ties in Croatia today is still of a very high standard, and a tie would make a highly appropriate choice for a souvenir of your visit.

There are some very good clothes shops in the centre of Zagreb where you can buy an assortment of ties, including the high-end **Boutique Croata**.

way, the pieces of lace that are produced can often be very different from one another. However, all the patterns originate with the same geometric structure which forms the base.

Pag lace is surprisingly light but at the same time strong. If at all possible, pieces of the lace should be bought in Pag itself. Not only can you be sure of paying a better price than elsewhere but you will be helping to keep alive a tradition which is over a century old.

Prices vary according to the size of the piece you buy, but if you consider that a table centrepiece measuring 10 cm (4 in) in diameter takes a good 24 hours to make, you will have some idea of the labour involved.

The only place to buy lace in Pag is at the **Lace gallery and shop** in the old part of town.

Lucky Jewellery

There is one item of jewellery which can only be found in Croatia or, more precisely, only in Rijeka. This is the *morčić* or small Moorish figure. The figurine, in the form of a black character wearing a turban, was originally produced as earrings but today you can also find tie-pins and brooches. The *morčić* has become the symbol of the city and, in 1991, it was proclaimed the mascot of Rijeka. A legend dates the origins of the figurine to the city's unexpected liberation

from a Turkish siege during the 16th century. It was shown that a determining factor in the victory was the contribution of the women of Rijeka and it is said that their men decided to give them a gift of special earrings made to represent the invaders who had been forced to flee for their lives.

In fact, it seems more likely that the *morčić* originated in the 17th and 18th centuries as a local reproduction, made from decidedly poor materials, of a figurine set with stones which was very popular with the Venetians. The figurine represented the connections between Venice and the East and the mystery that this part of the world symbolized for them at the time. The figure soon became a symbol of good luck among the Istrian people and

One of many jeweller's shops in Croatia

Another little-known fact is that the inventor of the fountain pen was an engineer from Zagreb. In 1906, one Eduard Slavoljub Penkala patented a mechanical pencil and a year later a pen with a reservoir of ink, called the "mechanical pen", which revolutionized the way people wrote.

The inventor opened the first factory for the production of fountain pens in Zagreb in 1911. Within a short space of time it became an enormous success and developed into one of the most important manufacturing centres for writing instruments, producing fountain pens which were exported all over the world. There could not be a more appropriate place to buy this everyday item than Zagreb itself.

Ties on display in a shop in the centre of Zagreb

Local Produce

The gastronomic specialities and local produce of Croatia are as varied as the landscape of Croatia.

Among the country's best-known natural products, one of the most important is lavender. Lavender is sold dried in small bags or as essence in bottles. It can be found more or less all over the country but is particularly linked with the island of Hvar (see pp130–33), where its colour and scent can nearly overwhelm the senses when the shrubs are in flower. The scent is particularly pungent when you browse the lavender

Paški sir, the sheep's cheese of Pag, sold on the island

stalls near the port, where you can buy any number of cosmetic products made with lavender.

The gastronomic specialities of Croatia also make excellent souvenirs. Many places have their own particular speciality. Among many items worthy of mention are the mustard (in traditional containers) made in Samobor, near Zagreb, the honey from Grohote, on the island of Šolta, and cukarini biscuits from Korčula.

Another unmissable delicacy is the delicious truffle found around Buzet, overlooking the Mirna valley in Istria (although these are only available in season). Other delicacies include pršut (a type of smoked ham) and kulen (a type of smoked sausage) found in Slavonia.

However, the most highly valued product is cheese. Croatia produces a range of its own cheeses, and the most well-known is paški sir, a mature cheese made from sheep's milk, produced on the island of Pag (see pp104–5). It is still made according to traditional methods and the grazing pasture for the sheep, full of aromatic herbs, is said to give it a distinctive flavour.

To buy the cheese on the island just look for signs with the name of the cheese, "paški sir" outside the farmhouses.

Seller of essence and lavender bags on the island of Hvar

ENTERTAINMENT IN CROATIA

Although Croatians speak a language which is most likely completely unknown to the average visitor, the country still manages to offer a surprisingly varied range of accessible and engaging entertainment for visitors of all age groups. A choice of opera, ballet, folk music festivals, disco nightclubs, cinemas, casinos, tennis, football and basketball matches should be sufficient to satisfy anyone. The settings for many of these entertainments are often memorably spectacular, too. Performance details are readily available from weekly or monthly magazines of events and from tourist offices and websites. Tickets are usually easy to come by, and can be bought at venue ticket desks or often in advance from local tourist offices. Read ahead to see what's on and where to go.

The ornate interior of the Croatian National Theatre in Zagreb

Information and Tickets

For information concerning dates, times, prices and booking details of the various festivals, shows, theatre performances and musicals, it is best to get in touch with the relevant local tourist information office in Croatia. All these offices can provide details about the cultural events happening in their part of the country. Another good source of information can be the Internet. The Croatian National Tourist Board's website is www. croatia.hr.

Posters announcing forthcoming events are often displayed all over cities and towns and these are often useful for finding out about the more important or more popular shows.

For information concerning theatre performances, you can also go to the theatre box office itself, where you can usually buy tickets on the spot.

Theatre and Dance

Plays are generally performed in the Croatian language which, unless you speak it, can marginalize the theatre as an evening's entertainment for all but the most ardent thespians. There is, however, an important reason why you should nonetheless check out what's on at the theatre in any town you happen to be in. High-class performances of opera and ballet, for which not knowing the language is not a barrier to enjoyment, are put on by Zagreb's **Croatian National Theatre,** Zadar's **Croatian National Theatre,** Rijeka's **Croatian National Theatre Ivan pl Zajc** and Split's **Croatian National Theatre**.

For a more unusual form of drama which also has the advantage of being accessible to visitors, especially families with younger children, consider a visit to the unique Zagreb puppet theatre, the **Zagrebačko kazalište lutaka**.

They put on performances almost every weekend.

Croatia's many traditional festivals not only have particular dishes associated with them, but dances too. The most famous of these is undoubtedly Korčula's sword dance, traditionally enacted in the town centre on the evening of St Theodore's Day, July 29th. Such is the attraction of the *Moreška*, as it is known, that this costumed 15th-century dance is now performed outside of that holiday date – every Monday and Thursday at 9pm throughout July and August, sometimes even in June and September as well. Tickets at the event, or in advance from an agency, are not terribly expensive. It is obviously touristy, but still worth seeing as they really do swing those swords around. At any festive occasion in Croatia, there are several famous folk dances you may well come across: the *poskočica*, where couples weave themselves into intricate configurations; the *kolo,* a pan-Slavic circular dance and the *drmeš,* a type of speeded-up polka.

Costume drama in Dubrovnik, at the Rector's Palace

Musicians playing traditional Croatian music

Music

Whilst Croatia has nurtured classical composers and does have many aspiring rock bands, unfortunately few people outside of Croatia have ever heard of them. But don't let that put you off.

Croatia does have a rich tradition of folk music and these bands play all along the Adriatic at summer open-air concerts, on holiday festivals and even in hotel lobbies to entertain tourists after dinner.

Unusual instruments to look out for are the *tamburica*, a sort of Turkish mandolin, in Slavonia and the *citra*, a poignant-sounding type of zither (a horizontal stringed instrument). You will also come across variations on the folk theme, such as *klapa* – five- to ten-part harmony singing, mainly by males – or lively *lindo* dance music from the Dubrovnik region accompanied by the *lijerica*, which is a three-stringed instrument. The traditional songs of the Međimurje in the north of Croatia are very beautiful.

For a wide range of musical styles, global, local and avant-garde, the **Aquarius Club** in Zagreb is one of the top places in Croatia. Otherwise, be sure not to miss the music and pyrotechnics of Dubrovnik's **Summer Festival**, held over five weeks between July and August, and anything at all going on in the evening at Pula's ancient and stunning **Roman amphitheatre**.

Nightclubs

Cafés, bars and pubs all over Croatia often put on live music, especially at weekends. But if, after a few drinks, you want to party on into the night, then the capital or the coast in summer are the places to be. Entrance prices vary between about 50 and 100 kuna and venues open around 10pm, although most people arrive fashionably late, towards midnight or later.

Winter closing times are 11pm from Sunday to Thursday and midnight on Friday and Saturday, but in the summer clubs go on into the early hours of the morning. Open-air bars on the Adriatic coast will serve until 3am; open-air discos stop at 5am.

Younger Croats simply don't have the cash to go out as often as they would like – but if there's a Croatian band on and it's a weekend they'll be out in force, dressed-up and fully made-up. Weekday parties in the coastal resorts are therefore going to be predominantly for holiday-makers. Where you will find plenty of locals almost any-time are the multipurpose entertainment complexes in Zagreb or Split, where all their café-bars, cinemas, discos etc are usually crowded with youngsters.

Zagreb, Rijeka, Split, Pula and Dubrovnik all have well-known discos and nightclubs, though times and conditions change so frequently that they should be checked out locally beforehand.

Zagreb has the ever-popular **Aquarius Club** which although 4 km (over 2 miles) from the city centre has dancing to commercial, techno and Croatian bands on a terrace overlooking Lake Jarun. **Green Gold Club** is for serious party people – five clubs in one, open 24 hours a day, 365 days a year, with VIP areas often frequented by local celebrities. **Boogaloo Club**, a popular place for young people, always tries to be up-to-date in the Croatian and world music scene and hosts international DJs. **Močvara**, in a disused factory on the banks of the river Sava, is a trendy place, home to gigs, exhibitions and performances of an alternative, off-beat kind.

Café-Disco Bar Marinka, located on the lower deck of the boat *Arca Fiumana*,

The amphitheatre in Pula, summer venue for spectacular concerts

Carpe Diem beach club, Hvar

moored on Rijeka's waterfront, mixes alt, rock, funk and indie music with live performances by local bands. If you prefer a big, techno party house teeming with teenagers, the **Colosseum** in otherwise staid and stately Opatija is the place to go.

Split boasts several clubs with open-air terraces looking out to sea, the best of which are the two-storey **O'Hara** and the palm-filled **Tropic Club**. The **Hemingway Bar** offers a wide selection of drinks, especially cocktails, good music and occasional live performances.

Rock Club Uljanik has Pula's liveliest alternative concerts in a vacant building above the shipyards. Out of town are **Aruba Club**, a lounge bar and disco, and **Summer Club**, for pop/house partying.

Dubrovnik is diverse in what it offers: **Culture Club Revelin** takes over the Revelin fort with high-volume techno; **Night Club Fuego** is casual, relaxed and plays a range of music; **Club Lazareti** is popular and holds concerts, parties and events.

On the islands, Hvar has become a fashionable centre for nightlife and developed a bit of a reputation as a party island. Early evening activity centres around Hvar town harbour, in bar-cum-clubs like **Carpe Diem** where the dancers warm up before heading up the tree-covered hillside to a big old Venetian fort that has been converted into an amazing venue, with tented structures hosting plays, concerts and an open-air nightclub, **Veneranda**.

Papaya Club, on Zrće beach on the island of Pag, hosts the world's leading DJs. Less fashionable but just as much fun is the **Faces Club**, on the island of Brač, near Bol.

Casinos

As you would expect, the capital Zagreb has the most casinos and as with the rest of Croatia they are found in the more upmarket hotels. (There are "casinos" in lesser hotels but they are usually not worth visiting.) Try those at the **Hotel International, Hotel Westin** and the Golden Sun Casino in the **Hotel Antunović**. Any casino will have an array of slot machines along with a number of card tables where stakes are relatively low. Normally you can wear just smart casual clothing and walk straight in. However, it might be worth calling ahead beforehand – the most upmarket casinos may ask to see your passport before you can enter.

Cinema

Most large towns in Croatia have a cinema. Zagreb has several multiplexes, such as **Cinestar** in Avenue Mall and Branimir Centar and **Cineplexx** in Kaptol Centar. **Kino-teka** shows cult and art films. Tickets cost from 20 to 40 kuna and films are shown in their original languages with Croatian subtitles. You can expect to see the latest Hollywood hits. Conditions can be more basic in smaller towns where you may come across rows of wooden chairs, rather like being back at school. Neither will things be so luxurious in the summer open-air cinemas which are more atmospheric: the films too might not be your first choice but the experience is worth trying.

Spectator Sports

Tito's post-war Yugoslavia, of which Croatia was a part, consistently put out strong teams in handball, football (soccer), basketball and water polo. Since 1991, when Croatia broke away to become an independent nation, this small country of only 4.5 million people continues to excel in those sports and has added tennis to its sporting repertoire. If you love tennis then go to www.croatiaopen.hr to find out the latest news on the ATP Croatia Open Championships, held at Umag in July.

Croats, just like so many other Europeans, love their football. The 1990s saw now legendary

The Hotel Westin in Zagreb, home to a casino

Croatian players like Štimac, Boban and Šuker rise as international stars as Croatia for the first time became a serious footballing nation: quarter-finalists in the 1996 European Championships and, two years later, third at the World Cup, 1998. Although they haven't scaled those heights since. If you want to see a game during your stay, try either Dinamo Zagreb at the **Maksimir Stadium** on the capital's east side or Hajduk Split at the **Poljud Stadium**, Split. Matches are traditionally held on Sunday afternoons throughout most of the year, with only a short holiday break in the summer.

Like football, the country's top two basketball teams are in Split – KK Split who have been European Club Champions many times – and Zagreb – with rival contenders, Cibona. Those familiar with the game will know the names of the local stars on the international scene, such as Čosić, Petrović, Kukoč, Tabak and Rađa, and that Croatia was the third best team at the Toronto World Cup in 1994.

If you want to see a basketball game the Cibona team in Zagreb, hosts top quality matches at the **Dražen Petrović Basketball Centre** every Saturday evening from October to April – tickets are sold on the door.

The Cibona basketball team from Zagreb during a match

DIRECTORY

Theatres

Croatian National Theatre
Trg Gaje Bulata 1, Split.
Tel (021) 306 908.

Croatian National Theatre
Široka ulica 8,
Zadar.
Tel (023) 314 552.

Croatian National Theatre
Trg maršala Tita 15,
Zagreb.
Tel (01) 488 84 18.

Croatian National Theatre Ivan pl. Zajc
Uljarska 1, Rijeka.
Tel (051) 337 114.

Zagrebačko kazalište lutaka
Ulica baruna Trenka 3,
Zagreb.
Tel (01) 48 78445.

Music

Dubrovnik Summer Festival
Placa, Dubrovnik
(ticket office).
Tel (020) 321 509.

Roman Amphitheatre
Tourist office: Forum 3,
Pula. *i* (052) 212 987,
219 197.

Nightclubs

Aquarius Club
Aleja Matije Ljubeka bb,
Jarun, Zagreb.
Tel (01) 364 02 31.

Aruba Club
Šijanska cesta 1a, Pula.

Boogaloo Club
Ulica grada Vukovara 68,
Zagreb.
Tel (01) 631 30 22.

Café-Disco Bar Makina
Putnička obala bb,
Rijeka.

Carpe Diem
Riva, Hvar.

Club Lazareti
Frana Supila 8, Dubrovnik.

Colosseum
Ulica maršala Tita 129,
Opatija.

Culture Club Revelin
Svetog Dominika 3,
Dubrovnik.

Faces Club
near Bol, Brač.

Green Gold Club
Radnička cesta 52,
Zagreb.
Tel (099) 256 33 23.

Hemingway Bar
8 Mediteranskih igara 5,
Split. **Tel** (099) 211 99 93.

Močvara

Trnjanski nasip bb,
Zagreb.
Tel (01) 615 96 67.

Night Club Fuego
Brsalje 8, (near Pile Gate),
Dubrovnik.

O'Hara
Uvala Zenta 3, Split.
Tel (095) 504 99 09.

Papaya Club
Zrće Beach, Novalja,
Pag.

Rock Club Uljanik
Dobrilina 2,
Pula.

Summer Club
Medulin, Pula.

Tropic Club
Bačvice bb, Split.
Tel (098) 569 135.

Veneranda
On the hill above Riva,
Hvar town, Hvar.

Casinos

Hotel Antunović
Zagrebačka avenija 100a,
Zagreb. **Tel** (01) 387 05 30.

Hotel International
Miramarska 24, Zagreb.
Tel (01) 615 00 25.

Hotel Westin

Izidora Kršnjavoga 1,
Zagreb.
Tel (01) 554 52 71.

Cinema

Cineplexx
Kaptol Centar,
Nova Ves 17, Zagreb.
Tel (01) 563 38 88.

Cinestar Novi Zagreb
Avenue Mall, Avenija
Dubrovnik 16, Zagreb.
Tel (01) 643 84 04.

Cinestar Zagreb
Branimir Centar, Kneza
Branimira 29, Zagreb.
Tel (060) 323 233.

Spectator Sports

Dražen Petrović Basketball Centre
Savska cesta 30,
Zagreb.
Tel (01) 484 33 33.

Maksimir Stadium
Maksimirska 128,
Zagreb. **Tel** (01) 238 61 11.
w gnkdinamo.hr

Poljud Stadium
8 Mediteranskih igara 2,
21000 Split.
Tel (021) 585 200
w hajduk.hr

OUTDOOR ACTIVITIES

One of the keys to Croatia's tourist success is that it is blessed with such bountiful natural resources – waterfalls, islands, hills, rivers, lakes, canyons, mountains, pine woods and verdant parks – all soaked in dependable Mediterranean sunshine. To its credit, Croatia has responded well by providing a good infrastructure backed by a multitude of organizations to get visitors climbing and rafting, sailing and surfing, hiking and biking throughout its wonderfully diverse topography. There are also less energetic activities to be enjoyed. Croatia has several thermal spa centres that can be a bit utilitarian but are getting better as retreats for unwinding after some activity. Finally, of course, the coastline and myriad islands have a glittering choice of beaches for sunworshippers.

Sailing along the Croatian coast

Sailing

The Croatian coastline has many natural harbours, ports and marinas, making it a real haven for sailors. As a result, the best way to fully appreciate the rugged beauty of Croatia's Adriatic coastline is not by car but by yacht or motorboat. With clean, clear sea, steady, moderate winds, waters in which it is easy to anchor and well-equipped marinas open all year round, a sailor's life is made easy in Croatia. If possible, avoid July to August, unless you really want to spend the time with every weekend admiral in Europe. May to June or September to October are more peaceful, cost less and what is more the weather is still good.

The Croatian National Tourist Board (www.croatia.hr) lists over 140 companies with some 2,700 boats available for hire, typically rented out on a weekly basis from 5pm Saturday to Saturday next at 9am. The most important decision for the holiday maker is whether to go "bareboat" or "skippered". The former requires that you show a valid licence with at least 2 years' experience on it and register the crew. You are then free to sail off on your own. "Skippered" means that for about another 130 euros per day, plus food, you'll have a local in charge who knows exactly what he or she is doing. Prices vary depending on the size of boat and time of year. The British company **Nautilus Yachting**, for example, will arrange a week "bareboat" on an 11-metre (36 ft) boat sleeping six for around 2,200 euros, while the Croatian company **Club Adriatic** has a few 4-berth 10-metre (33 ft) craft for around 1,800 euros, again for seven days.

Anyone sailing to Croatia in their own boat must report to the nearest Harbour Master's Office on arrival if it is over 3 m (10 ft) in length and has an engine over 4 kW.

From Umag to Dubrovnik, Croatia has 50 marinas with everything a sailor could want: refuelling and repair services, water and electrical hook-ups, medical assistance and surveillance, cafés, bars and restaurants. Marinas are classified according to the level of service they offer and charge accordingly. The Adriatic Croatia International Club, also known as **ACI Marinas**, runs a chain of 21 marinas to which you can take out a yearly contract for use of all facilities and discounted berth fees. In addition there are plenty of temporary moorings available. Or you could simply overnight in a deserted bay.

Another way to experience the combination of sailing and Croatia's unique coastline is to enroll on a special holiday to learn how to sail. **Adriatica.net** offers holidays for sailors of all different levels of experience, although there are plenty of other similar companies.

Coastal radio stations give weather updates in both Croatian and English. Useful radio stations include Radio

Mooring in the harbour at Makarska

Rijeka UKW channel 24, Radio Split UKW channels 07, 21, 23, 81 and Radio Dubrovnik UKW channels 07 and 04.

Windsurfing

Most coastal resorts offer windsurfing courses and boards for hire, but serious surfers will enjoy two places in particular: Bol, on the island of Brač, and Viganj on the Pelješac Peninsular, close to Orebić. Both resorts have many renowned windsurfing clubs, offering kit and courses from beginner to expert. Also, note, both places play annual host to international championship events in July.

The windsurfing season runs from early April to late October and the westerly winds are at their peak in the early afternoon. Conditions are ideal in late May/early June and in late July/early August – though the latter, of course, is in the high season.

Windsurfing, a very popular sport along the Croatian coast

Diving

Although Croatia may not be the Caribbean or the Red Sea, it nonetheless has its fair share of interesting dive sites. Nature has fashioned plenty of underwater caves from the porous karstic limestone along the coast, to which you can add the further attractions of sea walls and shoals of fish and, at greater depths, shipwrecks and corals. Lošinj Island has all the above features and is probably the most comprehensive dive site in Croatia. If fish are your interest,

The clear waters off Croatia, rich in marine life and coral

try Vis – thanks to its military background the island was never commercially fished and consequently has the richest marine life. The best underwater caves are around the beautiful Kornati Islands, while interesting shipwrecks can be found near Rovinj (*Baron Gautsch*, 1914 passenger ferry), Dubrovnik (*Taranto*, 1943 merchant ship) and the Pelješac Peninsular (*S57*, another merchant casualty of war, from 1944).

There are, however, rules and regulations about who can dive where. To dive at all, you will need to show a current diver's card issued by an internationally recognized diving organization. For a small fee, this is then given a year-long validation by the **Croatian Diving Federation** or any of its agents – which could be an authorised tourist agency or the nearest diving club to your hotel. Diving clubs

abound in the Adriatic and are useful not only for hiring equipment but also for going on guided tours with English-speaking instructors.

Areas off limits to divers are around military installations, protected cultural monuments and some, but not all, nature reserves. Diving is forbidden in Krka and Brijuni parks for example but, with a permit, is allowed in the Kornati National Park and the islands of Mljet. Check beforehand if you intend to be adventurous.

Fishing

The Adriatic Sea is one of the richest in Europe and draws all kinds of fishermen. In order to go fishing you will need a licence. These are issued by tourist offices, authorised agencies and diving centres and clubs which have an arrangement with the Ministry of Agriculture and Forestry. The cost of a licence is not terribly great and depends on its duration – you can purchase licences valid for 1 day, 3 days, a week or 30 days. The licences permit fishing with a rod and line or a spear gun and it is possible to fish everywhere except in the protected areas of the marine parks (that is, Kornati, the Brijuni islands, Krka and Mljet). Along with the licence you will receive a list of the areas which are off-limits and indications of the number of each fish species that you are allowed to catch.

Locals showing the wide variety of fish and shellfish in the Croatian sea

Hiking

Croatia is criss-crossed with countless hiking paths and trekking trails – marked by a white dot within a red circle painted onto a tree or rock. Contact the **Croatian Mountaineering Association (HPS)** for information about the many local walking clubs, maps and the national whereabouts of mountain huts for simple overnight accommodation. The best time of year for hiking is between April and October. However, be aware that the removal of unexploded mines is still taking place in the conflict zones of the 1991–95 war, so don't wander off established trails. See the Croatian Mine Action Centre website (www.hcr.hr) for specific information.

Top trails would have to include the Premužić ridge path, heading for 50 km (31 miles) at around 914 m (3,000 ft) through the Velebit massif, a short distance east of the central Dalmatian coast, and offering breathtaking views both into continental Croatia and way out to sea; the gorges and beech forests of Paklenica

National Park, 40 km (19 miles) northeast of Zadar; Mt Ilija above Orebić for superb mountain coastal scenery; the fortified hill-towns of the Istrian interior; Samobor and the Risnjak National Park in central Croatia and the Zagorje Castles district in the northern counties.

Free Climbing

As with hiking, climbing is also best pursued from April to October – after which there's the prospect of a sudden snowfall or being blasted by the bura, a strong cold wind from the northeast. Croats may not be thought of as Alpinists but they have scaled the Himalayas many times, have their own Croatian Mountaineering Association and plenty of home mountain ranges in which to practice their sport. Again, the Paklenica National Park is popular, having more than 400 climbing routes to choose from. Cetina Valley near Omiš in central Dalmatia is another prime destination for climbers. Should you want to climb and spend time at

Abseiling down a rock face in summer

the beach as well, consider heading for the peaks on the islands of Brač, Vis, Mljet, Krk, Hvar, Cres and Lošinj plus those on the peninsulars of both Istria and Pelješac.

Cycling

Cyclists, like hikers, get the full benefit of the outdoor fragrances, riotous bird-song and chance encounters with the locals that their sport brings. Regional tourist boards in Croatia have worked hard to promote a sensible series of designated bike routes. The national parks and nature reserves lead the way with clearly marked bike trails taking you in a circular tour back to where you began. The Plitvice Lakes provide scenic cycling at its European best. Similarly circuitous routes exist on the islands of Rab, Hvar and Mljet where out-of-the way beaches and restaurants come into the picture, too. Istria tourist board has also been prominent in looking after cyclists by running rural trails out of and back into Rovinj, Labin and Novigrad. You can find more details at www.istra. hr. Hiring bikes can be the best way to get around the island and find secluded bays. Expect to pay around 10–15 euros a day for bike hire.

Hikers on one of the paths in Paklenica National Park

Clay court tennis, a popular sport in Croatia

Tennis

After football, tennis is Croatia's most popular sport. Almost every town, holiday hotel and camp site will have the necessary facilities – usually plenty of excellent clay courts. Two of the best-equipped clubs are the **Tennis Club Pećine** in Rijeka and the **Tennis Club Smrikve** in Pula. If you enjoy watching tennis, the ATP Croatia Open Championships are held at Umag in July. At any tennis club in Croatia you're likely to be reminded of the achievements of their best-known sportsman: Goran Ivanišević, who is perhaps most famous internationally for winning the Men's Singles at Wimbledon in 2001.

Golf

Golf is becoming increasingly popular in Croatia. There are five major courses: **Golf & Country Club Zagreb**, **Golf Centre Novi Dvori** near Zagreb, **Golf & Country Club Dolina Kardinala**, near Karlovac, **Golf Adriatic** near Umag and **Spa & Sport Resort Sveti Martin** near Čacovec, as well as several smaller locations with golf facilities.

To play at a Croatian golf club you may need to show a membership card issued by the national federation from your home country. This will indicate your handicap, which may be required prior to

A golfer on a practice course

you tee-ing off. It's a good idea to check what identification you'll need in advance.

Whitewater Rafting

This most accessible of the extreme sports began in Croatia around the late 1980s, opening up remote canyons and rivers known before only to kayakers and fishermen. The most rewarding places to raft through wild scenery on waters clear down to the river bed itself – and innocent of vicious rapids or huge waves – are the Dalmatian rivers of Zrmanja, near Zadar, and Cetina, near Omiš, and the rivers Dobra and Kupa, near Karlovac in central Croatia. Agencies like **Kompas** in Zagreb organise trips with guides and all the gear. Otherwise try the website www.activeholidays-croatia.com

Relaxation

Several spa resorts offer natural thermal springs and treatments. They emphasise the relaxation aspect more than the treatment but have excellent sporting facilities *(see Thermal Spas Tour pp216–17)*.

DIRECTORY

Sailing

ACI Marinas
M Tita 151, Opatija.
Tel (051) 271 288. **W** aci.hr

Adriatica.net
W adriatica.net

Club Adriatic
W clubadriatic.com

Nautilus Yachting
W nautilus.hr

Diving

Croatian Diving Federation
Dalmatinska 12, Zagreb.
Tel (01) 484 87 65.
W diving-hrs.hr

Hiking

Croatian Mountaineering Association
Kozarčeva 22, Zagreb.
Tel (01) 482 36 24.
W hps.hr

Whitewater Rafting

Kompas
W kompas.hr

Tennis

Tennis Club Pećine
Šetalište XIII divizije 33, Rijeka.
Tel (051) 421 782.

Tennis Club Smrikve
Stinjanska cesta 91, Pula.
Tel (052) 517 011.

Golf

Dolina Kardinala
Tel (01) 370 11 34.

Golf Adriatic
Tel (052) 707 100.

Golf & Country Club Zagreb
Tel (01) 653 11 77.

Golf Centre Novi Dvori
Tel (01) 334 07 77.

Kempinski Golf Adriatic
Tel (052) 707 371 111.

Spa & Sport Resort Sveti Martin
Tel (040) 371 111.

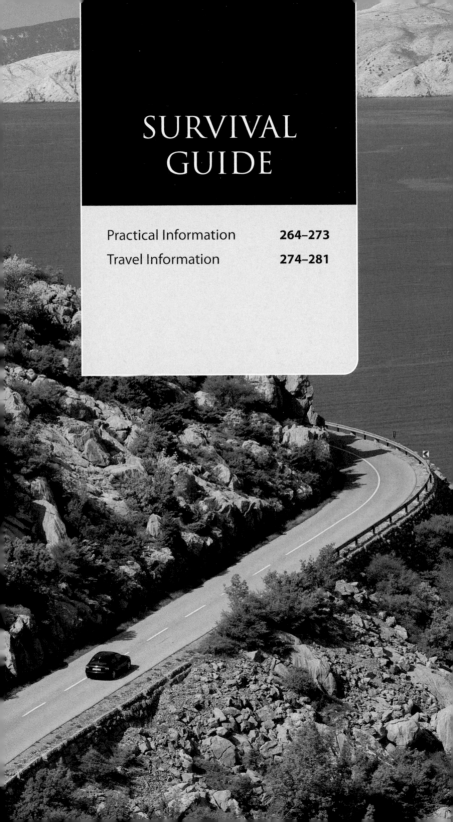

SURVIVAL GUIDE

PRACTICAL INFORMATION

In Croatia, tourism is an important source of revenue (accounting for approximately 15 per cent of the GDP in 2014) and every effort is being made to foster the growth and development of the industry. Since independence in 1991, a number of measures have been taken to encourage visitors, including simplifying border formalities and introducing tax reductions on items destined for export. Hotels and historic buildings damaged in the war have been rebuilt and modernized, and road and maritime links have been improved, both internally and with neighbouring countries. The country has reaffirmed itself as a popular holiday destination, able to offer tourist facilities of international standard at competitive prices. Croatia joined the European Union in 2013, though many of its pre-existing regulations and practices already fell in line with EU standards.

When to Go

The busiest, most popular time to visit the Croatian coastline are the summer months of July and August. With its crystal clear seas, combined with thousands of islands and bays for exploring and swimming, the coast is a major attraction. In addition, the summer weather is reliably sunny, another important aspect for many.

In the peak season, hotels and resorts are at their busiest, so if a quieter holiday is preferred, it would be better to choose the months of May, June or September, when the weather is still fine but resorts are not so crowded. Another advantage of travelling out of peak season are the low prices on offer. Spring and autumn are the best months for hiking, climbing and mountain biking.

Inland Croatia is home to a number of thermal spas, and it is possible to combine a few days of therapeutic treatment or relaxation (see pp216–17) with visits to cities and towns with their rich historical and artistic heritage.

Unlike nearby Slovenia, Croatia's facilities for winter tourism are not yet well-developed, although there are a few ski slopes, such as in Platak, the Medvednica and the Bjelolasica mountains.

Zagreb, the capital, offers numerous attractions and is a great destination the entire year round.

Visas and Passports

To enter Croatia, visitors need to have a valid passport. People from countries in the European Union, the US, Canada, Australia and New Zealand do not need a visa and may stay for up to 90 days. Croatian authorities have signed a bilateral agreement with EU countries, according to which EU citizens need only carry an identity card to enter Croatia.

To check whether you require a visa, visit the website of the Croatian Ministry of Foreign and European Affairs (www.mvep.hr) for a list of countries whose citizens require visas. If you need one, seek advice from the Croatian Embassy in your home country.

All foreign citizens must register with the local police within 48 hours of arrival in the country. Failure to do so may result in a fine or even expulsion from the country. In practice, if you are staying in a hotel, the reception staff will take care of this procedure for you.

People travelling with pets must ensure that their pets have been microchipped and carry an International Pet Passport as well as all the necessary documents verifying that their pets' vaccinations are complete and up to date, particularly with regard to rabies.

Customs Information

There are no restrictions on personal effects brought into Croatia by travellers and customs regulations are as for all EU member states. It is permitted to carry into or out of Croatia, 200 cigarettes or 50 cigars, 1 litre of spirits, 4 litres of wine, and 50 millilitres (one bottle) of perfume or essence.

On entering the country, high-value items such as radio equipment, computers, photographic equipment, video cameras and other recording equipment and portable televisions must be declared. Arrival in the country by boat must be reported to the Harbour Master's Office along with the number of people on board and all equipment.

Foreign and local currency and cheques may be freely taken in and out of the country by both foreign and Croatian citizens with foreign residence, but transfers of 10,000 euros or more must be declared.

Bottle of Croatian wine

Tourist Information

Every town and city has a tourist office, called Turistički Ured, Turistička Zajednica or Turistički Informativni Centar. These state-run offices provide information on sightseeing, excursions and transport and will often help visitors to find accommodation in hotels or private rooms (see pp222–3).

◀ A sweeping Adriatic coastal road, Senj

However, in smaller cities and towns, these offices are open during summer only.

Additionally, there are county and regional tourist offices, managed by the Ministry of Tourism.

Alternatively, you can contact the **Croatian National Tourist Board** in your home country before leaving. The Croatian Ministry of Tourism has set up information offices in all major countries to publicize the attractions Croatia has to offer. The website of the Croatian National Tourist Board is particularly helpful.

Tourist asking for help and directions

Admission Prices

Most state-run museums and historical sites charge an entrance fee between 10 kn and 70 kn. Children are normally entitled to a 50 per cent reduction in admission prices. Churches are usually free, though if there is an adjoining bell-tower or treasury, you may have to pay to visit them.

Opening Hours

Public offices open from 8am to 4pm or 9am to 5pm on weekdays. While most other office businesses more or less follow these standard opening times, these hours may vary for other businesses, such as pharmacies (see pp268–9), banks (see pp270–71) and post offices (see pp272–3), the bigger ones of which are also open on

Saturdays. Shops are usually open 8am–8pm (see p250), while cafés tend to open quite early.

Note that many museums and other cultural attractions are closed on Mondays. During summer, most have extended daily opening hours, and in coastal resorts, some close in the afternoon (when visitors are most likely to go to the beach) but open in the evening.

Language

Croatia is called Hrvatska in the national language, Croatian (hrvatski). It is a Slavic language and is written in the Latin script. Croatian is not an easy tongue to learn, but since most people in the country have studied at least one other foreign language, visitors should be able to make themselves understood in most circumstances. Italian, German and English are widely spoken while French is less common. Young Croatians generally speak very good English.

Etiquette and Smoking

Smoking is very common in Croatia (an estimated 30 per cent of the population smokes), but is officially banned in all enclosed public spaces, except for cafés that have approved air conditioning systems. While most establishments in Zagreb adhere to this law, it is frequently ignored in the south of the country. All the same, in summer, you can sit at the outdoor tables to avoid the smoke in closed spaces.

Taxes and Tipping

The practice of tipping, usually calculated at 10 per cent, is widespread in Croatia, even in restaurants, where a service charge is normally included in the price. When paying in bars or in taxis it is expected that at least the sum will be rounded up. It is also customary to tip the tourist or museum guides after a tour has ended.

In department stores, supermarkets and shops, the prices for goods are fixed. Bargaining, especially aggressive haggling, is not generally part of Croatian street-market culture..

Travellers with Special Needs

In Croatia there is a great awareness of the problems faced by the disabled particularly because of the war of independence which left many people with disabilities. Stations, airports, larger hotels and restaurants above a certain standard, and the main public offices in larger towns are accessible to those in wheelchairs. However, facilities at the ports are not so good.

Disabled visitors are entitled to a 50 per cent reduction in ticket prices at most state-run museums. For further information, contact the **Hrvatski savez udruga tjelesnih invalida** (HSUTI), the Croatian organization for the disabled, which has its headquarters in Zagreb. Also useful is the **HUPT** website, which provides information on accessible beaches and accommodation.

Pedestrians walking on a stone bridge in Ploce Gate, Dubrovnik

Travelling with Children

Tourist complexes such as large hotels and resorts usually provide facilities for children, such as playgrounds, pools and babysitting services. However, these may be harder to find in smaller towns and inland regions less visited by tourists.

When travelling with Croatia Airlines on domestic flights, children under 2 years of age go free, while those between 2 and 12 years of age get a 50 per cent discount. Children are also entitled to a 50 per cent reduction in tickets prices for most state-run museums.

Gay and Lesbian Travellers

Homosexuality is still rather taboo in Croatia. Same-sex couples should refrain from public displays of affection so as not to cause offence. You can find out more at www. friendlycroatia.com.

Travelling on a Budget

Low-cost accommodation is available in most destinations in the form of youth hostels and private rooms to rent. Decent youth hostels can be found in the cities of Zagreb, Split, Dubrovnik, Rijeka, Pula, Zadar and Šibenik, as well as on the islands of Hvar and Lošinj. Some, but not all, come under the Croatian Youth Hostel Association (www.hfhs.hr) umbrella group. Many hostels are part of the Hostelling

Conventional clothing worn in church by both men and women

A secluded beach on the Dalmatian coast

International group (www. hihostels.com) and if you plan to stay in these it is worth joining and acquiring a membership card before setting off.

An International Student Identity Card (www.isic.org) entitles you to discounts on travel expenses such as 25 per cent off train tickets.

What to Take/Wear

In summer you will need light cotton clothing with a jacket or pullover for the evenings, plus swimwear. In winter you will need woollen jumpers and a warm coat. Also be sure to pack at least one pair of decent walking shoes as some of the medieval towns have unevenly paved or cobbled streets.

Although it is rarely necessary to dress in formal clothes, clothes which are neat and tidy will be appreciated. For example, trainers are not suitable for dining in an upmarket restaurant.

Croatia is quite a religious country, so, when visiting churches, make sure you have your thighs and shoulders covered (that goes for both men and women).

Forms of Greeting

Croatians tend to be quite reserved with strangers. Attempting a few words in the local language will be appreciated. The forms used vary according to the person you are addressing: he or she may be a *gospodin* (a man),

a *gospođa* (a married woman) or a *gospođica* (a young single woman).

Greetings vary for the different times of the day: *dobro jutro* (good morning), *dobar dan* (good afternoon or good day), *dobra večer* (good evening), *laku noć* (good night). *Bok* (hi) and *ciao* are informal greetings. *Doviđenja* is commonly used to say goodbye to people you are not familiar with.

For polite requests use *molim* (please) and *hvala* (thank you). For more vocabulary, see the Phrase Book *(pp295–6).*

Naturism

Croatia is a popular country for naturism, where it is practised freely at designated places and resorts that are outstanding for their quality and high standards. Naturism has a very long tradition in Croatia. In fact, the first vacation resort for naturists was opened in Rajska plaža (Paradise beach) on the island of Rab in 1934.

Today there are many nudist beaches that are marked "FKK" (German for "free body culture"). There are about 20 official naturist resorts offering accommodation along the Croatian coast (mainly in the form of camping). The majority are in Istria and some even have Blue Flag (clean beach) status. These places are appropriately screened, allowing guests to enjoy the absolute freedom and peace the surrounding nature has to offer. British tour operators offering naturist holidays in Croatia include **Away with Dune** (formerly Dune Leisure).

Time

Croatia is one hour ahead of Greenwich Mean Time (GMT) in winter, and two hours ahead in summer.

Electricity

The electric current supplied is 220V, 50Hz all over the country. The standard European two-pin plugs are used throughout Croatia.

Responsible Tourism

Visitors can support local communities by shopping for local seasonal produce at markets such as the daily covered markets in Zagreb, Rijeka and Pula, the vast open-air market in Split, and many other smaller markets in towns and villages.

Visitors can buy local specialities direct from producers in various destinations, such as *paški sir* (sheep's cheese) on the

island of Pag, lavender oil and dried lavender on the island of Hvar, *pršut* (prosciutto), dried figs throughout Dalmatia, *tartufi* (truffles) in Istria, and wine in all the major wine-producing regions (you can visit vineyards and taste their wine before purchasing).

Visitors can take part in eco-friendly activities such as hiking, mountain biking, sailing and rafting – a greener alternative to fuel-guzzling motorboats for example.

Croatian ethical tour operators include the Makarska-based **Biokovo Active Holidays**, who organize outdoor adventures sports, including hiking and mountain biking on Mount Biokovo and rafting down the River Cetina near Omiš, and the Dubrovnik-based **Adria Adventure**, who specialize in sea kayaking and hiking holidays. The UK-based ethical tour operators arranging holidays in Croatia include **Responsible Travel** and **Swim Trek**.

Trogir market, Dalmatia

DIRECTORY

Tourist Information

Croatian National Tourist Board
Iblerov trg 10/IV, Zagreb.
Tel (01) 469 93 33.
W croatia.hr

Embassies and Consulates

American Embassy,
Ulica Thomasa Jeffersona 2, Zagreb. **Tel** (01) 661 22 00. W http://zagreb. usembassy.gov

Australian Embassy
Centar Kaptol, Nova Ves 11/3rd floor, Zagreb.
Tel (01) 489 12 00.
W http://croatia. embassy.gov.au

British Consulate
Dubrovnik
Vukovarska 22.
Tel (020) 324 597.
Split
Obala Hrvatskog Narodnog Preporoda 10/III. **Tel** (00 385) 21 346 007.

British Embassy
I. Lučića 4, 10000 Zagreb.
Tel (01) 600 91 00.
W gov.uk/government/ world/organisations/ british-embassy-zagreb

Canadian Embassy
Prilaz Gjure Dezelica 4, Zagreb.
Tel (01 488 12 00.

Irish Honorary Consulate
Miramarska 23, Zagreb.
Tel (01) 631 00 25.

Services for the Disabled

Hrvatski savez udruga tjelesnih invalida
Šoštarićeva 8, Zagreb.
Tel (01) 481 20 04.
W hsuti.hr

HUPT (Croatian Paraplegic & Tetraplegic Association)
W hupt.hr

Naturism

Away with Dune
Tel 01371 879 686.
W awaywithdune co.uk

Responsible Tourism

Adria Adventure
Tel (020) 311 545.
W adriaadventure.hr

Biokovo Active Holidays
Tel (021) 679 655.
W biokovo.net

Responsible Travel
Tel (01) 273 823 700. (In the UK)
W responsibletravel. com

Swim Trek
Tel (01) 273 739 713. (In the UK) W swimtrek. com

General Information

W visit-croatia.co.uk

Ministry of Tourism
W mint.hr

Weather Forecast
W meteo.hr

Zagreb Information
W zagreb-touristinfo. hr

Personal Security and Health

Croatian public health services meet the standards of those elsewhere in Europe, and in general, tourists run no serious health risks. There are no endemic diseases but tourists should take care against insect bites and over-exposure to the sun. Tap water is drinkable all over the country. In inland regions, de-mining along former lines of confrontation is not complete. Therefore, travellers should not stray from known safe routes in these zones. The crime rate is comparatively low, and there is little street crime, although visitors should take the usual precautions in busy places to protect valuables.

A Croatian policeman with a police car

Police

Regular Croatian police (*policija*) officers wear dark blue uniforms and keep a relatively low-profile presence. In addition, there are the seldom seen Intervention Police (who wear blue military-style uniforms) and the Special Police or SWAT (who wear khaki military-style uniforms). If you are a victim of crime, you should report this to the local police station and obtain a police statement.

What to Be Aware of

The level of safety on the roads and in public places is good, and the police are deemed responsible for the protection and safety of the country's visitors as well as its citizens. Croatia has a relatively low crime rate, and violent crime is comparatively rare. If a petty theft occurs, it is more likely to happen in crowded areas such as bus and railway stations. It is highly unlikely that the police will create any problems

for foreign visitors on holiday in Croatia unless, of course, the law is broken in some way. However, it is advisable to carry your identification documents, such as a passport, with you as the police have the right to ask for identification.

According to an international agreement, if a tourist is held for questioning or detained for whatever reason, he or she has the right to contact a diplomatic representative of his or her country (an embassy or consulate, *see p267*) and receive assistance in appointing a local lawyer, preferably English-speaking.

Any eventual costs and the lawyer's fee are the responsibility of the accused.

In an Emergency

In case of emergencies, the appropriate services to call are listed in the directory opposite. For accidents or other medical emergencies, go to casualty (*hitna pomoć*). There are general hospitals in all the

main cities while rural towns and the islands are served by local doctors. People can be transferred by ambulance or helicopter to the nearest hospital in case of any emergency.

Lost and Stolen Property

Precautions for avoiding theft and loss of documents and personal belongings are the same as in any other country, so use your common sense. You should avoid leaving objects of value and money unattended and keep an eye on your luggage and bags, particularly in crowded areas. Do not wear showy, expensive jewellery that could attract the wrong kind of attention.

When you travel, it is always a good idea to make a photocopy of your personal documents and keep it in a separate place; in this way it will be much easier to obtain a duplicate. In the event of loss, report the circumstances to the police as soon as possible.

Hospitals and Pharmacies

All the main cities have a hospital, and the standard of health care is on a par with other EU countries. For less serious problems, visit a pharmacy (*ljekarna*), which can be identified by the green cross above the door. Croatian pharmacists are highly qualified and can dispense medication not usually available over the counter back home. Although it

An ambulance driving past a hospital

Aerial view of people sunbathing on a Dalmatian beach

is easy to find all the more common over-the-counter medicines in pharmacies without too much difficulty, it is best to carry an adequate supply of any prescription medicines you may need.

Some medicines are not known by the commercial names given to them in their country of origin, but by the active ingredients contained in them. This may cause difficulty for a pharmacist trying to comply with the request of a foreign visitor. In any event, it is useful if you can produce a legible prescription written by your own doctor as proof that you are authorized to take a particular medicine.

Pharmacies are usually open all day (8am to 8pm) or in the morning or afternoon, depending on the day.

Minor Hazards

Most of the problems that visitors suffer from in Croatia are those common to tourists anywhere else.

To prevent sunstroke, you should drink lots of liquids and avoid strenuous sports or activities at the hottest time of the day. Make sure to use sunscreen creams with a high sun protection factor.

A change in diet can cause stomach upsets, which are often a nuisance but can usually be treated quickly. In Croatia there is no risk of dysentery or similar illnesses.

On the beaches and near the coast, the most common problem is probably irritating insect bites, particularly from mosquitoes, and it is a good idea to take some anti-histamine cream and insect repellent with you.

Tick-borne diseases can be a problem in rural areas in late spring and throughout the summer. Anyone spending a lot of time outdoors should take precautions, such as wearing long-sleeved tops and using insect repellent. Seek medical advice if bitten.

For hikers and climbers venturing inland, there is the possibility of encountering snakes, so take the appropriate serum with you if you are planning such a trip. However, most minor ailments and disturbances can usually be avoided with a little care and common sense.

Boat travel is a common means of transport for connections between the coastal towns and cities and obviously the only means of getting to virtually all the islands. Unfortunately many people suffer from seasickness and people who are susceptible should take some kind of travel sickness pill before embarking on a sea journey. It is advisable to keep to the central areas of the boat where any pitching and rolling is felt less, and to go on deck where fresh air and a visible horizon may help.

Travel and Health Insurance

Foreign tourists do not pay for emergency medical services if the Health Care Convention has been signed between Croatia and the country they come from. This is the case for all countries in the European Union including the UK, Ireland and Italy, and all EU citizens should carry a European Health Insurance Card (EHIC), available from the UK Department of Health or from a main post office. If you come from a country that has not signed the Convention, you must pay for health services according to a standardized price list.

It is, however, advisable to take out an insurance policy to cover medical assistance. The policy should also include repatriation by air-ambulance, as well as the refunding of any medical expenses that are necessary. All visitors have a right to emergency medical assistance, but certain medical services must be paid for.

Activities such as diving, rock climbing and in some cases, even hiking or motorcycling, are often not included in travel insurance cover, as they are regarded as dangerous activities. Check the insurance policy details; it may be necessary to pay a surcharge to cover these kinds of sports.

DIRECTORY

Emergency Services

Police
Tel 192.

Fire
Tel 193.

Ambulance
Tel 194.

General Emergency
Tel 112.

Breakdown Service (Automobile Club)
Tel 1987 w hak.hr.

Rescue at Sea
Tel 195.

Information
Tel 18981.

Banking and Currency

The Croatian currency is the kuna, which in May 1994 took the place of the dinar. It is in fact a very old currency; coins displaying the kuna were known to be in use in Slavonia in 1256. It is not difficult to change money into kuna at bureaux de change and banks throughout the country. Visitors need to pay for everything in Croatian kuna, even though hotel room prices are (confusingly) almost always posted in euros. Although Croatia joined the European Union in 2013, it will take several years before it officially adopts the euro, if indeed it adopts it at all.

Banks and Bureaux de Change

Money can be changed from one currency to the other in banks and authorized bureaux de change or exchange offices. Banks are usually open from Monday to Friday from 8am to 7pm and on Saturday from 8am to 1pm but times can vary, so always check in advance if possible. However, in the smaller towns, some banks may close in the middle of the day from noon to 3pm and on Saturdays they may shut a little earlier than large, city branches.

Exchange offices have more flexible timings and are open until late in the evening in tourist areas. A commission is charged on the exchange, which varies from 1 to 1.5 per cent at the exchange offices. These charges are lesser or almost non-existent if you change money at a bank.

You can also change foreign currency in post offices and tourist agencies. If possible, avoid changing money at hotels or camp sites where the exchange rates are less favourable. Do not be tempted to change money

One of the many ATMs found in all main towns and cities

at stations and ports or along the roads with people who are not authorized. Finally, if you hold on to your original receipts you can re-convert any unused kuna banknotes back to the orignal currency at the end of your stay. However, only banks offer this kind of a service.

ATMs

Automated Teller Machines (ATMs) are now widespread throughout the country, even in remote villages on the islands. Not every ATM accepts all forms of credit and debit cards, so it is best to check that the logo of the card you want to use is on the machine (*bankomat*) before making a withdrawal. Remember to always shield the ATM machine from strangers when feeding your PIN into it.

Traveller's Cheques

Traveller's cheques are not accepted anywhere in Croatia.

Credit and Debit Cards

The most commonly accepted credit cards are MasterCard, American Express, Visa and Diners. Credit cards can be used in almost every shop, resort, hotel and restaurant. Of course, there are always exceptions, so check the signs on the door of the establishment to see which cards they accept. If there is no sign, ask in advance to avoid unpleasant surprises.

In the event of the loss or theft of your credit card, it is extremely important to report it immediately so that the card can be blocked. This can be

DIRECTORY

Banks, Exchange Offices and ATMs

Zagrebačka banka
ⓦ zaba.hr

Hrvatska narodna banka
ⓦ hnb.hr

Lost or Stolen Credit Cards

American Express
Tel 1 905 474 0870
(collect call).
ⓦ americanexpress.com

Diners Club
Tel 1 702 797 5532 (collect call).
ⓦ diners.com.hr

Eurocard–MasterCard
Tel 1 636 722 7111 (collect call).

Visa
Tel 0 800 220 111 (wait for the second dial tone, then enter 866 654 0125).

Hrvatska narodna banka in Zagreb

done by calling the relevant card's emergency number (which is usually a number providing a 24-hour service, seven days a week). Inform your bank before departure that they do not block your card due to unusual activity.

Currency

The kuna is divided into 100 lipa (the word "lipa" means a linden tree). The Central Bank issues banknotes of 1000, 500, 200, 100, 50, 20 and 10 kuna, featuring Croatian heroes. Coins come in denominations of 5, 2 and 1 kuna, and 50, 20, 10, 5, 2 and 1 lipa. The local abbreviation for kuna is kn, but the international abbreviation is HRK.

The Croatian currency was formerly closely linked to the German mark and until 31 December 2001, prices for accommodation, especially private rooms, were always quoted in marks. However, the mark was replaced by the euro in January 2002 when it became the common currency of the European Union. The government tries to keep rates of exchange steady, which helps travellers and also helps to present an overall image of stability to potential foreign investors.

The euro is now accepted in all banks and bureaux de change.

Banknotes

The Central Bank issues banknotes of 1000, 500, 200, 100, 50, 20 and 10 kuna. Notes bear the portraits of famous Croats such as Stjepan Radić and Josip Jelačić.

20 kuna

50 kuna

100 kuna

200 kuna

Coins

The kuna is divided into 100 lipa. The coin denominations are 5, 2 and 1 kuna and 50, 20, 10, 5, 2 and 1 lipa. The 20 and 50 lipa coins are silver-coloured and the 10 and 5 lipa coins are bronze-coloured.

| 1 kuna | 2 kuna | 5 kuna |

| 1 lipa | 2 lipa | 5 lipa | 10 lipa | 20 lipa | 50 lipa |

Communications and Media

Croatia has good communication systems and well-functioning public services such as the post and telecommunications. The news and information network is well organized, although most visitors (unless they speak Croatian) will face the obvious language barrier. However, foreign television programmes can be received via satellite and it is also easy to find foreign newspapers and magazines with newsagents, although they might be available a little later than they would be at home. Internet use is also widespread in Croatia.

Public telephone booth in a Dubrovnik side-street

International and Local Telephone Calls

Calling Croatia from abroad is very easy: after dialling the international code (00 world-wide), dial the international country code (385), followed by the area code without the initial zero (Croatia is divided administratively into counties, each with a corresponding code) and finally the number of the subscriber. To telephone abroad from Croatia, dial the international code (again 00), followed by the international code of the country (for the UK it is 44), then the area code (omitting the initial zero) and finally the subscriber's number. The international codes for other English-speaking countries are as follows: the US and Canada, 1, Australia, 61, New Zealand, 64 and Ireland, 353.

When making local calls from a landline within Croatia, you need to include the area code when dialling, unless you are calling from within that area. There is a list of Croatian area codes in the directory on p273.

Numbers beginning with the code 060 are information services. These services can be dialled up from anywhere within Croatia, using the same code.

Mobile Phones

In Croatia several companies offer mobile phone services (GSM network): Tele 2, with the code 095; T-Mobile, with the codes 097, 098 and 099; and Vipnet, with the codes 091 and 092. The HT GSM network covers approximately 98 per cent of the country.

Check with your mobile phone service provider before you leave to see whether they have a roaming agreement with the Croatian networks.

If you expect to be in Croatia for more than a week, purchasing a local SIM card to use in your mobile phone may be worthwhile. You will need your phone to be unlocked in order to use the new SIM card.

Keep in mind that it is illegal to use a mobile phone while you are driving.

Public Telephones

There are fewer public telephones in Croatia now, but they do still exist. Pay phones in Croatia are operated by telephone cards (*telefonska kartica*) that are available in units of 15, 30 and 50 (1 unit = 1 kuna) and can be purchased from tobacconists, newsagents and news kiosks.

It is cheaper to call from a public phone rather than from your hotel, as hotels generally apply a supplement to any calls which are made from their rooms.

Internet

Internet and email facilities are widely available in Croatia, and it is easy to find Internet cafés with speedy connections in most places, even on the islands.

If you want to use a laptop computer, you will find that many hotels and hostels offer free Wi-Fi to their guests. Some cities (such as Rijeka and Osijek) also have hotspots with free Wi-Fi in public spaces. Ask at the relevant local tourist offices for the exact location of these zones.

Postal Services

The Croatian national postal company HP operates a network of post offices, with branches in all towns, and offers a wide range of services, including the sale of stamps and telephone cards, fax facilities and postal

Surfing the net at an Internet café in Dubrovnik

Typical newspaper kiosk in Valpovo

services of all kinds. If you are sending ordinary post, stamps *(marke)* can also be bought at newsagents *(kiosk)*. Note that unless airmail is specifically requested, postcards and letters will be sent overland.

Letters and cards can be posted at post offices or the roadside yellow post boxes. The costs vary according to the type of correspondence and the destination. Post offices are open 7am–7pm Monday–Friday, and 7am–1pm on Saturday. During summer months, the post offices in the tourist resorts extend their opening times until 10pm.

A practical and straight-forward way to receive post while on holiday is to use the *poste restante* service. Any correspondence sent to the following addresses will be held until it is collected by the addressee. In Zagreb, the address is Poste Restante, 10000 Zagreb, Croatia and in Split, Poste Restante, Main Post Office, 21000 Split, Croatia.

Entrance to a post office (HP) in Dubrovnik

Newspapers and Magazines

The top-selling national daily newspapers are *24 Sata*, *Jutarnji List*, *Večernji List* and *Slobodna Dalmacija*, all in Croatian. British, Italian and German newspapers and magazines are usually readily available at newsstands in all the major resorts and cities. Also look out for the very informative English-language *In Your Pocket* bi-monthly guides, available for various destinations including Split, Dubrovnik, Rijeka, Zadar and Zagreb.

Television and Radio

The main Croatian radio and television company is *Hrvatska radiotelevizija* (HRT). There are four national TV channels: HRT1, HRT2, HRT3 and HRT4, all of which broadcast foreign and domestic programmes. Other television stations are RTL, RTL2, Doma and Nova TV, as well as about 20 private regional channels. Almost all programmes including films and other foreign productions are broadcast in their original language, with Croatian subtitles. The radio has daily news in both English and German. Many hotels have satellite television and hotel guests will have access to a wide range of European stations.

Croatian radio stations broad-cast in Croatian only, apart from some traffic reports. On the Second Channel (at RDS-HRT2), reports on news in general are given in English, German and Italian.

DIRECTORY

Area Codes

Bjelovarsko-Bilogorska: 043
Brodsko-Posavska: 035
Dubrovačko-Neretvanska: 020
Istarska: 052
Krapinsko-Zagorska: 049
Ličko-Senjska: 053
Karlovačka: 047
Koprivničko-Križevačka: 048
Međimurska: 040
Osječko-Baranjska: 031
Požeško-Slavonska: 034
Primorsko-Goranska: 051
Šibensko-Kninska: 022
Sisačko-Moslavačka: 044
Splitsko-Dalmatinska: 021
Varaždinska: 042
Virovitičko-Podravska: 033
Vukovarsko-Srijemska: 032
Zadarska: 023
Zagreb: 01
Zagrebačka: 01

Useful Numbers

Information for International Calls
Tel 11802.

International Operator
Tel 901.

Speaking Clock
Tel 18095.

Directory Enquiries in Croatia
Tel 11888.

Weather Forecast and Traffic Conditions
Tel (072) 777 777.

Post Offices

Dubrovnik
Vukovarska 16.
Tel (020) 362 068.

Split
Kralja Tomislava 9.
Tel (021) 406 705.

Zagreb
Jurišićeva 13.
Tel (01) 662 64 52.

TRAVEL INFORMATION

Most visitors take a direct flight from the UK to Zagreb, Split or Dubrovnik and there are useful internal flights between the three main airports. During the summer months, numerous charter flights operate and the smaller airports in Croatia open. Many tourists visiting the country come from nearby Germany, Italy and Austria, which are all well connected by road or sea. These visitors often use their own transport, usually car or motorbike. A great deal has been done to develop and improve all means of transport and the country now has good connections to the rest of Europe and the world. It is also possible to get to Croatia by train, for those who prefer this form of transport – this is a much slower method, although the network is being modernized.

Arriving by Air

The national airline company, **Croatia Airlines**, links Croatia's main airports with the rest of Europe. The major European destinations are Amsterdam, Athens, Barcelona, Frankfurt, Berlin, Brussels, Copenhagen, London, Munich, Paris, Rome, Podgorica, Tel Aviv, Istanbul, Skopje, Zurich, Sarajevo, Venice and Vienna.

Other European airlines offering scheduled services to Croatia include **British Airways** (which operates both a summer and a winter service between London Gatwick and Dubrovnik, making Dubrovnik a year-round city break destination), and Star Alliance members Lufthansa, Austrian Airlines, Brussels Airlines, Air France, TAP Portugal, Turkish Airlines, SAS Scandinavian Airlines and Swiss International Airlines. Flying time from London is 2 hours 10 minutes and from Frankfurt 1 hour 30 minutes. The no-frills airline **EasyJet** flies to Dubrovnik from London Gatwick and Stansted;

to Split from Bristol, London Gatwick and Stansted; and to Zagreb from London Gatwick. **Jet2.com** flies to Dubrovnik from Belfast, Edinburgh, Leeds, Manchester and Newcastle; and to Pula and Split from Manchester. **Monarch** flies to Dubrovnik from London Gatwick, Birmingham and Manchester. **Wizz Air** flies to Dubrovnik and Split from Luton airport; and **Ryanair** flies to the cities of Osijek, Pula and Rijeka from Stansted, and to Zadar from Stansted and East Midlands airport.

From Dublin, **Aer Lingus** flies direct to Dubrovnik. Since there are no direct flights from the US or Canada to Croatia, travellers will need to change at one of the main European hubs such as London, Rome or Frankfurt, and then take a further connecting flight to Croatia. There is a daily flight to Zagreb from Rome Fiumicino, for example, as well as five flights a week to and from Split, and two flights a week to and from Dubrovnik.

There are also flights to Zagreb from Australia and New Zealand that have stopovers at major Asian and European airports.

Air Fares

The air fares on scheduled flights to Croatia vary according to the airline and the time of year. Fares tend to be higher in the summer. From the UK there are regular scheduled flights from Gatwick and Heathrow to Zagreb, with connections to Pula, Dubrovnik, Rijeka and Split, as well as direct flights from Gatwick to Dubrovnik. There are charter flights to Croatia from a wide range of UK regional airports during the summer months (May– September). Note that it is possible to get discounts on ticket prices by booking them through price comparison websites such as Kayak, Zugu, Momondo and Skyscanner.

Transport from Airport to Town

Croatia has three main airports. Zagreb airport is 15 km (9 miles) from the centre of the city and is connected by a bus service to the central bus station in Držićeva; the journey takes about 25 minutes and runs from the city to the airport from 4:30 or 5am to 8pm and in the opposite direction from 7am to 8pm (or before and after Croatia Airlines flight departures and arrivals). The airport at Split is

Croatia Airlines plane at Split airport

24 km (15 miles) from the centre of the city and is also connected by a regular bus service, which runs to the seafront promenade, in front of the ferry port. The journey takes about 30 minutes. Dubrovnik airport is 22 km (14 miles) from the city and is connected by a regular bus service, running to the main bus station, with a stop at Pile Gate which is just outside the fortified old town. The journey time for this service is about 20 minutes.

Package Deals

A number of tour operators offer package holidays where the price includes flights (usually charter flights) and accommodation. There are also several UK tour operators offering package holidays such as **Light Blue Travel**, **Balkan Holidays** and **Thomson Holidays**. **Saga Holidays** organizes tours for the 50-plus age group. **Adriatic Holidays** offer sailing holidays including 7- and 14-day trips along the Dalmatian coast, taking in a number of the surrounding islands and Dubrovnik, Split, Zadar and Pula.

Arriving by Train

You can travel from London to Zagreb by train, via Paris, Milan and Venice – a trip of around 30 hours. An alternative route goes via Brussels and Ljubljana in Slovenia. You can also travel from London to Paris, then take an overnight train from Paris to Bologna, followed by a train to the Italian port of Ancona, from where there are regular overnight ferries to Split. **Rail Europe** and **European Rail** can supply information.

Connections from other European cities include the Intercity Munich–Zagreb (which takes 9 hours); the Eurocity "Mimara", which covers the Frankfurt-Munich–Salzburg–Ljubljana–Zagreb route (12 hours), and the Intercity "Croatia" taking the route Vienna–Maribor–Zagreb (6 hours 30 minutes). Vienna–Rijeka takes 8 hours.

Driving along the Magistrala coastal road

There are rail connections from Italy too. From Venice, there is a direct sleeper train daily to Zagreb. There are regular trains to Zagreb from Belgrade (four a day; 6 hours 15 minutes) and Budapest (two a day; 6 hours).

The headquarters of the **Croatian Railways** (Hrvatske Željeznice) is in Zagreb.

Road signage at the Slovenian border

Arriving by Coach

Croatia is also accessible to other countries by coach. International coaches connect Croatia with the bordering states and also with France, Switzerland, Germany, Austria, Slovakia, Bosnia-Herzegovina and Montenegro.

From Germany there are almost daily services from Berlin, Cologne, Dortmund, Frankfurt, Mannheim, Munich and Stuttgart to Zagreb and the coastal cities, covering the stretch from Rijeka to Split.

Many Italian cities such as Bologna, Florence, Milan, Rome and Trieste are also connected to Zagreb by coach. The main Zagreb bus station is called **Autobusni Kolodvor Zagreb** in the capital. The SAF Autoservizio Friuli Venezia Giulia runs services

four times a day in the summer and twice in winter from Trieste to Pula in Istria. From Trieste you can also get to Rijeka by coach which runs four times a day.

Eurolines run a service from the UK to Croatia. Buses depart from London's Victoria station to arrive in Zagreb 32 hours later, with a change in Frankfurt, Germany.

Arriving by Road

Travelling to Croatia by car (or by motorbike) is popular with tourists coming from the neighbouring countries. There are six main border crossings between Croatia and Hungary, 23 frontier points between Croatia and Bosnia-Herzegovina, eight frontier points between Croatia and Serbia and two between Croatia and Montenegro.

Traffic coming overland from Italy enters Croatia via border crossings with Slovenia, all classified as international and open 24 hours a day, all year round. Rabuiese-Muggia, towards Savudrija, is the crossing point for Istria; Basovizza-Pesek, for Rijeka and Dalmatia; Fernetti-Villa Opicina, for those going towards Zagreb.

People driving to Croatia need to carry a valid driving licence, the car's log book (if appropriate) and a green card. For insurance purposes, on entering the country, any prior damage to the car which has not yet been repaired must be declared.

Arriving by Sea

Croatia's main international ferry connections are with Italy via the ports of Ancona, Bari, Venice and Trieste. The main Croatian maritime company is Jadrolinija *(see p279)* which runs services between Ancona and Split (three times a week). The crossing takes nine hours. Ancona–Zadar runs three times a week, an 8-hour journey, and Bari–Dubrovnik runs three times a week in winter and six times a week in summer (taking 10 hours by night; 7-and-a-half hours by day for the journey). In peak season (mid-July to mid-August) the Ancona–Split ferry also makes a stop at Stari Grad on the island of Hvar. **Blue Line** is another Croatian company running regular 10-hour ferry services between Ancona and Split, and seasonal ferry services between Ancona and Hvar, and Ancona and Vis. Ferries are well equipped with restaurants, bars and duty free shops.

One of the ships that connect Croatian ports with the rest of the Adriatic

Venezia Lines operate in the Northern Adriatic and link the northern Adriatic coasts of Italy and Croatia, though they run in summer only (April–September). Regular catamaran lines run between Venice and the Istrian towns of Poreč, Rovinj, Pula and Rabac, and also between Venice and Mali Lošinj on the island of Lošinj. **Trieste**

JADROLINIJA
Symbol of the maritime company Jadrolinija

Lines also run a fast catamaran in the Northern Adriatic, connecting Trieste, Rovinj and Pula, from late June to mid-September. The Italian ferry company **SNAV** runs a fast daily Croatia Jet catamaran service between the cities of Ancona and Split from mid-June to late September (the journey time being 5 hours).

DIRECTORY

Croatian National Tourist Board

Suite 4C, Elsinore House, 77 Fulham Palace Road, London W6 8JA.
Tel (020) 8563 7979 (from UK).
Ⓦ croatia.hr

Airlines

Aer Lingus
Tel 0871 718 2020 (from UK).
Ⓦ aerlingus.com

British Airways
Tel 0844 493 0787 (UK).
Ⓦ britishairways.com

Croatia Airlines
Tel 0844 371 0310 (UK); (01) 667 65 55 and (072) 500 505 (in Croatia).
Ⓦ croatiaairlines.com

EasyJet
Tel 0330 365 5000 (UK).
Ⓦ easyjet.com

Jet2.com
Tel 0333 300 0042 (UK).
Ⓦ jet2.com

Monarch
Tel 0333 003 0100 (UK).
Ⓦ monarch.co.uk

Ryanair
Tel 0871 246 0000 (UK).
Ⓦ ryanair.com

Wizz Air
Tel 0907 292 0102 (UK).
Ⓦ wizzair.com

Package Holidays

Adriatic Holidays
Tel 01865 339 481 (UK).
Ⓦ adriaticholidays.co.uk

Balkan Holidays
Tel 0845 130 1114 (UK).
Ⓦ balkanholidays.co.uk

Light Blue Travel
Tel 01223 568 904 (UK).
Ⓦ lightbluetravel.co.uk

Saga Holidays
Tel 0800 096 0074 (UK).
Ⓦ http://travel.saga.co.uk

Thomson Holidays
Tel 020 3451 2688 (UK).
Ⓦ thomson.co.uk

Coaches

Dubrovnik bus station
Tel (060) 305 070 (Cro).
Ⓦ http://libertas dubrovnik.hr

Eurolines
Tel 0044 871 781 8178.
Ⓦ eurolines.com

Split bus station
Tel (060) 327 777 (Cro).
Ⓦ ak-split.hr

Trieste bus station
Tel 0039 040 425 020.
Ⓦ autostazione trieste.it

Zagreb bus station
Tel (060) 313 333 and (01) 611 278 9 (Cro).
Ⓦ akz.hr

Railways

Croatian Railways
Tel (060) 333 444 (Cro).
Ⓦ hzpp.hr

European Rail
Unit 25, Tileyard Studios, Tileyard Road, London N7 9AH.
Tel 020 7619 1083 (UK).
Ⓦ europeanrail.com

Rail Europe
193 Piccadilly, London W1J 9EU.
Tel 0844 848 4064.
Ⓦ raileurope.co.uk

Ferry Services

Blue Line
Tel (0045) 3672 2001.
Ⓦ blueline-ferries.com

SNAV
Ancona, Italy.
Tel 0039 071 207 6116.
Ⓦ snav.it

Trieste Lines
Viale Miramarer 9, Trieste, Italy.
Tel 0039 0923 873 813.
Ⓦ triestelines.it

Venezia Lines
Trg Matije Gupca 11, Poreč.
Tel (052) 422 896.
Ⓦ venezialines.com

Getting Around Croatia

The transport system within Croatia is reasonably efficient, particularly if you are travelling by road or by sea. Connections between the mainland and the islands are excellent, and thanks to an extensive bus network, even smaller, lesser known towns can be easily reached. Although using air travel to get around the country is not that common, domestic flights link the major towns. Travelling by train is fine only if you have plenty of time as the rail network is small due to the mountainous terrain, and is in need of modernization. Train travel takes much longer than the time it takes to cover the same distance by road.

Biking in the mountainous terrain of Croatia

Green Travel

In Croatia, when it comes to green travel, the most positive moves have been seen in Zagreb where, as of 2007, the ZET (Zagreb Municipal Transit System) started using bio-fuels in public transport vehicles. Zagreb has a taxi company called Eko Taxi that markets itself as "low-emissions", and there are now marked cycle lanes in parts of the city, making it a bicycle-friendly destination.

Cycling in rural areas is growing in popularity, and cycling holidays are now available in Istria and parts of Dalmatia (mountain biking in the latter case). Hiking is also popular, with both Croatians and foreign visitors. The best seasons for hiking are spring and autumn. Organized hiking holidays are also available.

Last but not least, sailing is one of the most environmentally friendly ways of exploring the Croatian coast, using the power of wind as opposed to that of a motor.

Domestic Flights

Croatia Airlines runs regular connections between the three major airports in the country – Zagreb, Split and Dubrovnik. There are also connections between these airports and other secondary airports, such as the airports at Osijek, Zadar, Rijeka (on the island of Krk), Pula and Brač, which is open only in the summer months.

Travelling by Car

Cars drive on the right in Croatia and safety belts should be worn in both the front and back seats. Children under 12 must sit in the back.

The speed limits are 50 km/h (30 mph) in towns, 80 km/h (50 mph) outside built-up areas, and 130 km/h (80 mph) on the motorways. Cars towing caravans must not exceed 80 km/h (50 mph).

Road signs are generally more or less identical to those found in the rest of Europe.

Note that it is illegal to drive when drunk over the 0.5 per cent limit.

Service stations are open daily from 7am to 7 or 8pm, but in summer they are open till 10pm. On the main roads in the larger towns and cities and on major international routes service stations are open 24 hours a day. All the usual petrol types are available: Eurosuper 95, Eurosuper 98 and Eurodiesel.

Roads and Tolls

As part of a vast programme of improvements to the country's infrastructure, the national motorway (autocesta) network is being extended, necessitating the building of several impressive viaducts and tunnels. Croatia's motorways are now regarded as among the most modern and safest in Europe. The new A1 motorway connecting Zagreb and Split opened in 2007, and a section from Split to Ploče in 2012, with an eventual extension planned all the way down the coast to Dubrovnik for 2015.

On certain stretches of motorway drivers pay a toll (by either cash or credit card): Zagreb–Karlovac, Zaprešić, Krapina, Varaždin–Goričan, Zagreb–Oprisavci, Rijeka–Delnice, Zagreb–Split. There is also a toll to pay for the bridge to the island of Krk and the Učka Tunnel.

Parking

As elsewhere in Europe, car parking is an ever-increasing problem in most cities. Some hotels have parking spaces reserved for guests. If you are travelling by car it is worth checking this in advance. Likewise, in many smaller coastal towns, the seafront promenades are closed to traffic through the summer season, severely reducing parking spaces.

Where indicated, a parking ticket must be clearly displayed inside the windscreen. If you park in a no-parking area, your vehicle can be forcibly removed by officials.

Town traffic in the charming city of Osijek

Breakdown Assistance and Traffic Information

Emergency road services are provided by the local Automobile Club, **HAK**, which can be reached 24 hours a day all year round by dialling 1987 (preceded by 003851 for calls from outside Croatia). The service provides repairs (a charge will apply) on the spot or in a garage (subject to transport), the removal of damaged cars and transport up to 100 km (62 miles) distance.

The HAK also provides useful information on road and maritime traffic, motorway tolls, any temporary diversions, the prices of petrol, ferry times, possible alternative routes and general assistance for those travelling by car. Their website provides useful information and links.

Road Conditions/Hazards

Croatian roads are of a decent standard, comparable to those in most EU countries, while the newly constructed motorways are superior to most. However, the picturesque Magistrala (coastal highway), which runs down the Adriatic from Rijeka to Dubrovnik, twists and turns and can be extremely slippery when wet. On the islands and in rural areas, the roads may be narrow and poorly surfaced.

Car Hire

Car rental agencies can be found in all the main towns and cities, airports and holiday resorts. A valid driving licence is required and the driver must be at least 21 years old. Besides the well-known large multinational rent-a-car companies such as **Avis, Budget** and **Hertz**, there are many local independent companies as well.

The larger companies, however, offer the option of leaving the car in a different town from the collection point. Not all rental companies are able to offer this flexibility and there is always an extra charge for this service.

Entrance to the main railway station in Zagreb, Glavni kolodvor

Trains

Although the railway network in Croatia is slowly being modernized, travelling by train is not very popular except in the area around Zagreb. However, all the main Croatian towns and cities are linked by rail, with the exception of Dubrovnik, where there is no railway station at all.

The main railway station is in the capital city (Glavni Kolodvor Zagreb). There are trains to Rijeka with connections to the Istrian towns; to Split, with a branch line for Zadar and Šibenik, serving the Dalmatian coast; to Osijek, to the east and Varaždin, to the north.

The following journey times can be expected: 4 hours for Zagreb to Rijeka, 6 hours from Zagreb to Split (or 8 hours 30 min by night), 2 hours for Zagreb–Varaždin, and 4 hours 30 minutes for Zagreb–Osijek. Express services operate on some routes. Croatian Railways (Hrvatske Željeznice) has its main office in Zagreb (*see p276*).

Travelling by coach to the city of Dubrovnik

Buses

Buses are a convenient means of transport. The national bus service covers an extensive network with numerous connections and destinations, although tickets will be more expensive than on trains.

Suitcases and larger rucksacks will need to go into the luggage storage compartments below the bus and incur a surcharge.

Services are divided into "intercity" (direct connections between the larger cities) and the regional services (with connections between the smaller towns and the main cities).

There are daily connections between the towns and cities of Croatia and night buses cover the longer routes.

For information, go to the local bus station (*autobusni kolodvor*) and consult the timetable. *Vozi svaki dan* indicates the daily services, while *ne vozi nedjeljom ni praznikom* shows which services do not run on Sundays and public holidays. The main bus station in Zagreb is the **Autobusni kolodvor Zagreb** in Zagreb the main station in Split is **Autobusni kolodvor Split.**

Coach Tours

The travel agency **Atlas** offers a choice of coach tours, such as the 8-day escorted "Highlights of Croatia" which includes Dubrovnik, Split, Trogir, Zadar, Zagreb and Plitvice and the 10-day "UNESCO Heritage Sites and National Parks of Croatia". Atlas also runs regular 1-day trips from Dubrovnik to nearby destinations such as Ston and Korčula, Mostar (in Bosnia-Herzegovina) and the River Tara (in Montenegro).

Island Ferries

The majority of ferries and catamarans connecting the mainland and the islands are run by the state-owned company, **Jadrolinija**. These ferries can transport both passengers and vehicles.

The Croatian ferry network is divided into five districts. In the Rijeka district, Cres and Lošinj are connected to the mainland by the Valbiska–Merag and Brestova–Porozina routes. There is also a ferry running from Rijeka to Mali Lošinj, with stops at Cres, Unije and Susak en route. The island of Rab is connected to the coast by the Jablanac–Mišnjak route and with the island of Krk by the Lopar–Valbiska route. Finally, the island of Pag is connected to the coast by the Prizna–Žigljen route, while Novalja on Pag is connected to Rijeka with a stop at Rab Town en route.

In the district of Zadar, there are connections to the cities of Preko, on the island of Ugljan,

Bribinj and Zaglav, on the island of Dugi Otok and from Biograd to Tkon on the island of Pašman.

In the district of Šibenik, the town is connected to the islands of Zlarin and Prvić.

In the Split district there are connections between Split and the islands of Brač (Supetar), Korčula (Vela Luka), Hvar (to Starigrad), Šolta (Rogač), Vis (to the port of the same name) and Lastovo (to Ubli). There are also connections between Makarska and Sumartin (island of Brač), between Ploče and Trpanj on the Pelješac peninsula, between Orebić and Dominče (on the island of Korčula) and between Drvenik and Sućuraj (island of Hvar).

Finally, in the district of Dubrovnik, the main connection is between Dubrovnik and the island of Mljet (Sobra), while there are also small ferries running between Dubrovnik and the Elaphiti islands of Koločep, Lopud and Šipan.

Ferry Frequency

Ferry services run frequently in the high season (July and August), but are significantly reduced outside the summer months. On some short routes,

such as Jablanac–Mišnjak and Drvenik–Sućuraj, ferries sail non-stop so as to cope with the long queues that tend to form in the middle of the day.

For those travelling without a car or motorbike, high-speed catamarans connect Split to the surrounding islands of Brač, Hvar, Vis, Korčula and Lastovo with the most frequent services from June to September. The crossing times range from 45 minutes to Hvar to 2 hours 30 mins to Lastovo.

In addition to Jadrolinija, there are several small private companies that operate certain routes. **G & V Line** runs catamarans from Dubrovnik to Mljet and from Zadar to several small nearby islands. **Linijska nacionalna plovidba** runs catamarans from Split to Brač and Šolta, and from Pula to Zadar (summer only), as well as ferries from Valbiska (on Krk) to Lopar (on Rab) and from Drvenik (on the mainland) to Dominča (on Korčula). **Miatours** runs hydrofoils from Zadar to the nearby islands, while **Rapska plovidba** runs ferries from Jablanac (on the mainland) to Mišnjak (on Pag), and from Rab Town (on Rab) to Lun (on Pag).

DIRECTORY

Airports

Brač
Tel (021) 559 711.
W airport-brac.hr

Dubrovnik
Tel (020) 773 100.
W airport-dubrovnik.hr

Osijek
Tel (060) 339 339.
W osijek-airport.hr

Pula
Tel (060) 308 308.
W airport-pula.hr

Rijeka
Tel (051) 841 222.
W rijeka-airport.hr

Split
Tel (021) 203 506.
W split-airport.hr

Zadar
Tel (023) 205 904.
W zadar-airport.hr

Zagreb
Tel (060) 320 320.
W zagreb-airport.hr

Driving

HAK
Tel 1987. Tel (072) 777 777 (traffic information).

Car Rental

Avis
Tel (01) 467 36 03.
W avis.com.hr

Budget
Tel (062) 300 331.
W budget.hr

Hertz
Tel (072) 727 277.
W hertz.hr

Buses

Autobusni kolodvor Zagreb
Information
Tel (060) 313 333.
W http://akz.hr

Autobusni kolodvor Split
Information
Tel (060) 327 777.
W ak-split.hr

Coach Tours

Atlas
Izidora Kršnjavog 1, Zagreb.
Tel (01) 241 56 11.
W atlas-croatia.com

Ferries

Jadrolinija
Riva 16, Rijeka.
Tel (051) 666 111.
W jadrolinija.hr

G & V Line
Tel (020) 313 119.
W gv-line.hr

Linijska nacionalna plovidba
Tel (021) 352 527.
W lnp.hr

Miatours
Tel (023) 254 300.
W miatours.hr

Rapska plovidba
Tel (051) 724 122.
W rapska-plovidba.hr

Getting Around Zagreb

The city of Zagreb has developed a good, efficient transport network which, by means of trams, buses and a funicular railway connecting the Lower and Upper Towns, ensures good connections between all the central and suburban districts. Trams run at regular intervals and there are some night services also. Gradec, the old town, has many areas which are pedestrianized and closed to ordinary traffic, making this a pleasant, pollution-free zone to stroll around. There is no underground system in Zagreb.

White façade of St. Catherine's Church, Upper Town, Zagreb

Walking

Zagreb is a very large city and visitors will need to use some form of public transport to get around. However, the best way to visit the centre, that is the areas of Kaptol and Gradec (together these are known as Gornji Grad or Upper Town), is to walk there. Walking is especially rewarding in the old centre of Zagreb with its venerable churches and imposing buildings.

It is a good idea to equip yourself with a map of the city before setting off. Maps can be obtained from any tourist office. If you are lost and need assistance, you can always ask the locals for directions. They are generally friendly and helpful to tourists, although there may be a barrier to understanding if you are not familiar with the Croatian language; this is where your map may prove useful.

Trams

The company that runs the capital's public transport is the Zagrebački Električni Tramvaj, known as **ZET**. The network of electric trams is efficient, with frequent services covering a wide area.

A total of 15 tram routes run during the day (starting at around 4am and ending at midnight) and four lines run at night (midnight to 4am).

The routes operating during the day are:
1 Zapadni kolodvor–Borongaj;
2 Črnomerec–Savišče;
3 Ljubljanica–Žitnjak;
4 Savski most–Dubec;
5 Jarun– Kvaternikov trg;
6 Črnomerec–Sopot;
7 Savski most–Dubrava;
8 Mihaljevac– Zapruđe;
9 Ljubljanica– Borongaj;
11 Črnomerec–Dubec;
12 Ljubljanica–Dubrava,
13 Žitnjak– Kvaternikov trg;
14 Mihaljevac–Zapruđe;
15 Mihaljevac–Dolje;
17 Prečko–Borongaj.

All the lines run frequently during the day with intervals of 6 to 10 minutes between trams, depending on whether it is a weekday or public holiday. On Sundays and other holidays tram numbers 3 and 8 do not run.

The four tram lines that run at night pass every 20 to 40 minutes on these useful routes:
31 Črnomerec–Savski most;
32 Prečko–Borongaj;
33 Dolje–Savišče; and
34 Ljubljanica–Dubec.

The main hub for tram stops is Trg bana Jelačića, where seven different tram routes intersect.

Buses

There is an intricate network of bus connections with numerous routes branching out to the various termini: Britanski trg, Jandrićeva, Jankomir, Savski most, Ljubljanica, trg Mažuranića, Črnomerec, Mandaličina, Zaprešić, Kaptol, Petrova, Svetice, Dubrava, Kvaternikov trg, Glavni kolodvor, Žitnjak, Sesvete, Borongaj, Mihaljevac and Velika Gorica.

Tickets

Tickets for trams and buses can be bought on board all buses and some trams, and from newsagents or kiosks. The basic ticket is for a single journey. It must be punched in the machine as soon as you get on board and is valid for 90 minutes from that time. Tickets cost 10 kuna each. There is also a one-day ticket that costs 40 kuna, a good idea if you intend to make various trips

One of many tram lines serving the entire city

during the day (these tickets are valid until 4am on the following day). Monthly season tickets are also available. A useful website is www.zagreb-touristinfo.hr. Travelling without a ticket is punishable with a fine of 210 kuna.

Funicular Railway

An interesting method of transport is the *uspinjača*, a steep funicular railway that has been in operation since 1890. At 66 m (216 ft), this is one of the shortest climbs in the world and takes a little less than a minute to climb up from the Lower Town to the Upper Town, arriving close to the Lotrščak tower. Departures are from Tomićeva street, right in the centre, and the cable cars leave every 10 minutes from 6:30am to 10pm (midnight in summer). The price of a single ticket is 4 kuna.

Funicular railway connecting the Lower and Upper Towns

Cable Car

The Žičara is a cable car that connects Zagreb with Sljeme, the highest peak in the Mount Medvednica range, in a journey time of 20 minutes. The system has been in operation since 1963; however; it is currently closed for renovation as a new cable car is planned. Until this has been completed buses will connect Zagreb with Sljeme.

Taxis readily available in all the big cities of Croatia

Taxis

In Zagreb, as in any other large city, taxis can be found readily. There are several small private companies, such as **Eko Taxi** (a fleet of hybrid vehicles); the long-established and experienced **Radio Taxi Zagreb;** and **Taxi Cammeo**, with its smart uniformed drivers. All of their vehicles are licensed, with meters on board. Taxi fares vary from company to company, but you can expect to pay 10 kuna as the basic starting rate and then 5 kuna for every kilometre of your journey.

Car Rental

In the capital, it is also possible to rent a car by contacting one of the main car rental companies such as **Budget**, **Hertz** and **Avis**. Assistance while you are on the road is provided by the Croatian Automobile Club, which can also offer advice on routes *(see pp278–9)*.

Cycle Hire/Bike Tours

Being fairly flat and even, Zagreb is a bicycle-friendly city. There is a network of clearly marked bicycle lanes connecting most of the main attractions, except for the medieval quarter of Gornji Grad. There are several companies offering bikes for hire in the city centre, and some companies, such as **Zagreb by Bike**, also arrange guided tours by bicycle.

DIRECTORY

Trams

ZET
Tel (01) 365 15 55, (060) 100 001.
w zet.hr

Taxis

Eko Taxi
Tel 1414 and (060) 77 77.
w ekotaxi.hr

Radio Taxi Zagreb
Tel 1777, (060) 800 800.
w radio-taksi-zagreb.hr

Taxi Cammeo Zagreb
Tel 1212.
w taxi-cammeo.hr

Car Rental

Avis
Oreskoviceva 21, Zagreb.
Tel (01) 467 36 03.
w avis.com.hr

Budget
Radnička 45, Zagreb.
Tel (062) 300 331.
w budget.hr

Hertz
Vukotinovićeva 4, Zagreb.
Tel (072) 727 277.
w hertz.hr

Bike Tours

Zagreb by Bike
Meeting point: Trg bana Josipa Jelačića 15 (in the backyard), Zagreb.
Tel (098) 188 33 44.
w zagrebbybike.com

General Index

Acknowledgments

Fabio Ratti Editoria would like to thank the following staff at Dorling Kindersley:

Map Coordinator
Dave Pugh.

Senior DTP Manager
Jason Little.

Publishing Manager
Anna Streiffert.

Managing Art Editor
Marisa Renzullo.

Publisher
Douglas Amrine.

Dorling Kindersley would also like to thank all those whose contribution and assistance have made the preparation of this book possible.

Principal Author
Leandro Zoppè was born in Venice and graduated in Political Science from Padua University. At present he lives in Milan where, as a historian, he works as a freelance journalist and writer of tour guides and historical, artistic or naturalistic books.

Contributors
Božidarka Boza Gligorijević, Public Relations Manager for the Croatian National Tourist Board in Milan; Graeme Harwood, author and gourmand.

Text Revision
Sanja Rojić (University professor), Iva Grgic (University professor).

Checking of Practical Information
Lucia Čutura, Viktor Jovanović Marušić, Jane Foster.

Senior Editor, UK Edition
Jacky Jackson.

Proof Reader
Alessandra Lombardi, Stewart J Wild.

Indexer
Helen Peters.

Fact Checker
Katarina Bulic.

Revisions Team
Louise Abbott, Claire Baranowski, Marta Bescos, Sonal Bhatt, Nadia Bono-mally, Jonathan Bousfield, Louise Cleghorn, Karen DSouza, Anna Fischel, Anna Freiberger, Prerna Gupta, Kaberi Hazarika, Juliet Kenny, Sumita Khatwani, Kathryn Lane, Carly Madden, Sam Merrell, Nataša Novakovic, Susie Peachey, Lucy Richards, Ellen Root, Julie Thompson, Priyansha Tuli, Vinita Venugopal, Ajay Verma, Dora Whitaker.

Special Thanks
Croatian National Tourist Board, Zagreb, in particular the director Niko Bulić; Croatian National Tourist Board, Milan, in particular the director Klaudio Stojnic and the public relations manager Božidarka Boza Gligorijević; the regional and local tourist boards of Croatia; Vinko Bakija (director of the tourist office, Supetar, island of Brač); Zdravko Banović (tourist office, Split); Daniela Barac (tourist guide in Crikvenica); Nikša Bender (marketing manager of the tourist office of Dubrovnik); Maja Boban (tourist guide of the environs of Zagreb); Ankita Boksic Franchini (tourist office, Split); Tanja Bunjevac (tourist office, Varaždin) Rujana Bušić (tourist guide in Vinkovci); Vanja Dadić (tourist guide in Šibenik); Mirjana Darrer (public relations manager of the tourist office in Dubrovnik); Marchese Doimo Frangipane di Aiello del Friuli; Danijela Duić (tourist guide in Karlovac); Jurica Duževič (director of the tourist office in Stari Grad, island of Hvar); Daniela Fanikutić (tourist office, Poreč); Ennio Forlani (director of the tourist office of Vodnjan); Vesna Gamulin (tourist guide in Dubrovnik); Miljenko Gašparac (guard of the Risnjak National Park); Boris Gržina (front office manager of the Hotel Esplanade in Zagreb); Vesna Habazin and Snježana Hrupelj (tourist guides in the area of the thermal spas); Mladenka Jarac-Rončević (Croatian Consul in Italy); Zoran Jelaska (tourist guide in Split); Vesna Jovičić (tourist guide in Pula); Darko Kovačić (tourist guide in the Lonjsko Polje Nature Park); Darko Kovačić (director of the tourist office, Omiš); Stanka Kraljević (director of the tourist office in the town of Korčula); Vlasta Krklec (Museum of Krapina); Tonći Lalić (tourist guide in Makarska); Damir Macanić (director of the tourist office in Osijek); Damir Mihalić (tourist office, Varaždinske Toplice); Josip Mikolčić (tourist office, Virovitica); Danijela Miletić (tourist office, Zagreb); Smiljan Mitrović (tourist guide in Zadar); Franjo Mrzljak (director of the National Museum of Naïve Art, Zagreb); Andro Krstulović Opara (former Croatian Consul in Italy); Ottone Novosel (tourist guide in Križevci); Ankica Pandzic (director of the Museum of Croatian History in Zagreb); Danika Plazibat (Meštrović Gallery, Zagreb); Gordana Perić (tourist office, Zadar); Ante Rendić-Miočević (director of the Archaeological Museum, Zagreb); Mladen Radić (Director of the Museum of Slavonia, Osijek); Ljubica Ramuščak (Civic Museum of Medimurje, Cakovec); Ljiljana Sever (tourist guide in Varaždin); Josipa Šipek (director of Hotel Coning in Trakošćan); Doris Staničić (tourist guide in Osijek); Alka Starac (Archaeological Museum of Istria, Pula); Branka Tropp (director of the tourist office in Varaždin); Đuro Vandura (director of the Gallery of Ancient Masters, Zagreb); Klara Vedriš (Gallery of Modern Art, Zagreb); Vjenceslav Vlahov (tourist guide in Zagreb); Igor Zidić (director of the Gallery of Modern Art, Zagreb); Marko Zoričić (director of the tourist office in Opatija).

DK wishes to thank Lady Beresford-Peirse of the International Trust for Croatian Monuments for her time and invaluable suggestions.

Photography Permissions
The publisher would like to thank all the museums, the local corporations and associations, hotels, restaurants, shops and other places of interest for their co-operation and their kind permission in allowing their establishments to be photographed.

Additional Photography

Adriano Bacchella, Nataša Novakovic, Aldo Pavan, Lucio Rossi, Rough Guides/Tim Draper, Tony Souter, Leandro Zoppé

Picture Credits

Key to positions: a=above, b=below/bottom, c=centre, f=far, l=left, r=right, t=top.

The publisher would like to thank the following individuals, associations and photograpic agencies for permission to reproduce their photographs:

360 Degrees, Dubrovnik: 233tl, 241br.
Adriatic Luxury Hotels: Excelsior Hotel 229br; **Alamy Images:** Tibor Bognar 220-1; Europe/Peter Forsberg 281tr; JadroFoto 133tr; Kuttig - Travel - 2 132cla; Laraclarence 130cla; Lightworks Media 272cla; Nino Marcutti 2-3; Ian Middleton 86-7; Paul Prescott 129tc, 129bl; Phant 131tl; QEDimages 94br; toto 235c; Jason Wallengren Photography 235tl; Marcus Wilson-Smith 256tl; **Aldo Pavan, Aura Agency, Milan:** 28cl, 48bc, 70br, 99crb, 114cla, 138cl, 138cr, 140tl, 141b, 142cl, 142crb, 143clb, 237cl, 250cl, 254cla, 255tl; **Archaeological Museum,** Zagreb: 33br, 169c, 192c; **The Art Archive:** 37br; **Hotel Aurora:** 226bc; **AWL Images:** Walter Bibikow 15tl; Alan Copson 18.
Bevanda: 232cla, 239tr; **Bora Bar:** 238bc.
Corbis: Reuters/Matko Bijlak 234cla; Seth Joel 272cl; **Croatia Airlines:** 274bl; **The Croatian National Tourist Board Archives, Milan:** 23clb, 24bc, 25tr, 27cl, 28br, 29cla, 30–31 (all), 33, 36t, 37cb, 40tl, 48tr, 100crb, 108cla, 109cr, 114br, 115tl, 117cl, 136t, 137tr, 137br, 139 (all), 140cr, 140bl, 141tl, 141c, 142tr, 142bl, 143tl, 143cra, 143br, 146c, 149ca, 152c, 152br, 153tl/c, 164tl, 179bl, 190tl, 198br, 204cl, 205br, 206cl, 216ca, 217tr, 252tl, 253tc, 255br, 257tr, 259cl, 259br, 261bc, Dubrovnik-Jesuit monastery/Sergio Gobbo 266bl, 271 (all), 276c, Luka Tambaca 277cl, 278bc, 281cl; **Croatian Railways:** Dragutin Staničić 278tr.
Doimo Frangipane: 181ca, 181cr; **Dreamstime.com:** Airborne77 12tc; Josef Bosak 182-3; Chasseur 90; Dabidy 12bl; Deymos 212-3; Dziewul 13bl, 126crb; Ed Francissen 67br; Petr Goskov 15br; Inavanhateren 101tl; Jasmina 154; Matej Kastelic 14bc; Oleg Kozlov 10cla; Martin Kubát 127tr; Iv Merkas 173bc; Adrienn Orbánhegyi 128tr; Photoinsel 270bl; Tomislav Pinter 46-7; Rahela 132bc; Sanja1977 11tr; Nikolai Sorokin 10br; Sergey Uryadnikov 60bc; Dariusz Szwangruber 127bc; Whitewizzard 126tr; Xbrchx 14tl, 19bc, 93crb; Zatletic 202.
Esculap Restaurants: Fish Restaurant Proto 233br, 242bc; Restaurant Nautika 243tr.

Falkensteiner Hotels & Residences: Hotel Iadera 230tl; **Fosa:** 244tr; **Fresh Sheets, Dubrovnik:** 222br.
Gallery Of Modern Art, Zagreb: 8–9, 168b; **Gallery of Old Masters,** Zagreb: 170–71 (all); **Getty Images:** Danita Delimont 172; David C Tomlinson 50; Matthew Williams-Ellis 15tr; **Giaxa:** D. Fabijanic 232br, 243bl.
Robert Harding Picture Library: Stuart Black 78-9; Gunter Lenz/Image Broker 262-3.
Image Bank, Milan: 58br, 88cl, 89br, 93tl, 151br, 157cr, 166tl.
Karmen Hotel: 223br; **Kod Ruze:** 248tr.
Lesic Dimitri Palace Hotel: 222cla; **Marco Lissoni:** 24br, 72cr, 116cl, 253br, 254br. **Maistra Hotels, Resorts & Campings:** Hotel Lone 223tl; Monte 241tr; Hotel Monte Mulini 228br; **Mali Bar:** 247tr; **Hotel Marina, Krk:** 227tr; **Meštrović Gallery,** Zagreb: 24tr, 163cr, 163bl, 163br; **mondadori archives:** 22bc, 25cr, 34tl, 35tr, 35bc, 39 (all), 40cr, 40bc, 41 (all), 42tl, 42bl, 42br, 43cb, 44tl, 123tl, 163cl, 181cla, 198tr, 199cra, 199crb, 199bl, 210br, 237tlc, 259tc; **Hotel Mozart:** 225tc; **Museum of croatian history,** Zagreb: 42cb, 43tr, 43clb, 44crb, 160cl.
National Museum Of Naive Art, Zagreb: 25bl, 160bl, 165tl; **Nin Tourist Board:** Angelo Pijaca 102crb; **Nishta:** 246br; **Natasa Novakovic:** 161cr, 194cla, 196cl, 197crb.
Office of the President of the Republic of Croatia: 45tc.
Paklenica National Park: 22cl, 103c, 103b, 103tr, 260 (all); **Pet Bunara:** 245br; **Andrea Pistolesi:** 113tr.
The Regent Esplanade Zagreb: 224tl. **The Strossmayer Gallery:** 170cb;
Superstock: Funkystock/age fotostock 158bl; Bjanka Kadic/age fotostock 13tr; Hemis.fr/Hemis.fr 144-5; Henryk T. Kaiser/age fotostock 94tr.
Tourist Board of Konavle/visit.cavtat-konavle.com: 153br; **Tourist Board of Krapina-Zagorje County:** 216crb, 216bl; **Tourist Board Opatija:** 69tc, 69br..
Hotel Vestibul Palace: 225bl, 231bl; **Vinodol:** 246tl; Vuglec Breg: 249bl.
Zagreb City Museum: 162bl; **Zagreb Municipal Transit System (ZET):** Goran Kekic 280bl.

Front Endpaper:

Dreamstime.com: Chasseur Lbc; Jasmina Lcl; Zatletic Rcr; **Getty Images:** Danita Delimont Rtrl David C Tomlinson Lbl. Jacket Front and spine – **Getty Images:** Sylvain Sonnet.

All other images © Dorling Kindersley.
For further information: www.dkimages.com

Phrase Book

Pronounciation

c – "ts" as in rats
č – "chi" as in church
ć – "t" is a soft t
đ – "d" is a soft d
g – "g" is a hard g as in get
j – "y" as in yes
š – sh
Ž – shown here as "zh", sounds like the "J" in the French name, Jacques
"aj" – shown here as "igh", sounds like "I" or the "igh" in night.

In Emergency

Help!	**Pomoć!**	**po**moch
Stop!	**Stani!**	**stah**nee
Call a doctor!	**Zovite doktora!**	**zo**veetey **dok**torah
Call an ambulance!	**Zovite hitnu pomoć!**	**zo**veetey **heet**noo **po**moch
Call the police!	**Zovite policiju!**	**zo**veetey poleets**ee**yoo
Call the fire brigade!	**Zovite vatrogasce!**	**zo**veetey vatroh**gast**say
Where is the nearest telephone?	**Gdje je najbliži telefon?**	gdyey yey n-igh-**bleez**hee telefon
Where is the nearest hospital?	**Gdje je najbliža bolnica?**	gdyey yey n-igh-**bleez**hah **bol**nitsa

Communication Essentials

Yes	**da**	dah
No	**ne**	ney
Please	**molim vas**	**mol**eem vas
Thank you	**hvala**	**hvah**lah
Excuse me	**oprostite**	opros**tee**tey
Hello	**dobar dan**	**do**bar dan
Goodbye	**dovidenja**	dovee**djen**ya
Goodnight	**laku noc**	**lak**oo noch
Morning	**jutro**	**yoo**troh
Afternoon	**popodne**	po**pod**ney
Evening	**večer**	**ve**cher
Yesterday	**jučer**	**yoo**cher
Today	**danas**	**da**nas
Tomorrow	**sutra**	**soo**trah
Here	**tu**	too
There	**tamo**	**tah**moh
What?	**što?**	shtoh
When?	**kada?**	**ka**da
Why?	**zašto?**	**zash**toh
Where?	**gdje?**	gdyey

Useful Phrases

How are you?	**Kako ste?**	**ka**koh stey
Very well, thank you	**Dobro, hvala**	**do**broh, **hvah**lah
Pleased to meet you	**Drago mi je!**	**dra**goh mee yey
See you soon	**Vidimo se**	**vee**deemoh sey
That's fine	**U redu**	oo **red**oo
Where is/are…?	**Gdje je/su?**	gdyey yey/soo
How far is it to…?	**Koliko je daleko do…?**	**ko**likoh doh dalekoh doh…
How can I get to…?	**Kako mogu doći do…?**	kakoh mogoo dochee doh…
Do you speak English?	**Govorite li engleski?**	go**vo**reetey lee **eng**leskee
I don't understand	**Ne razumijem**	nay raz**oom**eeyem
Could you speak more slowly please?	**Molim vas, možete li govoriti sporije?**	**mol**eem vas, **mozh**etey lee go**vo**reetee sporiyey
I'm sorry	**Žao mi je**	**zha**oh mee yey

Useful Words

big	**veliko**	**vel**eekoh
small	**malo**	**mah**loh
hot	**vruć**	vrooch
cold	**hladan**	**hlah**dan
good	**dobar**	**do**bar
bad	**loš**	losh
enough	**dosta**	**dos**tah
well	**dobro**	**do**broh
open	**otvoreno**	otv**oh**renoh
closed	**zatvoreno**	zatv**oh**renoh
left	**lijevo**	**lee**yevoh
right	**desno**	**des**noh

straight on	**ravno**	**rav**noh
near	**blizu**	**blee**zoo
far	**daleko**	da**le**koh
up	**gore**	**go**rey
down	**dolje**	**dol**yey
early	**rano**	**ra**noh
late	**kasno**	**ka**snoh
entrance	**ulaz**	**oo**laz
exit	**izlaz**	**eez**laz
toilet	**WC**	**Veyt**sey
more	**više**	**vee**shey
less	**manje**	**man**yey

Shopping

How much does this cost?	**Koliko ovo košta?**	**ko**likoh ovoh **kosh**ta
I would like…	**Volio bih…**	**vol**ioh bee…
Do you have…?	**Imate li…?**	**ee**matey lee…
I'm just looking	**Samo gledam**	Samoh gledam
Do you take credit cards?	**Primate li kreditne kartice?**	**pree**matey lee cred**eet**ney cart**eet**sey
What time do you open?	**Kad otvarate?**	kad otva**ra**tey
What time do you close?	**Kad zatvarate?**	kad zatva**ra**tey
This one	**Ovaj**	ov-igh
That one	**Onaj**	on-igh
expensive	**skupo**	**skoo**poh
cheap	**jeftino**	**yef**teenoh
size (clothes)	**veličina**	vele**chi**nah
size (shoes)	**broj**	broy
white	**bijelo**	bee**yel**oh
black	**crno**	**tsrn**oh
red	**crveno**	**tsr**venoh
yellow	**žuto**	**zhoo**toh
green	**zeleno**	**zel**enoh
blue	**plavo**	**pla**voh
bakery	**pekara**	**pek**arah
bank	**banka**	**ban**kah
books hop	**knjižara**	knyee**zh**arah
butcher's	**mesnica**	**mes**nitsah
cakes hop	**slastičarna**	**slast**eecharnah
chemist's	**apoteka**	ap**oh**tekah
fishmonger's	**ribarnica**	**ree**barnitsah
market	**tržnica**	**trzh**neetsah
hair dresser's	**frizer**	**freez**er
news agent's/ tobacconist	**trafika**	**traf**eekah
post office	**pošta**	**posh**tah
shoe shop	**prodavaonica cipela**	prodava**on**itsa tseepelah
supermarket	**supermarket**	**soo**permarket
travel agent	**putnička agencija**	**poot**neechka agents**ee**yah

Sightseeing

art gallery	**galerija umjetnina**	galer**ee**yah oomyetneenah
cathedral	**katedrala**	kated**ral**ah
church	**crkva**	**tsrk**vah
garden	**vrt**	vurt
library	**knjižnica**	knyee**zh**neetsah
museum	**muzej**	**moo**zey
tourist information centre	**turistički ured**	too**reest**eechkey **oo**red
town hall	**gradska vijećnica**	**grad**skah veeyech**neet**sah
closed for holiday	**zatvoreno zbog praznika**	zatv**or**enoh zbog **praz**neekah
bus station	**autobusni kolodvor**	aooto**boos**nee **kol**odvor
railway station	**željeznički kolodvor**	**zhel**yeznichkih kolodvor

Staying in a Hotel

Do you have a vacant room?	**Imate li sobu?**	**ee**matey lee **so**boo
double room	**dvokrevetna soba**	dvok**rev**etnah **sob**ah
single room	**jednokrevetna soba**	**yed**nokrevetnah **sob**ah
room with a bath	**soba sa kupatilom**	**sob**ah sah koo**pat**eelom
shower	**tuš**	toosh

porter	**portir**	portir
key	**ključ**	klyooch
I have a reservation	**Imam**	eemam
	rezervaciju	rezervatseeyoo

Eating Out

Have you got a table for…?	**Imate li stol za…?**	eematey lee stol zah
I want to reserve a table	**Želim rezervirati stol**	Zheleem rezerveeratee stol
The bill please	**Molim vas, račun**	moleem vas, rachoon
I am a vegetarian	**Jasam vegeterijanac**	yahsam vegetereeyanats
waiter/waitress	**konobar/ konobarica**	konobar/ konobaritsah
menu	**jelovnik**	yelovneek
wine list	**vinska karta**	veenskah kartah
glass	**čaša**	chashah
bottle	**boca**	botsah
knife	**nož**	nozh
fork	**viljuška**	veelyooshkah
spoon	**žlica**	zhleetsah
breakfast	**doručak**	doroochak
lunch	**ručak**	roochak
dinner	**večera**	vecherah
main course	**glavno jelo**	glavnoh yeloh
starters	**predjela**	predyelah

Menu Decoder

bijela riba	beeyelah reebah	"white" fish
blitva	bleetvah	Swiss chard
brudet	broodet	fish stew
čevapčići	chevapcheechee	meatballs
crni rižot	tsrnee reezhot	black risotto (prepared with cuttlefish ink)
desert	desert	dessert
glavno jelo	glavnoh yeloh	main course
grah	grah	beans
gulaš	goolash	goulash
jastog	yastog	lobster
juha	yoohah	soup
kuhano	koohanoh	cooked
maslinovo ulje	masleenovoh oolyey	olive oil
meso na žaru	mesoh nah zharoo	barbecued meat
miješano meso	meeyeshanoh mesoh	mixed grilled meats
na žaru	nah zharoo	barbecued
ocat	otsat	vinegar
palačinke	palacheenkay	pancakes
papar	papar	pepper
paški sir	pashkih seer	sheep's cheese from Pag
pečeno	pechenoh	baked
piletina	peeleteenah	chicken
plava riba	plavah reebah	"blue" fish
predjelo	predyeloh	starters
prilog	preelog	side dish
pršut	prshoot	smoked ham
pržene lignje	przhene leegnyey	fried squid
prženo	przhenoh	fried
ramsteak	ramsteyk	rump steak
ražnjići	razhnyeechee	pork kebabs
riba na žaru	reebah nah zharoo	barbecued fish
rižot frutti di mare	reezhot frootee dee marey	seafood risotto
rižot sa škampima	reezhot sah shkampeemah	scampi risotto
salata	salatah	salad
salata od hobotnice	salatah od hobotneetsey	octopus salad
sarma	sarmah	cabbage leaves
sir	seer	cheese
sladoled	sladoled	ice cream
slana srdela	slanah srdelah	salted sardines
škampi na buzaru	shkampee nah boozaroo	scampi in tomato and onion
školjke na buzaru	shkolkay nah boozaroo	shellfish in tomato and onion
špageti frutti di mare	shpagetee frootee dee marey	spaghetti with seafood

sol	sol	salt
tjestenina	**tjest**eeneenah	pasta stuffed with meat and rice
ulje	**ool**yey	oil
varivo	**var**eevoh	boiled vegetables

Drinks

bijelovino	bee**yel**oh **vee**noh	white wine
čaj	ch-igh	tea
crno vino	tsrnoh **vee**noh	red wine
gazirana mineralna voda	ga**zee**ranah meener**al**nah **vod**ah	sparkling mineral water
kava	**kav**ah	coffee
negazirana mineralna voda	ney**gaz**eeranah meener**al**nah **vod**ah	still mineral water
pivo	**pee**voh	beer
rakija	rak**ee**yah	spirit
tamno pivo	tamnoh **pee**voh	stout (dark beer)
travarica	trava**reet**sah	spirit flavoured with herbs
voda	**vod**ah	water

Numbers

0	**nula**	**noo**lah
1	**jedan**	**ye**dan
2	**dva**	dvah
3	**tri**	tree
4	**četiri**	**chet**eeree
5	**pet**	pet
6	**šest**	shest
7	**sedam**	**se**dam
8	**osam**	**o**sam
9	**devet**	**de**vet
10	**deset**	**de**set
11	**jedanaest**	**yed**anest
12	**dvanaest**	**dvah**nest
13	**trinaest**	**tree**nest
14	**četrnaest**	**chet**rnest
15	**petnaest**	**pet**nest
16	**šestnaest**	**shest**nest
17	**sedamnaest**	**se**damnest
18	**osamnaest**	**o**samnest
19	**devetnaest**	**de**vetnest
20	**dvadeset**	**dvah**deset
21	**dvadesetijedan**	**dvah**desetee **ye**dan
22	**dvadesetidva**	**dvah**deseteedvah
30	**trideset**	**tree**deset
31	**tridesetijedan**	**tree**deseteeyedan
40	**četrdeset**	**chet**rdeset
50	**pedeset**	**pe**deset
60	**šezdeset**	**shez**deset
70	**sedamdeset**	**se**damdeset
80	**osamdeset**	**o**samdeset
90	**devedeset**	**de**vedeset
100	**sto**	stoh
101	**stoijedan**	stoh**ee**yedan
102	**stoidva**	stoh**ee**dvah
200	**dvjesto**	**dvee**stoh
500	**petsto**	**pet**stoh
700	**sedamsto**	sed**am**stoh
900	**devetsto**	**de**vetstoh
1,000	**tisuću**	**tee**soochoo
1,001	**tisućuijedan**	**tee**soochoo ee**ye**dan

Time

One minute	**jedna minuta**	**yed**na mee**noo**tah
One hour	**jedan sat**	**ye**dan saht
Half an hour	**pola sata**	**pol**ah sahtah
Monday	**ponedjeljak**	pon**ed**yelyak
Tuesday	**utorak**	**oo**torak
Wednesday	**srijeda**	**sree**jedah
Thursday	**četvrtak**	**chet**vrtak
Friday	**petak**	**pet**ak
Saturday	**subota**	**soo**botah
Sunday	**nedjelja**	**ned**yelyah